The Reluctant Escapologist

Adventures in Alternative Theatre

Mike Bradwell

Foreword by Mike Leigh

N
H
B

NICK HERN BOOKS
London
www.nickhernbooks.co.uk

A Nick Hern Book

THE RELUCTANT ESCAPOLOGIST
first published in Great Britain in 2010
by Nick Hern Books Limited,
14 Larden Road, London W3 7ST

Cover designed by Ned Hoste, 2H
Front cover photograph by Nobby Clark,
with Mike Bradwell (and Cass Patton) in *Oh What!*, Hull Truck, 1975.
© Nobby Clark/Arenapal.com
Back cover photograph by David Harrison (www.davidharrison.info)

Typeset by Nick Hern Books, London
Printed and bound in Great Britain by
CPI Antony Rowe, Chippenham, Wiltshire

A CIP catalogue record for this book
is available from the British Library

ISBN 978 1 85459 538 6

Mike Bradwell

Mike Bradwell trained at East 15 Acting School. He played Norman in Mike Leigh's award-winning film *Bleak Moments* and worked as an underwater escapologist and fireater with Hirst's Charivari and as an actor/musician with the Ken Campbell Roadshow.

He founded Hull Truck Theatre Company in 1971 and directed all their shows for ten years including his own devised plays *Oh What!*, *Bridget's House*, *A Bed of Roses*, *Ooh La La!* and *Still Crazy After All These Years*. Hull Truck toured nationally and internationally and was the first British fringe company to be invited to the National Theatre and to create work for BBC Television.

Mike has directed over forty shows for the Bush Theatre where he was Artistic Director between 1996 and 2007, including *Hard Feelings* by Doug Lucie, *Unsuitable for Adults* by Terry Johnson, *The Fosdyke Sagas* by Bill Tidy and Alan Plater, *Love and Understanding* by Joe Penhall (also at the Long Wharf Theatre, New Haven), *Dogs Barking* by Richard Zajdliz, *Dead Sheep*, *Shang-a-Lang* and *Little Baby Nothing* by Catherine Johnson, *Howie the Rookie* by Mark O'Rowe (also Dublin and Edinburgh Festivals, PS 122 New York, The Magic Theatre, San Francisco, and European tour), *Normal* by Helen Blakeman, *Flamingos* by Jonathan Hall, *Blackbird* by Adam Rapp, *Resident Alien* by Tim Fountain (also New York Theatre Workshop, European and Australian tour), *Airsick* by Emma Frost, *When You Cure Me* by Jack Thorne, *adrenalin... heart* by Georgia Fitch (also Setagaya Theatre Tram, Tokyo), *The Glee Club* by Richard Cameron (also Duchess Theatre, London, Galway Festival and national tour), *The Girl With Red Hair* by Sharman Macdonald (Royal Lyceum, Edinburgh and Hampstead Theatre), *Crooked* by Catherine Trieschman, and *Pumpgirl* by Abbie Spallen (Edinburgh Festival).

Other work includes *Mrs Gauguin* and *Mrs Vershinin* by Helen Cooper (Almeida, Riverside and Kampnagel, Hamburg), *Tuesday's Child* by Terry Johnson (Stratford East), *The Cockroach Trilogy* by Alan Williams (national and international tour), *The Dalkey Archive* by Flann O'Brien (Long Wharf Theatre), *The Empire* by DC Moore (Royal Court Theatre and Drum Theatre, Plymouth), and productions at the Tricycle Theatre, West Yorkshire Playhouse, King's Head Theatre, Hampstead Theatre, and for the Science Fiction Theatre of Liverpool, the National Theatre of Brent, the Rude Players of Manitoba and the Royal Court Theatre, where he was Associate Director. In addition, Mike has written and directed for film, television and radio including *The Writing on the Wall*, *Games Without Frontiers*, *Chains of Love*, *Happy Feet* and *I Am A Donut*.

Contents

Foreword

Here he is, in all his glory! Tough as an old scrotum, and soft as a baby's bum, that unique, lovable mass of unhinged madness and profound sanity—Mike Bradwell himself, in appearance somewhere between Falstaff, Burl Ives and Winnie-the-Pooh—the magician of Shepherd's Bush, and the inventor of the real Hull Truck. Guru, observer, critic, commentator, historian and chronicler of all things countercultural, and of our alternative theatre in particular, the ultimate outsider's insider; poet, piss-artist, cynic and romantic; inspired director, writer and teacher; actor, fire-eater, vaudevillian, joker and jester; anarchist, exploder, debunker, activist, entrepreneur, visionary, fantast, dreamer, realist and surrealist; inspired manager and practical man-of-the-theatre; passionate nurturer of young talent, loved by generations of actors, writers, directors, designers and techies; partner, daddy, brilliant cook, loyal friend and consummate cheeky bugger... in short, your definitive reluctant escapologist, whatever that may be!!

Towards the end of this brilliant account of his epic forty-year journey, Mike tells us, 'I don't believe that theatre is safe in the hands of grown-ups', and it is his healthy, eternal youthfulness that makes the book so inspiring.

Before I had read it, Mike asked me if I would consider writing a quotable supportive sentence. I wasn't sure what would suit, so he suggested, 'Buy this book. It is a work of genius. Laugh? I almost shat.'

Well, I've read it, and it gave me diarrhoea. It is as hilarious as it is informative. It is a masterpiece. Read it, and you too are guaranteed a truly moving experience.

Mike Leigh
London, April 2010

Acknowledgements

I would like to thank everybody who helped, informed and sustained me during the making of this book, especially Dudley Sutton, Chris Jury, Alan Williams, Mia Soteriou, Robin Soans, Philip Jackson, Dave Hill, Jane Wood, Sue Timothy, Tara Prem, Susannah Doyle, Matt Applewhite, Tim Fountain, Tony Bicât, Susanna Bishop, Natasha Diot and Jane Fallowfield. I would like to thank Catherine Itzen, James Roose-Evans, Jinnie Schiele, Julian Beck, Judith Malina, Abbie Hoffman, Peter Ansorge, John Tyrtell, Pierre Biner, Howard Goorney and Jean-Louis Barrault, whose books I pillaged on the way. I would like to thank Alan Plater and Kerry Crabbe for allowing me to quote from their plays. I would like to thank Nobby Clark, Gordon Rainsford, Sheila Burnett, Jonathan Player, Nicky Pallot, John Haynes, Jane Wood and Alastair Muir for letting me use their photographs. I would like to thank Chez Betty for the coffee and The Captain for the music. I would like to thank Nicola Wilson who made me keep going. And I would like to thank Helen Cooper and Flora Bradwell who were there every step of the way.

M.B.

*

The author and publisher gratefully acknowledge permission to quote extracts from the following:

'Woodstock' by Joni Mitchell, by kind permission of Alfred Music Publishing; *AC/DC* by Heathcote Williams (© 1972) and the *Complete Works of Antonin Artaud*, translated by Victor Corti (© 1971), by kind permission of Calder Publications (UK) Ltd; 'Les bourgeois' by Jacques Brel, by kind permission of Éditions Jacques Brel; 'High Windows' from *High*

Illustrations

Unsuitable for Adults by Terry Johnson, Bush, 1984 (photo: Nicky Pallot)

Meeting the Crown Prince and Princess of Japan, Tokyo, 1982

Filming *Happy Feet*, Scarborough, 1989

Flann O'Brien's Hard Life by Kerry Crabbe, Tricycle Theatre, 1985
    (photo: Sheila Burnett)

Love and Understanding by Joe Penhall, Bush, 1997 (photo: Alastair Muir)

Shang-A-Lang by Catherine Johnson, Bush, 1998

Howie the Rookie by Mark O'Rowe, Bush, 1999 (photos: Alastair Muir)

Resident Alien by Tim Fountain, Bush, 1999

Blackbird by Adam Rapp, Bush, 2001 (photo: Raphie Frank)

The Glee Club by Richard Cameron, Bush, 2002
    (photo: Gordon Rainsford)

adrenalin... heart by Georgia Fitch, Bush, 2002
    (photo: Gordon Rainsford)

A Carpet, a Pony and a Monkey by Mike Packer, Bush, 2002
    (photo: Gordon Rainsford)

Crooked by Catherine Trieschmann, Bush, 2006
    (photo: Alastair Muir)

Outside the Bush, 1997 (photo: Jonathan Player)

Every effort has been made to trace and acknowledge the owners of the various pieces of material in this publication. Should the publishers have failed to make acknowledgement where it is due, they would be glad to hear from the respective owners in order to make amends.

Introduction

This book tells the tale of the two theatre companies I have run: Hull Truck from 1971 to 1982 and the Bush Theatre from 1996 to 2007—and of the people who inspired me to run them in the way that I did. It also offers in part, a partial, personal and totally biased history of alternative theatre in Britain over the last forty years or so, and of its part in my downfall.

I subscribe to the 'Shankly Protocol'. I believe that theatre is not a matter of life and death; it's much more important than that. Real theatre must have the same dirty, corruptive influence as rock 'n' roll. Real theatre must be sexy, subversive, dangerous and fun, and in constant opposition to the Establishment. The day the music died was not the day that Buddy Holly, Ritchie Valens and the Big Bopper were killed in the plane crash. The music died on the day that Elvis joined the US Army.

I believe that a functioning theatre is as important, and as necessary, to the spiritual and physical well-being of any community, as a school, a hospital, a police station, a library, a sports centre or a prison. The essential bargain of theatre is that a group of human beings get together with another group of human beings and collectively they try to find ways to enrich the experience of being human. The theatremakers that I most revere all appear to believe this too.

Joan Littlewood and her Theatre Workshop company constantly sought to make popular, provocative and radically political entertainment for the widest possible audience. Julian Beck, Judith Malina and The Living Theatre wanted theatre to be become the revolution itself. They demanded 'Paradise Now' and would accept no substitute. Mike Leigh, through his unique improvisation techniques, took truth and honesty in acting on to a higher plane and made, and continues to make, some of the most compassionate drama of all time. And Ken

Campbell was the visionary embodiment of the Great God Pan, for ever searching for the most astonishing, remarkable and mind-bending caper of them all. Together they have inspired generations of directors, actors and writers and hopefully they will continue to do so for many years to come.

Apparently we are now living in a new theatrical golden age. The West End is booming. New classless audiences are flocking to the National Theatre, courtesy of the Travelex £10 ticket scheme. Subsidised non-elitist playhouses in both London and the regions offer a cornucopia of multicultural diversity and popular, yet challenging entertainment. There is, we are told, a renaissance in playwriting. There are more new plays being performed than ever before, with thrusting new writers appearing, and being celebrated daily. Some of them are even women, a couple of whom are so especially talented that they have been allowed to play in the biggest boys' playground of them all—the Olivier Theatre. Exciting performance and site-specific groups are springing up in catacombs and abandoned glue factories everywhere. The theatre god is in her heaven and all is right with the world.

An alternative version might be that the whole thing is a cosy conspiracy of mediocrity perpetrated by a circle jerk of Oxbridge directors, venal producers and supine middle-aged, middle-brow and middle-class dead white male critics foisting their suspect and overhyped metropolitan taste on the long-suffering, culturally browbeaten theatregoing public. The West End is sagging with Sixties musicals whose popularity is boosted by millions of pounds' worth of free reality-TV advertising, bought and paid for by licence-fee payers, and dedicated to helping Andrew Lloyd Webber or Cameron Mackintosh find a new Nancy.

Both commercial and subsidised boutique theatres continue to offer marketing-friendly event theatre: tricked-out and often anodyne revivals both classical and modern, stuffed with British and American film stars and directed by high-flying, high-profile movie directors.

Whichever of these views you subscribe to there is, however, one undeniable statistic, and that is that, in the last twenty-five years, the biggest single area of growth in theatre, and indeed most other walks of life, has been in the relentless expansion of the administrative and entrepreneurial classes. Indeed it seems that the history of the last fifty years of British theatre forms a perfect arc. The first twenty-five years were devoted to the struggle of artists and practitioners to get their hands on the means of production. The second twenty-five were spent watching management and executive claw them back. Such was the increase in administrative personnel that theatres have had to build extra floors to cope with the new departments overrun with chief executives, corporate events coordinators, marketing managers, diversity-compliance monitors, development consultants, finance officers, risk assessors and their myriad staff, all of whom believe that their worth in the marketplace is much greater than that of the artists whose endeavours their jobs were created to support. Theatre boards are stuffed with bankers, wealth creators and similar parasites recruited from the crime scene that is the City of London and who readily endorse the overblown salary claims. It is now common practice for individuals to be paid more to advertise a play than to write one. This has got to stop.

Joan Littlewood's old theatre, the Theatre Royal, Stratford East, currently has a full- and part-time staff of eighty-six before you even get to the creative personnel. In 1959, apart from Joan, the Theatre Workshop company had an entire administrative staff of three, although Mrs Chambers and Mrs Woolmer shared the cleaning duties, and many different wines, beers and spirits could be had from Mrs Parnham in the Long Bar, and tea, coffee, chocolates and snacks were available from Mrs Murphy in the snack kiosk. And this was at the same time as they were producing *A Taste of Honey*, *The Hostage* and *Fings Ain't Wot They Used T'Be*.

The extent to which even alternative theatremakers have rolled over and become complicit in all this corrosive practice is well illustrated by the case of one London profit-share fringe theatre that boasts two Artistic Directors, two Programming Directors, a Development Director, a Development Coordinator, three Development Officers, two Marketing Officers, a Head of Press, two Education-project Directors, a Youth-leader Project Manager, and at least a dozen other odds and sods. One imagines that there is not much profit left to share with the writers, directors and actors after this lot have had their cut. Maybe they believe that, by having them all, they will be able to attract Arts Council subsidy, in the same way that primitive tribes in New Guinea used to build crude wooden models of televisions, aeroplanes, fridges and the like in the hope that the gods would send them the real stuff. In the first two years of its existence the Bush Theatre mounted seventy-seven productions with a combined artistic, technical and administrative staff of just two.

And has all this freebooting expansionism resulted in better theatre? I seriously doubt it. What has happened is that the preoccupation with market efficiency and economic growth has begun to subordinate all other values. Morality, truth and honesty have no market price and are therefore considered to be almost irrelevant. Theatre development departments, in constant search for more sponsorship, compete with each other to climb into bed with the most unsuitable commercial organisations. Does anyone really believe that Shell underwrote the

National Theatre Connections Scheme because of an overwhelming desire to encourage Mark Ravenhill or Simon Bent to write pithy new drama for teenagers? Surely the transaction is an attempt by Shell's PR department to gussy up their tarnished image as one of the planet's leading environmental polluters. And might not a value-added bonus be that no Executive Producer or CEO would be likely to allow the production of a show that, for example, might suggest that Shell were allegedly complicit in the arrest and execution of Ken Saro-Wiwa, the Nigerian environmental activist? You don't bite the hand that feeds you.

Even more worrying is that, these days, it seems that even the most radical theatremakers would prefer to find themselves safely tucked up inside the glittering Kunstpalasts of Establishment Theatre pissing out, rather than outside them pissing in. They seem to be keener to allow themselves and their wares to be trafficked into the tawdry brothels of the West End and the subsidised temples of consensus culture, rather than to conspire to tear them down. Maybe it's all to do with school fees.

The current financial meltdown means that there are likely to be swingeing cuts in public expenditure for many years to come. Whichever government is in power, the subsidised arts seem to be in for a kicking. Even the future of the Arts Council itself is uncertain. Faced with much-reduced budgets it is to be hoped that theatres use this as an opportunity to shed all the surplus layers of overpaid and unnecessary executives, administrators and consultants, rather than reduce the money spent on the art. I doubt that this will be the case. Similarly I suspect that the big organisations like the National Theatre, the Royal Shakespeare Company and the Royal Opera House will remain untouched while small radical and experimental companies will, as usual, bear the brunt of the cuts.

If this book has any purpose it is to remind theatremakers that it is possible and even desirable to make their theatre outside the warm embrace of the theatrical Establishment, either commercial or subsidised. Between 1966 and 1974 over two hundred itinerant alternative theatre companies sprung up all over Britain, presenting entertaining, provocative and incendiary new work throughout the country. Perhaps the time had come to go on the road again.

In the early days of punk, the fanzine *Sideburns* published a drawing of three guitar chords with the caption:

Here's a chord. Here's another. Here's a third. Now form a band.

My version would go:

Find a play. Squat a building. Steal a van. Now make a show.

We may indeed be living in a new golden age of theatre, but even if we are, I would still like to think that, lurking in a dark alleyway round the back of every new £15 million glass-and-steel culturally non-elitist Shopping Mall Playhouse and Corporate Entertainment Facility, is a gobby and pretentious twenty-year-old with a passion for real theatre, a can of petrol and a match.

The Reluctant Escapologist is dedicated to all those who think that they should have been in it, and equally to all those who are glad to discover that they are not.

1

Games for May

On 12 May 1967 I went to a concert at the Queen Elizabeth Hall. The Pink Floyd were performing *Games for May—A Space Age relaxation for the climax of spring*. The Floyd at that time was very much Syd Barrett's band, and they and psychedelia were about to become big. Mark Boyle did the liquid-light show, and there was, for the first time anywhere, a rudimentary quadraphonic sound system. They played all Syd's songs: 'Interstellar Overdrive', 'Astronomy Domine', 'Arnold Layne', 'Bike' and 'See Emily Play'. They played a toy xylophone, a rubber duck and a hacksaw. There was a bubble machine and flower children. I sat on the front row. A man dressed up as an Admiral gave me a daffodil. I psychedelically ate it. Go with the flow...

After the gig I went to the UFO Club in Tottenham Court Road and saw a mediocre R-and-B band called The Paramounts magically transform themselves into Procol Harum to play their new song 'A Whiter Shade of Pale' for the first time in public. Earlier that day I had auditioned for East 15 acting school. I did a speech from David Halliwell's *Little Malcolm and His Struggle Against the Eunuchs*: the bit where Nipple goes down Leeds road t' gasworks and describes it as 'a surreal kaleidoscope pageant of insubstantial seemin' '. I ended up under a chair.

Because I had had a haircut for the audition the guy on the door at UFO thought I was the pigs.

Next morning I staggered out into the grey London dawn tripping the light fandango and doing cartwheels across the floor and then hitched back to Scunthorpe. It took me two days.

When I got home there was a letter to say that I had been accepted at East 15 for a place on the Directors' Course. I had to turn up in October with tights, a fencing mask, a cape, a pair of wellington boots and a copy of Onions's *Shakespeare Glossary*.

1

East 15 was the only drama school I had applied to, partly because it was the only place I thought would let me in, partly because the adverts said they were looking for 'lively minded, argumentative, inventive, exquisite, vulgar, idealistic, talented students who want a livelier theatre', but mainly because of Joan Littlewood.

At the Edinburgh Theatre Conference in 1963, when Ken Tynan, John Calder and Jim Haynes had staged the first happening in the UK, experimentally pushing a nude woman about in a wheelbarrow, Joan had famously declared that 'all drama is piss-taking and we are all here to take the piss' which had impressed me enormously. Also I had joined the Young Communist League and Youth CND at the age of fourteen, and I had heard that she was both a Pacifist and a Communist.

I had seen her groundbreaking production of *Oh What a Lovely War* in the West End and knew something different was going on. The actors had a quality I had never seen in Rep. They were real. They could dance and they could sing and they talked to the audience not at them. They seemed to own the show and could move from comedy to tragedy at the drop of a hat, and I wanted to know how they did it. Like everyone else I had heard stories of how Joan worked with improvisation on this, and other productions like *The Hostage*, *Fings Ain't Wot They Used T'Be* and *A Taste of Honey*. Improvisation was pretty much derided at the time by actors and directors who were both sceptical and scared of it, probably because very few people knew what it was or how to do it. I was also intrigued to read of Bill Gaskill's attempts to get Olivier to improvise during rehearsals for *The Recruiting Officer* at the National. It seemed to me to be risky and revolutionary, and East 15 was the place to find out about it.

I had always wanted to work in theatre. My father, a Lincolnshire farmer, had a love of variety and circus, and as child I saw great comedians like George Formby, Jewel and Warriss, Norman Evans, Tommy Cooper, Tony Hancock, Chic Murray, Jimmy Clitheroe, The Crazy Gang and the best of them all, Jimmy James. He even took me to see Buddy Holly and the Crickets live on stage at the Doncaster Gaumont, watching askance as the Teds jived in the aisles. My sister became a baby ballerina doing Panto with the Christine Orange Pippins, and I got to work backstage in the school holidays eventually becoming a student ASM at Lincoln Theatre Royal (where Michael Billington was Publicity Manager) and at Scunthorpe Civic Theatre. From the age of fifteen I worked as a stagehand on everything from Pinter to *Puss in Boots* and I saw and read as many plays as I could. I was inspired by Chekhov and his declaration that he made theatre in the hope of influencing audiences to make a new and better life for themselves. Later I was excited by Peter

Brook's Theatre of Cruelty experiments at LAMDA and by the *Marat/Sade* at the Aldwych. Productions of Edward Bond's *Saved* at the Royal Court and Halliwell's *Little Malcolm* made me realise that theatre had a duty to provoke as well as to entertain and that it could and should be as exciting as rock 'n' roll.

In 1966 I left school, saw Dylan go electric at Sheffield City Hall and joined the newly founded Scunthorpe Youth Theatre. Oddly enough, the first time I had been called on to improvise was at my audition, when director Philip Thomas asked me imagine myself to be an old Jew whose house is burning down. We did a production of the Appalachian witchcraft play *The Dark of the Moon*, which the local newspaper the *Star* described as 'an important step forward in the weaving of the cloak of cultural maturity towards which Scunthorpe has so long aspired'.

Phil Thomas was a local Drama lecturer and an inspiration to many. After the production a few of us went up to the Edinburgh Festival in his old Mini, driving through the night. We saw ten shows in two days, including the original Oxford student production of *Rosencrantz and Guildenstern are Dead*. Philip thought it was a wank. At the old Traverse on the Lawnmarket we saw plays by Arrabal and Heathcote Williams and were inspired by Liverpool poet Adrian Henri, who was dressed up as Père Ubu.

Phil insisted I apply for drama school, but first I signed up to do an Economics course at Doncaster Technical College, possibly because the LSE at the time was a hot bed of radical student action and I thought Doncaster Tech might be too.

This was a big mistake. I spent a miserable winter sitting in the college refectory with fellow students John Lee, who was to be a founder member of Hull Truck, and Richard Cameron, now an important playwright. We were like Scrawdyke and the Dynamic Erection Party in *Little Malcolm*, planning the overthrow of civilisation and trying to pull secretarial students on day release from the Yorkshire Coal Board over endless plates of beans and chips. We also joined the Doncaster Poetry Society and got to listen to Roger McGough, Seamus Heaney, Hugh MacDiarmid and Adrian Mitchell. We planned to take a satirical review to Edinburgh but never got round to writing it. I briefly fantasised a career as a sensitive contemporary folk singer/songwriter and hung around Scunthorpe Folk Club for a while in the vain hope of being invited to sing. All of which was getting me nowhere. In London the Counter Culture, inspired partially by the legendary Ginsberg, Ferlinghetti and Corso gig at the Albert Hall in 1963, was starting to get itself together with the birth of the underground newspaper *International Times*, the UFO club and the Indica Gallery where John met Yoko. And theatre was at the heart of the movement. At the Freak Out organised to launch *International Times* at the Roundhouse, Peter Brook's RSC actors turned up with the express intention of sorting out Charles Marowitz, who had accused them of failing to take sides in their production of *US*. In Europe the exiled Living Theatre had begun to work on their adaptation of *Frankenstein* through 'impassioned discussions and psychedelic improvisations'. And who exactly was Grotowski and what did he do?

Sitting in the Doncaster Tech College canteen I had scant opportunity to see the best minds of my generation destroyed by madness, starving hysterical naked, dragging themselves through the negro streets at dawn looking for an angry fix, and I was hardly likely to. I applied to East 15. I had realised that if you work in theatre you can really piss off grown-ups, and if you're lucky you might get a shag.

The Summer of 1967, the Summer of Love. 'Tune In. Turn On. Drop Out.' In San Francisco the Beats became Flower Children and held the first Human Be-In in Golden Gate Park. To a soundtrack of the Grateful Dead and Jefferson Airplane, Ken Kesey and the Merry Pranksters handed out tabs of Owsley's best LSD at the Acid Tests. Jimi Hendrix blew everyone away at Monterey. Protest against the Vietnam War grew. The San Francisco Mime Troupe made radical street theatre as students burnt their draft cards. In New York 700,000 marched on the United Nations. Abbie Hoffman and his Guerrilla Theatre Situationists invaded the Stock Exchange, burnt dollar bills and declared the end of money. Antonin Artaud's demand for 'the poetry of festivals and crowds with people pouring into the streets' seemed to be coming true.

'If you're going to San Francisco be sure to wear some flowers in your hair.' If you were going to Scunthorpe High Street such a manoeuvre would be singularly ill-advised. Where I come from you were considered queer if you used adjectives.

I spent the Summer of Love playing Azdak in the Youth Theatre production of Brecht's *The Caucasian Chalk Circle*, trying to grow a beard and get into Grusha's knickers. I walked about wearing a policeman's cape, Indian beads and a ten-gallon hat from a junk shop, and bored everybody shitless banging on about Timothy Leary. Psychedelic drugs were totally non-existent, and so I experimented with smoking dried banana skins—'electrical banana is going to be the coming phase'—crushing up morning glory seeds and snorting foxgloves. 'Make Love Not War' was the order of the day but free love had, as yet, sadly failed to find its way up north. Richard Cameron maintains that it was not until the mid-Eighties that you could get into a girl's brassiere in Doncaster without putting down a deposit on a council house.

At the Edinburgh Festival I saw a Swedish marionette version of *Ubu Roi* and the Traverse production of *Ubu Enchaîné*. I slept under the Forth Bridge. I bought a copy of Artaud's *Theatre and Its Double*. I saw Café La MaMa doing *Tom Paine* and the Soft Machine performing *Lullaby for Catatonics* with Mark Boyle's Sensual Laboratory and the Epileptic Flowers, two experimental danseuses who experimentally shagged a beach ball.

Most remarkable of all was Jean-Claude Van Itallie's *America Hurrah*, performed by Joseph Chaikin's Open Theatre. The three short plays *Interview*, *TV* and *Motel* were a direct attack on America and the American way of life. They were angry and violent and uncompromising, and they tackled everything from consumerism to the Vietnam War head on. *Motel* ended with the actors dressed as grotesque carnival dolls, representative of Middle America, trashing a motel bathroom and daubing slogans on the walls to the sound of heavy-metal feedback. I enthusiastically fantasised running a guerrilla theatre troupe that broke into people's homes, smashed up their TV sets and forced them to watch significant political drama. 'Up Against the Wall Motherfuckers.'

On 8 October 1967 I set off with my leotard, wellington boots and Onions's *Shakespeare Glossary* for East 15. I believed that theatre could change the world... and I still do.

Joan Littlewood founded Theatre Workshop in Manchester in 1945 with Ewan MacColl, Gerry Raffles, Rosalie Williams, John Bury and Howard Goorney. Joan and MacColl had worked together before the war in the Workers' Theatre Movement and Theatre of Action. They performed Socialist agitprop theatre and their influences were Meyerhold, Piscator, *Commedia dell'Arte* and subsequently Stanislavsky and Rudolf Laban. For their pains they managed to get themselves blacklisted by the BBC for Communist sympathies.

Theatre Workshop was very much an ensemble company and functioned as a collective. Joan preferred to work with actors who didn't look or think like actors, and would have nothing to do with the 'calcified turds' of the Repertory or the West End. She believed in constant training and in stretching the company by doing daily voice and Laban movement classes: discipline unheard of in British theatre at the time. They experimented with European design and lighting techniques. They studied classical texts including Aeschylus, Sophocles and Aristophanes. They initiated and researched contemporary projects. They worked on ways to combine Stanislavsky naturalism with Meyerhold's expressionism, British music hall and taking the piss. They designed and built the sets, made the costumes, put up the posters and sold the tickets. They borrowed and they blagged and they travelled in an old lorry playing wherever would have them. They were frequently broke. The Arts Council would not fund them because of their politics, so they all took part-time jobs to pay for the shows. Sometimes they picked tomatoes and sold them round Manchester from a barrow. Sometimes they had to sing for their supper. They often lived communally, sharing what food they had. They were trying to make genuine, popular, socially relevant, entertaining theatre for the people.

Their repertoire drew on the European classics including Molière, Lorca and Lope de Vega, Elizabethan and Jacobean drama, and Ewan MacColl's own plays, notably *Uranium 235*: a protest piece about the hydrogen bomb. Gradually they evolved their own style and began to find an audience. Gradually their unique work began to be recognised, but not by the critics. The company toured Czechoslovakia, Scandinavia and throughout Britain. They gate-crashed the Edinburgh Festival. Joan always maintained that the term 'fringe' was invented to describe their unofficial Festival appearance. They were frequently homeless, but they had an early champion in the form of the colourful queer Socialist MP Tom Driberg, who also wrote the William Hickey gossip column in the *Daily Express*. Driberg let the nomad troupe camp and rehearse in the grounds of his home, Bradwell Lodge in Essex, where they also ran workshops and summer schools. He even wrote a play for them.

In 1953 the company moved into the Theatre Royal, Palace of Varieties, Stratford, London, E15. 'Ours is Chaucer's Stratford, rather older than Will's,' said Joan. They hired it for twenty quid a week. The move caused a schism in the company. Ewan MacColl thought they were betraying their roots and soon drifted off to spearhead the British Folk Music revival. The company lived in the dressing rooms and cooked in the Gallery bar while they presented fortnightly Rep. They kicked off with *Twelfth Night*, hoping to attract a local audience from the market in Angel Lane. Hardly anybody came, but over the next couple of years they gave them everything from Shakespeare, Shaw and O'Casey to *Hindle Wakes*, *Celestina* and *The Alchemist*. They worked eighteen hours a day, seven days a week, fuelled by strong tea and Benzedrine. The company believed that only the best was good enough for the people but the people stayed away. A whole bunch of new actors joined, including Dudley Sutton, Brian Murphy and Yootha Joyce, who also ran the box office. Richard Harris and Maxwell Shaw walked in off the street. All were rigorously schooled in Workshop techniques. Slowly the word got around and audiences ventured out to Stratford East. When Joan produced a memorable *Richard II* with Harry H. Corbett, even the critics plucked up the courage to risk the arduous journey to the wastelands at the far end of the Central Line. Unsupported by the Arts Council, who still thought they were a bunch of Commies, and to the chagrin of the theatrical Establishment, the company were invited in 1955 to represent England at the Théâtre des Nations in Paris. Lacking funds for transport costs they were offered money by a West End impresario in exchange for a hefty poster credit. Joan told him to fuck off. The actors took the ferry, carrying the set, props and costumes for *Arden of Faversham* and *Volpone* with them.

Back home Joan played *Mother Courage* in the British premiere of Brecht's play. Brecht would only grant permission for the production if she took the part. Gracie Fields, who was his first choice, wasn't available. Joan was reluctant to do it, and apparently she was terrible. Despite her work being constantly labelled as Brechtian, Joan was never a big fan. She thought he was humourless. 'I hate the cunt,' she once said.

In 1956 Theatre Workshop produced *The Quare Fellow*, Brendan Behan's extraordinary anti-capital-punishment prison play. Joan and the company fashioned the piece from Behan's wild and chaotic text. The result was revolutionary. *The Quare Fellow* opened in the same month as John Osborne's *Look Back in Anger* at the Royal Court, and these two productions arguably changed British theatre for ever.

Whilst it is impossible to determine whether Theatre Workshop or The English Stage Company had the greater influence on future theatre practitioners, it would nonetheless be true to say that, whereas the Royal Court concentrated on producing important plays, Stratford East made socially significant popular theatre and had better jokes. Despite Joan's lifelong distaste for the glittering shithouse of the West End, the company were broke, so *The Quare Fellow* transferred to the Comedy Theatre, where it ran for three months.

The next year Joan, Gerry Raffles, designer John Bury and actor Richard Harris were taken to court by the Lord Chamberlain, charged with wilful improvisation. The play that caused the trouble was Henry Chapman's *You Won't Always Be On Top*. The play is set on a building site, so Bury had transformed the theatre into one, with the actors mixing real concrete and laying real bricks. There had been the usual improvisation during rehearsals, but this continued organically into performance, thus deviating from the text that had been licensed by the Lord Chamberlain, who sent in spies. They reported the company for criminal deviation, contrary to the Theatres Act of 1843.

In a sequence involving the opening of a public lavatory Richard Harris illegally impersonated Sir Winston Churchill while appearing to take a piss. If the company lost the case there was a chance that the theatre might be closed down. The Workshop managed to get a top-notch barrister to act for them for free. Fortunately the presiding magistrate, who had been a builder by trade, liked the play. He fined them fifteen pounds and told them not to do it again, and the Lord Chamberlain was made a laughing stock for bringing the charges. It would be another decade before the ludicrous farrago of state theatre censorship was done away with, but his Lordship had not yet finished with Joan.

Brendan Behan, after drinking his commission fee and after being motivated at gunpoint by Gerry Raffles, had managed to write sufficient of *The Hostage* for the company to go into rehearsals. They pieced together the play from improvisation, Brendan's anecdotes and rebel songs, and created an anarchic *Commedia* masterpiece populated by hookers, nutters, ne'er-do-wells, drag queens and the IRA. Brendan, often in the audience and often drunk, often joined in the show. The Lord Chamberlain reluctantly licensed the script after demanding that 'the builder's labourer is not to carry the plank in the erotic place and at the erotic angle that he does, and the Lord Chamberlain wishes to be informed of the manner in which the plank in future is to be carried'.

Joan, in homage to the comrades in Sloane Square (she called them the living dead), inserted a sequence in which the two most boring characters in the play were unceremoniously stuffed into a dustbin marked 'Return to the Royal Court Theatre'. The English Stage Company was giving its *Endgame* at the time.

Shelagh Delaney was nineteen when she wrote *A Taste of Honey*. She had been taken to a Rattigan play at Manchester Opera House and had been sufficiently inspired to write her own. Although the style was naïve, the use of language was electric, and Joan spotted the talent straight away. She produced the play, again with improvisational input into the script from the company.

The plot is simple, but the story of a teenage girl first made pregnant by a black boyfriend who deserts her, and then cared for by a gay art student, was groundbreaking for the time. The Arts Council, waking up to what was going on, gave Theatre Workshop a grant of £150 towards the production but demanded ten per cent of all future profits from the play in return. Against Joan's better judgement both *The Hostage* and *A Taste of Honey* transferred to the West End.

After fifteen years the company had become an overnight sensation. Their new-found fame brought a new set of problems, and several actors were lured away by lucrative offers from the commercial theatre and television. Joan was desperately juggling three separate casts, two in the West End and one back at Angel Lane. The situation was further complicated with the arrival of Frank Norman's play, *Fings Ain't Wot They Used T'Be*.

Norman was an ex-con, whose abrasive novel *Bang To Rights* had been celebrated by the glitterati. Joan decided that *Fings* should be a musical and roped in Lionel Bart, a musical prodigy from Stepney who had once been a member of Tommy Steele's backing group The Cavemen and had written Cliff Richard's catchy number-one hit 'Living Doll'. Joan turned the script inside out, and the actors added new scenes and dialogue with Frank and Lionel joining in the improvisations and writing new songs on the hoof. *Fings* was a triumph and for the first time the theatre was packed with people who had never been to the theatre before, including cockney villains revelling in the celebratory tale of cockney villainy. Max Bygraves took a heavily sanitised version of the title song to the top of the charts, and soon the nation was singing about how 'Once our beer was frothy but now it's frothy coffee', rather than how 'Once in golden days of yore ponces killed a lazy whore', reducing Bart's hymn to the glories of prostitution to a bit of a generational nostalgic moan. *Fings* went straight into the West End. *The Hostage* went to Paris and Broadway. *A Taste of Honey* was to be made into a film. Brendan had become a household name, and his Rabelaisian antics filled the gossip columns. Joan sensed trouble ahead. 'Success is going to kill us,' she said.

She had to cast and train another company for *Make Me An Offer*, the Wolf Mankowitz musical set down the Portobello Road. She recruited Roy Kinnear, Sheila Hancock and Victor Spinetti, who was doing stand up in a strip club. Despite Mankowitz's reluctance to change a word of his script, the show was a success, as was Stephen Lewis's *Sparrers Can't Sing* with Barbara Windsor. Both shows made the journey up west, making a total of five transfers in two years.

'They will soon be naming the junction of Charing Cross Road and Coventry Street, Littlewood Corner,' wrote Bernard Levin.

It was all too much. Joan was exhausted and felt that the company's standards were being eroded and that the work, which soon came to be caricatured as a cheeky, cockney, nostalgic knees-up, was a far cry from the original Socialist blueprint set down in 1945. The Arts Council still wouldn't subsidise the company—between 1945 and 1961 they gave them less than £5,000—and they were still demanding their ten per cent royalty for *A Taste of Honey*.

'When you have to live by exporting bowdlerised versions of your shows as light entertainment for sophisticated West End audiences you're through,' said Joan in 1961, and she quit and went off to Nigeria. She returned in 1963 to direct *Oh What a Lovely War*, possibly her greatest triumph.

Gerry Raffles had heard a radio broadcast by Charles Chilton combining the verbatim testimony of the soldiers in battle with the jingoistic songs of the First World War. He commissioned a script. Joan threw it out, put together a company of Workshop regulars and started again. The cast was initially unimpressed with what they thought was the sentimentality of the songs, but, by juxtaposing them with the terrible statistics of the war dead and naturalistic scenes showing the reality of life in the trenches, they created a bitter satire on the sheer waste and incompetence of the Capitalist war machine and a moving tribute to the lives that were needlessly sacrificed. Add to this Joan's brilliant device of presenting the entertainment as a seaside Pierrot Show while coldly projecting details of the casualties on a moving news panel and you have a production that horrifies, moves, offends and entertains the audience in equal measure. It was the culmination of everything Theatre Workshop had striven for. The final message of the futility of war and the politics that cause wars chimed with the British audience still affected by the Cuban missile crisis. Arguably the show contributed to the growth in support for the Campaign for Nuclear Disarmament. *Oh What a Lovely War* ran for over a year in the West End and then went round the world. Forty-five years later it is performed regularly, particularly in schools and by youth theatres and, although frequently and misguidedly accused of sentimentalism, it has nonetheless become one of the important political plays of the twentieth century.

The Fun Palace was a dream that Joan had cherished for years. She had been inspired by the eighteenth-century Vauxhall Pleasure Gardens and wanted to create a twentieth-century version on the Isle of Dogs. Here there would be plays, music, clowns, diversions, dancing, eating, drinking, arts and crafts, raree shows, charivari, fireworks and general rollicking. Partly educational, partly recreational, the Fun Palace would be a cultural amusement park for the People. A contemporary William Morris utopian playground:

> In London we are going to create a university of the streets—not a gracious park, but a foretaste of the pleasures of the future. The Fun Arcade will be full of games that psychologists and electronics engineers now devise for the service of industry, or war. Knowledge will be piped through jukeboxes. In the music area— by day, instruments available, free instruction, recordings for everyone, classical, folk, jazz, pop, disc libraries—by night jam sessions and festivals, poetry and dance.
>
> In the science playground/lecture demonstrations, supported by teaching films, closed circuit television and working models, at night an agora or Kaffeeklatch where the Socrates, Abelards,

Mermaid poets, the wandering scholars of the future—the mystics, sceptics and sophists—can dispute till dawn. An acting area will afford the therapy of theatre for everyone.

Joan enthusiastically set out to raise money for the development of the Fun Palace despite the project being lampooned in the press as some kind of Littlewood cheeky-chappie, cockney theme park—all jellied eels, pearly kings and doing the Lambeth Walk. She made a film version of *Sparrers Can't Sing*, which featured the Kray Twins' henchmen and a bunch of local faces as extras. She made a few commercials, and she agreed to direct what was supposed to be a West End blockbuster musical.

In the short years since *Fings Ain't Wot They Used T'Be*, Lionel Bart had become a household name and the most successful musical-theatre composer in the world. He had written *Lock Up Your Daughters*, *Blitz*, *Maggie May* and biggest of them all, *Oliver!*, which ran in the West End and on Broadway for years. He seemed to have the Midas touch and was now a millionaire living a millionaire's lifestyle. A new musical written by Lionel and directed by Joan Littlewood seemingly couldn't fail. The show was about Robin Hood and his Merry Men and was called *Twang!*:

The very next morning I regretted it. I found I was under contract to one or two good songs and no script, not even the outline of one.

The whole project was fatally misconceived from the start as a Ziegfeld Follies-style production with thirty showgirls, a full orchestra and baroque settings by Oliver Messel, who was supposed to be good at forests. Joan put together a company of old Workshop 'nuts' including Barbara Windsor and James Booth, and on the first day of rehearsals abandoned what little script there was and started improvising. War broke out between the creative team, and soon Bart was rehearsing one show while Joan worked on another, and Paddy Stone choreographed a third. *Sgt Bilko* writer Harvey Orkin sat in the stalls desperately thinking up new gags which Joan instantly dismissed. The script, costumes and casting were changed by the hour. Howard Goorney, playing Guy of Gisburn, famously went for a piss in one rehearsal only to find on his return that he was no longer in the scene. 'Christ, Joan,' he said, 'it's a good job I didn't go for a shit or I'd be out of a job.'

Tensions worsened when Joan accused Lionel of being out of his skull on acid. She walked around with a script folder on which she had written 'Lionel's Final Fuck-Up'. There were rumours of a gangland stand-off between the Twins who backed Joan and the Soho villains who backed Lionel. The production opened in Manchester and in chaos. Unable to make it work, Joan walked and took her name off the poster.

The producers brought in Burt Shevelove, a Broadway play doctor, to fix the show. He didn't. *Twang!* eventually opened at the Shaftesbury and ran for less than a month. Bart had sold the rights of *Oliver!* to finance the fiasco. He lost a fortune.

The Fun Palace was finally killed off when Newham Council decided it needed the proposed site for a sewage pumping station which remains unbuilt to this day.

In 1967 Joan was back at Stratford East.

East 15 Acting School is not at Stratford East. It's not in East 15 at all. It is based in Debden in Essex in a Georgian house called Hatfields.

Workshop member Margaret Bury founded the School in 1961 in order to pass on Joan's principles and techniques to a new generation. Joan had disappeared to Nigeria, and the company had no idea when or if she was going to return.

Maggie Bury (or Margaret Greenwood at the time) had joined the company in the late 1940s after attending a summer school. She toured with them throughout Britain and Europe playing a variety of parts including Lysistrata, and in 1948 married actor/designer/director John Bury. When the company moved into the Theatre Royal Maggie and John lived in the prop store while Joan and Gerry lived in the top dressing room. The School was originally based in the Mansfield House Settlement in the East End but was now housed in a spacious but freezing mansion with a newly opened theatre. Converted by the students from a medieval tithe barn, the Corbett Theatre was named after benefactor Harry H. Corbett (rather than Sooty's tiresome manipulator). Maggie lived in an apartment on the premises and strode the grounds in a leather trench coat and thigh-length boots, accompanied by two smelly dogs, looking every inch a sadistic KGB Commissar from a Bond movie.

I arrived at the School aged barely nineteen, shy, terrified and with no idea about what to expect or what I was doing there. It very soon became apparent that what I wasn't doing there was a Directors' Course. This was because there wasn't one. There was another directing student called Matthew Higham, and the idea seemed to be that we would do the first-year Acting Course as well as absorbing directing wisdom by stage-managing the third-year shows and then play it by ear.

My fellow lively minded, argumentative, inventive, exquisite, vulgar, idealistic, talented students who wanted a livelier theatre, were a mixed bunch. Maggie clearly shared Joan's proclivity for actors with diverse and colourful backgrounds. There was Tony Shear, an ex-morphine addict who had just got out of jail in the States for kiting cheques. There was Alan Ford, a market trader, stand-up comic, pub-singer and all round cockney geezer. There was a pastry cook from Scarborough, a captain from the Israeli Army, a toff from Eton, a lapsed member of the Provisional IRA and a woman from Canada with a spastic monkey. There were several students for whom English was not even close to being their second language. There were some forty of us altogether.

In the year above were Annabel Scase, whose parents David and Rosalie were founder members of Theatre Workshop; David Casey, who was the grandson of the great Jimmy James and son of James Casey who wrote *The Clitheroe Kid*; Oliver Tobias who went on to be, er... *The Stud*; and Alison Steadman, who even then was head and shoulders ahead of the rest.

The course consisted of classes in Acting, Speech, Laban Movement, *Commedia dell'Arte*, Singing, Fencing and Dramaturgy. Acting tuition was based on Stanslavsky's *An Actor Prepares* and was built around a variety of improvisation exercises.

So much of this stuff has now become the common currency of an actor's training that it's important to emphasise how revolutionary it was seen to be at the time and with what suspicion it was regarded. Despite *An Actor Prepares* having first been published in 1937, Stanislavsky was a closed book to most English theatre practitioners and his work was often pejoratively and purposely confused with The Method and Strasberg's Actors Studio, which involved Americans and mumbling. Bill Gaskill and Keith Johnstone at the Royal Court, Peter Brook, and Joan had been using improvisation techniques for years, but the majority of English actors, directors and drama schools distrusted the practice, despite having no real idea what it entailed. It's also true to say that a majority of actors believed that theatre shouldn't dabble in politics or discuss social issues. For the first half of the twentieth century British theatre was unassailably a middle-class activity. The plays were middle class, representing middle-class values to middle-class audiences, and as most of the roles available were middle class so were the actors. It was almost impossible to find an actor with a regional accent even to play the comical maid. There were times when even the best drama schools were regarded as little more than finishing schools offering training in elocution and deportment. Regional theatres staged either weekly or fortnightly Rep with actors rehearsing in the day and performing at night plus matinees. There was barely enough time to learn the lines and block the play, and there was certainly no time for experimentation or subtext analysis. This produced a rigidity in thought and an unwillingness to countenance change. Actors did not think it necessary or important to work on their craft, and any suggestion that they should would have been met with derision.

Unfortunately English actors were widely considered to be the best in the world, and equally unfortunately they believed their own publicity. Thus Improvisation, Units and Objectives, Laban Efforts and Character Research were clearly unnecessary and possibly dangerous. The idea that theatre should have any purpose other than entertainment was probably subversive. The ridiculous regime of the Lord Chamberlain ensured that theatre could never seriously discuss sex, religion, politics, the royal family or homosexuality, or engage with topics even remotely socially relevant; since all scripts had to be approved several months in advance of production by a coterie of retired army officers, creating dialogue through improvisation was theoretically illegal.

By 1967, however, the Establishment in theatre and everywhere else was starting to crumble.

Our first-year acting tutors were Robert Walker and Richard Wherret, both ex-students, and they cheerfully announced that their job was to break us down. There was no mention of putting us back together again. Their aim was to make us lose our inhibitions, to become unafraid of making fools of ourselves and to learn once again to play as children.

Each day began with a warm-up. This usually started with a physical stretch and shake-out session and then progressed into games. These could include kids' party games like Grandmother's Footsteps, Hide and Seek, British Bulldog or Blind Man's Buff. There were ornate sophistications. A Rob Walker warm-up would often start like this:

ROBERT. Right, Timothy, I want you to go into the bogs and toss yourself off. Go on, don't be a cunt, just go and do it.

Exit TIMOTHY.

Right, Cordelia, I want you to go and watch him.

Exit CORDELIA *in tears.*

Everybody else, we're playing tig. Last one to touch Jane's tits is 'it'!

Further inhibition-busting exercises included The Wanking Donkey, in which you had to pretend to be a wanking donkey, and Making Love to a Chair, which was equally self-explanatory.

Improvisation classes were mainly devoted to what have now come to be known as Theatre Games or Theatre Sports. These took many forms, but the emphasis was on spontaneity and preferably comic invention. A basic exercise would involve everybody sitting in a circle. One person mimes an object and then passes it on to the next person, who changes it into something else, thus an umbrella becomes a telescope and then a banana or a hand grenade. In another version of this an actor creates a physical sequence of movement, which is copied and mutated by the next actor. So climbing a ladder becomes digging a hole. A game similar to Statues involved everyone contorting themselves into grotesque positions and a chosen actor then describing them as exhibits in a museum. This gave everyone ample opportunity to comment on the physical peculiarities of their fellow students. There was an exercise that involved everybody swapping clothes and impersonating each other and several that involved groping about in the dark. Some involved snogging. There were Trust Exercises where you jumped off a table and the others caught you. There were Status Exercises involving servant-and-master domination games. There were exercises in instant characterisation along the lines of 'You're a vicar and you meet Marilyn Monroe and a tramp at a kosher deli.' The purpose of this kind of improvisation is for the actor to adapt to the circumstances and come up with instant dialogue. As an exploration of real character or motivation it's a complete non-starter. Alongside all this frenzied spontaneous activity we were also studying *An Actor Prepares*.

Stanislavsky concerned himself with truth in acting as opposed to the mechanical representation and demonstration practised in most European theatre at the time. He placed great emphasis on the power of imagination and the importance of Emotion Memory—how an actor conjures up parallel emotions from his own life to those experienced by the character he is playing. Accordingly we spent many hours sitting in a circle trying to conjure up traumatic episodes from our childhood that might come in handy. Everyone seemed to have a tragic tale to tell. Even the Old Etonian had been expelled for consorting with domestic staff. We learnt about Concentration and Observation, The Unbroken Line, The Inner State, and Units and Objectives.

Working on a text an actor breaks down each scene into sections—units of action that chart the journey of the character. The actor then decides what is the character's objective in each unit—that which the character seeks actively to achieve. What the character wants. There are different objectives for each unit and a super-objective for the entire play. We spent many hours deconstructing texts and breaking them down into units and objectives.

Workshop actor Dudley Sutton recently told me of Joan Littlewood's take on the subject:

> I reckon the most important thing about Joan—and what differentiated her from the Royal Court—was that the objectives we sought always had to be non-intellectual, physical and forward-moving—she reckoned (and I seem to remember this from rehearsals for *The Dutch Courtesan*) that there were only four

real questions: Who's got the food?, Who's got the power?, Who's got the money?, Who's got the sex? With these clearly in mind, she reckoned, you could walk into any play, well armed against bullshit directors.

During the rehearsals for *The Quare Fellow*, Joan had devised a series of improvisations in which the actors spent weeks living the life of prisoners in Mountjoy Gaol. They used the roof of the theatre as an exercise yard, marching round and round, and being drilled by the screws. They improvised slopping out, cleaning the cells and the day-to-day sheer boredom of the prison existence. Only after the circumstances and relationships had been fully explored did Joan introduce the text. East 15 had its own version of this that invariably involved being peasants.

Taking as the starting point *The Weavers* by Gerhart Hauptmann, Lope de Vega's *Fuente Ovejuna*, or any play involving a downtrodden mob, the students would create meagre hovels in the school grounds and live in them in character, unrelieved poverty and deepest misery. Everyone wore peasant clothing and lived on peasant food cooked on peasant fires, usually in winter, while imagining what it felt like to be oppressed. In later years this extreme form of improvisation became an East 15 trademark, and students spent weeks living on acorns and road kill and scavenging in the dustbins of Loughton as they recreated life in a Stalinist gulag or the Somme. Eventually Health and Safety kicked in when students started to go down with dengue fever, trench foot and dhobi's itch.

An Actor Prepares takes the form of a fictional account of a young actor, Kostya, learning acting at some late-nineteenth-century Russian conservatoire or drama school: 'Today the Director asked us to repeat the exercise in which we searched for Maria's lost purse.' *An East 15 Actor Prepares* would more likely be: 'Today the Director asked us to repeat the exercise in which Lavinia performed The Wanking Donkey.'

Jean Newlove taught Laban Movement in what had once been a Scout hut in what had once been an orchard in the grounds of the School. A trained dancer who had worked with the Kurt Jooss ballet, Jean had assisted Rudolf Laban at Dartington Hall during the war and helped him to set up The Art of Movement studio in Manchester. After introducing Laban techniques to the Theatre Workshop company at their summer school she joined the company at the same time as Maggie. She acted with the company for many years and was their movement teacher and choreographer for *The Hostage* and *Fings Ain't Wot They Used T'Be*. She had been married to Ewan MacColl and they had two children, Hamish and

Kirsty. Kirsty MacColl became a successful recording artist who was tragically killed in a boating accident. Joan was their godmother.

Rudolf Laban was an Austro-Hungarian dancer, choreographer and movement theoretician. He was the founder of the Free Dance movement and created pacifist and political ballets. He was appointed to choreograph the opening ceremony for the 1936 Berlin Olympics but fell foul of Goebbels who banned the performance after seeing a dress rehearsal. Laban escaped to Britain in 1938. He invented a new language and theory of movement, and it fell to Jean to pass it on to us. It was not the easiest of tasks. Although some of the first year had had some dance training (and in some cases military training), most of us were terribly unfit and almost all of us were smokers. For several weeks we coughed and wheezed our way through a series of stretching and spatial awareness exercises. We worked on balance and extending our range of movement, we worked on different rhythms like skipping, running, hopping and jumping, and then we did it backwards. In pairs we improvised imaginary sword fights and games of tennis, and in groups we wrapped ourselves into bizarre structures and created weird human machines by crawling over each other's bodies. Some of it was painful. Quite a lot of it was sexy. After all, Laban had been influenced by Freud. After a few weeks we had not unsurprisingly lost all our physical inhibitions. Then we had to make a model of an icosahedron.

An icosahedron is a twenty-sided crystal-like structure with which you can illustrate the possible planes of movement around the body. First we made small-scale models out of sticks and glue. It was like a class *Blue Peter* project. Then we made a full-sized one out of bamboo garden canes and string. Then we took turns to stand inside it, experimenting with how far we could stretch up and down, backwards and forwards and from side to side, exploring the planes of movement. Then we did it standing on one leg. As you moved inside the icosahedron, the theory was that you started to get a sense of your range and began to learn how to use the space around you. I fell over.

Laban analysed human movement and broke it down into eight Efforts based on whether the energy used was direct or indirect, sustained or broken, or strong or light. A movement that is light, direct and sustained is called a 'Dab', for example. A movement that is light, indirect and sustained is a 'Float'. The eight efforts are 'Floating', 'Flicking', 'Gliding', 'Dabbing', 'Wringing', 'Slashing', 'Pressing' and 'Thrusting'. Jean showed us exercises that taught us the essence of each effort.

Next Jean made us analyse which was our personal predominant effort. All the boys immediately assumed they were Thrusters, but Jean swiftly outed a few closet Floaters and the odd Dabber. The next step was to move around the room switching from effort to effort on Jean's command. Then we did it adding sounds that corresponded to the efforts and then we did it switching efforts and sounds while singing 'I am the very model of a modern Major General' from *The Pirates of Penzance*. Gradually we were able to move from one effort to another with ease. The value in all this is that you start to break away from ingrained patterns of movement and extend the range of the physical possibilities for any character you are playing. The efforts are in fact a form of shorthand used to illustrate various physical archetypes, not dissimilar to the stock characters in *Commedia dell'Arte*. The next stage was to take a pure effort and construct a character suggested by the physical movement. A Floater for example might be a Poet or a Guru whereas a Thruster might be a Politician or a Soldier.

It's a useful way to unlock the physicality of a character, although every character is obviously a combination of several efforts, some of them contradictory. Like all systems it is only one of the tools in an actor's toolbox, but combined with the Stanislavsky approach it certainly provides a comprehensive framework for the actor to work with.

Although Joan Littlewood pioneered the idea, the use of the Laban technique is now widespread. Drama Centre was created around the Laban system of character analysis. I have, however, worked with a number of actors who have become fundamentalist about Laban. This is a big mistake.

Voice was not at the time one of East 15's strongest suits. Theatre Workshop had benefited from Ewan MacColl's singing and musical talents, and he and Jean Newlove had been working on a way to incorporate Laban Efforts into vocal training. Perhaps because of this singing background Joan always had her actors work with Bel Canto teachers, and Maggie Bury followed her lead. The results were not totally successful, not least because it takes seven years to master Bel Canto and the course was only three. It's a system better suited to the training of opera singers. The Head of Speech was Julian Gardiner. He had a series of bizarre exercises designed to bring out your potential. The first thing you had to do was 'make the baby'. This involved trying to find the pure sound that a baby makes before acquiring bad vocal habits—like speech, for example. It roughly goes EEAAGGHHHHHH and done properly can be heard as far away as Theydon Bois. The next stage was 'the bow and arrow', which meant making the baby and then shooting it across the room. This goes EEAAGGHHHHhhhhhhhhhhhhhhhhhhhhhhh. Julian would assist in the process by standing behind you and goosing you as you let your arrow fly. The girls said that he occasionally became conspicuously overexcited while making the baby with them. It worked if you could sing, but I couldn't and it didn't. Julian also wrote bogus Edwardian light operettas based on the works of Arthur Wing Pinero. Every year Maggie announced that the school would be producing one of them, and every year the third-year students threatened to go on strike rather than perform in this nonsense. Julian would then threaten to die, and Maggie would burst into tears and emote, and before they knew it the thirds were all dressed up in bonnets and straw boaters singing 'So Hurrah for the Dean and good old Dandy Dick' while miming a jolly punt. It was hardly cutting edge.

Also teaching Speech was Vincent Clinton Clinton-Baddeley. Clinton was an experienced actor of the old school and a polymath. He wrote thrillers chronicling the adventures of Dr R.V. Davis, the amateur detective. He wrote pastiche Victorian Pantomimes in verse and ran a record label specialising in the recording of English verse-speaking, much of which he read himself. In 1935 he had appeared in a short film, *The Fairy of the Phone*, made by the GPO Film Unit to promote the benefits of owning a telephone, in which he played an unlikely potentate surrounded by nubile retainers of unspecified gender. He was a personal friend of Quentin Crisp and John Gielgud. He had shoulder-length white hair, and he resembled a very wise old eagle.

The only way to impress Clinton was to impersonate him. A typical lesson would start with 'Dear boy, today we will attempt the Chorus speech from *Henry Vee*' and off you would set with a polite, apologetic and inaudible 'O for a muse of fire,' etc. Clinton would be on his feet in a flash. 'No no no no, like *this*, dear heart.' It was like watching Macready. 'O FOR A MUSE OF FIRE, THAT WOULD ASCEND THE BRIGHT-EST HEAVEN OF INVENTION. Now you, dear boy...' and the only way out was to follow him around the room parroting his interpretation of the speech and punctuating it with appropriate gesture. Actually he was on to something. What he was illustrating was the fact that the speech has to come from some kind of internal passion, a need to communicate the information to the audience. You really had to see the very casques that did affright the air at Agincourt to make the audience believe they could too. Exhausted Clinton would sink back into his wing chair. 'That was almost quite good, old fruit. Do come to tea on Friday.' He had a butler. A lot of students thought his classes were a bunch of bollocks, but I loved them. Clinton was very much the real thing.

George Harvey Webb was the school dramaturg and a brain on a stick. He was a Classics scholar and an historian and a fiddle player. He had been a member of Ewan MacColl's folk band and had played Irish jigs in

Joan's production of *The Hostage*, both at Stratford East and in the West End and was in the band on *Fings Ain't Wot They Used T'Be*. He had also played fiddle for Aleister Crowley's bogus black masses in the Conway Hall in the Thirties. George claimed that he had been dramaturg to Theatre Workshop, but Joan would never admit to it. She had once encountered one in Germany:

> I had always wondered what a dramaturg did for a living and soon found out. He undertakes the research in which the Workshop involves the whole company. The result is handed to the actors with a strong suggestion to how the work should be interpreted. I didn't like the sound of it.

Brecht had sent one over to work with her on *Mother Courage*, but she swiftly banished him from rehearsals.

Joan called in George as an expert when she was working on Elizabethan or Jacobean texts. His knowledge of language, contemporary manners and social history was consummate. She installed him in an upper room in the pub over the road and consulted him whenever she needed information or clarification. She wouldn't let him speak directly to the actors as she thought that he would confuse them. She had a point.

George had great Theatre Workshop stories. He was once charged with minding Brendan Behan. George's job was to keep Brendan away from the Press, who were actively trying to provoke him into acts of wild and Fenian misbehaviour in the hope they could get copy out of it. One night in a quiet pub miles away from Fleet Street, Brendan went for a piss. On his return George noticed that he was behaving shiftily and had his coat buttoned up tight. George eventually persuaded him to open his jacket and found he had a loaded revolver stuffed into the waistband of his pants. 'Some fecker from the *News of the Screws* gave it me in the jakes.' George wrapped it in a parcel and threw it into the Thames.

He also told of Jean Genet coming through British Customs. 'Have you anything to declare?' said the officer. '*Moi, je suis pederast*,' said Genet. George lived in Highgate with a brood of feral children all of whom were educated at Summerhill. Occasionally they would all turn up at East 15 wearing combat fatigues and carrying machetes. Perhaps they were planning to run away and join the Viet Cong. I subsequently discovered that he had once been Ken Campbell's Latin master.

With George we read the classics: the Greeks and the Romans, the Elizabethans and the Jacobeans, Tragedy and Comedy, Carolean Masques and Miracle Plays: the entire canon. George illuminated them all, deconstructing obscure textual passages and explaining everything from the social order of Ancient Thebes to Venetian sewage disposal and from *The Shepherd's Calendar* to the fact that Restoration actresses didn't wear any knickers. He would frequently diversify into Magick, Religion, Philosophy and Quantum Physics. George was the first person I met who could explain Schrödinger's Cat. He taught us about Aristotle and Plato, Sophocles and Aristophanes, Plautus and Menander, Saint Augustine and Erasmus.

To better appreciate the Dionysian Rites in *The Bacchae* he took the whole first year into Epping Forest and after a bit of improvised Eleusinian chanting and free dance we became a pack of demented Furies chasing the girl with the monkey around for several hours. Emerging into a clearing, muddy, exhausted and waving pointed sticks, we were stopped in our tracks by a police car. Someone had called in to complain about a bunch of Satanists having an orgy and sacrificing some virgins. They were not far wrong. George just explained that we were from East 15. I got the impression this had happened before.

George's function was to open our minds. He certainly opened mine.

We did two productions in the first term. First we did some short Chekhov pieces. Matthew Higham and I did *The Unexpected Guest*. Matthew had no lines and I was terrible. Then we did Dürrenmatt's *The Visit*, in which I was even worse. I think I played the retired Judge as, in Laban terms, a 'Wringer'. I did, however, get to work at Stratford East.

In 1967 Joan had returned to the Theatre Royal, now marketing itself as 'the swinging nite spot in East London', to mount four shows. The first of these was Barbara Garson's *Macbird!*—an American satire about President Lyndon B. Johnson and his supposed involvement in the Kennedy assassination. Joan had thrown out the script as usual and made her own. The curtain went up on what looked like an RSC production of the Scottish play with RSC witches and RSC acting until Brian Murphy popped up and said, 'I bet you thought you were in the other bloody Stratford for a minute.' The writer spent every evening in the theatre bar telling anyone who would listen that this wasn't the play she had written. Joan then did an adaptation of Vanbrugh's *The Provok'd Wife*, which she called *Intrigues and Amours*, and which she followed up with *Mrs Wilson's Diary* by *Private Eye* satirists Richard Ingrams and John Wells. The play was an 'affectionate lampoon' but still attracted the attention of the Lord Chamberlain—Joan had had to turn the Theatre Royal into a club to get away with the scurrilous *Macbird!* as his Lordship felt he had to protect the heads of friendly states. There was delay of six months before the licence was granted for *Mrs Wilson's Diary* as Harold Wilson and his cabinet censored the script. They cut eight scenes, mainly those involving Foreign Secretary George Brown getting pissed.

Although it was hardly political dynamite, the show transferred to the Criterion. When George Harvey Webb congratulated Joan, she told him she didn't want to be remembered as the woman who directed *Mrs Wilson's Diary*.

The School got a call from Mark Prichard, the Production Manager at Stratford East, asking if there were any students who wanted casual work on the next show, *The Marie Lloyd Story*. Someone must have told him about my experience at Lincoln Rep and when he discovered I had worked as a hemp-set fly man I was in. There was a vacancy on the fly gallery as someone had dropped a cut cloth on Marie Lloyd at the Tech. I did half a dozen shows a week as a casual so had the opportunity to see how the show grew in performance. The actors had an incredible rapport with the audience and passages changed every night. The show didn't always work but it was always alive and never ever boring. There was a dreadfully, castrated polite version of music hall on the BBC called *The Good Old Days*. The Workshop show gave audiences the real thing.

There was always barracking from the punters. Some were plants and some were not. In one scene Avis Bunnage as Marie walked on wearing a new straw hat. A wag in the Circle shouted out, ''Ere, Marie, I like your new titfer!' To which Marie replied, 'Yeah, nice, isn't it. Mind you, I prefer my ole felt.' There was a blizzard of handkerchiefs every night as Avis sang 'The Boy I Love is Up in the Gallery'.

In the bar afterwards I used to watch Joan give notes and joke with the cast and audience, but I was too shy and self-conscious to join in. Eventually she asked me what I was doing there. I told her I wanted to start my own company and that I was at East 15. 'Fuck that,' she said. 'Just go and do it.'

The Marie Lloyd Story was possibly the last great production Joan did. A programme note read: 'This season of Theatre Workshop at the Theatre Royal owes nothing in the way of support, cooperation or even sympathy to the Arts Council of Great Britain nor to Newham Council.'

In America one hundred thousand people marched on Washington to protest against the Vietnam War, and Abbie Hoffman and Allen Ginsberg tried to levitate the Pentagon. In a piece of guerrilla ritual theatre Ed Sanders and the Fugs led the exorcism: 'OUT DEMONS OUT. OUT DEMONS OUT.' Ginsberg rang a Tibetan bell. The Flower Children chanted, 'OM AH HUM OM AH HUM OM AH HUM', and according to Abbie, 'The ground beneath us vibrated. The granite walls began to glow, matching the orange of the new sun, and then, before our very eyes, without a sound, the entire Pentagon rose like a flying saucer in the air.'

At East 15 we were perfecting our 'Slashing' in 'I am the very model of a modern Major General.'

At Christmas I went back to Scunthorpe to work on the Panto. During one Saturday matinee there was a robbery backstage. The police were called. The Wicked Baron did it.

In the second term we had to perform self-directed Shakespearean scenes, and I was determined to make an impact. I had been cast as Malvolio in the yellow-stockinged, cross-gartered *Twelfth Night* subplot. Egged on by George Harvey Webb, I came up with a revolutionary interpretation based on exhaustive text analysis. Malvolio clearly has a stiffy. The Bard even supplies the actor with the suitable Laban effort:

> Some are born great, some achieve greatness and some have greatness *thrust* upon them.
> Go off. I discard you. Let me enjoy my private.

It's all there in the Folio. Obviously a certain amount of Emotion Memory was required to pull this off, but the performance was well received and clearly impressed certain members of staff, although I was referred to as a 'cock actor' for the rest of my time at the School. It was in fact a breakthrough of sorts. I had felt very much an outsider during my first term and now seemed to have proved myself in some way. It was quite an odd way to have to do it though.

Everyone at East 15 had to do a turn. In addition to the classes and productions there was always a huge amount of extra-curricular activity. Every week or so there would be a call for a group to put on some form of entertainment. This might be at a Derby and Joan club or at a works canteen or in one extreme case the German Embassy staff Christmas party. People worked up music-hall songs or stand-up or magic acts or anything that could be trotted out at the drop of a hat. Although I am certain that the School used us as unpaid fundraisers, it was a great opportunity to go out and be bad somewhere. Despite a tendency to deteriorate into cockney knees-up with Alan Ford conducting a spirited version of 'I can't get my winkle out, isn't it a sin? The more I try to get it out the further it goes in', these impromptu gigs taught us how to deal with every kind of audience and situation.

I spent occasional weekends working at the theatre at Stratford. Well, not actually in it. The area round Angel Lane was being cleared to make way for new flats. The Theatre Royal stood in the middle of a ghost town. From the day that Theatre Workshop had arrived at Stratford they had been plagued with local kids breaking into the theatre. Joan had ambushed them and set them to work transforming the rubble from the demolition into an adventure playground and community of the streets. A bunch of us from East 15 went along to help. The kids built dens and took over derelict houses and painted and decorated them. There were festivals and picnics and dressing up, marching bands and orchestras, and George Harvey Webb played his fiddle. There were parades and pageants and Lionel Bart and sometimes a donkey. The kids made up their own plays and put them on, making props and costumes and posters and tickets. Eventually Joan took over the old school playground and started the Playbarn Project in an abandoned church hall where she held drama classes. Although the original Fun Palace had been killed off by bureaucracy and prejudice, the spirit was alive and kicking off in the derelict streets around the Theatre Royal. What was happening was educational in the true sense of the word—and without an options analysis or a risk assessment or an access appraisal or a cultural diversity action strategy in sight.

On 17 March I joined eighty thousand others to march against the war in Vietnam. Down Charing Cross road chanting 'Ho Ho Ho Chi Minh' and 'Hey Hey LBJ! How many kids did you kill today?' I was spat at by an elderly woman who instructed me to get my fucking hair cut. After Trafalgar Square the march turned left past Vanessa Redgrave and set off towards the American Embassy. I don't think anyone had any particular idea of what to do when they got to Grosvenor Square, but the Embassy was surrounded by a cordon of police and they were spoiling for a ruck. The Pacifists at the front decided to sit down, which meant that marchers were backed up to North Audley Street. They pushed forward into the Anarchists. The Anarchists pushed forward into the police lines. Smoke bombs were thrown. This is what the pigs had been waiting for, and the whole thing kicked off. Grosvenor Square was sealed and mounted police charged the demonstrators, clubbing everyone in sight. I saw a hippy girl dragged into a Black Maria by her hair and smashed the window with my fist. There were two hundred arrests and many hundreds injured.

It was the day after the My Lai Massacre when American troops of the First Battalion, Twentieth Infantry Regiment, under the command of Lieutenant William Calley, gang raped and murdered five hundred and four civilians, including women, children and babies who they suspected of being Viet Cong. The incident was covered up by one Major Colin Powell.

By the spring of 1968 the UFO Club had been closed down, the scene had moved on and I went with it. Middle Earth happened at weekends in a vast warehouse in Covent Garden. John Peel was the house DJ. Middle Earth had three stages and launched the new wave of British psychedelic bands, such as Dantalian's Chariot, The Crazy World of Arthur Brown, The Creation, Tomorrow, and The Deviants. Captain Beefheart and the Magic Band played there after first being deported for arriving at Heathrow with a strange appearance, no work permit and only two pounds and ten shillings between them. Mark Bolan's Tyrannosaurus Rex (with Steve Peregrin Took on bongos, Chinese gong and pixiephone) played frequently and indeed also did a gig at Loughton Technical College next door to East 15, with David Bowie doing a silly mime act.

Also in Covent Garden was the Arts Laboratory. Founded by Jim Haynes, who also founded the Traverse Theatre in Edinburgh, and Jack Henry Moore, who had been DJ at UFO, the Arts Lab was for two short years the centre of the alternative arts movement in London. The Lab was in another old warehouse in Drury Lane, and for five shillings or whatever you could afford you could spend all day and night doing your thing in the theatre, cinema, gallery, macrobiotic café, bookshop and crash pad. Jim described it as 'an Energy Centre where anything can happen'.

The Arts Lab in many ways resembled an all-year-round Edinburgh Fringe venue where bands and theatre and films from outside the mainstream Establishment could get a gig and an audience. In the cinema you could see Kenneth Anger's *Scorpio Rising* or Warhol's *Chelsea Girls* or Tod Browning's *Freaks*, lying in the dark on a foam rubber mattress. You could sip a Mu tea while listening to Principal Edwards Magic Theatre or The Third Ear Band or experimental electronic music from Ron Geesin. You could go to a lecture on Wilhelm Reich or Herbert Marcuse. In the theatre space I first saw the new radical and experimental companies that were starting to emerge.

People Show was founded in 1966 at the Abbey Arts Centre in Barnet by Jeff Nutall, Mark Long, John Darling, Laura Gilbert and Syd Palmer, to present a performance piece called *People Show Number One* for a single performance in the basement of Better Books in Charing Cross Road. They also played UFO and Middle Earth. Their work was a combination of happening, music hall, Grand Guignol and rock 'n' roll. They were Britain's first experimental visual theatre company, and their work has directly or indirectly influenced almost everyone working in theatre since. When they became company-in-residence at the Lab, Jim Haynes said, 'their work is outside the profession. Outside the scope, and outside the laws which define theatre in this country.' They were also described as 'the biggest all-out gas of London's intrepid new dream scene' and 'a jam session for all the senses'. A typical People Show scenario went:

> *The theatre is dark. On stage are:*
> *An animal carcass.*
> *A motorbike.*
> *A life-sized corpse doll.*
> SYD *in black mac, shirt and trousers.*
> LAURA *in school uniform gymslip, lisle stockings, hat, hair in ribbons.*
> *A spot roams slowly over these to give the effect of somebody looking it over with a gigantic flash lamp.*
> *At first* LAURA *and* SYD *are stock still and separate.*
> SYD *smoking (red dot in the darkness).*
> LAURA *reading* Jackie.
> SYD *and* LAURA *slowly start to move round the set stalking one another. Spot does not follow them, but occasionally reveals them:*
> *Talking.*
> *His face buried in her belly.*
> *She caressing his closed eyes.*
> *During this section two voices previously recorded and collaged (add music, play separate and simultaneous, swell, fade) come through house loudspeakers.*

People Show were the Swinging Sixties answer to Tristan Tzara's Cabaret Voltaire.

Portable Theatre was founded by Cambridge English graduates Tony Bicât and David Hare, who saw the established theatre as 'an outmoded pastime for the privileged elite'. Their first production was an adaptation of Kafka's diaries called *Kafka Insideout*, for which they managed amazingly to get Arts Council funding, the first fringe company to do so. They followed this up with *Gentleman I*, John Grillo's play about schizophrenia, and *Strindberg*, David Hare's play about, erm… Strindberg. Soon joined by writers Howard Brenton and Snoo Wilson, they set off round Britain to épater the bourgeois in a Volkswagen camper van. According to Tony Bicât, the company shared a belief that

> by taking plays to new places we would in some way help the revolution, the revolution that surely, given the state of the country, could not be far off. The irony was that we would all of course have wanted different revolutions and, almost certainly, have been amongst the first to be shot.

They toured with Brenton's *Christie in Love* and *Fruit*—a play of slander, lies, torture and perversion in high places, which ended with instructions on how to make a petrol bomb. The poster for *Christie in Love* read 'John Reginald Halliday Christie killed women and then he fucked them'. They were done for obscenity in Brighton.

Snoo Wilson's *Pignight* and *Blow Job* followed, and then Hare's *How Brophy Made Good*, about a left-wing intellectual who says 'fuck' on the telly. Their aim was confrontational—'to shake the audience and therefore the Establishment'—and they opened up the circuit that countless touring companies including my own Hull Truck were soon to follow.

Freehold grew out of the Wherehouse/La MaMa company founded by Nancy Meckler and La MaMa tyro Beth Porter. Meckler's work reflected the experimental physical theatre work of the American avant-garde troupes in the early Sixties. The ideas seemed to come from an interpretation of Artaud and the search for a non-verbal gestural theatre, which was grabbing a lot of attention at the time. The first Wherehouse show at the Lab was the alternatively titled *Alternatives*, which told the story of a young girl's childhood, and how she is shaped and repressed by both her family and the education system into obeying the rules and conventions of straight society. The play unfolded through a series of childhood games and rituals, the sub-Laingian notion being that there is a deeper and purer form of instinctive communication available to children before they become corrupted by the mind-forg'd manacles of man. After *Alternatives* Meckler formed Freehold, taking half the Portable Theatre Company with her. The new company would create performances from material evolved through extensive improvisation process and long rehearsal periods. They would follow a rigorous physical training regime in order to follow Grotowski's instruction that they should 'emerge from themselves'.

Pip Simmons Theatre Group started out at the Arts Lab with productions of *The Underground Lovers* and *Conversation-Sinfonietta* by French Absurdist Jean Tardieu, but they later hit their stride with *Superman*, which combined cartoon characters with rock music to satirise American politics and counterculture; Superman started out by fighting for civil rights but ended up by advocating fucking in the streets. The Pip Simmons Group had clearly been much influenced by the work of American companies such as The Open Theatre and The Living Theatre, but they soon established their own confrontational style, provoking audiences throughout Europe with seminal productions

27

Do It!, *Alice in Wonderland* and *The George Jackson Black and White Minstrel Show*, culminating in the brilliant *An die Musik*. In *The George Jackson Black and White Minstrel Show* they used the Coon Show format to confront the audience's inherent racism. Casting the audience as slave owners, the company held an auction in which the blacked-up minstrels cajoled the punters to buy them. The actors then spent the interval chained to their owners. Pip Simmons really fucked off the liberals.

The Arts Lab also hosted early productions by Steven Berkoff (*In the Penal Colony*), Jeff Moore's dance company Moving Being, and Lindsay Kemp (*Pantomime Turquoise*). Jane Arden's *Vagina Rex and the Gas Oven: a poperatic documentary*, with its use of strobe lighting and psychedelic *mise en scène*, was the first play to come out of the Women's Liberation Movement and was a resounding underground hit.

The Arts Lab Movement spread, as Jim Haynes intended, and soon there were Labs in Manchester, Birmingham, Guildford, Leeds, Portsmouth, as well as The Combination in Brighton and the Rock Factory in Edinburgh. David Bowie founded the Beckenham Arts Lab, announcing, 'There isn't one pseud involved. It's alive and new and healthy and it matters more to me than anything else.'

Around the same time I saw Jerome Savary's company Le Grand Théâtre Panique perform an improvisation/circus/happening loosely based around Arrabal's *The Labyrinth* at the Mercury Theatre in Notting Hill Gate. This was a very jolly carnival spectacular set in a lavatory in the middle of a maze of washing lines with sheets hung out to dry. There was a parade with flutes and drums and confetti. A nude man flew overhead on a swing, his bollocks dangling above the heads of the punters. A drag queen sang in Spanish. A woman had a wank. Topless divas invited you to tango. A large black man in an Afghan coat paraded a sacrificial goat, and a small boy wandered around in clown make-up. In the middle of it all, Savary himself pelted the audience with incense-filled smoke bombs. Everybody joined in the frolics, and a great time was had by all.

Back at East 15 Mike Leigh arrived to direct a production with the first year. By now the year had been split into groups A and B. We were assured that these groupings were no indication of any kind of preferment, but they definitely weren't alphabetical and all the *jeunesse dorée* were in group A. Naturally I was in group B, which meant doing Thomas Dekker's *The Honest Whore* with Mike, while the rest did Marston's *The Dutch Courtesan* with Helen Gold, who subsequently became a Sanyasin and changed her name to Prem Vashti. Mike had just left the RSC, where he had been assistant to Peter Hall and Trevor Nunn, and had been bounced off a production of Ann Jellicoe's *The Knack* (with John Shrapnel and Derrick O'Connor) by John Barton. Barton held a different opinion as to what constituted comedy, and the RSC had signally failed to recognise Mike's unique talent. Thirty years later Terry Hands admitted:

> Mike should have been given a corner to do his own thing in his own terms. In our defence, there was a strain of charlatanism at the RSC at that time, centred around people like Michael Kustow and Charles Marowitz.

All I knew about him was that he had directed the first ever production of *Little Malcolm and His Struggle Against the Eunuchs* and that he devised what he called Improvised Plays.

Mike and David Halliwell had been at RADA together and, in an attempt to get their hands on the means of production, started a theatre company, Dramagraph, in 1965. In some ways they were pioneers of the whole fringe movement. Mike directed and designed *Little Malcolm* at Unity Theatre and Halliwell played Scrawdyke. The original title was *One Long Wank*, but they were prevailed upon to change it, as no newspaper would print the advert. The show ran over four hours because Halliwell refused to cut a word. The production was not a success, but the play (without Mike) went on to the West End and Broadway and arguably became one of the seminal plays of the century.

Mike and I shared the same sense of humour, and we got on straight away. He also respected that I wanted to be a director and did all he could to encourage me. He had a built-in bullshit detector and a different take on improvisation, seeing it as a way to get to the truth of character and situation as opposed to an exercise in coming up with a punchline. He did not tolerate fools gladly. He didn't tolerate fools at all.

The Honest Whore is a dreadful bunch of Jacobean bollocks, with an involved and convoluted plot concerning love, thwarted love, death, feigned death, whoredom, madness, feigned madness and drapery. Mike concentrated on the drapery, creating a Jacobean street market out of a few bolts of cloth. The play is set in Milan, which turns into London halfway through when everybody ends up in Bethlem Hospital. I played Roger the Pander in Madame Fingerlock's Brothel, and a lunatic.

> *Enter* ROGER THE PANDER *with a stool, cushion, looking glass and chafing dish.*

> ROGER. I had wont to get sixteen pence for fetching a pottle of hippocras. (*Sees ruff.*) There's thy ruff. Shall I poke it?

I was on a hiding to nothing even with George Harvey Webb's priapic dramaturgy. Kenneth Williams would have found it a struggle. I feared that I would have to pull the Malvolio stunt, but Mike made me come up with a proper character. I thought of Johnnie, the old drag queen who had played Dame in *Dick Whittington* in Scunthorpe. I came up with a back-story and subtext. We set up an improvised scene where Madame Fingerlock and Roger were doing a moonlight flit from the brothel. We hastily bundled stool, cushion, looking glass, ruff, chafing dish and everything else in the rehearsal room into a suitcase. On the way out I took a swig from a stray can of Coke someone had left behind. I retched and spat the whole lot out. Someone had pissed in the can. Mike kept it in.

After *The Honest Whore* Mike went on to direct *Individual Fruit Pies*—an improvised play with the third year.

Mike had started devising plays through improvisation a couple of years earlier with the kids at the Midlands Arts Centre in Cannon Hill Park in Birmingham. He had arrived at the idea after seeing Brook's production of the *Marat/Sade* and discovering that the actors had spent weeks observing mental patients and creating fully rounded and organic characters through an extensive rehearsal process. He wondered if it was possible to create whole plays using this method. There had been improvised drama since *Commedia dell'Arte*, in which spirit Joan Littlewood had produced *Sam, the Highest Jumper of Them All* at Stratford East in 1960. Although William Saroyan was the credited playwright, he freely admitted that the play was made up, written, and directed on the stage of the Theatre Royal, Angel Lane, Stratford, London. *Sam* consisted of a cast of one-dimensional stereotypes acting out comic routines in a scenario provided by the playwright. Even now a great deal of improvised drama is constructed in this way.

Mike uniquely began with creating three-dimensional characters with the actors, based on people they knew, and letting the story unfold through their interaction. In terms of truth and honesty the piece was an inspiration, and I continually pestered Mike to tell me how his process worked. Eventually he did.

> *Les bourgeois c'est comme les cochons*
> *Plus ça devient vieux plus ça devient bête*
> *Les bourgeois c'est comme les cochons*
> *Plus ça devient vieux plus ça devient cons.*

> (Jacques Brel)

On 2 May 1968, after months of protest and occupation, the French authorities closed down the University of Paris at Nanterre and expelled all the students. The next day the police beat and tear-gassed students demonstrating in protest and then occupied and closed down the Sorbonne. There were 596 arrests. All the next week students, teachers, anarchists and revolutionaries fought pitched battles with the police and the CRS in the streets around the Rive Gauche. The protesters built barricades from cars, café tables, advertising hoardings and building materials. The CRS attacked the barricades with tear-gas grenades and clubbed students and bystanders. The protesters retaliated by ripping up and throwing cobblestones and petrol bombs. Over 1,500 students were injured, over 1,000 were arrested and sixty cars were burnt. The police were accused of acting as *agents provocateurs* and provoking the riot. There were rumours of over thirty dead in secret police morgues.

Shocked by police brutality and Government overreaction to the student protests, the Parti Communiste Français came out in support of the students and, with major left-wing trades unions the Confédération Generale du Travail and the Force Ouvrière, called a one-day general strike.

On 13 May over a million students and workers marched through Paris. The police stayed away. Guerrilla theatre companies burned effigies of De Gaulle and Prime Minister Pompidou, who quickly announced the release of the imprisoned demonstrators and the reopening of the Sorbonne.

Next day the students took back the Sorbonne and declared it an autonomous People's University. Julian Beck and Judith Malina of The Living Theatre joined the occupation and issued a communiqué from the Popular Action Committee: Artaud's letter to the Chancellors of European Universities.

> The race of prophets is extinct. Europe is becoming set in its ways, slowly embalming itself beneath the wrappings of its borders, its factories, its law-courts and its universities. The frozen Mind cracks between the mineral staves which close upon it. The fault lies with your mouldy systems, your logic of 2 + 2 = 4. The fault lies with you, Chancellors, caught in the net of syllogisms. You manufacture engineers, magistrates, doctors, who know nothing of the true mysteries of the body or the cosmic laws of existence. False scholars blind outside this world, philosophers who pretend to reconstruct the mind. The least act of spontaneous creation is a more complex and revealing world than any metaphysics.

On 15 May Jean-Louis Barrault, Artistic Director of the Théâtre de France-Odéon, was tipped off that the protesters were about to occupy his theatre. He was advised by Andre Malraux's Ministry of Culture to open the doors and start a dialogue. After the evening performance of the Paul Taylor Ballet Company, 2,000 students and workers led by the Becks and members of The Living Theatre waving black Anarchist flags and singing the Internationale took over the building. Barrault, who considered himself to be a supporter of the avant-garde and who was broadly sympathetic to the students' demands, tried to open negotiations. The *Enragés* leader Daniel Cohn-Bendit declared that there would be no discussion:

> The Théâtre de France is an emblem of bourgeois culture. The Odéon will from now on be a forum for political debate. Theatre must become a major weapon against bourgeois society.

The same day factories and schools closed all over France.

On 16 May, the hastily formed Commission de l'Information de l'Odéon sent out a call to all entertainment professionals, workers and students to join them in the theatre to celebrate the downfall of reactionary Capitalist entertainment and to debate the future of Revolutionary Art. Maoists, Trotskyites, Existentialists, Situationists, Sparticists, Anarchists, Anarcho-Syndicalists, workers, poets, actors, intellectuals, students and Ionesco turned up. The walls of the theatre were covered with revolutionary posters:

LE SEUL THÉÂTRE EST DE GUÉRILLA.
BE REALISTIC: DEMAND THE IMPOSSIBLE.

The dressing rooms and offices became dormitories and kitchens. There were Molotov cocktails in the orchestra pit. Couples fucked on the roof. Le Grand Théâtre Panique performed in the square outside.

For the next week debate and discussion continued twenty-four hours a day dominated by rival extremist factions jockeying for power. The students gradually become isolated as their spontaneous movement was annexed by factionalist agitators. Over four hundred action committees were formed with very little action taking place.

'In '89 they took the Bastille, in '68 they have taken the floor,' said some wag. Julian Beck said that it was the greatest theatre he had ever seen.

The Ministry of Culture accused Barrault of siding with the students, ordering him to leave the building and threatening to cut off the electricity supply. Barrault refused. He declared that he was staying on to protect the theatre and called on Malraux to back him or sack him. By the end of the week there were over a thousand people squatting in the Odéon. Ten million workers were by now on strike and the country was paralysed. French radio and television closed down in sympathy. De

Gaulle called for a referendum, which provoked more rioting and an attempt to burn down the Bourse. He then disappeared from Paris. De Gaulle had gone to sound out the loyalty of the Army and his Generals. Half a million strikers marched through Paris chanting 'Adieu De Gaulle'.

On 28 May the Odéon squatters broke into the costume store and shat on the costumes. Barrault burst into tears. 'Twenty years of work destroyed. And for what? For nothing. Why? Pure hate and for nothing.'

He finally realised that the Government had set him up. Unable to risk further CRS brutality after the riots on the Left Bank, they had sanctioned the occupation of the Odéon as a distraction and as a focus for the protest to prevent their occupation of the Académie, the Senate or the Louvre.

De Gaulle returned and announced the dissolution of the National Assembly and immediate elections. He threatened to declare a state of emergency and to use the Armed Forces on demonstrators and strikers if they didn't return to work. In Paris there were orchestrated demonstrations in support of De Gaulle. Thirteen-year-old Nicolas Sarkozy tried to join the right-wing marchers but was banned by his mum. The strike collapsed.

On 5 June Bobby Kennedy was assassinated in Los Angeles.

At East 15 we were supposed to be working on scenes of our choice from twentieth-century drama, but a group of us, inspired by recent events, decided to devise a programme of more incisive cutting-edge work. One was a piece of agitprop about political assassination involving a twenty-foot puppet Uncle Sam made out of chicken wire and toilet rolls, which was supposed to crash to the ground symbolically when shot. At the crucial point in the drama the poorly designed mannequin stubbornly refused to budge and hung above the stage throughout the rest of the show, swinging like a corpse on a gibbet. This proved to be a bit of a distraction during the more sensitive passages of The Winslow Boy.

Our second effort was a ludicrously pretentious adaptation of Genet's Our Lady of the Flowers, which we performed semi-naked as a piece of what we fondly imagined to be Artaudian Ritual Theatre to a track from The Pink Floyd's Saucerful of Secrets. We succeeded only in making ourselves unpopular, which at the time seemed to us to be a bit of a result.

On 14 June, my twentieth birthday, I decided to hitch to Paris to join the Revolution. It took me a week. When I got there the occupation of the Odéon was over and demonstrations were banned. The Government claimed that a group of Kanangais, a militant extremist group similar to the Weathermen or the Red Brigade, were holed up in the Odéon and making bombs. They sent in the CRS to 'protect' the students. The police had taken the Sorbonne the day before and flown the *tricolore* from the flagpole. There was still a whiff of tear gas in the air and endless debate and discussion in the École des Beaux Arts, but there was a profound sense that the circus had left town. I saw agitprop street theatre in the rue Mouffetard and the whole area was still covered in posters and graffiti. The scars of battle were still visible on the streets. I was stopped and searched several times. There were groups of cops on every street corner. In the Vieille Grille I spent the night talking politics with actors from the Théâtre de l'Épée de Bois. 'Take the theatre onto the streets and the streets into the theatre.' They were setting off to join The Living Theatre in Avignon *pour continuer la lutte*.

The Gaullistes won the election. The workers returned to work and the students mostly returned to their studies. The workers had secured a minimum wage, a forty-hour week and increased retirement and pension benefits. The students had secured the wholesale reform of the education system. There were significant advances in Women's and Gay rights, and abortion was legalised. The Revolution was postponed. Money was not abolished. The world did not end.

Jean-Louis Barrault was eventually sacked by André Malraux, who blamed the whole thing on the death of God.

Whatever happened was of sufficient significance for President Nicolas Sarkozy to express his desire forty years later to liquidate the legacy of *Les Événements*, which he claimed, had led to 'intellectual and moral relativism and hedonistic individualism'.

At the Avignon Theatre Festival, the Mayor, after being accused of permitting 'amusements for the mentally sick', banned *Paradise Now*, the visionary new work from The Living Theatre. Julian Beck declared: 'Theatre is the Wooden Horse by which we can take the town.'

And with his inspiring words ringing in my ears I headed back to Scunthorpe to direct the Youth Theatre.

2

Who Put the Cunt in Scunthorpe?

It was not easy to make revolutionary theatre in Scunthorpe in the summer of 1968, but the Youth Theatre had a fucking good shot at it. I had decided to produce *The Devils* by John Whiting and had serious hopes that this would successfully offend the local bourgeoisie. Originally produced by the RSC in 1961 and based on Aldous Huxley's *The Devils of Loudon*, the play tells of the seventeenth-century French priest Urban Grandier and his alleged black magical and sexual shenanigans with a bunch of Ursuline nuns. It was made into a film in 1971 by Ken Russell with Oliver Reed, Vanessa Redgrave and old Littlewood actors Dudley Sutton and Murray Melvin. *The Devils* afforded a large and largely teenage cast the opportunity to indulge in witchcraft, torture, rape, Sapphic masturbation, mass sexual hysteria and demonic possession. It afforded me the opportunity to practise all the techniques I had learnt at East 15. These included Dionysian Ritual, Emotion Memory, Units and Objectives, Laban Efforts and The Wanking Donkey; and culminated in an enthusiastically improvised group exorcism in the car park of the local council Cycling Proficiency Testing Centre, next door to the Civic Theatre. The cast took to all this like ducks to water.

One of the lads had an auntie who claimed to be a white witch so a group of them hitched off to Wootton Bassett in Wiltshire to interview her. They came back with a book of dubious spells and tales of nicking a Ford Cortina, which they eventually abandoned in a lay-by outside St Neots. Auntie the Witch told them that the best way to raise the Devil was to walk three times widdershins round a village church graveyard at midnight. We tried this out but all that happened was that Gerry Fillingham, an apprentice fitter at the Appleby Frodingham Steelworks, started speaking in tongues and we got a letter of complaint from the vicar. A couple of the sixth-formers had been on an educational exchange trip to France in May and had found themselves on the barricades at the sit-in at Montelimar Lycée. They were constantly on the look-out for some action, so when Russian tanks invaded Czechoslovakia bringing an end to the Prague Spring, the Youth Theatre staged a demonstration in support of Party Chairman Alexander Dubček by picketing the Russian delegation who were visiting the Scunthorpe Folk Dance Society's International Folk Dance Festival. Wearing their nun's and priest's costumes they handed out publicity leaflets for *The Devils* while chanting 'Dubček! Dubček!' and 'We will fight. We will win. Paris, Scunthorpe, Rome, Berlin.' This act of civil disobedience succeeded only in getting up the nose of Councillor Glynn Roberts, the Chairman of the Parks and Libraries Committee who had organised the international folksy extravaganza and was also in charge of funding the Civic Theatre where we were about to perform. The Russians were Ukrainians from Grimsby.

We also produced our own underground newspaper modelled on *International Times*: *POKE*, a Magazine of the Arts. This contained some wistfully prurient fifth-form poetry about love, a review of the new Mothers of Invention album, a drawing of Councillor Roberts shagging a goat and, bizarrely, a bad review of our own show which hadn't opened yet, saying that it was a shower of self-indulgent shit. I think we put that in to throw people off the scent as to who were the perpetrators of this vile canard. In retrospect it was probably for the best that *POKE* only ran to one issue. Actually I think it only ever ran to one copy.

In Chicago Abbie Hoffman, Jerry Rubin and the newly formed Yippies staged a Festival of Life to coincide with the Democratic Convention and to protest the Vietnam War. They ran a pig for President and circulated rumours that they were planning to spike the water supply with acid and have a public Fuck-In.

> The life of The American Spirit is being torn asunder by
> The forces of violence, decay and the napalm-cancer fiend
> We demand The Politics of Ecstasy.
> We will create our own reality. We are Free America.
> We will not accept the false theatre of the Death Convention.
> DO IT!!!

Thousands turned up for a free concert in Lincoln Park. On the orders of Mayor Daley the police charged the crowds with billy clubs and tear gas. Hundreds were arrested and injured over several days of brutality. Abbie Hoffman, Jerry Rubin, David Dellinger, Tom Hayden, Rennie Davis, John Froines, Lee Weiner, and Black Panther Bobby Seale were indicted with crossing the state line to incite a riot. They all faced long prison sentences. They became known as the Chicago Eight.

Turning up to rehearse at the theatre one day we found the building locked and the Theatre Director missing. We couldn't raise him on the phone but after several frustrating enquiries to the Parks and Libraries Department, the caretaker arrived with a message from Councillor Roberts: the theatre was closed until further notice and the production was cancelled. No explanation. Nothing.

We repaired to the Cycling Proficiency hut to review the situation. The solution was simple. We would occupy the Civic Theatre. One of the *Enragés* from Montelimar climbed in through the bog window and let us in. We phoned Roberts and told him that we were sitting in until the production was reinstated, and then we began rehearsing. Roberts dispatched the caretaker back to evict us. We refused to budge so he went for the police. A singularly bored copper wandered over from the police station, took one look and announced that it was nowt to do with him. The kids hung out of the dressing-room windows singing '*Les bourgeois c'est comme les cochons*'. Banners appeared on the walls: '*LES OUVRIERS AU THEATRE NON. LE THEATRE AUX OUVRIERS OUI*' and '*GLYNN ROBERTS BAISSE CHEVRÈS*'. After rehearsals I sent the younger kids home, but a couple of the Montelimar lads stayed to man the barricades in the front-of-house office. I headed off to the Theatre Director's house. His wife let me in. At first he refused to tell me what was going on, but he suddenly burst into tears. He had been arrested and charged with embezzlement. He had overpaid himself by two hundred pounds and had been caught. He was suspended from duty and not allowed near the theatre. He had also been sworn to silence, as Roberts did not want the matter made public. He also told me that he thought Roberts was using the situation to censor the show, as he did not approve of the content of the play or indeed the idea of the Youth Theatre in general.

Next morning I was called to a meeting at the central library. I told Roberts that I knew all about the situation with the Theatre Director and unless the production was reinstated I would go to the local press with the story. I can't imagine why I thought they would be interested for a second but it seemed to work. Roberts vacillated for a while but eventually he agreed. I think he was frightened of being made to look a fool. We had won and the kids were ecstatic. It was a small victory, but it brought them together as a company, and they had learnt a lesson on the persuasive power of demonstration and direct action.

One of the greater glories of theatre is its ability to steal children.

The Devils played to packed houses, mostly of adoring parents, who must have been impressed to see their children writhing around in the throes of demonic possession. To be fair I suspect that the people on stage had a better experience than the people in the audience, but the kids had had a good time and worked hard and were justifiably proud of their achievement.

Mike Leigh drove over from Manchester to see it in his clapped-out Deux Chevaux. He had recently moved there to attempt to write a conventional play and was living in a cheap flat above a halal butchers in Slade Lane. I don't think Mike was particularly taken with the production, but he was caught up in the ebullient spirit of the company and later invited me over to Manchester to assist him with the last few days of rehearsals for *Big Basil*, an improvised play he was devising with the Manchester Youth Theatre.

Big Basil was the story of a five-foot-tall, gobby fifteen-year-old who fancied himself as a hard case. In some ways the character was the teenage prototype for Johnny, David Thewlis's character in *Naked*. Basil has a series of adventures involving school, teachers, parents, shoplifting, and girls, culminating in a teenage party that goes wrong. I kipped on Mike's floor and directed the party scene using a freeze action technique nicked from *Rowan and Martin's Laugh-In*. The play had been devised with the young cast developing characters that they knew from school. The late great Steven Pimlott played the teacher. He and Mike spent hours playing convoluted word games based on the more obscure lyrics of Gilbert and Sullivan.

On 26 September 1968 Theatre Censorship was finally abolished in the United Kingdom, thus ending the ludicrous reign of the Lord Chamberlain and his band of small-minded philistines who had effectively stifled all sexual, political and religious debate in Playhouses for three hundred years. The gates of filth were flung wide the very next day as the tribal rock musical *Hair* opened at the Shaftesbury Theatre in the West End. The first night had been delayed pending the departure of the good Lord, who had refused to license the show proclaiming that:

> This is a demoralising play. It extols dirt, anti-Establishment views, homosexuality, free love and drug-taking and it inveighs against patriotism.

Hair was written by two New York actors, James Rado and Gerry Ragni, who had based the characters on a bunch of East Village acid freaks, primarily the feral street hippy gang The Motherfuckers. The play was anti-war, anti-authoritarian and advocated free love, free dope, and fucking in the streets. The title acknowledged that long hair was a badge of belonging to the tribe, a totemic symbol of coming out for the counterculture. The nudity was a testament to sexual liberation. Written in 1966 and developed using the improvisation techniques of Chaikin's Open Theatre and The Living Theatre, the show opened at Joe Papp's Public Theater in 1967 before moving on to the Cheetah Disco and Broadway.

By the time *Hair* hit England it had become sanitised and lost a lot of its bite. The scene had moved on, and the riots in Paris and Chicago and the murder of hundreds of unarmed demonstrators in Mexico City by the Fascist Government on the eve of the Olympics saw the movement beginning to take a more aggressive stance. It was beginning to dawn on us that love probably wasn't all we were going to need. The show, which had radical beginnings, had now become the banal and acceptable face of the youth revolution. They even dimmed the lights for the nudity. The songs by Galt MacDermot, rather than being blazing acid rock anthems of protest would have happily fitted into *Jesus Christ Superstar*. 'Let the Sunshine In' was hardly 'Up Against the Wall Motherfuckers'.

The West End cast included Oliver 'Stud' Tobias, who had dropped out of East 15 to do the gig. No one at the school could remember him being either overtly political or particularly psychedelic. *Time Out* used to list *Hair* as a costume drama set in the mid-Sixties.

The producers of *Hair* gave East 15 students loads of free tickets. Maybe they hoped the girls would get their tits out for the Love-In audience participation finale. *Hair* ran for five years at the Shaftesbury, attracting coach parties from all over Britain, possibly even Scunthorpe. Bells, beads and kaftans had by now become high-street fashion.

The second-year acting tutor was Gunduz Kalic, a radical Turkish director who had to flee to Britain when his company was threatened by the Turkish Government. He was tall, rangy, smoked liquorice paper roll-ups and fancied himself as a stud muffin. He lived in a caravan in the orchard. Gunduz was a great believer in popular theatre, making drama accessible to the widest possible audience; his first project was a tour of prisons with a new road show. We played Pentonville, Wandsworth, Wormwood Scrubs and Holloway. Holloway was the most depressing show we ever did. The girls were howled off whenever they made an appearance and the boys were constantly heckled with shouts of 'Show us your cock'. They really were tough gigs, and we quickly learned that we were a bunch of smart-arses and not nearly as funny or as irresistible as we thought. After the gig in Pentonville we all went for a kebab in a local Turkish café. Gunduz, speaking Turkish, told the waiter we were on a day out from a lunatic asylum.

On 28 October I went to see the Mothers of Invention in concert at the Festival Hall. After ten minutes of baffling atonal music and what seemed like random dialogue about overthrowing the diatonic system and eating meat, Frank Zappa announced, 'We're doing a play.' And they were. The plot of what Zappa later described as 'a cheesy little psycho-drama' went like this:

The three talented members of the Mothers decide to quit and form a new band with a lot of discipline. They enlist fourteen members of the BBC Symphony Orchestra who march on as robots in evening dress. The remaining Mothers, coveting the robots' natty uniforms, try to join the new band but are rejected on account of their lack of ability to read music. Jimmy Carl Black, the Indian of the group, who is horny and wants to boogie all night long, wonders how he will get laid if they don't play rock 'n' roll and drink beer. Zappa advises him that he will not get any pussy in London unless he looks like a pop star so he is kitted out in a Mod a-go-go jacket, a feather boa and a Hendrix wig, and sent into the audience to hustle chicks. Roy Estrada appears as the Mexican Pope and hands out Smarties to the audience. The real Pope had banned the contraceptive pill for Catholics a few weeks earlier. Despite an impressive falsetto, the Mexican Pope is also rejected by the new band. Eventually the Mothers are reunited by their love of sentimental harmonies.

Zappa had supplied the scenario and the band improvised the dia-logue. It was the first time that he had worked with live orchestral music and the first time he had attempted a play, although much of his work features storytelling of life on the road. Musically Zappa admitted to being influenced by Edgar Varese and Erik Satie, and theatrically he seems to have been inspired by Jarry and the Absurdists. What I think significant is that theatre was then automatically considered to be at the heart of all forms of contemporary and underground culture, as well as being regarded as politically relevant.

During the course of the evening a liveried Festival Hall attendant told a section of the audience to sit down. 'Get those fucking uniforms outta here,' shouted some twat from the auditorium. Everybody cheered. 'Everybody here is wearing a fucking uniform, and you better not forget it,' rejoined Zappa. Everyone cheered some more. Freaks characteristi-cally had no problem in supporting diametrically opposed views without an intervening pause for reflection.

The ICA decided to produce *The Hero Rises Up* by John Arden and Margaretta D'Arcy, for four nights only, at the Roundhouse. This was a huge risk as the Roundhouse had up to then almost only been used for rock concerts and had proved to be the graveyard for Arnold Wesker's Centre 42. They even described the undertaking on their ornate publicity as 'an apparent lunacy on the part of this Institute, which only the most excessive Public Support can prevent from causing the Immediate Ruin of the Administrators'. Looking for free labour they called up East 15, and I went to work on the show as lighting-board operator.

The Hero Rises Up was an epic drama about the life and loves of Horatio Nelson. Arden said he wanted the audience to have:

An experience akin to that of running up in a crowded wet street on a Saturday night against a man with a hump on his back dancing in a puddle, his arms around a pair of laughing girls, his mouth full of inexplicable noises.

And with that aim in mind John and Margaretta had insisted on directing the piece themselves.

The experimental production was partly Brechtian, partly multimedia promenade theatre and partly *Carry On Admiral*. Henry Woolf played Nelson, and Ann Mitchell and Bettina Jonic played Lady Nelson and Lady Hamilton respectively. Four actors played the rest of the forty-odd parts and the Havering Youth Theatre were on hand as matelots, a mob, sea nymphs, dockyard workers, and to provide general frigging in the rigging. There was a traditional folk group, Pickwick's Paupers, who threw in the odd shanty, and Mark Boyle and the Sensual Laboratory, who was by now doing the lightshow for Jimi Hendrix, provided nautical oil slides and atmospheric visuals. An equally atmospheric sound track was composed and improvised by Boris Howarth, who played a deconstructed piano like a harp and had to hand a selection of whistles, wind chimes, water gongs, bells, mallets, thunder sheets, duck calls, and a glass organ that ran on Calor gas and spouted smoke. He had also recorded some genuine sea and boat sounds on HMS *Victory* in Portsmouth Harbour. All this stuff was amplified through twelve phased speakers ranged throughout the vast auditorium. The actors had absolutely no amplification at all and the acoustics were dreadful. Some of the show was to be presented promenade style and some of it wasn't, so the seating arrangements were at best arbitrary and the sight lines were dreadful. Apart from Brook's *The Tempest Experiment*, the Roundhouse had never mounted a full-length play before, and the technical staff, helpful though they were, had absolutely no idea what they were supposed to be doing. It was also freezing.

After the dress rehearsal the producers decided to cut the entire lighting plot as the lights on stage rendered Mark Boyle's experimental and expensive film of the sea going backwards invisible. Next day they turned up with a vanload of German pageant lamp follow spots, the kind of thing they use for the Edinburgh Military Tattoo or *Holiday on Ice*. The wheeze was that the Havering Youth Theatre would operate these from the gallery, only opening them up when a prominent character had a speech. The problem was that they failed to allocate specific actors to the kids, so most of the time Nelson was simultaneously blinded and illuminated by a dozen or so follow spots while Emma Hamilton was left in the dark or at best appeared to be drowning, dragged under by Mark Boyle's receding cinematic tide. Arden stood Canute-like in the middle of this nautical chaos, desperately trying to reassure everyone that all would be well, while Margaretta conducted noisy public rows with the producers about pretty much everything, but mainly that the ICA were failing to recruit the right sort of audience.

At the first performance Boris's amplifier blew up, so much of the atmospheric texture and dramatic punctuation failed to put in an appearance. Many of us believed this to be a bonus.

The next day John and Margaretta announced that from now on all performances would be free. They disagreed with charging punters seven and six, believing that theatre should be available to all without charge, and had accordingly invited most of the working class of Camden to that evening's press night. The ICA and the other producers countered that this was emphatically not the case; that admission charges would remain the same, that they had their investment to recoup and the backwards sea film to pay for, and that the Ardens could essentially fuck off. The actors carried on rehearsing in the hope of getting through the evening's performance unscathed but had to stop as an Anarchists' conference had been scheduled for the afternoon. At the half-hour call there was a kerfuffle in the foyer. John and Margaretta were staging a sit-down strike in protest against the ICA and bourgeois admission charges. They were picketing their own show with banners and leaflets and exhorting the punters not to pay. The front-of-house and box-office staff had no idea what to do, and when the entire working class of Camden turned up all became chaos. Eventually the audience, some who had paid and some who had not, were crammed into the auditorium. There were not enough seats so the critics ended up sitting on the floor or clinging to the pillars that supported the roof. Several left halfway through, mumbling curses. All things being equal, it was a good performance. During the curtain call Arden elbowed his way onto the stage with a white plastic bucket. He made a stirring speech about Free Theatre and then handed round the bucket asking for donations from those who got in free to make up the actors' wages. One of the producers rushed up to the lighting desk shouting, 'Black out! Black out the fucker!' I told him to sod off.

The reviews were terrible, the most charitable being the *Listener* which described it as a 'misguided production'. Personally I thought it was a heroic failure, but the consensus of opinion seemed to be that the Ardens couldn't direct Harold Wilson to Downing Street.

In December Jack Moore brought over The Human Family, a theatre company from Amsterdam, and together with Ken Kesey of Magic Bus fame they annexed the Drury Lane Arts Lab and organised a happening at the Albert Hall, *The Alchemical Wedding*. I worked on the crew, and a very peculiar evening it turned out to be. The event started with the Radha Krishna Temple and the entire audience doing the Hare Krishna chant and climaxed with John and Yoko getting into a white silk bag and staying there for three-quarters of an hour while nothing else happened at all. Then they got out and there was huge applause. Then a girl in the stalls took her clothes off, and some more people took their clothes off, then everybody clapped some more and then went home to speculate as to what had gone on in the sack. Later Yoko explained that this had been the beginning of Bagism, a movement inspired by *Le Petit Prince* in which 'one sees rightly only with the heart, the essential is invisible to the eye'. Lennon used the term again in the lyrics of 'Give Peace a Chance': 'Everybody's talking about Bagism, Shagism, Dragism,' etc., etc., etc. It certainly beat doing panto in Scunthorpe.

After Christmas my fellow directing student Matthew and I assisted on two third-year Shakespeare productions. Maggie Bury directed *King Lear* and Gunduz directed *As You Like It*. Working on *Lear* involved mainly driving around Essex in Matthew's beaten-up van pilfering scrapyards for bits of rusty old metal. These were to form the set designed by Maggie's faux-German boyfriend Wilf, or Manfred Hilke as he styled himself professionally. Wilf was an ex-student whom Maggie and husband John Bury had allegedly saved from a life of crime and now hung around the school looking disdainfully miserable and occasionally mowing the lawn. In his designer capacity he had also blagged several tons of Welsh slate flagstones, which we spent ages laying on top of the already stone floor of the Corbett Theatre. It was fortunate that the Duke of Kent had previously worked on building sites or we would still be there. Maggie wasn't interested in my ideas for the play, nicked from Peter Brook, nicked from Jan Kott's *Shakespeare Our Contemporary*, but I got to direct the rowdy knights in the rowdy knights' scene. The rowdy knights were a bunch of first-year lads and the disgruntled rump of the third year who had not been allotted speaking parts. In an attempt to lift events above the usual drunken rhubarb I tried to give them life histories and objectives, but to no real effect. In the end I wrote a bogus medieval drinking song called 'A Young Swain Poked It In', but even that failed to improve matters. I don't think I learnt much on *King Lear*. *As You Like It* was much more fun.

Gunduz was determined to make the play a contemporary entertainment, so, dramaturgically encouraged by George Harvey Webb, he decided that Duke Frederick was a gangster and that his courtiers were thugs, whereas Duke Senior was, George maintained, a drop-out and his courtiers were hippies. George seemed to be stretching a point by making the orchard a garage, but his interpretation was fully justified when the unconscious Charles the wrestler (played by me) was unceremoniously thrown into the back of an old Citroën and driven out of the doors of the theatre and off into the night. Charles the wrestler made a full recovery and joined the hippies in the forest where he was enthusiastically embraced by the first-year girls. We had decided to use 'living scenery', which meant that Arden was stuffed with students playing trees, flowers, snakes, bumblebees and God knows what. I got to direct all the forest activity, and it ended up looking like Woodstock. Now obviously this was all going on within a few months of *Hair* opening in the West End and the influences are clear, but the show played to packed houses of Essex schoolkids getting their first taste of Shakespeare. They raised the roof.

Despite all the above Gunduz gave the actors a lot of space and tended to help them find their own way through the play rather than imposing himself on every sentence. I thought this made good sense.

Matthew and I decided to put together a company made up of second-years to take three shows up to the Edinburgh Fringe. We decided on an all-male version of Genet's *The Maids*, a production of *Afore Night Come* by David Rudkin about a ritual murder in a Bromsgrove pear orchard, and Matthew was going to try his hand at an improvised play mysteriously titled *Loan*. We had no money and no venue, but we started casting and fund raising.

Tony Shear had a plan to run a 'stag'. This was an old scam of his from his criminal Canadian past and involved a rigged poker game, a large amount of drugs, and pimping the first-year girls from *As You Like It*. Alan Ford had a theory about knocking off a jeweller's in Chigwell. Matthew and I got a stall on Harlow market and tried to sell a load of particularly unattractive East German nylon cardigans. It rained. We didn't sell shit.

We drove up to Edinburgh to find a venue. The door of Matt's car fell off just outside North Berwick. We blagged our way in to see Max

Stafford-Clark, then running the Traverse, who was understandably unimpressed, especially when Matt asked him if he was 'the Wanker Royal around here'. By sheer luck we found a venue space in the Masonic Hall, paid our five pounds registration fee to the Festival Society, and we were all set. We had persuaded the Manchester Polytechnic Drama Department to come in with us. A friend of Mike Leigh's, Gerald McNally, who lectured there, wanted to do a production of *Macbeth* with his students, one of whom was Julie Walters. Mike had by now devised another play with the Youth Theatre called *Glum Victoria and the Lad with Specs* and another, *Epilogue*, for Sedgley Park Roman Catholic teacher-training college. He was also planning a venture called The Working Theatre with RSC tyro director Buzz Goodbody and the playwright Mike Stott. They collectively applied to run the new Hull Arts Centre but were turned down by Alan Plater and now had designs on an old electricity generating station in Rochdale.

I rejoined the second-year acting group for the *Commedia dell'Arte* productions with Maria Sentivany, the Hungarian mime tutor who had escaped the 1956 uprising. In addition to the performances at the Corbett we were also going to play the Roundhouse. We did two shows: *Albert*, a modern-dress *Commedia* about a bunch of misfits running away to join the circus, and *Mr Pucci*, a traditional show. Group B, with which I was now reunited, did *Mr Pucci*. Maria insisted that everyone tried out all the masks—including the girls who normally got a raw deal playing whores, cuckolding wives, young lovers, pert minxes and the occasional zanni. Obviously, twatting about with false noses was regarded as a uniquely male preserve in sixteenth-century Italy. I found that the mask I felt most at home with was *Il Dottore* and I created a character who was a bizarre cross between the Mad Hatter and Ken Tynan. I'm not sure that we had much of a scenario but neither I imagine did the original Venetian players. I came up with a *lazzi* in which *Il Dottore* lasciviously tried to persuade a large Australian woman to let him saw her in half as part of a magical entertainment, possibly to curry favour with the Doge. This included a lot of measuring her not inconsiderable chest, a bit of renaissance frottage and some jovial word play around the theme of 'Your saw' and 'You're sore'. And at the end we all did a merry and comic dance. We played Sunday afternoons at the Roundhouse and attracted a good crowd, so much so that we were invited back by George Hoskins, who was the venue manager at the time. Matthew and I took over the organisation of the gigs and briefly became Bradwell/Higham Productions. We even managed to bluff our way on to John Peel's late-night radio programme to promote the show. One Sunday Patricia, the large Australian woman, announced to me that she was going to try something new that afternoon. As usual we entered the scene comically from opposite sides of the vast Roundhouse stage and met in the middle. When I got there I saw that she had taken her ample tits out and painted the nipples mandrill mauve. The merry dance at the end was never merrier.

The Edinburgh project continued to take shape. George Harvey Webb knew a Scottish farmer who would let us live in his barn in the Trossachs, and Maria agreed to come and prepare refugee stew from an old Hungarian recipe.

In the summer term Maggie made me assistant to Caroline Eves, who was first-year tutor. I ended up teaching improvisation and acting classes and directing half the Shakespeare scenes. We spent a lot of time chasing round Epping Forest again. This was great experience for me and Caroline let me do pretty much as I pleased, but in retrospect I'm not convinced that the students were getting full value for money. The third-years were by now reluctantly battling through *Dandy Dick*, Julian Gardiner's latest musical, Julian conspicuously having failed to die yet again, and I wrote a letter to Grotowski.

I read *Towards a Poor Theatre* as soon as it came out, and although there was much of it I didn't understand I was fascinated by the process and the ideas:

> The actor makes a total gift of himself. This is a technique of 'trance' and the integration of all the actor's psychic and bodily powers which emerge from the most intimate layers of his being and his instinct, springing forth in a sort of 'translumination'.

> The education of an actor in our theatre is not a matter of teaching something: we attempt to eliminate his organism's resistance to this psychic process. The result is freedom from the time lapse between inner impulse and outer reaction in such a way that the impulse is already an outer reaction. Impulse and action are concurrent: the body vanishes, burns and the spectator sees only a series of visible impulses.

People were starting to get turned on to Grotowski, and I think 'turned on' is the correct phrase. The combination of mysticism, yogic discipline, shamanism and the ability to vanish chimed perfectly with the acid generation influenced by Carlos Castaneda, Timothy Leary and the *Tibetan Book of the Dead*. With Maria Sentivany a group of us had tried out some of the exercises in the book. They were incredibly physically demanding but no more so than some forms of yoga. The idea of discovering a form of total universal non-verbal communication was too good to miss, so I wrote to Grotowski to ask if I could come to Wrocław as an observer for three months in the autumn. Amazingly I got an immediate response saying that this might be possible. I had to fill in a form and apply for a visa. I had to be able to understand French and bring dollars. Further instructions were to follow. I went to Maggie with the plan. I think she was quite relieved, as she clearly had no idea what to do with me for my third year. She even suggested I spend some time with the Berliner Ensemble, where she reckoned she had contacts from the Theatre Workshop days. So it was determined I would spend one term with Grotowski, one term with the Ensemble and the final term back at East 15 telling them all about it: bingo!

In June 1969 The Living Theatre arrived for a season at the Roundhouse and we were finally going to see what all the fuss was about.

The Living Theatre was founded in New York in 1949 by Julian Beck and Judith Malina, who had both been students of Brecht's collaborator Erwin Piscator. They believed, like he did, that theatre could change the world. Their first production was Gertrude Stein's *Doctor Faustus Lights the Lights* at the Cherry Lane Theatre in 1951. Active Anarchists and Pacifists, they had a commitment to what they called avant-garde poetic drama and introduced American audiences to Pirandello, Brecht, Ezra Pound, Cocteau, Picasso, William Carlos Williams, Lorca and Jarry. They refused to charge admission and took up a collection in a tambourine. They were permanently broke and often hungry. They smoked dope, they enthusiastically practised free love, and they were arrested and jailed for protesting against the H-bomb.

In November 1956 they found a new home in an abandoned department store on 14th Street and 6th Avenue where they scored a big hit with Jack Gelber's *The Connection*, a play about jazz and smack. *The Connection* takes the form of a fake avant-garde documentary about 'the anti-social world of narcotics' as it was known at the time. For the production the Becks recruited a cast of actors, musicians, actor/musicians, Martin Sheen in his first professional role, and assorted hipsters, several of whom were junkies who apparently shot up on stage every night. Freddie Redd's jazz combo played live bebop, improvising along with the dialogue.

The message of the play, a bizarre fusion of Pirandello, hyperrealism and Charlie Parker, was that Capitalism is as addictive a drug as heroin.

The critics hated it. The *New York Times* thought it was 'nothing more than a farrago of dirt'. The *Herald Tribune* said it was 'completely tasteless'. Notices like these could have killed off the show and indeed the theatre, which was $25,000 in debt to the IRS until Norman Mailer and Allen

Ginsberg rallied to the cause in the *Village Voice* praising the play for being 'dangerous, true, artful and alive'. Ken Tynan said it was the most exciting American drama he had seen since the war and the show became a hot ticket. Despite this artistic and box-office success, The Living Theatre continued to teeter on the brink of bankruptcy. By now Julian had read Artaud's *The Theatre and its Double*, recently published in America for the first time, and his ideas were moving on. He no longer just wanted to make theatre; he wanted to make revolution.

In late 1961 in response to America and Russia resuming tests of the hydrogen bomb, Judith and Julian set out to organise a General Strike For Peace. The 14th Street Theatre became strike headquarters.

On 29 January 1962 the Becks led a march down 5th Avenue to Washington Square. A scant few hundred turned up, but the Movement grew, and there were sit-down demonstrations in Grand Central Station and at the Stock Exchange. At a strike benefit at the Village Gate the young Bob Dylan sang 'Blowin' in the Wind' for the first time. On 3 March Julian, Judith and company member Joseph Chaikin, who went on to found the Open Theatre, were beaten and arrested by cops at a demonstration in Times Square.

As well as all this radical activity The Living staged productions of Brecht's *In the Jungle of the Cities* and *Man Is Man* and experimented with what they called 'The Theatre of Chance', improvised drama inspired by the I Ching and the work of John Cage, which involved actors throwing dice to determine character, dialogue and plot.

In 1963 they produced *The Brig* by Kenneth H. Brown, the perfect play for where they had arrived at politically and artistically. Brown was an ex-Marine who had served in Japan. In 1957 he had been sentenced to thirty days' hard labour in the Mount Fuji Military Prison for being four hours late coming back from leave. *The Brig* was a graphic reconstruction of the overwhelming sadistic violence and brutality he experienced. The Becks saw it both as a political metaphor for American totalitarianism, and the dehumanising savagery of the armed forces as an opportunity to further their experiments with Artaud's Theatre of Cruelty and Meyerhold's theories of biomechanical acting.

The action of *The Brig* takes place over twenty-four hours. A new prisoner arrives and is abused and assaulted. The prisoners wash, dress and go through a gruelling exercise drill. They go on work detail. They get searched. They clean up their quarters. There is an inspection. They shower. They shave. A prisoner has a nervous breakdown. He is carried off in a straitjacket. A new prisoner arrives. Every action is conducted at the double with the prison guards screaming orders and the prisoners yelling back their responses. Throughout the prisoners are bullied, humiliated, threatened and beaten. The slightest infringement of regulations is punished by a punch in the stomach. It is harrowing, relentless, brutal and hellish.

Judith conducted the three-month rehearsal period under Marine Corps regulations. Some of the actors had military experience, and additionally the cast were sent to boot camp for lengthy drill and training sessions. They were aiming for 'Acting as a state of being, not a state of representation', hoping to realise Artaud's ambition of a theatre so violent that no one who witnessed it could ever contemplate or endorse violence again. Once again the critics failed to respond to the work. Most complained that *The Brig* wasn't a play at all and that it was anti-military and mindlessly violent. Once again the *Village Voice* recognised its worth and audiences picked up, but the company was still broke and seriously in debt.

On 15 October 1963 and without warning the landlord of the theatre served the company with an eviction order. Simultaneously the IRS sent in the bailiffs to repossess the theatre and to eject the actors. The IRS claimed the company owed $28,000 in unpaid back taxes, sequestrated the building and locked the lobby and box office. The Becks were convinced that the action was an attempt by the authorities to stifle them politically. They immediately organised a demonstration outside the locked theatre and began an occupation of the upper floors. On 19 October, with chanting pickets, television crews and police barricades on 6th Avenue, Julian announced through a megaphone that there would be a free performance of *The Brig* that evening. The audience avoided the police by climbing in up a fire escape and over the roof. The IRS cut off the electricity to the building but the performance went ahead. At the end of the show the police threw out the audience and arrested the company and supporters who had chained themselves to the set. The theatre was boarded up and closed down.

As a result of the 14th Street bust, Judith and Julian were charged with eleven counts of impeding Federal Officers in the performance of their duties and were sent for trial. Judith dressed up as Portia throughout, and they turned the proceedings into an anarchist panto, refusing to recognise the moral authority of the court. They were found guilty on seven of the original eleven charges and fined $2,500. In addition they were found guilty of contempt. Julian was given sixty days in jail and Judith thirty. They were put on probation for five years. The judge described them as 'misguided but sincere people who were unable to adjust to living in a complex society'. They appealed but in the meantime were allowed to go with the company on a prearranged tour to Europe.

The Brig opened at the Mermaid in London in September 1964. The reviews were mixed, ranging from tempered admiration to total abuse. John Russell Taylor writing in *Plays and Players* described the production as the 'Theatre of Nothing' and concluded that the play provided 'a supply of image material for armchair sadists and masochists'.

The show played to sell-out houses including a bemused Laurence Olivier, who nervously watched the production from the wings. After only three weeks of performances Mermaid boss Bernard Miles, under pressure from the theatre board and the American Embassy, cut short the six-week engagement and closed down the show. The cast demonstrated outside the theatre until Bernard paid them off. The company set off for Paris. The exile of The Living Theatre had begun.

In Paris the company, now living as a commune, began to work on *Mysteries and Smaller Pieces*, a collective collaboration that took the group's work in another new direction. There would be no more characters, no more set, no more costumes, nothing to get in the way of pure communication, no more theatre of intellect. They would from now on personify Artaud's 'vital sincerity'.

The idea behind *Mysteries* was to perform a modern version of the secret rites practised at Eleusis outside Athens as initiation rituals to the fertility goddess Demeter. The audience would become a congregation who, by participating in the ritual, would reach a state of transcendental awareness and raised consciousness. In preparation the company developed a series of exercises that involved Tantric Yoga, Biomechanics, Pranic Breathing, Mantra Chanting, Sex and Psychedelics, and researched the Kabbalah, the I Ching and the *Tibetan Book of the Dead*.

Mysteries and Smaller Pieces was a series of nine ritual games. The performance started with a solo actor standing in silence for at least ten minutes. This action was designed to provoke a reaction from the audience. The audience reaction frequently involved boredom and/or mirth. A bunch of actors marched in and mimed sequences from *The Brig* as others read out the words on the dollar bill. This led into a meditation in the dark, involving incense, candles and the singing of an improvised Indian raga which evolved into the ritualistic chanting of 'Street Songs', a poem by Jackson Mac Low, a mantra invoking the peaceful overthrow of the police, banks, the army, the draft, the state, prisons, racism and an end to the war in Vietnam and the abolition of money. The company then formed a circle and began to hum a chord, an AUM. Sometimes some of the audience joined in. Sometimes they didn't.

Then there was an interval.

Mysteries culminated in a ritual called 'The Plague'—*Theatre and the Plague* was Artaud's working title for the *Theatre and its Double*. In the midst of the audience the actors gradually developed the symptoms of bubonic plague and for over thirty minutes, or as long as it took, they twitched, cried, screamed, groaned, gobbed, shivered and eventually expired until all were dead and arranged in a lifeless human pyramid that resembled the death pits in Bergen-Belsen or the aftermath of Hiroshima. Sometimes the audience joined in with the dying. Sometimes they didn't. Julian reckoned that on a good night they had to bury fifty extra bodies. *Mysteries* opened in Paris and then toured Germany, Austria and Italy, where the show was banned in Trieste after an actor got naked.

When The Living Theatre revived *Mysteries and Smaller Pieces* in New York thirty years later, Ben Brantley in the *New York Times* wrote:

> When Judith Malina sits half-lotus before a candle, chanting for an end to social and economic injustice, you get a sense that on one level she has not moved from that position since 1964.

The Becks went back to America to serve their time and on their return the company, now numbering twenty-five-plus lovers, children and hangers-on, hit the road in a caravan of second-hand VW microbuses. With a repertoire of *The Brig*, *Mysteries* and an all-male production of Genet's *The Maids*, they travelled round Belgium, Holland, France, Italy and Germany. Their work had clearly hit a nerve and they played to both enthusiastic and outraged audiences and caused a nuisance everywhere they played. In September 1965 the Venice Biennale invited the company to make a new piece for the Festival. Julian proposed 'an elaborate spectacle with visual, musical and mechanical effects' loosely based around Mary Shelley's gothic novel *Frankenstein*. The company were given accommodation and rehearsal space in Spandau prison outside Berlin. The sole remaining prisoner was Rudolf Hess. Rehearsals and discussions began with a new intensity of purpose. The collective creation sessions turned into Laingian group therapy. Most of the company took acid and participated in what Julian called 'psychedelic improvisations'. Eventually a scenario evolved. Julian called it 'a leap into the abyss of our own helplessness'.

Played out on a three-storey scaffolding set with fifteen cubicles that served as a boat, an apartment block, a torture chamber, a gallows, an operating theatre, a cemetery, a brain and a metaphor for human society, *Frankenstein* begins with an even longer silence than *Mysteries*. For half an hour the actors silently meditate in order to levitate a woman lying in the middle of the stage. If she levitates the play is consummated. She doesn't levitate, so she is chased by the company, caught in a net, put in a coffin with the lid nailed down and paraded through the audience. Several of the actors protest and are hunted down and electrocuted, gassed, guillotined, hanged, disembowelled, garrotted, beheaded, crucified and shot. Frankenstein removes the victim's heart. The laboratory is constructed. The dead are raised. The workers, the Capitalists, the generals and the Marxists build the Golem from the body parts of the corpses. Paracelsus provides the third eye, Freud grafts on the penis, and Norbert Wiener supplies electricity. Dr Frankenstein instals the heart, and with suitable thunder, lightning and pyrotechnics, the Creature, played by seventeen actors hanging from the scaffolding rig, is born and staggers towards the audience:

> The creature who is formed at the end of *Frankenstein* not only menaces the public, it is the public, the creature simultaneously menaces civilisation and is civilisation, it is civilisation menacing itself.

> That is, we are both civilisation and the monster that threatens civilisation. Within us is the creature that raises his arms and breathes, notably changing and transforming, metamorphosing and waiting, and praying for the next development in man.

> (Julian Beck)

After the first performance of *Frankenstein* in Venice, The Living Theatre were expelled and banned from Italy. It might have been because of the nudity bust in Trieste, or it might have been because Julian gobbed at Festival Director Wladimiro Dorigo. The Living Theatre were big on gobbing. Whatever the cause the police ran them out of the country, escorting them to the Austrian border. In Provence they gave the second performance of *Frankenstein*, which lasted over five hours. Someone tried to firebomb one of their buses.

For the next two years The Living criss-crossed Europe performing their repertoire as the student protest movement continued to grow. They became perceived as leaders of the counterculture and acquired underground rock-star status. Gypsy Pied Pipers of the alternative, their dope and free-love lifestyle attracted many disciples who followed the company on the road.

In February 1968 the company moved into the abandoned Club Mediterranée in Cefalu, Sicily, and amongst the wooden huts, palm trees and bogus jungle of the African-themed holiday camp they began to prepare their masterwork: *Paradise Now*.

The company felt that that they needed to go further than they had in *Frankenstein* and *Mysteries*. They felt that nothing *really happened* between the spectator and the performer and were now determined to abolish the fourth wall altogether. Their aim was to make a piece that destroyed all barriers between the actor and the audience, so that everyone present became a genuine and involved participant in the action. And that action was the revolution. *Paradise Now* would not be a play about non-violent revolution; it would be the thing itself:

> To hasten the steps for non-violent revolution, the revolution that destroys the economy, that eschews the use of money, that starts the change. But symbols and theatre don't mean anything any more. Only action does…

After months of rehearsal and Reichian Orgone Therapy in the plastic jungle, Julian and Judith went into isolated retreat for a week and emerged with a plan for the show, a route map that illustrated the form of the play, 'the voyage from the many to the one and from the one to the many'.

What they came up with was essentially a poster-sized chart with two figures, a Hindu figure and a Kabbalistic Jewish figure, overlaid with a grid that mapped out the way to permanent revolution. There were eight rungs on this stairway to heaven and each rung or sequence contained a *Rite*, a *Vision* and an *Action*. The *Rites* were rituals or ceremonies that the actors performed to engage and provoke the audience. The *Visions* were illustrative tableaux vivants designed to lead on to the *Actions*, which involved 'free theatre' and were performed by the audience. Each rung was allotted an appropriate hexagram from the I Ching, an appropriate yogic meditation and an appropriate verse from the Kabbalah.

Rung One started with 'The Rite of Guerrilla Theatre'. When the audience are almost seated the actors appear amongst them, confronting individual spectators with a series of repeated statements or observations on the nature of social oppression:

> I am not allowed to travel without a passport.
>
> I am not allowed to smoke marijuana.
>
> I don't know how to stop the war.
>
> You can't live if you don't have money.
>
> I am not allowed to take my clothes off.

They start quietly but increase in intensity until they become hysterical screaming at the audience in rage and pain. They are not allowed to interact with the spectators, but maintain eye contact. During the last statement the actors strip down to 'as little as is legally permitted'. Judith believed that clothes were a badge of repression. 'The Culture represses Love.' The Rung concludes with the actors chanting the last few lines of R.D. Laing's *The Bird of Paradise*:

If I could turn you on
If I could drive you out of your wretched mind
If I could tell you
I would let you know.

What usually happened was that the punters were pissed off by the actors screaming at them and frustrated by their insistence on hysterically repeating the set pronouncements rather than engaging in discussion or any form of meaningful communication. So they shouted back and sometimes physically attacked the actors. Audience members frequently offered the performers marijuana and usually quite a few stripped naked in contrast to the company who wore G-strings and posing-pouches to avoid prosecution.

This generally sets up the tone for the evening's entertainment.

On the Second Rung the actors move amongst the audience blessing the punters and various parts of their body: 'Holy hand. Holy shirt. Holy leg. Holy nose. Holy asshole.'

On the Third Rung the actors sit in Hatha Yoga positions and cajole the audience into revolutionary activity: 'Form anarchist cells. Open the jails. Free the prisoners. Disarm the police. Abolish the army. Burn the money. Save the souls of the people.'

On Rung Four the actors perform 'The Rite of Universal Intercourse', in which the company grope, stroke, suck, lick and rub each other in a big pile. The audience are invited to participate and many do. 'Break the touch barrier. Drop your psychic. Fuck the Jews. Fuck the Arabs. Fuck means Peace. Psychosexual repression is impeding the revolution.'

In 'The Rite of Universal Intercourse', Judith maintained fifteen or twenty company members had orgasms every night on stage. There are no statistics available for relative punter satisfaction, but the actors often shagged members of the audience. Company member Jenny Hecht apparently thought it was her revolutionary duty and that it was politically unsound to refuse.

By the time we get to Rung Eight the actors enact their own death. They say goodbye to the world. They invoke the holy spark of I and Thou and they rise again. The company head for the exits, triumphantly carrying audience members on their shoulders:

Free the theatre. The theatre is the street, free the street. The theatre is in the street. The street belongs to the people. Free the theatre. Free the street. The emergency is now. Burn the money. Change the World. Change the World. Find a way. Make it work. Begin...

And the audience, thus transformed, go out into the night to make Permanent Non-Violent Anarchist Revolution...

The performances lasted four hours or longer, depending on the degree and intensity of audience participation. All barriers between stage and auditorium were broken down and the space was full of semi-naked people shouting, arguing, fighting, crying, screaming, drumming, dancing, chanting, gobbing and making out. Many stormed out in disgust and anger. Many disagreed with the company's politics and were incensed with their belligerent non-violence (non-violent belligerence?). The Living Theatre were not interested in intellectual debate. If you were not part of the solution you were most definitely part of the problem.

The company left Cefalu in May. Hearing of the student occupation of the Sorbonne and believing it to herald the dawn of the new political consciousness they were advocating in *Paradise Now* they immediately headed to Paris. They arrived on 12 May. 13 May was the day of the General Strike. On 15 May Julian and Judith led the occupation of the Odéon. After witnessing and participating in what Julian described as 'the greatest theatre I have ever seen', the company travelled to Avignon to finish rehearsing *Paradise Now* which they were scheduled to perform for the first time at the Festival in July.

The first performance of *Paradise Now* was disrupted by a Gaullist mob; the second ended with several hundred enthusiastic supporters and *Enragés* marching through the streets demanding radical change. After the third the Mayor banned further performances on the pretext that they might lead to violent demonstrations. The company withdrew from the Festival in protest and left town with a police escort.

At the end of August 1968 the company returned to America for a six-month tour. They arrived to find the country polarised by the Vietnam War, LBJ, Chicago and the Watts Riots. Their reception was equally polarised, ranging from evangelical adulation to violent hostility.

At Yale the students, some of them tripping, took their clothes off to gleefully participate in 'The Rite of Universal Intercourse'. When the company led the audience out on to the street Judith, Julian and eight company members were arrested for indecent exposure and disturbing the peace. They were bailed out by Dean Robert Brustein, who, however, along with the liberal academic intelligensia, found it impossible to come to terms with the company's methodology and politics. Brustein thought *Paradise Now* was tedious, that The Living had become a cult and that ultimately they were destroying theatre:

The Living Theatre treats us to a threefold fascism. The fascism of mercilessly inflicted vulgarity and boredom, the fascism of global intolerance, and the fascism of profound disrespect for human creativity and art.

(*New York Magazine*)

Everywhere they went on the road, leaders of the radical left turned out to see the performances. Ginsberg and Abbie Hoffman joined in New York. John Sinclair, founder of the White Panthers, met them in Ann Arbor, Michigan. In New Haven the black members of the company were hassled by the Black Panthers, who thought non-violence was a self-righteous cop-out and the true path of revolution was through armed struggle:

This is the United States of motherfucking America, and when you talk about revolution in this country you're talking about taking The Man's shit away from him. Shooting him with his own shit. You've got to get your shit together. The Man's got his shit together, that's why he's so strong. Get yours together, Jim, cause where it's at is bloody revolution.

At Berkeley students protesting the sacking of Herbert Marcuse were being tear-gassed in the streets as the company performed *Paradise Now*. The radical activists stayed away. They had already set up cells, fought the pigs, set up alternative lifestyle communes. They had heard it all before.

By the end of March 1969, the company were exhausted, deflated and broke. Several of them were ill with pleurisy and narcotic-induced brain damage. The tour had been shambolically organised and they had been ripped off by the hip promoters. Many shows were banned or cancelled and what money they had made had gone to pay back taxes. There was dissent in the group about the direction that the work was taking. The press had mainly been hostile. They had been worshipped and vilified in equal proportion by the public, declared irrelevant by the radical left and pretty much disowned by the liberal intelligentsia.

Jim Morrison of The Doors gave them $25,000 for their fares back to Europe.

At the beginning of June 1969 The Living Theatre arrived in London for a four-week run at the Roundhouse. I worked as a casual on the crew so helped with the get-in. The company were remote but exotic. They communicated in a private language that seemed to be made up of English, French, German, American and Hippy. Every request was prefixed by 'I love you, man, but...' (as in 'I love you, man, but move that fucking ladder'). Julian had a serene, ethereal quality. He looked like the love child of Gandhi and Ken Campbell. Judith was nuts. Initially they were all staying in dormitory rooms in a B&B off Praed Street, but soon moved out into squats in Camden or the dressing rooms of the Roundhouse, which they turned into a psychedelic boarding house. Some of the company stayed with Mick Jagger in Chelsea until Marianne Faithfull threw them out. There was a lot of dope around, but then there was always a lot of dope around at the Roundhouse.

Mysteries and Smaller Pieces already seemed rather dated. The techniques were by now familiar and indeed had already become part of the vocabulary of experimental theatre. I had even used some of the stuff myself in the abysmal *Our Lady of the Flowers* at East 15. One of the smaller pieces turned out to be a yoga exercise called The Lion. 'The Plague' was pretty impressive, even though I wasn't sufficiently transported to join in with the dying.

I thought *Frankenstein* was an amazing piece of visual and physical theatre that worked on an entirely visceral level. Some of the images were obscure and the metaphors opaque, but the power of the torture and execution sequences, the Grand Guignol assembly of the Creature and the sheer commitment of the performers was stunning.

Paradise Now was, however, something else altogether...

On opening night the Roundhouse was packed to the roof with an expectant audience of critics, freaks, the entire working class of Camden, the liberal intelligentsia and the terminally hip. From the first 'I am not allowed to travel without a passport' all normal rules of behaviour was suspended and all bets were off. Within five minutes there were arguments and walkouts as the actors screamed at the punters and refused to engage in reasoned debate. Encouraged to make 'free theatre' and join in the bacchanal, many of the audience left their seats and headed for the stage, at which point the police arrived and told them to sit down or the show would be stopped. Roundhouse manager George Hoskins, surrounded by semi-naked actors, tried unsuccessfully to calm things down until Julian suggested piling all the chairs on the stage and playing the rest of the show in the auditorium. At which point the police gave up. What followed seemed at first to be a series of random actions as the play and the audience freewheeled around the auditorium. I remember an overwhelming smell of sweat and patchouli as a young kid clearly off his tits on acid simulated buggery in 'The Rite of Universal Intercourse'. I remember being impressed as one of the actors tried to suck himself off. I remember rolling around in a pile of bodies. I remember a speech that went something like:

You've got to dig where it's at. Get it together. Dig where it's at. We've got to get it together and dig where it's at and COMMU-NICATE how we can fuck with this fucking country which is fucked. Dig it. Violence is counter-revolutionary so dig it. If you are sexually repressed you are going to have violence. So dig it. Make it real. Do it now. We better dig each other or WE'RE ALL FUCKED, MAN...

And then there was some drumming and Indian dancing. In fact Julian was conducting all this creative disorder like a circus ringmaster, and the company were so finely tuned to what was going on that they could change the mood and tempo at the drop of a hat. At one point Steve Ben Israel gobbed at a punter in the middle of a heated debate ('Fuck you, man!' 'Well, fuck you, man!' 'Well, fuck you too, man!'). The punter was about to twat him but within seconds Julian and several company members stepped in and enthusiastically gobbed on each other. 'It's only water, see. It's only water, man. Bodily fluids.' Soon they were all hugging each other and chanting about love being where it was at and getting it together and digging it. Many audience members were frustrated by the lack of intellectual rigour in the revolutionary arguments, but many others joined in and joyfully frolicked along with the show.

To see Bernard Levin cowering against a pillar as Rufus Collins, a six-foot half-naked sweaty black man, shouted 'What are you doing about the fucking starving in fucking Biafra, motherfucker?' was entirely worth the price of admission. At the end the company carried the audience shoulder high into Chalk Farm Road to storm the jails and release all the prisoners. I went for a kebab.

So what then was the point of it all?

Paradise Now seemed to me to most resemble an evangelical revival meeting, a psychedelic Billy Graham crusade. The Becks were charismatic preachers who, aided by their acolytes, sought to convert their audience by involving them in a series of ornate rituals and miracles. The converted were then blessed, baptised and born again, not as Christians, but as Pacifist Anarchists. They were then encouraged to go forth and multiply.

The company believed that the natural state of man was peaceful, loving, moral, altruistic and non-violent. Mankind had been repressed emotionally and sexually and driven psychotic by a Capitalist society based on the accumulation of wealth and power and this psychosis was responsible for war, hunger, poverty and all the ills of the world. We were outside the Gates of Paradise. If we could throw off the chains of repression and rediscover our natural uncorrupted selves, then we could abolish hunger, poverty, war, violence, and there would be no need for countries, governments, armies, police, rules or money.

The Living Theatre believed that a repressed society breeds despair and that despair breeds only violence. They believed in replacing this despair with hope. This may sound like the triumph of hope over reason, but then they believed equally that reason itself was nothing more than a construct of Capitalist bourgeois false consciousness, an obstacle on the path to nirvana.

> If I could turn you on
> If I could drive you out of your wretched mind
> If I could tell you
> I would let you know.

Proper theatre should always ask questions. The Living Theatre also tried to provide answers. It may well be that these answers were a bunch of naïve bollocks, but no more ludicrous than the belief that free-market fundamentalism leads to social democracy and that liberty can be achieved through shopping.

After a couple of weeks the crew and most of the staff at the Roundhouse thought that The Living Theatre company were a pain in the arse. They were unapproachable, arrogant and supercilious and you got the impression that they were very aware of their status as international superstars of the counterculture. They thought they were as cool as fuck, which, although understandable in light of all they had been through in the last few years, came as a bit of a surprise in terms of their avowed dedication to peace, love and understanding. They also didn't have much of a sense of humour either on or off stage, which would seem to me to be essential if you plan to spend your evenings gurning in a jock-strap.

Julian Beck once remarked to Joe Chaikin that one of the things wrong with the company was that many of them felt that they had become living examples of *homo superior*, the higher evolved human being invoked by Confucius and the I Ching.

Paradise Now is still one of the most amazing pieces of theatre I have ever seen. The visit of The Living Theatre to the Roundhouse in 1969 taught us what was possible. I know of at least four people who started theatre companies after being inspired by their work, and there must be dozens more. They walked their talk, and they never ever sold out. They believed in what they were doing and did it fearlessly in the face of overwhelming opposition and prejudice. They got up people's noses, and they went to jail for their beliefs. They were alive, and they were dangerous, the greatest exponents of the Theatre of Nuisance ever.

Rehearsals continued for Edinburgh. Matthew, who had been heavily influenced by *Paradise Now*, held a workshop in his parents' garden in Hampstead where everyone touched the flowers and the trees and each other. 'Holy Peonies. Holy Azaleas. Holy Lawnmower.' After half an hour we got fed up and went to the pub.

Three weeks before we were due to go to the Festival we were told by the Fringe Society that Manchester Polytechnic had pulled out of the gig and unless we could find the full rental or someone to share with us we would lose the venue. We scrambled round to raise the cash, but by now enthusiasm was wavering and several of the cast pulled out to do other jobs. Matthew and I were devastated, but worse was to come. I got a telegram from Grotowski.

ELT MICHEAL BRANDWELL E 15 ACTING SCHOOL

SON CONTENU STAGE AN OCTOBRE IMPOSSIBLE DAILLEURS SOMMES TOUS EN ANGLETERRE ET EN USA

SALUTATIONS GROTOWSKI

Instead I spent the summer restoring antique furniture in a garage in Highgate and doing a bit of minor dope-dealing to raise the two pounds and ten shillings to see Bob Dylan on the Isle of Wight. I hitched down in an ice cream van. As the sun set over Woodside Bay and Bob sang 'I ain't gonna work on Maggie's farm no more', I realised that neither was I.

Maggie Bury had failed to contact anybody at the Berliner Ensemble about the possibility of me working there, and, more significantly, the Lincolnshire Education Authority ruled that my travelling scheme could not be construed as being in full-time education and withdrew my grant. So I left East 15.

> By the time we got to Woodstock,
> We were half a million strong
> And everywhere there was song and celebration.
> And I dreamed I saw the bombers
> Riding shotgun in the sky
> And they were turning into butterflies
> Above our nation
> We are stardust (Billion-year-old carbon)
> We are golden (Caught in the devil's bargain)
> And we've got to get ourselves back to the garden.
>
> (Joni Mitchell)

Later that month half a million hippies, yippies, panthers, freaks, diggers, hog farmers, flower children and middle-class weekend revolutionaries turned up for three days of peace and music at the

Woodstock Music and Art Fair—an Aquarian Exposition held at Max Yasgur's farm in Sullivan county, upstate New York. Most of them got in free after the Motherfuckers tore down the fences. They turned up to see The Who, The Grateful Dead, Jefferson Airplane, Joan Baez, The Band, Sly and the Family Stone, Janis Joplin, Crosby, Stills, Nash and Young, Jimi Hendrix, Ravi Shankar, Joe Cocker, and Country Joe and the Fish—'Give me an F'. The organisers had originally estimated a crowd of sixty thousand, but love and revolution were in the air and everyone even vaguely aligned with the counterculture had to be there to recapture the original spirit of the San Francisco Be-Ins, celebrate the new age and get off their tits on acid. The ensuing traffic jam backed up the Interstate Thruway for twenty miles.

Despite no food, water, sanitation or proper medical facilities, despite a heatwave followed by a tropical rainstorm that turned the whole site into a sea of mud and despite being declared an official disaster area, Woodstock has come to be mythologised as a beacon of universal peace and harmony. Half a million stoned freaks almost successfully organising themselves into a self-supporting community of love in the mud for three days was celebrated as a victory over Capitalism and the death culture of the Pig Empire.

What it also was, was a marketing opportunity for hip Capitalism and the Woodstock Nation were the target market. Warner Brothers bought the film rights for $100,000. The subsequent movie was edited to remove all trace of anti-Establishment politics but included long sequences of nude frolicking. It made millions, as did the album, the second album, the video, the DVD and the Director's Cut. The whole thing was a gigantic promo for the millionaire bands, many of whom were signed by Warner Brothers and none of whom had played for free. The Festival was in profit long before the walls came down. Not a cent went back to the counterculture celebrated in the movie. Joni Mitchell, who wrote the national anthem, wasn't even there. Her manager had advised her that an appearance on *The Dick Cavett Show* would shift more units of her new album than singing to a few beatniks in a field.

In 1910 the brothers Karel and Josef Čapek wrote a play called *The Fateful Game of Love*, a satire on theatre in the style of *Commedia dell'Arte*. It has a predictably thin plot and is set in the world of a troupe of touring Italian players. Brighella, the villain, provokes a duel between love rivals Gilles and Trivalin for the hand of the fair and relatively unsophisticated Isabella. Scaramouche comically tells the audience that the theatre is on fire. Gilles is killed. Trivalin fucks off as Brighella gets the girl, having bribed her with loads of ducats. There's also quite a bit of scripted improvisation about the parlous state of Czech theatre in 1910. It remained justifiably unperformed until 1930 when Karel Čapek had become famous, and even then it was regarded as a bit of a dog. Maria Sentivany decided to revive it at the Roundhouse. Maria was determined to start a professional *Commedia* company to build on the success of *Albert* and *Mr Pucci* and recruited a cast of mainly ex-East 15 actors for her production. I was cast as Brighella and Mike Leigh, who had just returned from his writing sabbatical in Manchester, was persuaded, against his better judgement, to play Scaramouche. Sustained by Maria's refugee stew, we rehearsed in her freezing bed-sit and a school gymnasium. We didn't have a mask for Brighella so we bought a joke-shop false nose and painted it black with gloss paint. Brighella opened the play with something along the lines of:

> Here comes Pepe Nappo, also known as Gilles, our lyric talent; pale *amant de la lune* born at night under Virgo's sign while the pale moon hung in the path of shimmering Venus…

Mike as Scaramouche had pages and pages of interminable descriptive verse in praise of the baroque filigree work on a pair of duelling pistols. The show was booked for a week and went up at eleven at night. We arrived at the Roundhouse to discover that the reason we were playing at eleven at night was because during the day the BBC were filming a television variety show with Val Doonican. Not only that, it was *Val Doonican on Ice*.

The BBC had built an ice rink in the middle of the Roundhouse, which every night we had to cover with a tarpaulin and duckboards after Val and his rocking chair had wrapped for the evening. There was also a loud humming noise made by the machine which kept the ice frozen. When we asked if we could turn this off we were told we would sink. We sank anyway.

The very few people who came for the first couple of performances couldn't hear a thing. We fell back to playing whatever broad comedy we could find. Mike cut his long duelling-pistol speech down to 'My name is Scaramouche and here are the guns.' On the third night I was halfway through 'Here comes Pepe Nappo also known as Gilles' when my voice trailed into silence. All that could be heard was the penetrating hum of the ice machine. One by one the other cast members stuck their exaggeratedly comic noses around the edge of the set to see what was going on and then joined me on stage. For several minutes we stood there frozen on the ice in silent realisation. There was absolutely no one in the audience whatsoever. We were playing a thousand-seat theatre and nobody had turned up. Then from up in the gallery a lone voice rang out with 'Next actor please'. It was Derrick O'Connor. He took us to a late-night drinking den he knew and we drank late-night.

It was not a happy time: Mike's plan for The Working Theatre seemed to be heading for the rocks; Buzz Goodbody had become embroiled at the RSC; and Mike Stott was starting to break through as a playwright. Leigh was unhappy with *Monsters*, the play he had written in Manchester, and was determined to devote himself to improvised work on stage and on film. We fantasised about starting a company together devoted to devised work. It was to be called the Pig Theatre and would be based in Scunthorpe. Mike even got as far as designing the logo.

At the end of September the ICA brought over Grotowski's Polish Theatre Laboratory Company for ten performances at the National Portrait Gallery and I managed to get a ticket for *The Constant Prince*. The performance in fact took place in an old Public Baths in the East End. The audience, limited to forty, were bussed in by coach, which picked everybody up from outside the National Portrait Gallery.

Calderón's original play tells of a Portuguese Prince who is captured by the Moroccans and is ultimately tortured and martyred rather than let the town of Ceuta fall into Moorish hands. Grotowski cut the plot, several of the characters and most of the words, and transformed it into a ritual about the mortification of the flesh and the transformation of anguish into ecstasy. Sitting in a single row on hard wooden benches above the old swimming pool, we looked down on the empty performance area illuminated by arc lights on stands. I had seen photos of this production in *Towards a Poor Theatre*. They in no way prepared me for what was coming. A bell rings. A semi-naked man lies on a wooden dais, an operating table maybe. He is pushed and probed and examined by four figures in clerical dress. One might be a priest. One might be a king. One has an umbrella. One is a woman. They could be the Inquisition. The man is castrated, killed and then resurrected and clothed as one of torturers. Another man is brought in. He is the Prince, and likewise he is tortured by the others. He does not capitulate. He accepts his fate. He achieves ecstasy. He is killed and left naked on the stage. The performance ends abruptly as the lights go out. There is no curtain call.

The whole performance lasts less than an hour. The acting was unlike anything I had seen before or have seen since. The actors performed impossible feats of athleticism seeming at times to defy gravity as they moved and balanced on knees, arms, heads and shoulders. The whole thing was played at a hectic pace in a mysterious language of sound and gesture using screams, coughs, snorts, whistles, singsong, animal and bird calls and words which may have once been Polish but possibly not. As the Prince, leading actor Ryszard Cieslak contorted into unbelievable shapes, transforming his face into a series of masks and producing a series of paroxysms and spasms in every muscle of his body. He actually appeared to achieve the state of self-induced trance or ecstasy that Grotowski demanded: the public offering of himself. Conversely he seemed always to be in complete physical control of his movements. Every gesture was carefully planned and choreographed, nothing was improvised or spontaneous, The production was shot through with images from Catholic iconography and of profound suffering that could have come from the paintings of Goya or Canavesio. The effect this had, on me anyway, was purely visceral. I was physically shaken and disturbed, but I hadn't got a clue what was going on, who anybody was or what, if anything, the play was trying to say. It could have been about the schism between Catholicism and Communism in Poland. It could be seen as a meditation on the triumph of human spirit over suffering. Let us not forget that Grotowski's theatre was based only forty miles from Auschwitz. Is the Prince offering himself as a sacrifice to end oppression? Grotowski would certainly have considered all these interpretations, questions and answers irrelevant. The actor becomes a shaman, contacting primeval forces and passing on a mystical experience to the audience. And if you can describe or define a mystical experience it ceases to be mystical.

Peter Brook described this work as Holy Theatre. In Grotowski's case it was certainly monastic and in many ways puritan. I subsequently learnt about his rehearsal and preparation techniques from someone who had been to Wrocław as an observer. Rehearsals were conducted in silence. Only Grotowski was allowed to speak, and there was no discussion. No one else was allowed to voice an opinion. No one was allowed to smoke except Grotowski who (like Joan Littlewood) chain-smoked Gauloises. All improvisations were physical, and the meaning and nature of the work was never debated. There was a total emphasis on rigour, discipline and solemnity. The training made enormous physical and mental demands and was based on total fitness, self-abasement and a quasi-religious zeal. Grotowski had no time for jokes or humour. He insisted that 'private ideas of fun' had no place in the actor's calling. He frowned on personal nonchalance and triviality. I would not have lasted ten minutes.

Initially Grotowski conducted his experiments in great secrecy, but gradually news of his techniques spread, and Grotowski-inspired companies, most of them a pale imitation of the real thing, blossomed like flowers that bloom in the spring. In latter years the discipline and rigour of his work seems weirdly to have metamorphosed into a kind of New

Age therapy self-improvement programme. His influence can still be detected in the work of everybody from Peter Brook to DV8.

Seeing both The Living Theatre and Grotowski at work profoundly influenced me too, in as much as they also nudged me in a totally different direction.

Antonin Artaud was looking for a bomb to overthrow consciousness. He talked of a theatre that would be like 'an electric shock treatment galvanising people into feeling'. Like Grotowski he wanted to see the actors vanish and burn, and he dreamed of seeing them signalling through the flames. Artaud, the Becks and Grotowski were seeking a new language of sound and gesture that would transcend other forms of communication. This would not be a series of shared codes and signals used to establish character and narrative but a common primeval language communicating pure raw emotion. They wanted to make theatre that aspired to the condition of music, or possibly non-representational art, and that had no recourse to words, plot or intellectual coherence. Their overriding concern was to change the very nature and form of theatrical communication. Seeing their work made me realise that what interested me was not the nature of communication or a desire to change it, but rather what it was that was being communicated. I wanted to make theatre with words and three-dimensional characters and argument and metaphor and storytelling and jokes and life and laughter. Although I was suitably transported by ecstatically entranced actors signalling through the flames, I was far more engaged in who they were supposed to be and what it was that they were supposed to be signalling. I still believed that theatre could change the world, but I also realised that I was more inspired by the kids from Scunthorpe than by either a bunch of po-faced, self-aggrandising, acid-casualty revolutionaries or a piece of technically brilliant but ultimately humourless physical theatre perpetrated by a neo-Fascist guilt-ridden Catholic aesthete. It was therefore both timely and fortunate that late in 1969 Mike Leigh called me up and asked me to be in his new project.

3

Hello Sadness

Mike Leigh had been invited to devise and direct an improvised play for Charles Marowitz at the Open Space Theatre, and he wanted me to act in it. Marowitz was a smart-arse American director, impresario and critic, who came to Britain in the late Fifties to study at LAMDA. He had been Peter Brook's assistant on *King Lear* and the Theatre of Cruelty experiment at the RSC, but they fell out when Marowitz wrote a scathing review of *US*—the anti-Vietnam war piece—in which he accused Brook of sitting on the fence. At various times he claimed to have introduced Brecht, Artaud, Stanislavsky, improvisation, The Method, happenings and experimental theatre to England. He selflessly taught Joe Orton the true nature of comedy—'Listen, Joe, this isn't the fucking *Cherry Orchard*'—and apparently discovered Harold Pinter. He opened the Open Space in 1968 in a basement in Tottenham Court Road, a stone's throw from the original UFO club. The theatre was modelled on the Off-Off-Broadway playhouses of New York. The first production was *Fortune and Men's Eyes*, a gay prison play that, pre-1968, would never have got past the Lord Chamberlain owing to a flash of male nudity. The repertoire included new American writers including Jean-Claude Van Itallie, John Guare, Israel Horowitz, Leonard Melfi and, most significantly, Michael Weller. Marowitz famously directed the world premiere of Sam Shepard's *The Tooth of Crime*. His concept differed so much from that of the author that Shepard was excluded from rehearsals and Marowitz delayed the opening until he had left the country. New British writers whose work was produced there included Howard Brenton, Howard Barker, Trevor Griffiths and Stanley Eveling. Since the demise of the original Arts Lab in Drury Lane, the Open Space (along with the Almost Free, another venue run by a visiting American, Ed Berman) had become the centre for experimental work hosting visits from Albert

Hunt's Bradford College of Art Company, Pip Simmons Theatre Group, the Theatre of the Ridiculous and The Scaffold.

Marowitz's real preoccupation was his own work, which mainly involved deconstructed cut-ups or collages of Shakespeare. He basically altered the theme, character and structure of the plays to suit his own interpretation of them. *Hamlet* had Gertrude and the Ghost playing the Player King and Queen on film while Hamlet dressed as a tearful clown swung on a Meyerhold-inspired rope before stabbing the entire court. Marowitz opined:

> I despise Hamlet. He is a slob, a talker, an analyser, a rationaliser. Like the parlour liberal or the paralysed intellectual, he can describe every facet of a problem; yet never pull his finger out.

Lady Macbeth became the head of the witches' coven, and there were three Macbeths. *The Taming of the Shrew* was presented as a 'black Artaudian fable' reflecting atrocities in Northern Ireland. Marowitz's rationale for all this malarkey was that he objected to the reverence with which the plays were invariably treated. It's a shame that Will was not around to benefit from Marowitz's dramaturgical input.

The deal with Mike Leigh was that he and the actors would create a bunch of characters and improvise over a week's rehearsal time. At the end of the week Marowitz would check out what we had been up to and, if he liked what he saw, there would be a further three-week rehearsal period, after which the show would play at eleven o'clock at night at the Open Space for nine performances in March 1970. The cast Mike assembled for the initial workshop was Anne Raitt, who Mike knew from Peter Cheeseman's Victoria Theatre company in Stoke, Joolia Capple-man, who was Mike's girlfriend at the time and who had been in the Israeli Army during the Six Day War and also in *Number 4*, Yoko Ono's film of bottoms, Sarah Stephenson, who had been in *Individual Fruit Pies* at East 15, John Shrapnel, from the abortive production of *The Knack* at the RSC, and me.

We rehearsed in the Open Space and in Mike's flat in Cranleigh Street near Mornington Crescent. Mike's technique then was pretty much the same as it is today, but obviously the process was truncated, as we had to come up with something to show Marowitz in only a week. As usual each us came up with a character or characters loosely based on someone we knew and, working with Mike, built up a fictitious life history and background for this character. As usual the work was conducted in total secrecy, no one knowing what anyone else was playing.

My character, Norman, was based on a couple of people I knew from Scunthorpe. One was a painfully shy guy who hung around the folk club hoping to be asked to play and hoping to get a girlfriend. The other was a lad from the Youth Theatre who was very bright but had fucked up his A-levels and didn't know what to do. Neither of them was called Norman. No, actually one of them was. After a couple of days of solo character work Mike declared that Norman now had a brother who happened to be John Shrapnel's character. Shrapnel and I then spent some time working out our characters' now collective backgrounds and started to improvise scenarios of our home life. Simultaneously Mike was creating characters and scenarios with the other actors, or 'depicters' as Mike preferred to call us. At the end of the week Mike asked me how Norman could get to London, so I invented a story in which he hitched down for the weekend to go to an all-night gig at Cousins—Les Cousins' folk club in Greek Street. We set up an improvisation in which I, as Norman, wandered round the West End imagining it was my first trip to London. After a suitable interval I would return to the Open Space basement where Shrapnel was waiting back at home, and we would improvise the scene of Norman's return. I got a bus up to Oxford Circus and walked back in character. I was wearing an ancient military greatcoat and a bandana. It was January and freezing and getting dark, and Norman hadn't enough money for a cup of tea. It started to rain. On the zebra crossing on Charing Cross Road I looked the wrong way and barged into a couple nearly knocking them over. I muttered apologies. The couple were John Lennon and Yoko Ono. Fuck! I hadn't recognised them at first because they had just had their heads shaved after a visit to a Primal Screaming workshop in Denmark. What would Norman do? I stayed in character. I flashed the peace sign.

NORMAN. Ey up, John. On behalf of all the freaks in
    Scunthorpe, I'd just like to say it's great what you're doing
    for world peace.

Lennon mumbled 'Yeah', gave me a dirty look and they disappeared into the Soho twilight.

As Norman I headed back to the Open Space full of my adventure in the Smoke. Shrapnel was waiting for me. The deal was that Norman had disappeared to London without telling anyone. Leigh was hiding behind the sofa, his now customary position, notebook in hand, waiting to note the improvisation.

NORMAN enters.

SHRAPNEL. Where have you been, cunt-face?

NORMAN. I went to London and guess what? I met John Lennon.

MIKE LEIGH (off). Cut! Come out of character. Wanker!

Mike was furious. He thought that I had made the whole thing up for effect. We had to set up the whole improvisation again. Next time Norman didn't bump into anybody, Mike was happy and I never met John Lennon again.

After a week we had managed to create five organic characters and the beginnings of potential relationships between them. Annie Raitt was Sylvia, who had a retarded sister called Hilda played by Sarah Stephenson, and a monstrous best friend called Pat, played by Joolia. It was time to audition for Marowitz. Clearly he thought he knew all about the improvisation game so without any knowledge of what we had been doing he set up an improvisation of his own in which he was going to play a character. He announced that he was an American cop, that there had been a murder, that we were all suspects, and that he was going to interrogate us to test our alibis. It was totally inappropriate, inorganic and preposterous. We all went along with this charade as best we could and, remarkably, passed the test. We were on.

I had been living in an attic in Chingford since leaving East 15, but now I moved into Mike's living room in Cranleigh Street. From there Mike masterminded the production, and I became his general dogsbody. John Shrapnel dropped out and was replaced by Derrick O'Connor, also from *The Knack*. Mike decided that he wanted an older character in the play, possibly as Sylvia and Hilda's dad, and recruited George Coulouris. This was a major coup for two reasons. Firstly the idea of getting an elderly actor to agree to appear in a play with no script and no character for no money was nothing short of a miracle but more significantly George had been in the film *Citizen Kane* and had actually worked with Orson Welles. Mike was impressed and flattered. We also had to find a set and design and distribute publicity. Mike decided that the show should be called *IMPROVISED PLAY NO. 10 (which will have a proper title by the first night)*. He designed the poster which, with chums Paul and Esther Rowley, we silk screened at Camberwell College of Art and wrote the press release. in which he carefully laid down his working method at the time:

> *IMPROVISED PLAY NO. 10 (which will have a proper title by the first night)* is so called because it is being evolved from improvisations into a fully rehearsed play. It will not be a 'happening', an evening of impromptu acting or an arty movement show. It will not involve audience participation on the night.
>
> Mike Leigh is not, in fact, primarily concerned with improvisation for its own sake; his main interest is with characters and situations rather than with instant theatrical effects, and yet

while his plays are firmly routed in realism, he is nothing if not a rigorous stylist. But the form and discipline of a play must be, he insists, a function of its content.

His method as it has now evolved consists of each actor building a live character based on somebody he actually knows, Leigh then bringing these characters together by a slow, organic process of improvised situations until the actors have 'lived out' the lives of their characters over a given period.

At this late stage in rehearsals, Mike Leigh constructs a formal play from all the accumulated material, and this is then rehearsed. The play gets its proper title only when the time is ripe. Though nothing is ever actually written down, the play nevertheless has a proper dramatic structure. Each scene, each minute sequence of action, is as carefully rehearsed as it would had it come from a script.

Whilst for the actors being in one of the plays involves an approach quite different from the approach to an ordinary play, Leigh's aim is always that the audience's approach should be the same: they are watching a play and the fact that it has been created by an unusual process should not inhibit or influence their response to it. The rest is up to the play itself.

For Mike Leigh, this way of working is not a reaction against the written play as such, although it is, to some extent, a reaction against superficial writing, acting and direction. He doesn't regard it as a crusade in a general sense: it is simply one man's way of creating plays.

With the new cast we went back into the rehearsal room, which this time was in the church hall of St Mark's, Regent's Park Road, and again occasionally in Cranleigh Street.

Mike and I reinvestigated the character of Norman, once again without a brother. Again Norman came down to London with his guitar, but this time he decided to stay. Initially he lodged with his auntie in Croydon, but she threw him out so he moved into a squat. He told them he was from Doncaster because people used to laugh when he said he came from Scunthorpe. I spent hours getting into character in the kitchen of St Mark's playing the guitar badly and feeling lonely. After a few days Derrick O'Connor left the company to play Jimmy Porter at the Liverpool Everyman.

Eric Allan, who Mike had also known from the RSC, replaced him. We had to change the poster. Eric was and still is a wonderful actor. He had been in Brook's *US* and had first-hand experience of working with Grotowski. He had also been in Marowitz's cut-up *Hamlet*. He created a character called Peter, a repressed schoolteacher, who invites Sylvia out on a date. Eric went on to work with Mike many times.

Mike asked me why Norman would rent a garage. I invented a story in which the freaks in the squat decide to start an underground magazine. Norman is given the job of duplicating it on an old Gestetner. I got the idea from having to duplicate all the press releases for the show on the Open Space machine and being yelled at by Thelma Holt for spilling ink. Norman has to find somewhere to do the duplicating. He sees a notice in a newsagent's window about a garage for hire. He goes round. It's Sylvia's garage.

In the second week of rehearsals George Coulouris joined in. He was to play Sylvia and Hilda's dad. He seemed to be enjoying himself, went along merrily with the process and told spicy anecdotes about his days in Hollywood. At the end of the week he told Mike that it was as exciting as working with Orson. Mike was made up.

George never came back. We had to change the poster again. George wasn't replaced by anybody. Sylvia and Hilda were orphaned overnight.

Gradually a story line began to evolve. Norman hires the garage and now spends hours in there duplicating the magazine badly, playing 'Freight Train' badly and freezing to death. Sylvia invites him in for a cup of tea. He likes her. He meets retarded Hilda, who freaks him out a bit. He plays the guitar for her. She likes it. He meets Pat. She bullies him. He is embarrassed. He meets Peter. He bullies him. He is embarrassed. After each improvisation Mike talked through what had happened in the scene with each actor individually. He was always insistent that in these sessions actors refer to their character in the third person—*Norman* caught the bus, not *I* caught the bus—so as to be able to maintain a degree of objectivity about the character. Acting in an improvised play demands an extremely subjective involvement. When in character you feel what the character feels. When out of character you have to be able to analyse the character's emotional response to the events in the improvised scenes objectively. The post-improvisation debriefings enabled Mike to get a handle on what was going on subtextually, which in turn gave him clues as to which direction to take the story in and as to the nature of the politics of the final play. Mike's task was, of course, far more complex than choosing some characters, setting up improvisations and editing the results. The process is at least as exacting as creating plays in a more traditional manner, as I discovered when I came to do them myself. All decisions must be organic, but at the same time the director has to keep an overview of the themes he has chosen to explore. True, the script is a distillation of what has happened in the improvisations, but the resultant piece is not an *objet trouvé*, it's a totally thought out and crafted piece of work.

After three weeks Mike took a weekend off to write the 'script' based on the tale that had unfolded. What he came up with was a series of scene units, for example:

Saturday Night. About six o'clock

1) Sylvia alone
2) Norman (off) guitar
3) Hilda, Sylvia
4) Pat, Sylvia, Hilda
   Sylvia makes tea with Pat's help. Hilda stays alone.

What this was, of course, was a very bare outline for a story about five nervous, repressed and lonely people on one Saturday night in suburban London in 1970. The play was to be called *Bleak Moments*, though Mike had briefly flirted with the idea of calling it *Hello Sadness*. The plot is very simple:

Sylvia lives in her parents' old house in South London where she cares for her mentally retarded sister Hilda. She has a friend called Pat, a garrulous spinster, who works in the same office and who is similarly trapped by having to care for her bedridden mother. Sylvia has rented out the garage to Norman, a would-be hippy from Scunthorpe who uses it as an office in which to duplicate an underground magazine. One Saturday night Sylvia has a first date with a shy and sexually paralysed schoolteacher called Peter. They are going to a concert at the Fairfield Halls. Pat comes round to take Hilda to the pictures. They have some tea. Pat is excited about Sylvia's 'boyfriend'. They hear Norman playing 'Cocaine Blues' in the garage and ask him in for tea. Pat patronises and embarrasses Norman. Hilda overcomes her shyness and Norman is asked to play his guitar. Hilda is demonstrably enthusiastic. Pat is jealous of Norman's success with Hilda. Peter arrives and meets the assembled company. Pat and Hilda depart for the Rialto. Sylvia goes to change and drink sherry, mischievously leaving Norman alone with Peter. Peter patronises and tries to humiliate Norman about his failure to take A-levels. Sylvia returns and goes off with Peter to Croydon. Norman returns to the garage.

Later that night Pat and Hilda return from the pictures and Sylvia and Peter return from what has clearly been a painful evening. Hilda is sent up to bed. Peter goes for a piss. Pat recommends that Sylvia take Hilda to a faith healer. Pat leaves the 'love birds' alone. Sylvia and Peter drink some sherry and have a nervous conversation about Marshall McLuhan that Pat interrupts in search of her handbag. She leaves. Sylvia and Peter drink more sherry and play out their repressed love scene, which culminates in Sylvia suggesting that Peter might like to take off his trousers. Peter is terrified and departs. Sylvia, alone, hears Norman in the garage playing Dylan's 'She Belongs to Me'. She drinks more sherry. She invites him in. They talk. Norman has to leave to go to an all-nighter at Cousins. 'I didn't know you had relations in London?' says Sylvia. Norman leaves. Sylvia is alone.

For the last week of rehearsals we went back into the scenes and patterns of dialogue began to emerge. As we discussed and improvised events that happened between the scenes in the play (for example when Peter and Sylvia go to the concert, or Pat and Hilda go to the pictures), Mike even then used to say we would put them in when we made the film.

All the action in *Bleak Moments* takes place in Sylvia's front room, so Mike and I trailed around North London borrowing furniture for the set from friendly antique dealers, which we transported in the back of the Deux Chevaux, the driver's door of which was now held on with camera tape. We blagged a tea service from Woolworths in Tottenham Court Road, an electric fire from the London Electricity Board and a revolting carpet from Fay Weldon's husband Ron. Back at the Open Space all, however, was not well.

In an attempt to raise some extra cash Marowitz had decided to show the new and controversial Andy Warhol film *Flesh*. *Flesh* is a typical product of the Factory. Male hooker and superstar Joe Dallesandro is sent out by his wife to raise money for her dyke girlfriend's abortion. He turns a few tricks and walks on the wild side for a bit before going home, where his wife and her girlfriend have now decided to keep the baby, so Joe and the women go to bed together. And the coloured girls sing, etc., etc. It has the usual Warhol home-movie production values and was in fact written and directed by Paul Morrissey. Warhol's actual involvement was simply to franchise the brand. The film attracted a different clientele to the theatre who Marowitz himself described as:

> Clearly related to the raincoat brigades which manned the strip clubs and private cinemas in nearby Soho, a grubby, lascivious, anonymous tribe of respectable businessmen and commercial travellers plus a few cineastes, students, weirdos and perverts.

On 3 February thirty-two policemen and one superintendent raided the theatre, confiscated the film and projector and took down the details of the seventy-five assembled and furtive raincoats. The superintendent announced that there had been a complaint from a member of the public that the film was obscene and that a report would be sent to the Director of Public Prosecutions. Next day the shit really hit the fan. It appeared that John Trevelyan, the Secretary of the British Board of Film Censors, had in fact certified the film for showing in private members clubs, which the Open Space was, so the cops had fucked up. What the whole affair highlighted was that the battle was still raging between the old Establishment moral, and usually philistine, values epitomised by Mary Whitehouse and the advocates of the 'Permissive Society' championed by the likes of Ken Tynan. Soon questions were being asked in the House, and Home Secretary Jim Callaghan was forced to admit that there was no case to answer and that there would be no prosecution either for obscenity or for pornography. The Metropolitan Police, suitably humiliated, then decided to prosecute the theatre for the lesser offence of membership regulation infringement, and Marowitz and Thelma had to go to the High Court to get the film returned. It was with all this going on in the background that *Bleak Moments* opened at the Open Space on Monday 16 March 1970.

Mike Leigh describes the first performance as being 'absolutely charged, very precise, highly modulated, absolutely organic and impeccably acted'. Marowitz clearly thought it was a bag of shite, dismissing it as a trivia of talking, tea and sherry. One can only imagine that he had anticipated a rerun of 'The Rite of Universal Intercourse' from *Paradise Now*, or at least a bit of smack and buggery. Next morning we discovered that the critics didn't like it much either. Irving Wardle in *The Times* completely missed the point and, despite Mike's determination to explain exactly what we were up to, reported:

> What would you expect from a group of actors if you asked them to come on cold and improvise a play? First a long silence, and the performance of some non-committal physical task; then, sooner or later, a timid little speech thrown out in the hope of stimulating the others into some kind of dramatic response.

Wardle also wrote:

> The style of playing suggests a constant sense of dread, as though these people are making small talk in a town stricken with the plague. Their fingers writhe ceaselessly, their smiles switch on briefly over grimly fixed masks, every action they make is rigid with some unspoken obsession.

Which sounds a bit like Artaud to me.

B.A. Young's review in the *Financial Times* said much the same thing and the rest of the dailies were no better. Mike was furious and frustrated.

The same day as the notices came out I had to go for an interview for what was then called the ABC TV Regional Theatres Trainee Directors' Scheme. The deal was that if you won you got to work as an assistant at a Rep. I had applied months ago and forgotten about it. For the application you had to come up with a list of plays you would like to direct and write a review. I wrote a review of Edward Albee's *Tiny Alice*, which I precociously described as a play about an ornate burglar alarm, an opinion that I still hold. Weeks later I got a letter saying I was on the short list. There were six of us on the short list and places to be had at four theatres. The Reps were Birmingham, Glasgow Citizens', Leatherhead and the Prospect Theatre Company. The interviewing panel consisted of the Artistic Directors of the participating theatres, some execs from the television company, Ken Loach and B.A. Young, the critic of the *Financial Times* who had just given me a crap review in that morning's paper. My interview did not go well. I told them all about improvised plays. Greville Poke and Hazel Vincent Wallace from Leatherhead clearly thought I was insane. Ken Loach mysteriously asked me how it could be applied to Agatha Christie. Giles Havergal from the Citz asked me if I always quivered like an aspen. I didn't get the gig. Everyone on the short list apart from me had been to Oxbridge. The other failed applicant was Michael Coveney. As far as I know, none of the other finalists is still working in theatre. A couple of weeks later B.A. Young invited me to go with him to see the Marlowe Society production of *Measure for Measure* directed by one of the winners, a man called Keith (The Butcher) Hack. He asked me what I thought of the show. I told him I thought it sucked. The next week he invited Coveney, who as a result went on to work with him at the *FT* and has had a dazzling career as a drama critic. Where did I go wrong?

After the interview I headed back to the Open Space where Marowitz and Thelma were drinking champagne and there was a party going on. They were not celebrating the critical triumph of *Bleak Moments*. They had just got the print of *Flesh* back from the High Court and planned to show it four times a day.

For the rest of the week we played to small but appreciative houses. The show was only seventy-five minutes long, but the late start meant that we did not come down till after midnight, which made it difficult for people to get home. We were cheered by a review from Benedict Nightingale in the *New Statesman* who, despite admitting to a prejudice against improvised plays, realised what we were up to and reported:

By the end, we've a surprisingly full sense, not only of the individual characters on display, but of their attitudes towards each other. It's also clear how much they're inhibited from expressing these attitudes by social convention. Each watches each, with pity, exasperation, greed, frustration, through a polite barrier of smiling, scraping and evasion. It's amusing, touching, unpretentious and good.

Before this enthusiastic notice had time to kick in at the box office, Marowitz called Mike into his office. *Flesh* was playing to packed houses at every screening. The theatre was making a shed load of money, and they could make even more if they could show it five times a day instead of the current four screenings. *Bleak Moments* would have to make way to secure the financial future of the Open Space in particular and fringe theatre in general. We were being pulled off.

Everyone was devastated. We set about telephoning everybody we knew to boost numbers for the last couple of performances. Mike and his old school chum from Salford, Les Blair, who, like Mike, taught at the London Film School, cold-called everybody in the British film industry to persuade them to see the show. Mike was still convinced that we would one day make the film. A couple of them actually turned up, most significantly Bruce Beresford, who at the time was running the British Film Institute Production Board, and Tony Garnett, producer of Ken Loach's film *Kes*. This was nothing short of miraculous as Garnett even today has a profound loathing of theatre and would rather eat his own pancreas than be dragged into a playhouse. Garnett loved it and agreed with Mike that it would make a good film.

On the day of the last performance we got a genuine five-star rave review in the *Workers' Press*, the organ of the Socialist Labour League. It said:

The Open Space is a small theatre in the Tottenham Court Road. It achieved a certain notoriety recently when a large squad of policemen invaded it—not spurred on by any devotion to the arts, but to confiscate the print of a film showing there, Andy Warhol's *Flesh*. In spite of police pressure, powerfully supported by the resident Home Secretary, prosecution was dropped. I've not seen it yet but I went to the theatre to see a late-night play called *Bleak Moments*.

The audience was sparse to say the least. The reviews in the press had been bad. The play apparently lacked the sensational qualities associated with the 'avant-garde'. No sex, no nudes, no electronics.

It was dismissed. The management is taking it off at the end of the week. I think it is one of the most compelling pieces of theatre I have seen in a long time. I think its director Mike Leigh has a genuine and important talent... These are characters trapped and repressed, unable to communicate directly; eyes never meet, nervous laughter conceals pain; the most elementary routines of social intercourse become self-conscious tasks of anguish. Words don't communicate, they conceal, and they fill, as it were, the empty space, the silence that threatens them. Unease and self-consciousness is the condition. Loneliness the retreat.

Bleak Moments is an impassioned indictment against the kind of world that traps people in this way, divorces and separates them from feelings. It is performed with great sensitivity and absolute unsentimentality. Its style is direct and hard. It confronts us with pain and loneliness, not despairingly, but as a challenge.

It insists on the question, 'What kind of world do we have?'

It was a short-lived triumph. The next day *Bleak Moments* closed after half a dozen performances. Marowitz and Thelma ran *Flesh* for months and raked in a fortune until their original non-raincoat membership complained that they had joined an experimental theatre club dedicated to producing new plays and not an emporium for arty wank films. Years later we discovered that the original obscenity complaint that provoked the police raid was entirely bogus and had been orchestrated by the film's distributor in a desperate bid to drum up trade.

In Chicago the trial of the Chicago Eight reached its lunatic climax. The Eight had been charged with conspiring to cross state lines with intent to incite a riot, a recently concocted federal offence designed to curtail protest against the Vietnam War. Even before the trial started battle lines had been drawn.

The defendants were not allowed to vet potential jurors for bias or prejudice with the result that the jury was made up of the white middle class and middle-aged, one of whom believed that that the Eight should be convicted for their appearance and lifestyle, and another who thought that the demonstrators should have been shot by the police.

Yippies Hoffman and Rubin determined to turn the trial into a piece of guerrilla theatre to gain maximum publicity for the movement. What happened was certainly a farce.

Following the example of Judith Malina in *The Brig* trial they turned up in court wearing judge's robes and took the piss out of Judge Julius

As Dottore in *Mr Pucci* at the Roundhouse, 1969

As Norman in Mike Leigh's
Bleak Moments, 1971

The poster for
Improvised Play No. 10 at
the Open Space
Theatre, 1970. The
play was eventually
titled *Bleak Moments*

Davos the Flying Dane, Ken
Campbell and Bob Hoskins outside
the big top, Hirst's Charivari, 1971

Hirst's
CARIVARI
on
SOUTHSEA COMMON
in the
BLUE "BIG TOP"

A new show for the young in heart
with Ken Campbell's Crazy Gang.
Acrobatics on the Trampoline,
Suicide Dive into Fire, Under Water
Escape, Magic Theatre an untam-
able Rhinoceros and other acts,
accompanied by Chris Nicholls and
his band.

NIGHTLY 7.30 p.m.
Saturday 2 p.m., 5 p.m., and 8 p.m.
Matinees Wednesday 3 p.m.
Children and O.A.P.'s 30p. all seats
Adults 30p., 50p., 70p., 90p.

BOX OFFICE : PORTSMOUTH 25055

1971

The Untameable ──────
Rhinoceros, Hirst's
Charivari, 1971

The original Hull Truck company outside the
Coltman Street house, May 1972
(left to right: Mike Bradwell, Lisa Hicks, Nick Levitt, Dave
Greaves, John Lee, Steve Halliwell, Chris Levitt and Mark Allain)

Steve Halliwell and Cass Patton in *The Weekend After*
Next, Hull Truck, 1973

1972

As Dooley in *The Knowledge*, Hull Truck, 1974 ——————————

Peter Nicholson and Rachel Bell in
Granny Sorts It Out, Hull Truck, 1974

Mary East and David Ambrose in
The Knowledge, Hull Truck, 1974

Left to right: Mike Bradwell, David Hatton, Peter Nicholson in *Oh What!*,
Hull Truck, 1975

Bridget's House, Hull Truck, 1976
(right: Cass Patton and Rachel Bell;
below: Alan Williams)

The *Bed of Roses* company in the Hull Truck rehearsal room, 1977
(left to right, back row: David Threlfall, Mia Soteriou, Alan Williams, Kathy Iddon,
Heather Tobias, Robin Soans, Colin Goddard; front row: Mike Bradwell, Barry Nettleton)

Steve Halliwell and Derrick
O'Connor in *The Great Caper* by
Ken Campbell, Hull Truck, 1978

Lally Percy as Frances
Farmer in *The New Garbo* by
Doug Lucie, Hull Truck,
1978

Arbel Jones and Chris Jury in *Mean Streaks* by Alan Williams, Hull Truck, 1980

Left to right: Helen Cooper, Christopher Fairbank, Jim Broadbent and Philip Jackson in *Games Without Frontiers*, BBC TV, 1980

Hoffman and the whole legal proceedings by blowing kisses and trading insults with the prosecution. The joke soon turned sour. Bobby Seale had been refused his own Black Panther lawyer and consistently inter-rupted the Court demanding his right to defend himself and accusing the Judge of racism. Judge Hoffman initially ordered Seale to be chained and then bound and gagged with industrial tape. The image of a black man thus restrained in an American courtroom went round the world and did little to boost the credibility of American justice, freedom of speech or democracy. The exasperated Judge then sentenced Seale to four years for contempt. From that point on the now seven defendants and their lawyers refused to stand whenever the Judge entered. They declared they would not dignify his behaviour with any show of defer-ence to the Court or the legal system.

The defence called a bunch of star witnesses including Norman Mailer, Allen Ginsberg (who chanted), Dick Gregory, Timothy Leary, Phil Ochs, Arlo Guthrie and Rev. Jesse Jackson. The central contention of the defence was that there had been no conspiracy and that yippies couldn't organise a piss-up in a brewery. The Judge refused to allow any reference to Vietnam, race or politics in general. He sustained every objection made by the prosecution and dismissed every objection made by the defence. The trial was a parody of justice. All seven defendants were found guilty of inciting a riot and sentenced to five years. Abbie Hoffman and Defence Attorney William Kunstler were also done for twenty-four charges of contempt each. Kunstler was sentenced to four years. All the police officers charged with assault during the police riot were acquitted. Jerry Rubin inscribed a copy of his book for Judge Hoff-man thus: 'Julius—you radicalised more young people than we ever could. You're the country's top yippie.'

In April 1970 The Living Theatre split into four cells. Carl Einhorn went to Algeria to join Eldridge Cleaver; Rufus Collins went to India to study Kathakali; another group went to Berlin to work on environmen-tal protest; and the Becks eventually went to Brazil to work in the favelas, where for their trouble they were arrested, imprisoned and several members of the company were tortured.

Back in Cranleigh Street both Mike Leigh and Les Blair were trying to get films off the ground. Together they formed a company, Autumn Productions, to raise interest in, and money for, their projects. Once again we wrote to everybody in the British film industry from the Boulting brothers to Elizabeth Taylor. We were profoundly unem-ployed, but Mike was a member of the National Film Theatre so we spent days there watching movies. I was cinematically illiterate so it was an education for me to immerse myself in Truffaut, Pasolini, Eisenstein, Renoir, Chabrol, Fellini, Satyajit Ray, Buñuel, Godard, Bertolucci and rest of the all time greats. Just round the corner from Mike's flat, next door to Laurence Corner Army Surplus Stores, was a wonderful old cinema called the Tolmer. It was a dreadful fleapit, but it showed two different programmes every day and three different programmes every week. They showed everything from Ealing Comedies to The Three Stooges and Japanese Godzilla movies. They also showed old shorts like *Our Gang* and *Flash Gordon*. There was no discernible programming policy, and it certainly wasn't art house. It most resembled an ABC Minors Saturday morning picture club, but for adults. It cost something like one and six downstairs and half a crown upstairs. Downstairs smelled of piss and had winos. Mike and I practically lived there.

I also remember a trip to see the D'Oyly Carte Company doing *The Gondoliers* at Sadler's Wells. Mike was a huge Gilbert and Sullivan fan and told me gleeful tales of how, back in Manchester, he had seen the company perform drunken and mucky versions of the most popular choruses at the Press Club. After the performance at Sadler's Wells we went to the pub by the stage door, where Mike tried to engage comic baritone John Reed, who had just played the Duke of Plaza Toro, in a debate about the neo-colonial interpretation of the piece. John Reed was more interested in telling us how he had recently met the Queen Mother.

Mike had a unique sense of humour. He had recently read *Portnoy's Complaint* and enjoyed performing unspeakable acts of depravity with pork products whilst singing 'A dirty old Jew was making tea, he brew, he brew', and wearing an improvised yarmulka. In restaurants he would frequently order the chef's cock on toast. He wrote and drew cartoons for the London Film School magazine *Sinic*, including a strip called *Little Sergei* featuring the young Eisenstein as a baby filming from his pram as it careered down the Odessa Steps. We created a character called Chopper the Copper, a nude policeman whose knob was always at the same angle as his truncheon and we fantasised about getting it published in *Oz* magazine. Mike turned me on to the comic genius of Flann O'Brien and wrote a spoof piece for *Sinic* called 'A Tragedy for the Irish Cinema' about the Fergus MacPhellimey retrospective at the NFT and a rare screening of that veteran Irish director's seminal oeuvre *Blaidn' Bhallochs* late night at the Tolmer. Other *Sinic* articles entertained the notion of John Schlesinger disappearing up his own arsehole and expressed the hope that Jerry Lewis would die in his sleep.

A frequent visitor to Cranleigh Street was playwright David Halliwell who had recently caused a bit of a fuss with *K.D. Dufford hears K.D. Dufford ask K.D. Dufford how K.D. Dufford'll make K.D. Dufford*—a play described by Simon Gray in the *New Statesman* as being 'almost too vile to be tolerated'.

Keith Dufford is, like Scrawdyke in *Little Malcolm*, a bed-sit fantasist. Too socially inadequate to hold a conversation in the chip shop, Dufford sits at home reading the papers and imagining himself to be President Lyndon Johnson or El Cordobes, the Beatle of the bullring. Then he reads about Ian Brady, Myra Hindley and the murder of Lesley Ann Downey. Dufford murders an eight-year-old schoolgirl and immediately acquires an identity, status, celebrity and notoriety. There are books written about him, documentaries made and ballads sung. In the second half of the play the murder scene is repeated many times as different versions and interpretations of the action are explored. It's all pretty brutal and contains the stage direction 'DUFFORD *starts to hammer the wood up the child's vagina with a mallet*'. It is not, however, a play about sex or murder. It's about the nature of private fantasy and prurient public obsession and the way they feed on each other. With *Dufford*, Halliwell was decades ahead of 'In Yer Face' Theatre and the smack and buggery brigade. Think *Billy Liar* written by Sarah Kane.

Dufford also marked the beginning of Halliwell's preoccupation with what he called MVPD: multi-viewpoint drama. MVPD does pretty much what you might imagine, in that the action of a scene is repeated several times presenting it from the perspective of each of the protagonists in turn. The differences that occur between each version of the scene serve to illustrate that dramatic truth is relative. Halliwell used to maintain that in the story *Dog Bites Man* you show the incident from the point of view of the man, from the point of view of the dog and from the point of view of the bite. This is hardly a revolutionary notion, but Halliwell continued enthusiastically to embrace the genre for the rest of his life:

> I may of course be crackers but I think a day will come when almost all drama, including popular drama—even series on television—will be multi-viewpoint and people will look back and wonder why its validity was ever doubted. It'll be regarded as a liberating force in the same way that jazz was liberated by harmonics in the 1940s.

Always keen to get his hands on the means of production, Halliwell had formed a new writers' collective company, Quipu, to produce *Dufford* at the LAMDA Theatre. After producing another piece of MVPD, *A Who's Who of Flapland*, at the Green Banana in Frith Street, Soho, David was now exercised about Quipu's new home in the basement of a Greek restaurant at 49, Greek Street, where he was going to launch another revolutionary new idea: Lunchtime Theatre. In the evenings the basement would revert to its more usual role as Les Cousins' folk club where Norman and I spent many a jolly and formative evening.

The Royal Shakespeare Company at that time had a policy of employing the occasional token black spear-carrier. Three of them, Louis Mahoney, Oscar James and Alton Kumalo, who knew Mike from Stratford, approached him to run an Afro-Caribbean improvisation workshop in the basement of the Mangrove Restaurant in Ladbroke Grove. Mike asked me to help. One of the group members was a Bermudan actor called Earl Cameron, who had been one of the first black actors to break through into British film, notably in *Sapphire* and *The Pool of London*. After a few weeks Earl disappeared back to Bermuda to star in the Bermuda Arts Council's production of *Othello*, directed by Robin Midgley, who ran Leicester Phoenix. A couple of weeks later Mike got a call. Midgley had resigned, and the Bermuda Arts Council had decided that *Othello* might not be the most politically sound play for them. Could Mike think of another play for Earl Cameron to star in and come out to Bermuda to direct it for three months and a shit load of money? The same day he got a phone call from Halliwell asking him if he wanted to direct a play called *Thank You and Good Evening* with two weeks' rehearsal and no money for the Quipu Basement. He chose Bermuda, and Halliwell asked me to direct *Thank You and Good Evening*.

The deal in Bermuda was that Mike had to find a vehicle for Earl Cameron that could accommodate a huge cast of amateur actors, a large number of whom were white. He initially suggested *Macbeth*, which was instantly rejected. Cameron then ruled out Brecht's *The Caucasian Chalk Circle* on the grounds that Azdak didn't come on until after the interval. Eventually it was agreed that Mike would direct Brecht's *Galileo* with Earl as the eponymous astronomer. Mike had to fly out to Bermuda almost straight away. He had a reefer jacket and a pair of Burton's corduroy trousers but no tropical clothing, so we went round the corner to Laurence Corner, where he bought half a dozen second-hand army vests and a pair of Desert Rat shorts that almost reached his ankles. He dyed the vests in the bath. They came out pink.

Thank You and Good Evening was an odd first, and I suspect only, play by Michael Konrad Harding, who also did the publicity for Quipu. The title is based on David Frost's catchphrase. The whole thing took the form of a television quiz show in which the contestants were questioned, psychoanalysed and then rewarded with tranquillisers, electric shock treatment or a lobotomy. It was an absurdist social satire on the treatment of mental illness and, erm... television quiz shows. I suspect that Michael Konrad had personal experience of at least one of the central topics of his play. One of the Quipu regulars was Carl Forgione, an actor who had played David Frost in Joan Littlewood's production of *Mrs Wilson's Diary*, so he obviously became the quiz inquisitor. I roped in Dave Peart from Scunthorpe, a couple of mates from East 15 and an elderly but game actress called Irene Gawn for the lobotomy. Mike Leigh's chum Paul Rowley designed the set.

I spent time on character background, and we improvised round the text. I like to think it made a difference, but I suspect the play resisted all attempts at depth or subtlety. It was, however, only forty minutes long. The three lunchtime theatres that existed at the time were all in Soho. Ed Berman's Ambience was then in Frith Street. Soho Theatre was in New Compton Street. We were round the corner in Greek Street. We all competed for the passing lunchtime trade with hookers and strip clubs. Michael Konrad and I loitered furtively outside the theatre trying to drum up custom with earnest but ultimately pathetic cries of 'How about some Lunchtime Entertainment then?' And 'Why not see an interesting play?', while next door the spielers were offering 'See the beautiful Sabrina! See the dusky Ribena! They're NAKED and they DANCE!' One lunchtime a strip-club punter was stabbed to death about two feet away from us. We retreated indoors.

The play was not a big hit, but Halliwell seemed pleased with it and I enjoyed the gig and the eccentric venue and company. I stayed on to stage manage a couple of other shows including another piece of Halliwell MVPD called *Muck from Three Angles* and the first play from a young journalist working on the *Bradford Argus*, *Two Kinds of Angel*, by David Edgar. The two kinds of angel in question were a revolutionary Socialist and a dumb blonde actress who imagined themselves to be Marilyn Monroe and Rosa Luxemburg respectively and who shared a flat. Marilyn did a fair amount of pouting and Rosa unsurprisingly organised demos. *Plays and Players* looked forward to future plays from Mr Edgar, and who could blame them?

There was trouble in paradise. Mike Leigh was having a terrible time in Bermuda. The place turned out to be the last bastion of an Empire on which the sun was rapidly setting, rather than a funky tropical island in the sun. Earl Cameron wasn't interested in either Brecht or improvisation and was becoming increasingly paranoid. The rest of the amateur cast was largely made up of ex-pats who were into gin and yachting. Rehearsals could only take place in the evenings, so Mike had time on his hands. There was plenty of sea and sun. Mike does not do sea and sun. *Galileo* is a difficult play at the best of times, but with a recalcitrant Galileo, a frequently absent, tired and emotional cast and an impenetrable jungle of local politics the task became almost impossible. Mike was tempted to bail out but was persuaded, against his better judgement to stay—'Without question, the biggest mistake I have ever made.'

The torrent of filth unleashed by the departure of the Lord Chamberlain continued with the opening of Ken Tynan's evening of civilised erotic stimulation *Oh! Calcutta!* at the Roundhouse. The title derives from the French '*O quel cul t'as*'—'Oh what an arse you have.' The show, which survived an attempt to have it banned by the Dowager Lady Birdwood, turned out to be a bunch of not particularly funny and not particularly erotic sketches by a variety of authors both living and dead including the Earl of Rochester, John Lennon, Joe Orton and Sam Shepard. The cast, which included Arlene Phillips and Tony Blair's father-in-law Anthony Booth, got naked, and there was tasteful dancing and singing and simulated sex. The audience on the night I saw it were middle class and middle-aged, but there were sufficient of them for the show to transfer and to run in London for over two thousand performances. At the Roundhouse none of the actors got a stiffy, but it is a very chilly venue.

Far more exciting was *Cancer* by Michael Weller, which was produced at the Royal Court. Weller had had two earlier plays at the Open Space, *Now There's Just the Three of Us* and *The Bodybuilders*, but *Cancer* was, for me, a revelation and a definite influence on the work I was later to create with Hull Truck.

Cancer was the first naturalistic play set amongst and chronicling the foibles and confusions of the Woodstock generation. The characters are all extras in the revolution who, despite their hipness and enthusiasm for alternative politics, still have to cope with life, love and death in Nixon's America. Nothing much happens. A bunch of students share a flat. They have eight hundred and fourteen empty milk bottles. They argue about who ate the hamburgers. They have a possibly imaginary cat. They go on an anti-war demonstration. One of them gets drafted and decides to existentially join up. A couple split up. They are visited by a neighbour, the landlord, an encyclopedia salesman, two cops, a plumber, a milkman, an uncle and Santa Claus. They have fantasies. They tell lies. The two cynical smart asses, Mike and Cootie, wind up the nerdy mathematician into a self-immolation anti-war suicide pact. They fill his gas can with water. He burns his wrist. Space cadet Shelley sits under the table throughout, blowing peace bubbles. The characters are real, organic and authentic. The play is witty and affectionate. The writing has an almost Chekhovian feel about it. *Cancer* made me realise that I wanted to make contemporary drama about contemporary characters trying to make sense of the modern world. In America the play was retitled *Moonchildren* because they don't have cancer in America.

Back at Stratford East Joan was briefly back in business. The theatre now stood alone in the middle of what looked like a vast bombsite. Newham Council were set on redeveloping the area with tower blocks and offices, and the Theatre Royal was the last building standing. Gerry Raffles used to guard the theatre at night armed with a shotgun in case any bent property developer might accidentally knock down the walls of the now Grade II-listed building. The future of the company was again at risk, and Joan's programme reflected the situation. *Forward Up Your End* by Ken Hill was a satire on corruption in local government. Although set in Birmingham, the play could equally have applied to the good burghers of Newham. Joan followed this up with *The Projector*, a comic opera by William Rufus Chetwood. Joan had unsuccessfully tried to produce a piece based on the suspicious events behind the Ronan Point disaster a couple of years earlier, when a block of flats had mysteriously collapsed killing several residents. She had attended the inquiry but had been warned that any attempt to dramatise the actual events and personalities could be libellous. She was therefore fortunate to find *The Projector*, an obscure eighteenth-century play that satirised an historically parallel situation. Chetwood was for many years the prompter at Drury Lane and at Smock Alley in Dublin. He wrote a number of plays including *The Lover's Opera* and *The Generous Freemason. The Projector* opened on Friday 13 April 1733. The first and only performance had had to be abandoned when the actors were booed off stage by a gang of thugs hired by the tenement builder whose reputation for shoddy work is lampooned in the play. The play was never performed again until Joan's revival. *The Projector* was a Hogarthian tale of corruption, bribery and buggery in the style of John Gay's *The Beggar's Opera* and exposed the unscrupulous behaviour of contractor Van Clysterpump and a band of venal local dignitaries. Lord Aimwell, a character who in no way resembled Tom Driberg, hung around building sites in pursuit of horny-handed sons of toil, and there was a farting sergeant. The Stratford production was a popular success, even more so when it became clear that the whole thing was a spoof and had not in fact been written by William Rufus Chetwood, but by John Wells and Richard Ingrams from *Private Eye*, who had also been responsible for *Mrs Wilson's Diary*. In recognition of Joan's work the Arts Council again withdrew their grant.

In October 1970 the Royal Court hosted the 'Come Together' Festival, a celebration of the best new work of the British avant-garde. There were twenty different shows over a period of three weeks both upstairs and downstairs. The companies on show included The Freehold, The Brighton Combination, Portable Theatre, The Other Company, Cartoon Archetypal Slogan Theatre, People Show, Stuart Brisley, The Alberts, Theatre Machine, Pip Simmons Theatre Group, The Victoria Theatre, Stoke and The Ken Campbell Road Show. The list is a fair indication of where alternative theatre was at at the time.

Brighton Combination presented *The NAB Show*, a very free adaptation of Aristophanes' *The Wasps*. NAB stood for the National Assistance Board, which was the forerunner to the DHSS, which was a forerunner to the DWP. The play was a satire on the tortuous bureaucracy and endless form filling involved in getting the dole. The audience had to undergo a series of interviews and answer complicated questionnaires before being allowed to see the show. Marcel Steiner and Jim Carter were in the cast.

Nancy Meckler's Freehold continued the classical theme with their version of *Antigone*. They had clearly been influenced by both The Living Theatre and Grotowski. This was Sophocles for the Love Generation. The text was cut up and rearranged and, with references to Vietnam and Biafra, the play became a mouthpiece for the Peace Movement. Creon symbolised both America in particular and the Capitalist war machine in general, and Antigone represented the power of Peace and Harmony. The text eschewed any mention of gods, replacing the deities with a somewhat vague 'Commitment to Loving'. The acting was physically impressive and the invocation of the horrors of war were suitably horrific despite the fact that the actors all wore brown string vests. As an audience member you would have to have had a working knowledge of the text to have a clue who was who or what was going on. Whether or not this mattered is, of course, up for grabs.

Pip Simmons performed an adaptation of Chaucer's *The Pardoner's Tale* and a reworked version of *Superman*. People Show did a piece in the phone box outside the theatre. They offered sex, drugs and violence. You got a kiss, a sugar lump and hit over the head with a telephone directory. Peter Cheeseman's Theatre in the Round company from Stoke presented *The 1861 Whitby Lifeboat Disaster* by Peter Terson, which was the latest in a long line of documentary plays that had become the company's trademark. Theatre Machine played improvisational theatre games. The Alberts clowned and played peculiar instruments. The biggest hit of the Festival was, however, The Ken Campbell Roadshow.

Ken trained as an actor at RADA with Mike Leigh and David Halliwell. He had worked as a stooge for both Dick Emery and Warren Mitchell and was in the touring version of *Fings Ain't Wot They Used T'Be*. He acted in Rep, notably for Peter Cheeseman at Stoke where he, Mike Leigh and Annie Raitt were in a production of *Twelfth Night*. He had also written several plays, including *Anything You Say Will Be Twisted* about the highwayman Jack Shepherd and his own version of *Old King Cole*. A showman with a love of the bizarre and sensational, Ken was approached by Robin Pemberton-Billing, the Artistic Director of the Octagon Theatre in Bolton, to set up a company that would take theatre out into the community.

Pemberton-Billing's idea was that the Roadshow would go into pubs and clubs and drum up custom for the shows in the Rep. What in fact happened was that the punters preferred the capers of Ken and his team to what was on offer in the Octagon and continued to stay away in droves. After a dispute the company split from the Octagon and went back on the road, honing their skills in pubs and workingman's clubs. They performed *Bar Room Tales*, a collection of sketches and songs based on Urban Myths—the modern folk legends that people tell each other in pubs. The style was broad and rude and totally unpretentious. In the cast were Bob Hoskins, Dave Hill, Jane Wood and Ken. The Sloane Square sophisticates loved them.

Also at the Festival was the Royal Court's own production of Heathcote Williams's *AC/DC*, one of the seminal plays of the decade described by the *Times Literary Supplement* as 'the first play of the twenty-first century'. *AC/DC* is a visionary piece that defies analysis and sometimes even comprehension. It's a play about schizophrenia, synchronicity, ECT, telepathy, astral projection, the collective unconscious and quantum physics. It starts with three American freaks having a Mongolian cluster fuck in a photo booth in an amusement arcade and ends up with an epileptic ex-alcoholic dosser undergoing a trepanning operation to open his third eye. It rages against Psychic Capitalism: the vampiric power of the media to control taste and thought and thus enslave the population. It suggests that Fame is merely a measure of electromagnetic waste. It gives R.D. Laing and anti-psychiatry a good kicking and presents an alternative view of sanity. It's also ecologically prophetic.

The production was enhanced by the remarkable acting of Victor Henry and Henry Woolf. Tony Shear from East 15 was one of the shagging Americans. The play won the Evening Standard Award for Best New Play, and Heathcote won the George Devine Award for most promising new writer. The writing is extraordinary and the language is electric, probably best illustrated in Perowne's final speech when he says:

Heathcote was an eccentric Old Etonian poet, astral traveller and necromancer with a profound interest in sexual excess. Ken Campbell was a visionary prankster and Fortean from Ilford with a profound interest in ferrets and ventriloquism. Remarkably they were on the same cosmic journey.

Mike Leigh came back from Bermuda having just about survived Earl Cameron and *Galileo*. He described it as the worst production of anything ever. He had, however, some good news. Albert Finney was going to put up the money to make the film of *Bleak Moments*.

Finney and Michael Medwin had set up a production company, Memorial Enterprises, in 1965. They had produced Lindsay Anderson's *If...* and Finney's own film *Charlie Bubbles*, and, persuaded by Tony Garnett, they had agreed to finance the film version of *Bleak Moments* to the tune of £14,000. The only concession they asked for was that the film should be made in colour rather than black and white as Mike had suggested. Money was still tight, so the BFI Production Board put in a hundred pounds, not a huge investment, but it meant that the film could be made under the aegis of the BFI, thus qualifying for the reduced fee experimental film agreement with the unions. We would start rehearsing in January 1971 for four weeks and then shoot for six weeks.

The idea was to take the same basic story as the seventy-minute play version of *Bleak Moments* and expand it into a ninety-minute film by opening up the backstories of the central characters and incorporating some of the extra scenes we had discussed in rehearsals for the original show. Mike and producer Les Blair began to round up the crew and interview actors for the new roles. They recruited Bahram Manocheri, an Iranian graduate of the London Film School as cinematographer, and Roger Pratt, who later went on to shoot *Batman*, as his assistant.

Mike decided that Sylvia and Pat worked in an Accountant's Office and Chris Martin, Annie Raitt's real-life husband, was cast as their lascivious boss. Hilda went to a day-care centre for the disabled, so actors were cast as her colleagues. Pat's bedridden mother made an appearance. Mike cast the wonderful Liz Smith in what became her breakthrough role. There were further scenes in Peter's school, a gloomy off-licence and a deserted Chinese restaurant where Peter takes Sylvia to dinner. Reg Stewart from *Individual Fruit Pies* played a yobbish customer. We reworked Norman's background story and hit upon a commune in Acre Lane, Brixton, run by an old mate of Mike's called Malcolm Smith who ran a radical bookshop. Malcolm ended up playing himself in the film, and Donald Sumpter played a flashy communard. Eventually the original five of us got our contracts. We were to be paid the Equity minimum for filming, which was then forty pounds a week, but agreed to invest half of this into the picture in exchange for a share in the profits. Forty years later there were still no profits.

Art director Richard Rambaut found a suitably gloomy semi in Norwood, South London, and Mike, Les and I hunted for suitably bleak furniture and set dressing on Brick Lane market.

Rehearsals began early in the New Year back in the original church hall. The new actors began inventing life histories and creating characters in isolation, Mike gradually incorporating them into the central story. We needed a duplicator for the scenes in the garage so I found one somewhere in Essex and went to buy it in character with Don Sumpter driving around in the beaten-up dormobile that belonged to the commune. I also went to an all-nighter at Les Cousins in character although I didn't have the bottle to get up and play. I had written some songs for Norman. My favourite lyric was:

Took a walk down by the universe
Everything was looking worse.

We moved rehearsals into the location house in Norwood, and I spent days in the freezing garage trying to get the oil stove to work and playing

'Candyman' with the wrong chords. The night before filming Annie and Sarah slept in the house in character. Mike slept in the spare room.

The shoot started out painfully slowly; it was the first time that any of us had made a feature film, but the atmosphere was electric. Scenes were rehearsed on the set before a take. The dialogue was never written down, but a final version of the scene evolved organically.

Occasionally Finney turned up on location in his Range Rover with his stunt double bodyguard and tied up the location payphone making calls to his bookie. One day he brought his new wife. 'This is Mrs Finney.' It was Anouk Aimée. 'Call her Nookie.' They were both fascinated by the working process.

The lack of a significant budget called for improvisation in all departments. Film stock was expensive so Finney donated several cans of short ends from his recently completed movie *Gumshoe* to eke out the supply. This meant Mike and Bahram had to be very strict about the length of the takes. Sound equipment was equally rationed. There's a long tracking shot where Sylvia and Peter walk along the pavement talking. Out of shot the entire crew and cast hid behind a hedge stealthily passing a microphone from hand to hand to record the conversation as they passed by. Bahram lit the film beautifully using his own homemade lighting gear. Location catering was a takeaway from the Wimpy.

Bleak Moments was premiered at the London Film Festival in October 1971. Mike and Les and a crew of five had made a III-minute feature film for £18,500.

Unlike their theatrical colleagues, the film critics totally understood what we had been up, to and Mike was recognised as the talented auteur he indubitably is. He was variously compared to Olmi, Milos Forman, Antonioni, Eric Rohmer, Chekhov and, erm... Sam Peckinpah. Philip Oakes said it was 'one of the most loving films I have ever seen'. George Melly in the *Observer* thought it was 'a remarkable debut and a striking and entirely original first feature'. Roger Ebert in the *Chicago Sun Times* said that the film was a 'masterpiece, plain and simple' and that 'there have never been performances just like this before in the movies'. Nina Hibbin in the *Morning Star* perspicaciously wondered if *Bleak Moments* was going to be 'yet another casualty of the British film industry's attitudes and preconceived ideas about what the public wants'.

Despite all the fuss the film failed to find a distributor and was in danger of disappearing into the dustbins of Wardour Street until Contemporary Films came to the rescue and programmed *Bleak Moments* for a short season at the Paris Pullman. Broke as ever, I went along one night to busk the queue. There was no queue. The film went on to win both the Golden Leopard at the Locarno Film Festival and the Golden

Hugo in Chicago. It played the art-house circuit but has never had a general release. Tony Garnett invited Mike to make a television film, *Hard Labour,* with him at the BBC. Here Mike joined the rest of the serious British Film Industry in exile in White City. He didn't make another feature film for seventeen years.

4

The Untameable Rhinoceros

During the filming of *Bleak Moments* Chris Martin, who had played Annie Raitt's accountant boss, told me that Ken Campbell was looking for an actor/musician to take over from Andy Andrews for the final tour of *Bar Room Tales*. Andy had decided to become a proper musician. I had seen the show at the Theatre Upstairs as part of the 'Come Together' Festival, so I called Ken and asked him if I could join. My audition took the form of turning up to one of their gigs and coming second in a joke competition. The Roadshow at the time was Ken, Percy James Patrick Kent-Smith (later to become Sylvester McCoy), Dave Hill, Susan Littler, Jane Wood, Chris Martin and Bob Hoskins. *Bar Room Tales* was a mixture of songs and sketches culled from pub tall stories, and the shows were gleefully bawdy. The style was what Peter Brook called 'Rough Theatre', but what Ken cheerfully maintained was 'Uncle Acting'—the kind of stuff that pissed uncles do at Christmas when they play Scotsmen with a tartan car rug. The props and costumes were rudimentary, although Dave Hill had blagged fifty quid from the Arts Council for some Oxfam suits. We had a Woolworth's electric organ and my beaten-up old guitar from *Bleak Moments*, and we toured in an old VW Microbus with everything stashed in Tampax boxes on the roof.

The sketches included *The Phantom Hitchhiker*, *The Granny on the Roof Rack*, *The Man Who Disappeared Up His Own Arsehole*, *The Biscuit Tin*, *The Man on the Monument*, *The Chicken* and a couple of mini-musicals written by Dave and Andy, one tantalisingly called *The Inflatable Bra* and another *Queen Victoria's Coachman*, in which Hoskins played Queen Victoria but only on the gigs that paid proper money so Ken had to do the others.

The Inflatable Bra told the story of glamorous young actress whose Hollywood career had failed to take off, much to the consternation of her cigar-chomping agents Lou and Leslie, who lament:

93

Lou and me dear, we're worried to bits
Can't afford failures, only back hits.
Your face it is fine, everything fits,
All you need now is a bit more out front if you know what I
mean.

As this sketch predates readily available boob jobs by several decades,
our heroine (played by Sylvester McCoy) invests in an inflatable bra and
sets off on a plane to America. Halfway over the plane hits turbulent
weather:

But the plane had gone up too far
She'd forgotten all about her inflatable bra
And as the pressure went down
It forced out the front of her gown.

At this point in the entertainment Kent/Sylvester is sitting on Chris
Martin's knee while Ken operates a foot pump blowing up a vast bladder
under her blouse until it eventually explodes. That was pretty much it
really.

Ken had always been a fan of the original Crazy Gang, and to an
extent that was the secret of the Roadshow's success. What we were doing
was music hall and clowning in its most simple and honest form. What
you needed was 'bottle': the chutzpah and arrogance of spielers and
buskers to turn up often unwelcomed in someone's local pub and fart
about in disguises. It was a million miles away from Mike Leigh.

Rehearsals were a solitary affair for me as everybody else knew the
routines and had better things to do with their time. Ken, however,
decided that once I had learnt all the music we should try to come up
with some new material.

The list of suggested items went:

1) Song about how wonderful it is to get totally pissed going
   into Kent's drunk act

2) The landlady's son, the vicar and the potty

3) Hoskins as man with new false teeth clappering in pub

4) Rich Widow and Australian and Kangaroo

5) Victoria and fart?

6) Beethoven's Fifth in the Trenches

7) The turd in the hat

8) Nell Gwynn and her large fruit?

There was also a new song we worked on, the number that eventually
gave Kent his new name. The Roadshow used to rehearse in a pub in

Chorley. One night the landlord had a lock-in. In the early hours of the morning a bunch of nice old Chorley ladies taught Ken and the team an apparently famous local song called 'My Brother Sylveste'. Ken had collected the lyrics and presented them to me:

Have you heard about the Big Strong Man
Who lived in a caravan?
Have you heard about the Jeffrey Johnson fight
When the big black nigger fought the White?
You can bring all the heavyweights you've got
Cos we've got a little man to beat the lot.
He plays the organ in the belfry
And he wants to fight Jack Dempsey.
That's my brother Sylveste.
What's he got?
He's got a row of forty medals on his chest.
Big chest.
He killed forty darkies in the West.
He knows no rest.
Bigger the arm, the stronger the punch
Don't push, just shove, plenty of room for thee and me.
He's got an arm as big as a leg
And a punch that would sink a battleship.
Big ship
It would take all the Army and the Navy
To put the wind up... Sylveste.

I wrote a new verse and an arrangement for two chords and Kent became Sylveste and later Sylvester because nobody ever remembered Sylveste.

I subsequently discovered that 'My Brother Sylveste' was an Irish folk song apparently based on a Canadian marching tune. There were several extra verses, one about Japan and another about the sinking of the *Lusitania* and the tune was more or less right.

The *Beethoven's Fifth in the Trenches* routine needed more careful preparation. Ken had the notion that sometime during the First World War, probably about the same time both sides were singing *Stille Nacht* in no-man's-land, a similar incident took place in which soldiers on both sides took to playing the tunes of Beethoven's Fifth and Handel's Largo using the notes created by firing off their guns. Ken sought to recreate this poignant Wipers moment in the form of a Robert Service ballad using the sound of plastic toy machine-gun fire. The Robert Service bit wasn't too difficult:

When out of a night that was forty below
The Hun was heard to shout:
'Mein Gott, vat vas Beethoven
Vot vey vas banging out.'

The gunfire bit involved Ken, Sylvester and me spending a merry after-noon in Harrods' toy department brandishing a tuning fork and pestering the staff with requests for a Gatling in B flat. And so we were prepared.

The short tour was basically a week at the Sheffield Festival, a week at the Leeds International Children's Theatre Festival, a week at the Royal Lyceum, Edinburgh, as part of a Rock Festival, and a TV pilot to test out the newly completed BBC Pebble Mill Studios in Birmingham. More fascinating by far was the added possibility of joining a circus for the summer. Ken had been approached by his old mate Mike Hirst about the notion of collaborating on a new circus project. Everybody wants to run away to the circus, and the Roadshow were no exception.

First there was a try-out gig where a skeleton Roadshow cast played as half a lunchtime double bill in a nightclub on Kensington High Street called Toto's. A couple of charming but incredibly Sloaney actresses had persuaded the club owners to let them produce lunchtime cabaret and theatre in the hope of attracting sophisticated Chelsea office workers to enjoy a tasty and wholesome salad and a glass or two of Pinot Grigio while watching us perform *The Man Who Disappeared Up His Own Arsehole*. We shared the bill with Keith Johnstone's Theatre Machine, the seminal improvisation troupe who I had once seen warm up for The Pink Floyd at the UFO Club.

What happened was pretty much that nobody turned up. I think the largest house we had was twelve; at one particular lunchtime the entire house was Warren Mitchell who bought us champagne. By the end of the week we were swapping casts out of sheer boredom. Sylvester and me did some comedy improvisation games with Theatre Machine and Judith Blake and Roddy Maude-Roxby did *The Inflatable Bra* with us. *Beethoven in the Trenches* proved to be incomprehensible, as the Harrods machine guns never played the same note twice, so we ditched it. I don't think Toto's lasted for very long either, as one of the Sloanes became a Maoist and disappeared to Peking, where they promptly gave her her own TV chat show.

Mike Hirst was a man with a dream. Ken had met him at Colchester Rep where he used to be Master Carpenter. Hirst was one of that lost breed of showmen who could do anything. He had built sets for Joan Littlewood at Stratford East. He had built his own boat, built his own house and, at Colchester, apparently single-handedly built the entire theatre and most of Colchester. He was a tent master, a steeplejack, a stevedore, a lighting designer, an illusionist, a horseman, a worshipper of Pan and a trainer of performing pigs. He had built the stage and rigged the lights for the Isle of Wight Festivals. He was six foot four, had wild matted Afro dreadlocks and carried a lump hammer in his pocket. He looked like a cross between Frankenstein's monster and Jimi Hendrix, and he wanted to start a circus.

Hirst was ahead of his time. He wanted a circus without animals. It would be a cornucopia of tricks and stunts and phantasmagoria, a place of danger and of magic and of strange delights. There would be tumblers and jugglers and fireworks and dancing girls, and we, the Roadshow, were going to be the clowns.

Hirst had somehow sequestered the old blue Cinerama tent from the producers of *Hair* in Amsterdam. He had the lighting rig from the Isle of Wight, which he had taken in lieu of a fee, prudently dismantling it and smuggling it across the Solent in a borrowed tug, as Hendrix played 'All Along the Watchtower' in the gathering gloom. He had engaged a seven-piece band to play Nino Rota's score from Fellini's *La Strada*. He had borrowed some ancient bleachers from Big Bob Fossett. He had the Fabulous Flying Hendersons, a top-notch trapeze act flying in from Johannesburg, financial backing from Albert Finney and Princess Mbone of Uganda, and the whole thing was about to be erected on Southsea Common...

HIRST'S CHARIVARI—
THE CRAZY MUSICAL MAGICAL SHOW

But first came the tour. In Sheffield Dave Hill accidentally cracked my rib while beating me up as a tramp falsely accused of rape in a particularly witty routine. Ken and Sylvester had a fight live on BBC Radio Hallam. In a desolate and empty pub the next night only four pensioners turned up. We bought them drinks and offered to do requests. 'It's important to get to know your audience personally,' said Ken, unconvincingly. We were excited to see Portable Theatre's *Plays for Rubber Go-Go Girls* by Chris Wilkinson, in which Patricia Hodge spent some time wearing a rubber cat suit. Indeed Ken was so impressed that he later booked a private performance in his front room.

In Leeds we were part of an International Festival of Children's Theatre, which was a bit odd, as we didn't really do children's theatre. It turned out that we had been booked as roving minstrels and general troubleshooters, so we did a gig in a car park, a gig in the Playhouse foyer, a gig in the Playhouse bar, a gig in the *Yorkshire Post* office building, a gig in the Victoria Hotel ballroom, a gig in a pub and several gigs in the street. The festival had booked some of the leading companies from Europe including The Chesacoo Raree Show, The Malo Pozoriste Black Light Theatre from Zagreb, The Wim Zomers from Holland, Theatre Mobile from Burnley and the Coventry Theatre in Education Company.

The Wim Zomers were happy shiny people and everybody fell in love with them. Their show was considered to be quite radical even in Holland. They performed an agitprop piece, *Ants*, about conscription into the Dutch Army, which featured Peace Ants and War Ants, and then they turned out the lights and passed round a microphone so theoretically the kids could voice their opinions on the topic anonymously. They were devastated to learn that we no longer had conscription in Britain. Overnight they rewrote the show with the new topic—discipline in schools. All went well until the secret microphone bit. In the darkness a kid grabbed the mic:

> This is Eric Boocock from Cleckheaton speaking, and I don't care who knows and if I do owt wrong our teacher Mrs Arkwright gives us a belting and she's a fucking twat.

The Coventry Theatre in Education team was highly rated and also broadly speaking leftish, but they too came a cropper with the kids of Leeds. Their latest show, *Nothin' Ever 'Appens 'Ere*, was about newspapers and the power of the press to manipulate politics. It kicked off with lights up on a huge figure silhouetted behind gauze. The figure spoke in a booming RADA voice saying 'I AM AN EDITOR'. The unfortunate actor then assumed what he clearly felt was a butch and authoritative pose with one hand on his hip and the other vaguely pointing into the wings. With one voice the audience shouted out 'Yer great poof!' Whatever message the Coventry mummers were seeking to convey was lost in a barrage of catcalls every time the Editor opened his mouth.

The Chesacoo Raree Show were a *Commedia dell'Arte* troupe who didn't come from Bohemia as they claimed, but one of them had studied with Ladislas Fialka at the Theatre of the Balustrade in Prague. Personally I think the stuff we were doing in the Roadshow was a lot closer to true spirit of *Commedia* than their version of what was essentially a live Punch and Judy act, but they seemed to be going down well with the kids. So great was the response that they attempted a bit of good old-fashioned panto audience participation. Mr Punch was faced with a decision about who he should murder next so he asked the kids for advice. Now this appealed to the kids no end. 'Shall I kill zee babee?' He shouted in his not really from Bohemia accent. 'Shall I kill zee babee or shall I kill zee dog?' 'Kill the baby!' they shouted. 'Kill the dog! Kill the baby! Kill the dog! Kill the baby! Kill the dog!' It was total chaos.

Then, as the Rarees fought to calm things down in the dog/baby slaughtering debate, one still small voice rang out from the audience. 'Bring back the poof from yesterday!' It might have been Eric Boocock.

Theatre Mobile from Burnley presented a musical by Mark Wing-Davey based on T.S. Eliot's *Old Possum's Book of Practical Cats*. It was called *Cats*. Silly title, absolutely no future potential.

Also in Leeds, Ken and I saw an early performance of the Pip Simmons Company's raucous and sexy *Do It!*, their satirical take on Jerry Rubin's manual for a Yippie revolution. At the end Ken leant over to me. 'That's the kind of show you should be doing,' he said.

The gigs with the Roadshow were tough and I quickly learnt what Ken meant by 'bottle'. You had to show no fear and, as Joan Littlewood always said, 'Never apologise.' There was quite a lot of drinking involved too.

One of our drinking partners was Victor Henry, who came from Leeds and, out of work, propped up the Playhouse bar in the vain hope that fellow actors would buy him drink. Victor was undoubtedly one of the best actors of his generation and had done some remarkable stuff including Perowne in the original production of Heathcote Williams's *AC/DC* at the Royal Court. He was also mad, bad, and dangerous to know and was an agent of chaos everywhere he went. We were joined at the bar by Marcel Steiner of the Brighton Combination, a gentle giant of a man with huge moustaches and sideburns. He had the unique talent of being able to carry four pint bottles of Newcastle Brown between the fingers of each hand, a skill highly applauded by the Roadshow. It turned out that Marcel was also going down to Southsea to the Charivari. His girlfriend was the Wardrobe Mistress, and Marcel had been roped in to help put up the tent. He may have a part in the show. He may do a Gorilla Act. Victor's eyes lit up at news of the Charivari. This sounded like just the caper he was looking for.

As Marcel set off to put up the tent, the Roadshow headed for Edinburgh and the Edinburgh Pop and Rock Festival, where we were to open the new Royal Lyceum Studio Theatre. Hoskins was to join us for the gig as it paid proper money.

Bob's return meant that the parts got swapped around again, and Ken dropped out of *Queen Victoria's Coachman*. The sketch was a simple tale of a Royal progress.

Queen Victoria's off today in a brand new coach and four
Touring the countryside and we know what it's for.
To exercise her Royal prerogative she takes a ride,
Her prerogatives haven't been exercised since Prince Albert died.

Chris Martin played the lascivious coachman as Mick Jagger brandishing a suggestively long-handled whip.

> I was chatting up a lady-in-waiting,
> She gave me a glass of toddy,
> I knocked it back and then I knocked her off,
> The beer had a slightly better body.

Actually more Max Bygraves than Mick Jagger. The Queen progressed up the motorway to Newport Pagnell, where she had an adventure with a sturgeon and to Watford Gap where she inspected a rubber chicken for freshness by sniffing its arsehole—'Madam, could you pass such a test?'

Eventually the coachman, who had been dying for a piss all day, expires from a burst bladder, and Victoria passes a law allowing motorists to pee on their off-side rear wheel provided they declare 'I am about to urinate' in a voice to be heard at ten yards distant. Apparently this law is still on the statute books. With the drag on Bob Hoskins looked amazingly like Queen Victoria, except he had arrived in Edinburgh having grown a huge black beard. Ken made it quite clear that there was no way he was going to let Bob play the Queen as a bearded lady, but Bob was very proud of his growth and said he would only shave it off for an extra tenner. Ken gave him a fiver. Bob grumpily disappeared into the gents and only emerged at 'beginners' now sporting half a beard. Ken was furious but Bob stuck it out and got the extra fiver, which pissed everybody else off. The atmosphere backstage was poisonous, but the show was tremendous. This was the first time that I had worked with the whole team together, and what I saw was popular theatre at its best; actors working at the top of their game and providing dirty and gleeful entertainment that genuinely communicated with the punters. The only other event of significance that happened in Edinburgh apart from sharing the bill with The Strawbs was watching Evonne Goolagong win Wimbledon on assistant director Richard Eyre's TV. Ken christened Richard 'Pubes'—something to do with Dick Hair.

On the way down to Southsea we stopped off at Millets to buy tents, as Hirst had not managed to blag enough caravans. Bob already had his own superior tent, which he claimed was a souvenir from his days in the Norwegian Merchant Navy. We had run away to join the circus.

We finally pulled the van onto Southsea Common where the big blue ex-Cinerama tent was pitched at a crazy angle surrounded by a miniature Woodstock of living vans, tents and teepees. Hirst greeted us warmly. 'Oh, by the way,' he said, 'we've had a bit of bad luck. The Fabulous Flying Hendersons aren't coming, but I'm sure we'll be all right. Lavatory facilities are available across the road in the gents behind the Esplanade Café.'

As we pitched our tents and sorted out our Primus stoves, it gradually dawned on us that we were in fact IT, the entire show. There was Ken, Hoskins, Sylvester, Dave Hill, me, Judy Blake from Theatre Machine, who we had roped in at Toto's, Marcel Steiner, who had suddenly become very much part of the team, and Hugh Armstrong, an actor mate of the Roadshow who was supposed to be very good on a motorbike and who had just come back from Poona where he had been an orange devotee of free-love guru Bhagwan Rajneesh. And there was Chris Nicholls and his seven-piece band, who were all mysteriously accommodated in caravans. There was also a small army of riggers and chippies who had put up the tent and built the set and were now working on what looked like a three-tiered scaffold made out of old doors and ladders. They looked like the Grateful Dead road crew.

What they were in fact building was the front entrance to the tent which would serve as a living billboard. The idea was that every hour on the hour we would appear out of the doors and entertainingly caper about in an attempt to attract punters. The whole thing was to be decorated with garishly exaggerated paintings of the attractions available within in the style of a carnival freak-show booth. The edifice was topped off with a leering effigy of the god Pan: half-man, half-goat. It looked like a bizarre cross between a Pagan advent calendar and the set for The Living Theatre's *Frankenstein*.

These notional hourly caperings were in addition to doing two performances a day and three on Saturdays of a show in which no one, with the possible exception of Mike Hirst, had the faintest idea what it was they were supposed to be doing.

In fact there was a script of sorts:

A bare stage... Silence... Then in the distance we hear the sound of Nino Rota's circus music and as from nowhere the band and performers march in through the audience. They carry flaming torches and costume skips and grotesque heads on poles. They are like ethereal beings, these acolytes of Pan. What will they do? Do they really exist? As one they all blow fire, lighting a flaming brazier that is hoisted to the roof of the Big Top. Let the Charivari begin!

Now according to Lord George Sanger, the great British showman, Charivari goes like this:

All the clowns in the company took part, and many others who were not clowns, but made up as such for this act. After some preliminary tricks and fooling, a follow-my-leader line would be formed with the younger members in the lead, as they would usually be the poorer tumblers. The first one performed his best tumbling trick, the next had to outdo this or give place to a better man, and so on down the line with tricks of ever increasing magnitude and difficulty, so that to be the last in a line of tumblers in those days was to be accorded not only a position of honour but a position that it was extremely hard to maintain. And once the last man had maintained or had to cede his position, there was a furious rally in which everyone all over the ring simultaneously performed whatever trick he could do best, and everyone shouted their heads off and the big drum banged away like a cannon. After this the whole company and perhaps the audience too had to get their breath back.

This seemed a mammoth task for a company of devout smokers and drinkers with three forward rolls, two cartwheels, an unconvincing handspring and a headstand in the lotus posture between them. It was clear that we would have to go into serious gymnastic training as well as having to learn to breathe fire. The rest of Hirst's scenario was a combination of wishful thinking and a variety of ornate props that he had made.

1) Charivari
2) Fireblowing
3) Bob introduces...
4) Garth the Gorilla (Marcel for the kids)
5) Ballerina in cage with Tramp (Ken)
6) The Birds (UV sequence)
7) Fire Brigade (Hugh on bike)
8) Stilt Walking (for the kids)
9) The Identikit Routine
10) The Untameable Rhinoceros
11) Lois Fuller
12) Bubble Machine
13) Finale and Carousel

Then there was some malarkey involving handing out roses and leading the punters in a merry dance before disappearing like laughter among the leaves.

The situation needed careful planning so we went to the pub. We spent our first night under canvas and got bitten to shit by mosquitoes. Nobody slept a wink.

Training started the next morning with firebreathing lessons supervised by Master Carpenter Hywell Price, who had also spent time working fairground sideshows. Basically the way you blow fire is to take a mouthful of paraffin and blow it out over a flaming torch in the manner of playing a trumpet. 'You need to have a good embouchure,' said the trumpet player in the band, who had no intention of putting his mouth where his mouth was. 'Fuck off,' we said. We sat around on the edge of the ring, trying to persuade each other to go first when Bob arrived late because he was the ringmaster, and obviously it was the ringmaster's privilege to arrive late.

'So what's the score then, lads?' said Bob. 'Nothing to it,' said Dave Hill. 'You just get a gob full of paraffin and set fire to it.' 'Have you all done it?' 'Yeah sure, Bob, nothing to it, dead easy.' We were a bunch of lying toerags. 'Right then, I'll have some of that.'

Bob picked up the bottle of paraffin, took a big swig, raised his flaming torch and blew out a fifteen-foot jet of flame that catapulted him backwards across the ring and into the bandstand, singeing his eyebrows and his post-Queen Victoria beard. Bob picked himself up, grinned from ear to ear and said, 'Piece of piss. Now where are the fucking stilts?'

So with the firebreathing under our belts we started out on acrobatics. Hirst had hired the Drill Instructor from the local Territorial Army, but it was an uphill struggle. Sylvester and Hugh were quite good at vaulting, but the rest of us were pretty useless so we turned it into a comedy routine in which we all fell over a lot. The really top-notch sporto was Steve the prop maker, but he wasn't in the show. Well, not at this stage anyway.

Marcel was fine-tuning his gorilla act, for which he wore an old flying helmet, a pair of tights, a Marcel Marceau T-shirt and a pair of roller skates. He spent his days skating along the promenade intimidating holidaymakers with concupiscent gorilla behaviour until the police moved him on. Meanwhile, we worked on our stilt skills, which also rapidly became about falling over. 'The kids will love it,' said Hirst with little conviction.

The Ballerina and the Tramp came about because Hirst had borrowed a lion cage from somewhere. The idea was that Judy Blake performed some classical ballet in the cage while Ken as a sad Tramp figure looked on in rapture and then presented Judy with a rose through the bars. Judy hadn't done ballet since she was fifteen but gamely donned her tutu and Ken did his best as a refugee from *Les Enfants du Paradis* while the band played Dvořák's *Humoresque*. Hirst claimed that it was deeply symbolic of something, while Hoskins called it a paedophile's dream. There was also a notion that we should perform a traditional lion-tamer act with Hugh as the dashing lion tamer and the rest of us as lions. We spent a couple of days locked in the cage improvising lion scenarios with Sylvester as the keen one, Bob as the lazy one, Judy as the sexy one and Dave Hill as the deaf one, and doing a spot of half-hearted roaring until Ken declared the whole thing to be titty and we abandoned it.

Not being entirely convinced by the way things were going Ken decided that we should try some of the Roadshow material, although we were working without the full team. Bob and Sylvester worked up *Russian Roulette*, a sketch about two Russians fighting over the same woman (Judy). The whole thing was played in gibberish except when they used a rouble to toss up for who would shoot first. Instead of 'heads or tails?' Bob said 'Czar or Czar's arse?' Then they pretended to corpse themselves for ages, ditched the girl and gaily went off together. It went in.

The Untameable Rhinoceros was made of fibreglass and was built by prop maker Steve. It was life-size and a thing of beauty and in dim light you could almost believe it was real except that Steve himself was the front legs and driver because he could see and I was the back legs and couldn't. The Rhino came with an important announcement from Ringmaster Bob:

> A Rhinoceros of up to five tons in weight is able in favourable conditions to reach a speed of thirty-five miles per hour. It cannot be presented in the type of cage normally used for performing wild animals. Zoologists, in collaboration with modern technologists, have, however, devoted the past decade to researching ways of preventing the escape of larger animals without the use of steel bars. In association with the Royal Zoological Society, we have developed the New Psychological Cage, which safely confines the Rhinoceros without restricting the audience's view of the animal.

Throughout Bob's spiel the boys and girls of the company would be setting out a ridiculously flimsy barrier of garden canes as the lights slowly dimmed 'to avoid needlessly provoking the highly strung pachyderm'.

A roll on the drums. 'Ladeez and gentlemen, for the first time anywhere on the known planet Hirst's Charivari is proud to present... The Untameable Rhinoceros!!' And Steve and I would lollop around the ring for a bit as the band played the theme from *Daktari* with extra trombone work until with gathering speed we charged through the New Psychological Cage and gored the punters in the front row. 'The kids will love it,' said Hirst.

Our canteen was either the local pub or the Esplanade Café where we took our meals and flirted with the waitresses when we could afford it. We were all on twenty quid a week rising to thirty when the show opened. Over several breakfasts a sort of plan began to emerge. After Marcel's Gorilla and *The Ballerina and the Tramp*, Sylvester would finally get to do his drunk act. He would start as a plant in the audience and disrupt whatever act we had least confidence in, eventually ending up in the ring. He would then try to light a cigarette whilst drinking from a whisky bottle, which would of course contain paraffin. He would blow a tongue of flame and then hide in the audience again. We would all arrive as the Krazy Keystone Fire Brigade in Hugh's sidecar, fall over a bit comically and then go into *The Identikit Routine*. This involved an elaborate prop with all kind of cut-out faces and wigs and beards, and the audience were encouraged to made up a photofit of Sylvester, and then we all got back in the sidecar and chased him some more. No wonder he ended up on *Tiswas*.

No one had a clue what or who *Lois Fuller* was, or what we were supposed to do, or how to pronounce it, or her or both. Hirst explained. Lois turned out to be an exotic dancer from the turn of the century whose speciality was to dance magically with diaphanous silks in a sensitive way. We would be performing an homage to Lois, which Hirst would light magically and sensitively. As this was a uniquely female endeavour it would feature Judy Blake, Marcel's girlfriend Romaine from Wardrobe and Anna and Jennifer, who were either Hirst's nieces or stepdaughters or half-sisters and who were nubile, fourteen years old and off-limits.

After a week of gymnastics and living under canvas, we had to go to Birmingham for a Roadshow gig. We were to record *Bar Room Tales* in front of a live audience as a pilot for the Roadshow and as guinea pigs to test the brand new BBC Pebble Mill Studios. The gig reunited all the original team with Jane, Chris, Sue Littler and Andy Andrews returning and everybody got paid proper money, although Bob tried the beard trick again. The show was a huge hit, and we partied long into the night in the gay B&B that the BBC had mysteriously booked us into. Next morning at dawn we set off back to Southsea as several prominent television executives did a runner down the fire ecape.

I had only been a minor part of the Roadshow for a couple of months, but on the way back from Birmingham I think I realised as much as everybody else that a chapter in the history of the Roadshow had come to an end. We'd done the last ever performance of *Bar Room Tales* and the company were off in different directions. Ken had always said Bob Hoskins would be a star, and it was time for him to go off and be one. But first...

The tent site had been transformed while we were away. The billboard construction was finished and in place and had been brightly

painted with images of Garth, the Roller Skating Gorilla, the Ballerina
and the Tramp, the Untameable Rhinoceros, the Krazy Keystone Fire
Brigade and a huge leering figure of Pan that looked very much like Ken.
The words Hirst's Charivari were picked out in multicoloured light
bulbs. As we drove into the field Hirst waved us down. 'Great news! I've
decided to do an Aqua Show as well. We're going to dig a swimming pool
in the middle of the ring.' Sure enough, standing in the middle of the
ring was a mechanical digger.

'Thing is, I haven't told the Council about the pool, and the Watch
Committee are coming to inspect in a minute so I've told them it's a
prop for the show. Could you sort of, do something? Quick, they're
here!' and he was off.

Hugh was already in the driver's seat. 'The Inflatable Bra,' shouted
Ken, 'Kent, get in the fucking shovel.' And the rest of us climbed on the
JCB as Sylvester went up and down in the scoop and we sang:

Here I go; I've checked my knobs.
My juice is pumping and my engine throbs,
So I pulled my little joystick
And I shot off in the sky.

Incredibly the Watch Committee either fell for this ludicrous charade
or thought we were dangerous lunatics and should be left alone.

The other piece of news was that Victor Henry had arrived and got
himself a job looking after the Crazy Golf Course and was sleeping in
the Park Keeper's hut. 'Worrying times, lads,' said Victor in the pub that
night, happy to help us drink our BBC wages. 'Worrying times.' We
opened in a week.

In fact Hirst knew what he was doing with the Aqua Show idea, as
Ken was an expert in that now sadly neglected tributary of popular
entertainment. The story goes that, while at RADA, Ken answered an
advert in *The Stage*:

Wanted.

Actors that can swim.

Auditions at Oasis Swimming Baths, Endell Street.

Bring Trunks.

Ken applied, swam a length, dived off the springboard and was offered
the job of directing shallow-end activity in the Aqua Show in
Bournemouth. He was offered four pounds a week and crumpet, which
meant he got first crack at the Aqua Lovelies.

So we set out creating an Aqua Show. 'There are three basic ele-
ments,' said Ken. 'We need a daredevil stunt diver who can do a double
somersault tucked with pike from a thirty-six-foot-high board into a

mere five foot six inches of water possibly through fire. We need Aqua Goons, who are essentially clowns that swim, and we need some Aqua Lovelies for the dads.' It turned out that prop maker Steve, in addition to being a top-notch gymnastic sporto, was also a diving champion, so he became Stefan the Flying Swede and he was in. Despite the fact that in a real show the Aqua Goons are the most experienced performers, and that Sylvester couldn't swim, the Goon task inevitably fell to the Roadshow. More falling over comically but now into water. Hugh recruited two of the waitresses from the Esplanade Café to be our Aqua Lovelies. 'What we really need now,' said Hirst optimistically, 'is a Speciality act.'

I have often wondered why I volunteered to become an underwater escapologist. I think a lot of it was to prove to the Roadshow and myself that I had the bottle, the right stuff to do it. Another reason could have been that when I was about eight I saw an escapologist doing a drowning act off Skegness pier. He drew a big crowd and it was exciting and frightening at the same time. The Arcadia Theatre Follies even sang about it in the 'Skegness Calypso'.

My father said 'I'll teach you to swim'
On the beach at Skeggie.
He took me out in a boat and pushed me in
On the beach at Skeggie.
He said 'Now my son you must swim back'
On the beach at Skeggie.
But I'd a devil of a job getting out of the sack
On the beach at Skeggie.
Sitting in the sun, sitting in the sun, sitting in the sun
On Skeggie beach. (*Repeat ad infinitum.*)

So it was that I reluctantly agreed to escape out of handcuffs, locks and chains and a sealed mailbag under water twice nightly and three times on Saturday, and Hywell Price was going to teach me.

As the stage crew dug a pool ten foot by ten foot by five foot six deep in the middle of Southsea Common without permission and constructed a wooden stage that winched up in the interval and a thirty-six-foot diving board, we tried to become an Aqua Show in a week. Rehearsals shifted to the municipal baths, and we practised falling off the high board comically and hopefully not dying. The deal now was that after the Krazy Keystone firemen had chased Sylvester round the ring and round the audience they chased him up the ladder to the high diving board where he evaded capture and we all fell off. We all fell off three times to make it more exciting. Steve practised his daredevil routine.

Hugh directed the waitresses in a Tantric Busby Berkeley beachball duet and I learnt the hermetic secrets of escapology.

Hoskins was my spieler. He did the introductions and was responsible for making sure that the punters he dragged on stage to assist fixed the handcuffs and chains and tied the bag in the particular manner that allowed me to escape.

> Ladeez and gentlemen, at this point in the programme we were going to present the Great Pizmo but unfortunately he couldn't turn up so Mike Bradwell, a plucky young man from the company, has agreed at short notice to perform for you this evening the very trick what Houdini died doing. Thank you. Ladeez and gentlemen, I give you... Mike Bradwell.

Then Bob would invite someone on stage to test the 'standard police handcuffs' and the length of 'prehensile steel' chain that went around my arms and legs and 'the weakest part of Michael's body: his neck'. And then get someone else to examine 'the toughest lock in the world: the Chubb'. Next I was manhandled into the drawstring mailbag, which was then securely tied by yet another audience member, and then this little army of assistants would throw me in the water. In fact if everything was going well I should be out of the handcuffs and chains before I went in so all I had to do then was hold my breath as long as possible swanning about at the bottom of the pool before operating the release mechanism and emerging in triumph. Piece of piss.

Except we weren't allowed to rehearse it in the municipal baths and there was no water yet in the pond in the tent.

Watching us inventing comic ways of falling in and not dying was a lad called Dave, who was working there as a lifeguard. He had started working out some stunt dives with Steve, but when we discovered that he had also been runner-up in the All Dorset Trampolining Contest and he also had his own trampoline, we roped him in as Davos the Flying Dane. The climax of the show would be Steve diving blindfolded from the high board through a ring of fire blown by everyone in the company. We were all quite impressed.

Back at the tent site Victor was worming his way into the show. He had become Marcel's gorilla trainer. He had invented a miserable Chekhovian character that had seen better times at the Moscow State Circus but now through no fault of his own was reduced to playing the Charivari with his ungrateful charge Garth, who would now be presenting poses from classical art and literature. He sat mournfully on the edge of the ring and announced that Garth would now perform *Eros, God of Love*. Behind him Marcel enthusiastically mimed tossing himself off. 'The kids will love it,' said Hirst doubtfully.

In the dead of the night before we opened, Hywell and the crew stealthily crept into the War Memorial Gardens and, connecting a hosepipe to the council water mains, siphoned off the thousand or so gallons needed to fill the pool. The wooden stage was lowered; the double-purchase counter-weighted lifting system was checked and checked again. The Jimi Hendrix lighting rig was installed, and the tent was decorated with a collection of unlikely art-deco seaside backdrops that Hirst had salvaged from the set of Ken Russell's film of *The Boy Friend* that he had been shooting with Twiggy in the King's Theatre up the road. We all had costumes of Day-Glo tights, tie-dyed T-shirts, frock coats and top hats. Every hour on the hour we would caper comically on the three-storey living billboard throwing buckets of water over each other. We blew some fire. We handed out leaflets. The band played some circus music. The bubble machine filled the Southsea skies with rainbow soap-suds. The startled holidaymakers looked on in total disbelief. We were ready to rock.

We had two preview performances before the Grand Opening. During the first, the cantilevered stage refused to budge and it took the entire company and probably most of the audience thirty-five minutes to winch it up. Despite the wait, most of the audience stayed, and my escapology act was a triumph considering I had never rehearsed it in the pool. Hoskins successfully organised the ornate tying up, and I took a deep breath as I hit the water.

> Ladeez and gentlemen, plucky Michael has only thirty seconds to escape before the intense water pressure will cave his lungs in and he will expire. Volunteers from the St John's Ambulance Brigade are on hand in case of any emergency. Drum roll. Ten seconds, nine, eight...

And Bob and the audience began the countdown.

Underwater I had no idea of the drama unfolding above as I held my breath for as long as possible. Bob got to one minute and the audience held their collective breath as well. One-and-a-half minutes and Hywell nervously looked at his watch. The drum roll petered out. Bob, starting to panic, signalled to Stefan the Flying Swede and pointed into the pool. A woman screamed in the audience, 'Oh my God, he's going to die!' Simultaneously Hywell in full evening dress and Stefan hurled themselves toward the water just as I triumphantly broke surface and waved to the crowd. I had stayed underwater for over two minutes. 'I think we can build on that,' said Hirst.

The other major discovery we made in preview was that Hirst's brilliant idea of separating the kids from their parents and sitting them on a vast inflatable cushion meant that the kids could join in the action at any and every opportunity. Which they did.

At about 5 pm on opening night a vast black Daimler pulled into the showground and out of it emerged two huge black men wearing military uniform and wrap-around mirrored sunglasses. They looked like the Tonton Macoute and they were carrying a flag. 'This is the flag of Uganda and you will fly it from the flagpole,' they instructed Hirst. We didn't have a flagpole so Hywell was dispatched to fix it to the top of the tent. The backers were coming to the show. Princess Mbone turned up with an entourage, and Albert Finney was represented by his business partner Michael Medwin, who once played Corporal Springer in *The Army Game* and who arrived in a chauffeur-driven Roller smoking a fat cigar. Our fate was in their hands.

In many ways the show was a triumph. The tent was packed as we had papered all the B&B landladies and café owners and pretty much anyone we could think of. The kids indeed loved everything, to the extent of joining in with chasing Sylvester, trying to free the caged Ballerina and beating up the Untameable Rhinoceros with the sticks from the psychological cage. 'That's something you don't see every day,' said Campbell, 'two hundred kids on a bouncy cushion spanking the rhino.'

The Mayor of Portsmouth and the council VIP guests, clearly impressed, gasped when the stage rose up to reveal an illegally dug swimming pool on their municipal turf. They gasped at the nail-biting drama of the Houdini Escape. They gasped at Garth the Gorilla's living statue. They gasped at the gossamer magic of Lois Fuller. They gasped at the inflated charms of the Aqua Lovelies. They gasped at Stefan the Flying Swede's blindfold suicide leap into fire with pike. The audience gasped at everything. The backers left at the interval.

The *Portsmouth Evening Echo* reported:

> One of the most bewildering pieces of entertainment ever to come to Southsea is now showing at the Common. Sometimes it seemed that the company itself was not quite sure what was coming next.

For the first week everyone was in high spirits, and, although we could sense trouble ahead, visits to the pub after the show often ended up as a party in the tent. There's always a sense of roguery and frolic around any circus pitch, and the Charivari attracted a fair amount of groupie action. One night Hoskins and Victor went out on the pull to Nero's

(Portsmouth's leading nite spot), returning with a couple of strangely silent girls. They annexed the band caravan and invited me in to party insisting that I bring my guitar. After a few choruses of 'Freight Train' and 'Wild Rover', Hoskins demanded the blues so I launched into my version of 'St James Infirmary', a song essentially about hospitals and death. At the end of my suitably sensitive performance Victor grabbed me tightly by the shoulder, stared at me with mad tear-filled eyes and said, 'Fuck me, Michael; it's a good job they're deaf and dumb.' Victor and Bob also had a plan that involved them becoming Socialist burglars. They would break into government buildings, crack the safe, steal all the secrets and leak the documents to the press. This would bring about the downfall of Capitalism. I thought they were on to something.

Bookings were not good so we threw ourselves into publicity. From dawn to dusk we comically capered on the billboard and on the Esplanade. We even took the rhinoceros out for a stroll. From my position behind Steve I had no idea where we were going, but Ken gleefully led us onto the pier where we comically fucked off Bob Monkhouse who was suavely presenting Miss Southsea 1971 with a silver rose bowl and a ten-shilling voucher for top beauty-care products.

And I had a fan in the shape of Mr Patel who ran the Bel Shazzar Indian Restaurant ('Luxurious Food—Excellent Service') on Osborne Road. Whenever I passed by blowing bubbles and pestering holiday-makers to buy tickets Mr Patel would shout out, 'Mr Houdini, Mr Houdini, come to my restaurant where I will give you an appreciable discount because of your bag show.' And as the temperature rose and the storm clouds gathered I took frequent advantage of Mr Patel's bargain bhuna.

At the end of the week Hirst called a meeting. There was no more money. He had overspent on the Aqua Show. The backers had pulled out and the creditors were circling. We would not be getting our promised thirty quid a week. This week it would be twelve. Next would be profit-share. We had come so far that everybody decided to stay and pull the show together, but it was obvious that people were wobbling.

That night at the party in the tent after the pub, Bob punched the trombone player for pissing in the pool. 'Don't be a cunt,' he said. 'Bradwell has to fucking escape out of that!' I finally felt I belonged.

The punters who came seemed to be having a good time, but despite all our efforts there were just too few of them, and gradually people started to drift away. One of the tech crew left to help the Native American Indians occupying Alcatraz, taking an Aqua Lovely with him, and the band was reduced to a quartet by lack of funds and non-specific urethritis.

In the middle of the second week in the middle of the night a huge thunderstorm broke. In a howling gale and driving rain Hirst organised everybody into emergency crews to man the guy ropes to stop the tent from blowing away. The living billboard buckled and the painted doors of Pan were wrenched off and blown into the Solent. Stefan and Davos hung off the high-diving board to lash down the lighting rig, which threatened to topple into the pool. All the electrics blew and Hywell Price and the emergency generator sank into a sea of mud. The storm was right above us and a lightning bolt struck the Esplanade Café but somehow we held on and magically the old blue Cinerama tent survived the night. As the storm blew itself out everyone crashed on the kids' inflatable cushion. Next morning we discovered that our Millets tents and most of our belongings had blown away like laughter among the leaves.

This was all too much for Bob, who made his excuses and sadly left. Victor replaced him as ringmaster, which was what he had been angling for ever since the drunken nights in the Leeds Playhouse bar. The running order was rejigged with extra comedy falling-over, and the show limped on into the third week. The band was now a trio. Hirst spent most of the time in his caravan desperately appealing for more backers until the phones were cut off.

Victor made the most of being ringmaster, bringing to it a sort of malevolent glee until on the Wednesday between the matinee and the evening show he disappeared. Search parties were sent to all the local pubs but found no sign of him. We even checked the Crazy Golf. With the punters arriving and as Marcel entertained them with solo Gorilla stuff on what had been salvaged of the living billboard we rewrote the show yet again. Hugh would be ringmaster in the first half, Ken would spiel for my escape and Dave Hill would do *Russian Roulette* with Sylvester. All went smoothly until the interval. Most of the company and the trio were outside the tent having a fag as the stage was being winched up, when we heard a kerfuffle coming from the Big Top.

Victor, half-wearing his gorilla-trainer uniform and clutching a bottle of vodka, was sitting on the edge of the ring addressing the audience. 'Worrying times, ladies and gentlemen, worrying times. Let me tell you about this show. You know nothing. Why? Because you're a bunch of cunts.' Dave Hill and I look on in amazement. Hywell Price shifts uncomfortably. 'Hugh Armstrong is, as I speak, in his caravan rolling a joint and plating the Aqua Crumpet. The band are all pissheads and they're running back from the pub and they've all got the pox...'

Hywell launches himself at Victor, hoping to throw him comically in the pool but Victor punches him away and carries on. 'They're all a bunch of fucking dope fiends, ladies and gentlemen. Worrying times, worrying times indeed.' At which point Hirst and Dave Hill and several others overpower Victor, carry him out and lock him in the props van.

And that was pretty much the end of things really. The next day Victor left to join John McGrath as a founder member of 7:84 and Hirst sadly announced that the show would end on the Saturday.

Hirst's Charivari—The Crazy Musical Magical Show had been a glorious failure but Mike Hirst had pioneered a concept that years later would be echoed in the work of Cirque du Soleil, Archaos, Derevo, Circus Lumiere and countless other alternative circuses throughout the world. For everyone involved it had been an unforgettable experience that influenced all our future work. After Charivari anything was possible.

Marcel Steiner joined forces with Ken and Sylvester to launch the new Roadshow with *The Adventures of Sylvester McCoy—the Human Bomb*. Marcel played the Wild Man from Borneo, which was more or less Garth the Gorilla in a wig. Sylvester stuck a ferret down his trousers and a banger up his arse. Dave Hill went off to do Brecht with Bill Gaskill. Jane Wood joined Max Stafford-Clark's fledgling Joint Stock. Hoskins went off to be Hoskins. And I went off to start my own company, Hull Truck.

The *Oxford English Dictionary* defines 'Charivari' as a 'serenade of rough music with kettles, pans, tea trays and the like designed to be a nuisance'. And in the early sixteenth century the Council of Tours issued an edict forbidding its practice and threatened practitioners with instant excommunication. I can't say I blame them.

5

High Windows

When I see a couple of kids
And guess he's fucking her and she's
Taking pills or wearing a diaphragm,
I know this is paradise

Everyone old has dreamed of all their lives—
Bonds and gestures pushed to one side
Like an outdated combine harvester,
And everyone young going down the long slide

To happiness, endlessly.

(Philip Larkin)

Hull Truck was called Hull Truck because we lived in Hull and travelled about in a truck.

John Lee and Richard Cameron, mates from endless days in the Doncaster Technical College refectory, had both moved to Hull. John was at the University Drama Department and Richard was training to be a teacher. Throughout my time at East 15 I had made occasional forays to Hull to run workshops for the East Riding County Youth Theatre and to attempt to impress female drama students with my metropolitan sophistication. When the Pig Theatre idea with Mike Leigh collapsed I had many late-night stoned conversations with John about starting a touring theatre company, and Hull seemed the place to do it. Hull was cheap, it was easy to get the dole, and it was the last place on earth anyone in their right mind would go to found an experimental theatre troupe.

The idea was originally to have a company that made theatre for people of our own age about people of our own age. We would create plays through improvisation about characters that were familiar to our audience living in situations and relationships that they recognised. I felt that there was a whole generation whose stories were not being told in contemporary theatre, or, at best, they were being stereotyped. Every time you saw a student on stage or television they would be wearing a duffel coat and a college scarf. Stage hippies, if there were any, would wear beads and sandals and flash peace signs.

Our company would tour universities, colleges, theatres, arts centres and arts labs. The audience we were after were the *Rolling Stone* readers, the people who would go and see a rock band, but not necessarily a play. To counteract this Hull Truck plays would have music, and the company would also function as a band. This was probably as much to fulfil all our Grateful Dead and groupie fantasies as anything else, but the notion was to provide a live soundtrack that would complement and comment on the action. We claimed that our two big influences were Chekhov and Bo Diddley. We planned to be a nuisance.

The other element I was particularly interested in exploring was the way in which various esoteric and hip philosophies were impacting on people of my generation outside the hermetic world of the cool. Kids in Grimsby were now reading Timothy Leary and taking acid. Fifthformers were tuning in, turning on and dropping out. They had seen *Easy Rider* and *Woodstock*. They were being told to smash society, kill their parents, fuck in the streets. How easy was that when you were living with your mum on social security in Goole? And they were doing it to a soundtrack provided by a bunch of millionaire cokeheads sitting by swimming pools in Laurel Canyon churning out interminable doggerel about the pain of sharing Joni Mitchell with their drummer. They were Norman's people.

John Lee, Peter Edwards—another ex-Hull student who aspired to be our roadie—and I moved into a tiny attic in Willesden. It was from there that we planned our campaign.

We put an advert in *Time Out*:

> THEATRE/MUSIC GROUP now half-formed needs other half—musical actors and actresses—to create original material and tour college/university circuit. Must be orientated towards both acting and music and prepared to move up north after Christmas. Details contact Mike Bradwell 965 1108 evens before 10 pm

John Ashford, who was *Time Out*'s Theatre Editor, helpfully added that 'They plan to move to Hull which will be their equivalent of a cottage in the country in which to get it together.' Getting it together in the country was what all sensitive artists and musicians did at the time. It inevitably resulted in a concept album.

The company would be a collective in as much as everyone would be paid the same, which was nothing. Everyone would sign on when they got to Hull and hope that Social Security wouldn't find them a job. In Hull there was not much risk of that. The DHSS did more to subsidise arts in Britain than the Arts Council ever did. As a touring company though, we would need a van and some props so we set out to raise money. I cashed in some premium bonds. We bought some headed notepaper and stamps and once again wrote to rich and famous people for help.

B.A. Young gave us five pounds. Harold Pinter declined. Tony Garnett gave us a tenner. George Melly advised us to go to the Arts Council. Donald Pleasence gave us a fiver. Jonathan Miller and Albert Finney said they were broke. The London Rubber Company, makers of Durex, wished the venture every success, and John Cleese told us to fuck off. In all we raised about eighty pounds, most of which went on writing to another bunch of rich and famous people who didn't give us anything.

The first person to audition for Hull Truck was a young Northern Irish actor called Gerard Murphy. He couldn't play an instrument but we offered him the gig anyway. He turned us down for the Glasgow Citizens', who paid wages. He went on to be a magnificent Henry V for the RSC and to have a long and distinguished career. Next was a guy called Brian Routh, who played the harmonica. He brought along his friend Martin von Haselberg. They had both been thrown out of East 15 for being experimental. Brian was fine, but Martin was clearly nuts. Halfway through the audition they both lay on the floor, waved their legs in the air and shouted 'Kippana! Kippana! Look at you getting all high and mighty. Whoops Kippana!' They explained that they had a collective alter ego called Harry Kipper who occasionally took over. It was all part of their act. They called themselves The Kipper Kids. We asked Brian to join but he didn't want to break up the winning team. The Kipper Kids went to New York where they became successful and highly regarded performance artists. Martin von Haselberg turned out to be a German Baron. He married Bette Midler.

Mike Hirst called me up and offered me a gig fire-eating for Led Zeppelin's show *Electric Magic* at the Empire Pool Wembley. Hirst was providing the performing pigs. We spent my fire-eating fee on a company publicity brochure. We decided to call our first show *Children of the Lost Planet*. In it we promised to reveal the truth about 'the new, permissive, anarchist, drug-crazed, long-haired, Communist, hippy student love culture'. The style was purposely irreverent and cartoonic. We wanted to connect with the readers of *Zap Comix*, *Oz*, *International Times* and the *Furry Freak Brothers*. 'Keep On Truckin'' was the mantra of hip cartoonist Robert Crumb.

We auditioned a few more people and then, financed by some minor drug peddling, made a trip to Hull, where we recruited Steve Halliwell, a talented actor and musical genius who had been in the Youth Theatre, and a girl called Sue Riley, who had been in the Drama Department with John Lee and would-be roadie Peter Edwards. Pete had now christened himself Hangdog and bought a leather overcoat. We were well up ourselves. We persuaded the Drama Department to let us open our show in their brand new Gulbenkian Centre. Opening night would be 10 March 1972. Back in London we added to the team Mark Allain, who had been in *Hair* in Amsterdam, and a Canadian girl called Lisa Hicks who wrote sensitive folk ballads and was into the kabbalah. We were ready to rock.

We moved to Hull on 18 December 1971. It was the coldest place on earth. We rented a semi-derelict house in Coltman Street off Hessle Road near the fish docks in the poorest area of town. The fishing industry was in decline but the smell of fish was still in the air. Almost everybody in the street was on the dole. The corner shop sold single cigarettes. Mrs Fuller, our Dickensian landlady, also ran the Willow Plate Guest House in a slightly better part of town. We went to get the keys. Mrs Fuller was a well-built woman. She resembled Ursula, the pig woman in Jonson's *Bartholomew Fair*, crossed with Barbara Cartland. She lay on a gilded chaise longue wearing a quilted dressing gown and surrounded by farting dogs and Capo di Monte shepherdesses. Her mooncalf son fed her cream horns from a bag. He was called 'our Cess'. Mrs Fuller told us that she didn't stand for any funny business and neither did our Cess. The rent was six pounds a week. We had three rooms on the second floor plus a kitchen, a bathroom and a windowless attic that we planned to use as a rehearsal room. Most of the ground floor was boarded up and stacked with broken furniture. There were feral cats. At the back lived Mr White, a solitary man from Sunderland who played Jim Reeves records all day and sometimes all night. There was a solitary fan heater. The house backed on to a wasteland where the rag and bone men grazed their horses. Outside the house was a phone box. For the first year it was our office. Speedway House next door was the home of middle-aged biker and DJ, Ron Tex. Ron was also manager of a band called Alias B who lived in the house with him. The band were teenage bikers, and Ron was grooming them for stardom in much the same way that Tam Paton groomed the Bay City Rollers. We subsequently discovered that this involved industrial quantities of amyl nitrate.

Although Hull was a city in decline there was a lively, if idiosyncratic sub-culture. Most of the inner city residents had been shipped out to ugly and soulless housing estates with optimistic-sounding names promising orchards, meadows and the like. This meant that there was row upon row of decent two-up-two-down terraces in the centre of town that had been taken over by the student population from the University, Art School and several other colleges. There was an arty middle class. Philip Larkin was librarian at the University and Alan Plater, who became Hull Truck's first champion, had set up the Hull Arts Centre several years earlier. There was also an Arts Lab type venue called the Brick House and a healthy music scene. Local hero Mick Ronson and his band, The Rats, were now David Bowie/Ziggy Stardust's backing group, The Spiders from Mars. Genesis P. Orridge and his performance art music collective, Coum Transmissions, lived in a squat in the old town that you accessed through a polythene tunnel. Genesis was a university drop-out called Neil Megson. His girlfriend was called Cosmosis. One of the band members had recently married his dog Tremble in a secret ceremony in Beverley Minster. The most popular local band ironically called themselves Nothinevrappens. There were several thousand pubs, a disco called Malcolm's, a folk club, a jazz club, a couple of clubs catering for gentleman bikers and a transvestite dockers' speakeasy where you could get a cup of coffee spiked with rum at five o'clock in the morning.

Famous Hull celebrities past and present include William Wilberforce, Andrew Marvell, Amy Johnson, Brian Rix, Tom Courtenay, John Prescott and Fifties crooner David Whitfield, whose doorbell apocryphally played the first four bars of 'Cara Mia', his number-one gold disc. Old Mother Riley died while performing on stage at the Hull Tivoli Theatre in 1954 and who could blame her.

Things did not start well. Cleaning out the bathroom I pulled up a rotten floorboard and a bedraggled rat staggered out. This was too much for Sue Riley, who immediately phoned her parents. They came to collect her and took her back to Rochdale in a Morris Traveller. Sue was replaced by Dave Greaves, an incredible guitar player and another ex-Youth Theatre actor. Dave shared a pigsty with Steve Halliwell behind the Hull F.C. Rugby League ground on the Boulevard. On 9 January 1972 rehearsals began.

The original idea was that we would meet every morning at eight in the upstairs attic for a warm-up. Lisa taught yoga classes and I did East 15 Laban exercises. The days would initially be spent in one to one character work and research, and in the evenings we would rehearse as a band. Several things became obvious straight away: half the company were incapable of functioning in daylight; the attic studio was unusable because it had no windows and the feral cats shat in it; and the music was going to be magnificent. Steve, Dave and Mark were consummate musicians, and all the voices blended together perfectly. Within a couple of days they were working on three-, four- and five-part harmonies and arranging each other's songs. We quickly decided to get a set together that we could perform in local venues and hopefully make some money and publicise the play.

I started to work on building characters. I asked each of the actors to come up with a character or characters who were the same age and gender as they were and who could possibly be living in Hull in 1972. The only fixed idea I had was that at the time of the play some, if not all, of the characters would be sharing a house not dissimilar to the one we were living in.

John Lee came up with someone who had left the University but was still stuck in Hull. The character Ez had been a big fish in a rather small pond and was terrified of losing status if he moved on into the real world. He was a bit of a shit. Steve Halliwell decided on a friend from school called Kevin who was nice but dim, and desperate to be part of the alternative society. Mark's character Andrew was a philosophy and economics student who was unsure of his sexuality. He did a lot of drugs and was emotionally insecure, covering it up with love and peace. Lisa was Sandy, a rich Canadian girl studying English on a student exchange scheme. She was pissed off with everyone asking her if she was American. Dave played Toby from Sheffield, who was shy.

I worked with each actor in isolation creating life histories for the characters from birth up to the time of the play. I would see each actor for an hour or so a day, moving the story forward in yearly instalments. We then moved on to interior monologues, and the actors began to go out and about in rehearsal costume and in character. We improvised on location where possible. Lisa, Mark and Dave spent a lot of time wandering about the University campus and even attended lectures. Steve and Mark went to see Mott the Hoople in character. As always in the early stages no one knew who anyone else was playing, and everyone worked in isolation, so it was important that each evening everybody got together as a group to rehearse the music.

John's character Ez lived in a four-bedroom student house and I decided that each of the other characters would eventually move in. I set up improvisations to explore their arrival. First to arrive was Kevin. He had gone to a party in the house and had never gone home. His mother had thrown him out because he had dropped out of technical college and wouldn't get his hair cut. He idolised Ez. Ez ripped him off. Andrew moved in and then Sandy. I orchestrated the improvisations to expose the allegiances and conflicts between the characters. Sandy fancied Ez. Kev fancied Sandy. Ez had screwed Kev's previous girlfriend behind his back. Andy was hopelessly behind in his work. Toby fancied Sandy.

I discovered the importance of patience. There is always a great temptation to take the simplest and most obvious option when deciding on what to pursue and what to discard. Gradually a scenario began to emerge.

By now it was the middle of winter and snow was on the ground. We rehearsed in one of the rooms in Coltman Street burning broken furniture and banisters in the fireplace. We ran out of firewood so built a tent of blankets and rehearsed under that until it collapsed and blew up the solitary fan heater. Steve and Dave wrote a song about it.

Fell in love with a fan heater
Fell in love today
Fell in love with a fan heater
But it blew away.

Fell in love with fan heater
Better than chopping wood
Fell in love with a fan heater
Cos it looked so good.

It blew hot and cold and sundry
But I didn't even care
Cos me and my fan heater
We ain't going nowhere.

Fell in love with a fan heater
Fell in love today
Fell in love with a fan heater
But it blew away.

To cheer ourselves up we played a music gig at Hull Arts Centre as part of a fundraiser for a local homeless charity. Alan Plater heard us and became a great fan and supporter. The rest of the Arts Centre staff regarded us with deep suspicion. We were a bunch of scruffy hippies and they were real pros doing proper plays like *The Lion in Winter* and *Little Eyolf.*

After six weeks of improvisations I came up with the outline for the play.

Children of the Lost Planet starts with Sandy moving into the student house shared by Ez, Kev and Andy. Both Ez and Kev fancy her.

Everyone goes home for Christmas except Kev who spends Christmas Day with his mad aunties. He reads an article in *Rolling Stone* about Marrakesh and fantasises about hitching there. Ez says he will come along. Ez has his dole stopped and ponces money off Kev to score some Congo bush from Dooley the dope dealer. Sandy gets involved in a student-sit in at University. Ez mocks the impotence of student politics.

Toby from Sheffield comes around and fails to kiss Sandy and falls asleep. Kev refuses to pay for Ez to see Mott the Hoople so goes with Andy and gets bombed on mandrax. Ez seduces Sandy.

Kev is furious with Ez for sleeping with Sandy. Andy is furious with Ez for betraying Kev yet again. Andy has a bad trip and freaks out. Sandy comforts Andy and blames Ez. Ez and Kev make up and practise hitching in a field.

Essentially *Children of the Lost Planet* was a play about a group of young people living away from home for the first time, trying to live up to second-hand notions of love and peace and understanding, and finding themselves ill-equipped to deal with what was actually happening to them. Hopefully the audience would recognise aspects of themselves in the characters on stage and try to find a better way to talk to each other.

After deciding on the scenario we then rehearsed the play scene by scene, and the company wrote the songs and music. Sometimes the lyrics were written from the point of view of the character, sometimes they commented on the action.

> Well what a lonely three weeks
> What a let-down
> Christmas at home's not for freaks
> What have you found?
> Well man,
> It's so good to see your face
> It's a picture in this place
> And I saw lot of TV
> And I had myself a meal.

Roadie Peter (Hangdog) Edwards decided that Hull Truck and poverty was not the life for him so went back home to Wales where there was a welcome in the valleys and a job with the BBC. He was replaced by Nick Levitt, who managed, for thirty-five pounds, to acquire an old Bedford van with an extremely dodgy tax certificate. We amassed a set made up of broken furniture and rancid milk bottles and on 10 March 1972, we opened the show.

Remarkably B.A. Young sent a reviewer from the *Financial Times*, who reported that the play 'turned out unexpectedly to be a sensitive and sympathetic picture, with wit and comedy too'. It was the only review the show ever got.

As we had no reputation, no administration, no phone and no publicity gigs were hard to come by. We had a couple more in Hull, one in York, one in Sheffield, one in Coventry and a final one in London, so while waiting to embark on this extensive tour we decided to devise a kids' show. Mark Allain had written a couple of songs, and together we concocted a simple plot. Everyday we improvised, wrote and rehearsed five minutes' material, and at the end of ten days we had a show. *The Land of Woo* was on one level a pretty vague parable about law and order and freedom, but was more a slapstick romp with cartoon characters, ladders, paint, falling over, silly songs and he's-behind-you participation. There were a couple of characters who were shoemakers so every time they came on the kids got to shout out 'Cobblers...' And it was. Against all the odds, the show was a big hit and we played schools, orphanages, play schemes, posh kids' birthday parties and a nun's garage. The strangest gig was for the children of Asian refugees recently expelled by Idi Amin as part of the 'Africanisation' of Uganda.

The Government had housed several hundred of the entirely legal immigrants in an abandoned RAF camp in Lincolnshire. The conditions were terrible: it was little more than a detention centre. The refugees were charming, intelligent and slightly perplexed about their treatment by the police cadets who were in charge. The cadets were a bunch of ignorant racist thugs. They advised us not to eat lunch with the Asians because their food tasted like shit.

The Land of Woo was the first of many Hull Truck kids' shows and fulfilled the dual purpose of making us a bit of money and giving us the opportunity to work audiences. The shows were for entertainment purposes only; our main role model was the *Beano*. We made a conscious decision that we were on the side of the kids not the teachers and so any educational content was entirely by mistake. We actively sought to be the antidote to the more worthy Theatre in Education companies who did improving tales about weaving or personal hygiene. We wanted kids to see theatre as magic and subversive and fun, not as an extension of lessons.

In addition to *Land of Woo* we were doing gigs as a band, playing local pubs and clubs. We even recorded an *In Concert* session for BBC Radio

Humberside. We played Hornsea Floral Hall as support to Medicine Head and, dressed up as Vikings, were commissioned to write and sing a hymn to the incoming Mayor in the Lord Mayor's Parade.

Ye sons of Odin long ago
Stout men one and all
In long ships sailed the northern wastes
To this fair port of call.
And with them they did bring a tale
A legend handed down
That some day there would come a man
To rule this wayward town, wayward town.
All hail, all hail, wave the Holy Grail
And the *Daily Mail* across the land
To tell all men yet again and again
Hull's saviour is at hand, is at hand.
Hurrah for the City
Hurrah for the Mayor it has chosen
And Hurrah for the powers of common sense
In choosing Lionel Rosen.

God knows how we got away with it. The Junior Chamber of Commerce gave us a rosette.

Children of the Lost Planet worked with student audiences everywhere we played, but there was always a minority that objected to the language and content. An outraged punter in York wrote to the local paper suggesting that it should be made illegal to portray such depraved characters on stage. The most enthusiastic response to the show was at the International Student Film Festival at the London Film School. Mike Leigh had arranged the gig. The van broke down on the way and had to be abandoned in a pig farm outside Gilberdyke. We hitched to London with the props and costumes, and improvised a set from bits and pieces of borrowed furniture. We got a standing ovation and took up a collection. We thought we had made it. We were wrong.

At the end of June, the first company broke up. Lisa went back to Canada, and Dave and Mark went to London to become rock stars. They signed a contract with Island Records and for a short while had some success as Rainmaker. Their single got to eighty-something in the charts.

Summer came to Coltman Street, and Mr White, the Jim Reeves fan, had an appointment with destiny. Returning home from collecting the dole one day we were surprised to find a mob outside the house. Even Mrs Fuller had put in a rare public appearance, supported by our Cess.

As he was bundled into a Black Maria Mr White turned to the crowd and, sobbing, confessed that he had only done it because he loved the bairns. Mrs Fuller offered us his old room for an extra thirty shillings a week. The Yorkshire Arts Association under extreme pressure from Alan Plater gave us a grant of two hundred pounds. We bought another van and a telephone and planned the next season. I recruited two new company members, Cass Patton, who had just left the Drama Department, and Alan Williams. Alan Williams was eighteen, had hair down to his waist and incredible spots. He was and is one of the best actors I have ever worked with. He had been thrown out of Manchester Grammar School, where he knew Sir Nicholas Hytner before his voice broke. Mike Leigh had seen him play Che Guevera in a Youth Theatre production and had recommended him to me. With this new team we planned to devise a new kids' show, *Wimbo the Wonderdog*, that we would tour while devising the next main show, *The Weekend After Next*. We spent the rest of the YAA grant on publicity for the two shows.

Wimbo the Wonderdog was a vaguely ecological tale about a spaceman, Joe Flash, and his green dog, Wimbo, who discover that the future of mankind is threatened by litter, and a couple of surreal dustbin men who worship a Coca-Cola machine. After the obligatory hair raising adventures the earth is saved and everybody sings a song. We charged fifteen pounds per performance. I would love to claim that it was heavily influenced by *Endgame*, but it wasn't.

One of the drawbacks to devising plays in rehearsal is that it's impossible to describe either the characters or plot in the advance publicity you need to big up the show. The temptation is to make something up. This is a mistake as you can easily get stuck with a story you are unable to tell. I decided in advance that *The Weekend After Next* would be a tale about a student couple who go to colleges in different parts of the country and the strain this puts on their relationship. And so that's what we did.

The Weekend After Next was created over a ten-week rehearsal period in the Coltman Street house over the autumn of 1972. I used the same rehearsal techniques as on *Children of the Lost Planet*, with extensive background and character work and improvisation on location. Steve Halliwell and Cass Patton were the young student couple, Paul and Angela. After A-levels she goes to Hull to study painting and he goes to London to study graphic design. Angela rents a bed-sit from John Lee's wicked landlord Neal. Across the hall lives Alan Williams's character Gareth, a weirdo loner who collects Del Shannon records. Paul hitches to Hull to visit Angela every other weekend.

The play covers the events of three such weekends and chronicles the deterioration of the relationship brought on by separation and jealousy.

Neal eventually throws Gareth out, and Gareth gets a job gutting fish. Although the play evolved organically from the improvisations I was constantly aware that I was imposing a predetermined structure on the piece. I think this was a mistake. I also decided not to use songs and music, simply because the company, apart from Steve Halliwell, were not really up to it. There was, however, one remarkable musical event during the rehearsal period.

A couple of months previously *Rolling Stone* ran an article on a yet unsigned band, The New York Dolls, who they called 'the new darlings of the underground Warhol Fellini Satyricon set'. For no readily apparent reason they were booked on a very short British tour. And so it was that on 2 November the legendary lipstick killers did an almost unpublicised gig at Malcolm's Disco in Hull. So we all went along.

The Dolls made The Ramones look like Bucks Fizz. Afterwards I interviewed the band for an alternative magazine I occasionally wrote stuff for. They were charming and polite and wore women's clothing. I asked Billy Murcia, the drummer, what his dream was. He told me he wanted to die a rock 'n' roll death like Jimi and Janis. Two days later he did. He overdosed in a London hotel and a couple of groupies stuck him in a cold bath and poured hot coffee down his throat.

David Bowie wrote a song about it.

The Weekend After Next opened at the Gulbenkian Studio Theatre, Hull University, on 25 January 1973 and toured with *Wimbo the Wonderdog* until the end of March. The most significant touring dates were Birmingham Arts Lab, The Close in Glasgow and the Royal Court Theatre Upstairs as part of the Improvised Play season.

Clive Barker, who had been an actor with Theatre Workshop, saw the play in Birmingham and wrote that:

> The concentration of the actors on specific character truths avoiding generalised emotions invited comparison with the work Joan Littlewood was doing in the late 1950s and the work itself was the best I have seen in this genre since *A Taste of Honey*... They provide a stimulating alternative to the boring trivia and tricked-out classic 'interpretations' that the established theatres have to offer.

Clive's review unfortunately appeared in *Theater der Zeit* in Germany and so failed to have much impact on the box office.

The Close was the sixty-seat studio of the Glasgow Citizens' Theatre. The Citz at that time was one of the most exciting companies in Europe producing work of astonishing daring and beauty under the inspired

triumvirate of Giles Havergal, Philip Prowse and Robert David Mac-
Donald. Although the scruffy bed-sit world of *The Weekend After Next* was
worlds away from the usual programme of Genet-inspired drag-queen
versions of the classics, the Close audience were largely appreciative.
The Scottish critics' opinions were mixed, ranging from 'extremely
dreary' to 'tells it like it is in a refreshingly unpretentious and frequently
comic way'. George Harvey Webb, who was temporarily living close by,
came along to see the show. He told me he thought it was very pure. I
think he meant that it was too long and too slow. The week after we left
the Close burnt down, and never reopened.

Mike Leigh had convinced Nick Wright, who ran the Theatre Upstairs,
that it would be a good idea if the Royal Court hosted a season of Improvised Plays. Mike would devise a new play; Annie Raitt from *Bleak Moments*
would devise a new play; and Hull Truck would bring in *Wimbo* and *The
Weekend After Next*. Mike's play turned out to be *Wholesome Glory*, which introduced the characters Keith and Candice-Marie Pratt, played by Roger
Sloman and Alison Steadman, who were later to feature in *Nuts in May*.

How far informed critical opinion on the merit of improvised plays
had evolved since *Bleak Moments* can be judged by *Time Out*'s introduction
to the season:

> Improvisation is a snappy trendy word. It's a wide-open situa-
> tion, more real, totally of the present and all that. Anything
> might happen. Wow. Or so the theory goes. But as anyone knows
> who's gone to watch improvisations, what happens all too often
> is nothing at all. You sit around hopefully, usually somewhere
> cold, waiting for that sudden interaction, and then it's all over.
> Maybe the actors have had a great time and have discovered a lot
> of valuable things. But too often it is a private stage, and arro-
> gance to assume that there's anything there yet to offer an
> audience. You might as well have sat watching people on the
> Tube, who at least don't charge and tell you it's art.

Our opening coincided with *The Freedom of the City* by Brian Friel and
directed by Albert Finney in the Royal Court main house downstairs.
On Finney's press night there was a bomb threat and the police evacu-
ated both theatres and the performances were abandoned. It was not a
good omen.

How The London critics were not impressed with us. The *Telegraph* thought
we had chosen 'a theme of such uninspired monotony that only an
Osborne or Wesker could make it seem fresh, affecting or true'. Billington in the *Guardian* reported that:

Improvisation is an invaluable rehearsal weapon: it rarely, however, provides a satisfying source of new drama and *The Weekend
After Next* does nothing to disprove this... I think theatrical realism
should be reinforced by a Zolaesque scientific zeal or by some
underlying mythic quality.

B.A. Young in the *Financial Times*, while praising the acting, bemoaned
the lack of wit and outside references in the play blaming the 'Hull Truck
method of composition which can only create characters and moods'.
The general complaint seemed to be that there was no plot, no narrative
pyrotechnics and no inspirational speeches, just monumentally trivial
dialogue between insignificant characters for whom they didn't much
care. We provided neither a well-made play in the traditional sense nor
a piece of spontaneous extemporisation. There was still a deep suspicion of the validity of our creative process.

It's fair to say, however, that *The Weekend After Next* was not our finest
hour. The show would have benefited from a more rigorous editing
process; the company never gelled together as a unit. By determining
the theme in advance I had pushed the characters in directions they
would not necessarily have taken and concentrated on a relationship that
should have been just one part of the story rather than carrying the
weight of the whole play.

Wimbo the Wonderdog had, on the other hand, played to over five thousand kids all over the country including performances at both the
Theatre Upstairs and the Roundhouse. We returned to Hull to review
the situation.

The alternative-theatre scene in Britain had moved on apace in the two
years since the company was founded. In London the Bush, the Half
Moon, the Orange Tree and the Almost Free Theatres were up and running, and the Open Space still continued. Other groups and spaces were
starting out all over the country. The Arts Council had established a New
Activities Committee to try to find ways towards funding the growing
movement. As David Edgar once pointed out:

In those days it was just about possible to write a three-to-five
hander, at under an hour in length, so dreadful that nobody at
all would want to put it on. But it wasn't easy.

David also had a theory that all this upsurge in theatrical energy was a
product of the 1944 Butler Education Act in as much as it allowed many
young people from less privileged backgrounds admittance to further
education that their parents would never have received. This created a
pool of smart working- or lower-middle-class people for whom theatre

was their chosen art form, both as practitioners and as audience, and they were demanding something new and more socially engaged. I suspect that he was right.

The Arts Council had also finally decided to subsidise Theatre Workshop to the tune of forty grand, so Joan returned to Stratford East in March 1972 with *The Londoners*, a musical version of *Sparrers Can't Sing* with songs by Lionel Bart. She followed this with a new version of *The Hostage*, adapted to deal with a changed political landscape in which the IRA could no longer be regarded as vaguely romantic characters in a theatrical romp.

Gerry Raffles wrote a programme note:

> *The Hostage* is set in Ireland but it is not only about Ireland, but about any other small country in the world which has a large neighbour and suffers from chauvinism and intolerance. You can't help being involved in Irish political life when you work on or watch *The Hostage* but Brendan's sights were on a sickness, which is endemic throughout human history.

Despite this caveat the theatre was continually plagued by bomb threats.

There was talk of a film version, but the American producer was apparently dissuaded from making the movie on the advice of Princess Margaret. Next Joan directed *Costa Packet*—a musical about package tours with book by Frank Norman and music by Alan Klein and occasionally Lionel Bart, which, despite being a critical hit, was considered to be a disaster by everybody involved. In November 1973 she directed her last play at Stratford East, *So You Want to Be in Pictures* by Peter Rankin—a satire on the movie business set on the roof tops of Rome. Sylvester McCoy, who Joan had spotted busking with the Roadshow outside the theatre, played the lead. George Harvey Webb as usual played the fiddle. Then Joan left. Gerry carried on for another year, but in the end, frustrated once again by the Arts Council and the local authorities, he left too. Gerry died in April 1975. Joan was heartbroken and never went back.

The Weekend After Next company split up. Steve Halliwell went off to join Mark and Dave and become a rock star. Cass Patton went to work in fashion. Nick Levitt went off to be a roadie with art rockers Hatfield and the North, and Alan Williams went to Manchester Poly Theatre School where he lasted a term. Only John Lee and I were left from the original company. I decided not to launch immediately into a new devised piece but rather to cash in on the popularity of the kids' shows and train up a new team in performing skills. In the spirit of the Roadshow we would also put together a naughty pub/cabaret show that would incorporate stunts, magic and rock 'n' roll. I recruited a new company. Rachel Bell, David Ambrose and Mary East came from the University Drama Department, and Pete Nicholson from the Youth Theatre, having just been kicked out of LAMDA. They were a talented if slightly eccentric bunch. I wanted them all to become confident and consummate performers, used to working an audience, so that when we came to devise the next play they would approach it with a different energy. I also decided that I would act in both shows. We started to work on the new kids' entertainment.

Joe Flash and the Singing Caterpillar from Venus was billed as the sequel to *Wimbo the Wonderdog*, although Wimbo had departed for the great kennel in the sky. Joe Flash from Space Patrol had a new sidekick in the unlikely shape of intergalactic lavatory attendant Ramsbottom (me) who fought evil with a mop and bucket. Joe and Ramsbottom set off on a mission to rescue the Big Eyed Bean Sisters, Venusian entrants in the Europlanet Song Contest who have been kidnapped by the evil Dr Gloat. Dr Gloat, who wants to win the contest himself with his truly dreadful song about his pet vulture Leslie, has turned the sisters into a caterpillar. Caterpillars are, of course, ineligible for the competition. Our heroes come up with a plan that involves stealing Gloat's magic hat and a great deal of noisy audience participation. Good inevitably triumphs over evil and the Big Eyed Bean Sisters win the day.

The method of construction was slightly different for this piece in as much as we came up with the most ludicrous title possible and then invented a story to fit it. Again we improvised/scripted five minutes per day as well as rehearsing the scenes from the day before and working in the songs and routines. The show was possibly influenced by listening to too much Captain Beefheart.

Simultaneously we worked up the pub show, *The Macintosh Cabaret*—Macintosh because Dave Ambrose's posh compere was called Howard (The Toff) Macintosh and also in the sense of dirty raincoat. We obtained by mail order from the Supreme Magic Company, Bideford, Devon, several pamphlets revealing the secrets of Mentalism, Levitation, Psychometry and other astonishing stuff and studied them closely. Essentially I was aiming for an entertainment that was a cross between a cheap end-of-the-pier show and a fairground sideshow. There used to be a booth on the promenade at Cleethorpes, just down from Wonderland, that presented striptease and mock executions. The sign outside said 'Why go to Paris when you can get it in Cleethorpes?' This could be said to have had a significant influence on my work at this point. We concocted a vaguely offensive poster and a bill that promised:

YOU'LL THRILL to the rippling torso of
Mick O'Toole, Colossus of Rhodes
YOU'LL TINGLE to the startling powers of
Zondo and Griselda,
Master and Mistress of the Mystic Arts
YOU'LL TREMBLE at the Death Defying Feats of
Los Tros Dodos
YOU'LL HUM along with the melodies of
Whispering Sid Pratt
YOU'LL DANCE to the cool sounds of those hep cats
Uranus Rappaport and the Soular System
SEE
The Nude Tableaux Vivants
featuring
The Rape of the Sabine Women
in pulsating flesherama
WIN a fortnight's holiday for two in Guatemala with
Howard's Big Time Bingo

Mick O'Toole was John doing a muscle-man act. I was Sid Pratt singing a traditional folk song I had written about a maid, a swain and a serpent. Dave and Mary were Zondo and Griselda doing a mind-reading routine we got from the catalogue. We were all Uranus Rappaport and the Soular System, a doo-wop band singing covers of 'I'm not a Juvenile Delinquent' and 'Running Bear'. Los Tros Dodos was an invisible juggling act. The Nude Tableaux Vivants wore pink body stockings with knitted wool genitalia and performed scenes from Classical Art and Literature. Other acts variously included Pete Nicholson as a dreadful club comic called Cheeky Reg Cleethorpes, a flea circus, a country and western band, Chinese escapology and a *Generation Game*-style melodrama competition called *Daphne's Truncated Picnic*. We quite blatantly stole material from anywhere and anybody we could and took both shows on the road.

Over the summer of 1973 we played *Joe Flash* in schools, arts centres, community centres, adventure playgrounds, fields and car parks the length and breath of Britain. We hung a backcloth on the side of the van and played out of the back of it. We quickly learnt to rope off a stage area to avoid getting mobbed by swarms of over-excited kids. We played festivals in Oxford, York and Leicester, and miners' galas in Cotgrave and Durham. We played the Great Yorkshire Agricultural show, performing five or six times a day. In London we played in Regent's Park, at the Roundhouse and under the Westway on Portobello Road, where a bunch of dope fiends who claimed to be Vulcans joined in the Europlanet Song

Contest and decided they wanted to live with us. The *Times Educational Supplement* decided that the show was 'great fun'. Simultaneously we played *The Macintosh Cabaret* in pubs, clubs and anywhere that would have us, including a corridor at Bretton Hall College of Education as The Pink Floyd did their sound check next door. Although we didn't know it at the time we were opening up what eventually became the alternative-comedy circuit.

In Hull we were banned. We were booked in for a one-nighter at The Blue Bell pub. All was well until the landlord read the flyer and took it literally. He wasn't going to have nude rape in his pub. I explained the sketch to him but he was adamant. He then said he hadn't got a bingo licence either. I explained that that was a joke too—everybody had the same numbers—but he still banned the show. The *Hull Daily Mail* decided that we were peddlers of filth, which enhanced our reputation enormously. From then on the cabaret became 'The Show They Tried to Ban!!'

The first leg of the tour finished at the Bath Another Festival run by the Bath Arts Workshop. We were booked in to play *Joe Flash* in the parks and in a number of plastic polyhedral domes and to play the cabaret in pubs. Also involved in the Festival in one form or another were The Natural Theatre, The Phantom Captain, Landscapes and Living Spaces, Mr Pugh's Puppets, GASP Theatre, Chilly Willy, The Pink Fairies, King Crimson, Zoot Money, Wild Willy Barrett, Mike Westbrook, Strider Dance Troupe, Edgar Broughton, People Show, John Bull Puncture Repair Kit, Lumiere and Son, Welfare State, Hawkwind and Allen Ginsberg. We were accommodated in a selection of crash pads. There was a macrobiotic staff canteen.

One day we were just about coming to the end of not very good performance of *Joe Flash* in a black plastic polyhedric dome when something entirely strange occurred. The kids, by now bored shitless by days of experimental entertainment, were getting restless. They had been joined by their elder siblings, and things were starting to look dangerous. We cut to the last number and planned a quick getaway before missiles flew. We were belting out the sing-along chorus of 'We are the Space Patrol guarding the human race. We fight for the right as we wander through space. We fight evil face-to-face cos we are the Space Patrol bum ba ba bumba ba bum ba babum' when a hippy vision of loveliness sidled on to the stage.

HIPPY VISION (*sotto*). Keep going!

JOE FLASH. What?

HIPPY VISION. Keep going!!

RAMSBOTTOM. Why?

HIPPY VISION. Ginsberg's coming

DR GLOAT. Fucking hell!

CATERPILLAR (*brightly*). We are the Space Patrol (*etc., etc.*).

We were actually about to share a stage with Counterculture Superhero, Pentagon Levitator and Hippy Guru Allen Ginsberg. We ploughed on with the Space Patrol Anthem for twenty-eight choruses. By now the kids were on the brink of a riot. Ginsberg arrived wearing a kaftan and carrying a prayer mat and prayer wheel. He was accompanied by a very young, dazzlingly beautiful and supremely untalented guitar player. We retreated to the wings.

> *Enter* GINSBERG. *He sets up his prayer mat, spins his prayer wheel and chants.*

GINSBERG. Ohm Shanti. Ohm Shanti.

> *Enter* MUSICIAN *nervously. A Coke can hits the stage.*

Hi, I'm Allen and this is my new friend Eric and we're going to sing some songs about peace and love.

KIDS. Boo. Fuck off. (*etc.*)

> *The* KIDS *throw Coke cans.*

GINSBERG. Play the C chord.
(*Sings.*) 'Oh the World is a really nice place...'
Now play the F chord.

KIDS. Boo. Fuck off, beardie. (*etc.*)

> *Even more Coke cans.*

GINSBERG. 'I really like living in the world...' (*Ducks.*)
Willya just cut that out with the fucking cans!

We made our excuses and left; it was all too mortifying for words. In sombre mood we packed up the van and drove back to the macrobiotic staff canteen for tea. By the time we arrived Ginsberg was already tucking into a plate of alfalfa rissoles. He must have teleported himself. He flashed us the peace sign.

GINSBERG. Great gig, man.

HULL TRUCK. Yeah, great gig, Allen.

That night we performed *The Macintosh Cabaret* in The Hat and Feather pub. We got a standing ovation and ran out of encores. Ginsberg didn't turn up to see us.

Earlier in the year I had applied for an Arts Council grant to produce the next devised play. Sue Timothy, the Arts Officer, helped me to fill in the form. We made up a non-existent play with a bogus plot, but we did include a warning that the nature of the rehearsal process was such that everything was likely to change in the final version. It worked. We had enough to buy a proper van, some decent equipment and pay every-body fifteen pounds a week almost every week. I set out to devise the new show: *The Knowledge*.

Rachel Bell invented a character called Elaine who was on her first teaching job in a local secondary school. She wanted a conventional life and relationships. She didn't get either. John Lee wanted to play Doo-ley who was an ex-biker and who had spent time in both the Merchant Navy and the nick. He was now a mechanic and part time dope dealer. He was based on the bloke who fixed our van. Pete Nicholson was Jimmy, a working-class fantasist. He was sexually repressed and socially inarticulate. He had a collection of porn and extreme right-wing views. David Ambrose was Jamie, a public-school university dropout with a private income. He was a bit of a drifter, who had vague plans to become an antique dealer, but was more interested in getting stoned. Mary East invented Maggie, an acid casualty who was into UFOs, Pyr-amids, Erich von Däniken, Astral Projection, Telekinesis, Tolkien and the entire ragbag of hip esoterica. She was currently a devotee of Maharaj Ji, the grinning fourteen-year-old Divine Light guru whose particular pathway to enlightenment was called *The Knowledge*, hence the portmanteau title for the play. She was a kleptomaniac and a nympho-maniac and was borderline psychotic. Gradually I brought the characters together.

Elaine's nice flat is in the same house and over the landing from Jimmy's bedsit. Jimmy develops sexual fantasies about Elaine. He also fantasises that he is Gary Glitter. Jamie turns up on her doorstep. He is an old boyfriend from school days in Godalming. He temporarily moves in, sleeping on the sofa. In a head shop Jamie meets Maggie and brings her round. Elaine thinks she is ludicrous, especially as Maggie thinks all teaching is repressive—'the mind-forg'd manacles of man'. Jimmy is sus-picious of Jamie and terrified of Maggie and drugs. Jamie and Maggie go to visit a tramp who lives in a wardrobe and may be a divine avatar from outer space. (The tramp actually existed. He lived on Hessle fore-shore and waved at the trains. Mary and Dave visited him in character as part of the background improvisations). Maggie catches Jimmy wank-ing and tells him she thinks that Jamie is a 'homo superior'. Jimmy tells Elaine that Jamie is a homo. Jamie buys a second-hand ambulance from Dooley that doesn't work. Dooley repairs the head gasket on Elaine's

Habitat carpet. A cheque for thirty pounds and a Stonehenge paper-weight disappear from Elaine's flat.

Elaine suspects Dooley and Maggie. Jamie defends his friends. Jimmy wants to call the police. Eventually we discover that the paper-weight had apparently teleported itself into Maggie's flat. Elaine thinks Maggie may need help. Jamie goes off in his ambulance, and Elaine is left alone with Jimmy, who smugly tells her that she is better off without them.

The short sharp scenes were linked by narration from Dave Ambrose, introducing the characters to the audience and the songs that commented on the action. For example, Maggie's character was cele-brated by a pastiche Hawkwind number called 'Return to the Stars':

> Those we take will have minds like us
> With fully expanded consciousness
> All we need are the simple things
> Like the Tarot cards and the old I Ching.
> Everyone knows you've got to go with the flow
> So set the controls for the great unknown
> With Captain Kirk as Commander-in-Chief
> And Scotty on the engines for some comic relief.

I hoped that the show, with its more accessible style, would have the same appeal as *Children of the Lost Planet*.

With *The Knowledge* up and running, we now had three shows on the road simultaneously. We were often booked by Regional Arts Associations to open up local touring circuits. We would play for a week in the West Midlands or Southern Arts Region, doing kids' shows in the morning and afternoon in local schools or play schemes, and the cabaret or *The Knowledge* in a local arts centre or community centre in the evening. This made for some interesting evenings. We played the cabaret to a bemused audience of public school boys at Shrewsbury Public School, while at Hereford Technical College we performed *The Knowledge* to an audience of day-release police cadets who searched the van for drugs after seeing the show. In fact gigs for *The Knowledge* were harder to come by. The regional organisers thought that our work would upset the good folk of, for example, Basingstoke, failing to understand that that was the point.

In early 1974 we were booked to take part the 'Stopover' event in Birmingham. 'Stopover' was a two-week Festival of Experimental The-atre organised by DALTA, the touring wind of the Arts Council. DALTA quaintly stood for Dramatic and Lyric Theatre Association. The idea was to create the buzz of the 1970 'Come Together' Festival at the Royal

Court in the regions and showcase the experimental talent that the Arts Council was squandering taxpayers' money on. We shared the bill with The (now no longer Brighton) Combination, Welfare State, The Phantom Captain, People Show, Belt and Braces, Strider, Emil Wolk, The John Bull Puncture Repair Kit, John Dowie, The General Will and the newly formed Joint Stock. The list is a fair indication of the state of the game at the time.

After one performance of *The Macintosh Cabaret* in the Birmingham Rep Studio Pete Nicholson was berated by Noel Greig of The Combination for using the word 'poof'. Noel claimed it was offensive to 'we homosexuals'. We had claimed in a press release that Pete's character Cheeky Reg Cleethorpes had recently joined us from the northern club circuit and Noel was completely taken in, believing Pete to be a genuine sexist comedian rather than a satirical portrayal of one. Next night Cheeky Reg dedicated his closing number to shirt-lifters everywhere and belted out a rousing version of 'Born Free'. It was our first brush with Alternative Puritanism.

In The Gun Barrel pub opposite the Arts Lab in Tower Street we saw The General Will perform their non-sexist pub show. General Will were a Socialist agitprop company that had grown out of Bradford University. Most of their work was written in collaboration with local journalist-turned-playwright David Edgar. Their stated aim was to present a Marxist perspective of what was going on. What was going on apparently was the crisis of Capitalism. The General Will were engaged in framing the working-class response to it. Their style was cartoonic. In *The National Interest* the Tory Government were portrayed as Chicago Mafia. *Rent*, a play about the Housing Finance Act, was presented as a Victorian melodrama. In the pub show we were fortunate enough to catch David Edgar himself performing with the company. He wore a frock coat and a top hat and stood on a table to sing 'I am the man, the very fat man who watered the workers' beer'. It was an uplifting and inspirational experience. John Dowie also joined in with the show. John was very much the founding father of alternative stand-up comedy. Billy Connolly and Jasper Carrott came out of the folk-club circuit, but they were essentially singers or musicians who hid behind a banjo and did the odd routine. John stood up and did gags to an Arts Lab audience. It would be several years before the Comedy Store and Comic Strip unleashed their tsunami of alternative rib-tickling frolics on a grateful nation. Dowie's big influences were Spike Milligan and Marc Bolan. John, David, The General Will and Hull Truck all became firm friends.

Anthony Everitt of the *Birmingham Post* gave us the first proper review for *The Knowledge*:

Whilst other dramatists and companies deal with the entrenched positions or far-flung outposts of our changing society, the Hull Truck Company wanders intrepidly through no-man's-land documenting the shell-shocked, deserters, malingerers and cheerful non-combatants.

The characters of their plays are people caught between the safe worlds of successful private enterprise and obedient conformity. They are wandering off course, blindly believing that they know where they are and that for the most part everyone is out of step with them...

It would be easy to scoff at, condemn or patronise these characters. The honesty of the Hull Truck Company's work is that it does not exploit the peculiarities and incongruities but seeks a deeper understanding of how and why they live the way they do.

All of which, I have to say, was fair enough.

At Easter John Lee decided to pull out. He had a new relationship with Chris, a costume designer he had met at the Citizens' in Glasgow, and she had moved to Hull with her small son. He needed a proper wage and had had enough of life on the road. Living in a van and sleeping on other people's floors for months on end loses its charm after a while, and, to John, we had all become a colossal pain in the arse. He cut his hair and became a PE teacher, which must have been particularly galling for someone who had once imagined himself to be the Jerry Garcia of North Humberside. As we had no time to recast I took over as Dooley, reinventing the character with a slightly different background. We reinvestigated the scenes and discovered that the dialogue stayed pretty much the same. We also dumped *Joe Flash*—we had played it to over ten thousand kids throughout the country and the bookers were demanding a new show:

GRANNY SORTS IT OUT

Granny and young Waldo Wheeze have gone for a day out to Shrimping-on-Sea. Granny wants to paddle and go on the dodgems. Waldo wants to get up to mischief and play with his pet spiders.

But their peaceful day turns into a dangerous and exciting adventure when they meet up with the evil Ruby Rotten and her bumbling assistant Percy Prank, who are plotting to blow up the amusement arcade...

Who are the Black Hand Gang?

What is the fortune-teller's bizarre secret?

Who put the jellyfish in the swimming pool?

Who is the mysterious hot dog man?

The answers to these and many more exciting questions can be
found in *Granny Sorts It Out*,

Hull Truck's new musical for kids aged 5—11

Rachel was Granny. Pete was Waldo. Mary was Ruby Rotten, and Dave
was Percy Prank. I wrote myself out of this one. The working method
was exactly the same except we raided the local joke shop and bought a
truck load of squirty flowers, plastic spiders, whoopee cushions, stink
bombs, bloody fingers with nails through them, rubber bats and itch-
ing powder and improvised round them. We put the price up to
twenty-five pounds per show (twenty pounds in the Hull area) and the
bookings flew in.

Wythenshawe is nine miles out of Manchester. It is, or was, the biggest
housing estate in Europe. Local mythology has it that it is also the hard-
est. In 1971 the council built a vast new arts and leisure complex in the
middle of the estate. The Forum was one of Manchester's largest public
buildings and boasted a leisure centre, library, theatre, concert hall and
meeting rooms. The idea was that it would become a hive of artistic
endeavour and community spirit. In truth it was a vast and ugly concrete
box and was soon vandalised and covered in graffiti. The theatre was
administrated by the same team as the Library Theatre, but was programmed with mainly safe, middle-of-the road family-orientated
touring shows. I was surprised therefore to be offered a week's run of
The Knowledge. They also agreed to pay us three hundred and fifty quid,
which was more than we had ever earned before.

Not entirely believing the offer I called up the administrator Terry
Hawkins and explained the nature and content of the show, emphasis-
ing the amount of swearing and drug references in the piece. He told
me that he was looking for something thrusting and modern to shake up
the Wythenshawe audience.

We arrived at the theatre to find that, instead of using our brash Day-
Glo Robert Crumb-style posters, they had produced their own. Their
poster sported uniformly dull civic graphics and described the play as

A HILARIOUS HIPPY WHODUNIT!

We were greeted by supercilious Sloaney Assistant Stage Manager
Amanda, who went out of her way to be unhelpful and told us that she
was a) a Christian and b) hoping to go to RADA. The Forum Theatre
seated four hundred. Thirty-five people turned up. They were all senior citizens, presumably looking forward to an evening with Agatha

Christie. Half of them left at the interval and in the second half when I, as Dooley, announced that I had never seen a cunt in a bottle we were down to single figures. Robin Thornber wrote in the *Guardian*:

> I feel compelled to come to the defence of Hull Truck Theatre Company, if not to apologise to them. There were less than fifty people dotted about the auditorium of the Forum Theatre last night for the opening of their show *The Knowledge*. At the end there were twenty-two. One brave old lady stormed out shouting 'Tripe!' This was presumably because the script was liberally sprinkled with a present participle rhyming with Hulltrucking that you don't often hear on the telly. So firstly I should defend the play's language. The adjective was wielded with the greatest frequency by a character who was an ex-Merchant Navy motor mechanic who fancies himself as a bit of a hard case, and if anybody supposes that a man like that punctuates his speech in any other way, they don't use the same garage as me. Secondly, I have to say that there is no resemblance between the play's content and tripe. Tripe is dull, flabby and lifeless. *The Knowledge* is lively, tough and stimulating. It offered no pat answers but asked all the right questions, gently, honestly and clearly.

Next morning Terry Hawkins called me into his office in the Library Theatre. Despite the enthusiastic *Guardian* review he was pulling the show. 'It's no good for us,' he said, 'and it's no good for you.' He had had complaints from the audience, and they had complained to the council, who had complained to the Board. I told him that this was censorship. He replied that it wasn't. Some of our company were not members of Equity and Assistant Stage Manager Amanda, who was a provisional Equity member refused to work with non-union labour. If the show continued he would be operating illegally and the future of his theatre would be threatened, etc., etc., etc. It was clearly bollocks. We were devastated, but there was little we could do, although we did consider pushing Hawkins into the fountain in St Peter's Square. He paid us off, we drove to Wythenshawe, and we packed up the van. Then we made some phone calls. We called up Robin Thornber from the *Guardian* and met him in a pub and told him what had happened. He was scandalised and promised to write an article questioning the decision. We called up Equity, who were furious. There was a tacit agreement to turn a blind eye to non-union fringe companies working in union houses, though technically the Library were within their rights.

I also wrote to David Scase, Artistic Director of the Library Theatre, who apparently was away on holiday, although I subsequently discovered that he wasn't. David Scase was one of the original members of Theatre Workshop, joining the troupe aged sixteen in 1945 and flogging tomatoes from a barrow round Manchester to support the fledgling company. In my letter I pointed out that Hull Truck was also young touring company making experimental theatre for very little money and that our work and philosophy was very much inspired by Joan Littlewood. I asked him how he could justify the shoddy way we had been treated by his administration. I never received a reply.

Robin Thornber's piece appeared next day in the *Guardian* castigating the management of the Library for cowardice and moral panic. I called Howard Gibbins at the Bush Theatre. Gibbins was supposed to come to Manchester to see the show with a view to booking us for a run at the Bush. He had seen the review and Thornber's article. They had both appeared that morning in the London edition. On the spur of the moment I proposed that we drove to London and did an audition performance at the Bush on that Sunday night for a box-office split. Gibbins agreed. The show was a sell-out. Gibbins thought we had organised a claque, but we hadn't. He booked *The Knowledge* for a three-week run in November. It was a major turning point in the fortunes of Hull Truck and the beginning of my thirty-five-year relationship with the Bush Theatre.

The incident had deeper ramifications for Equity. The whole relationship between the union and the fringe was a mess. Equity operated a Catch-22 closed shop. You couldn't work in an Equity theatre or company without Equity membership, and you couldn't get Equity membership unless you worked in an Equity theatre or company that paid union rates. This excluded fringe companies as even those in receipt of Arts Council funding did not receive enough to pay actors Equity minimum.

Equity was unique among trades unions in as much as the vast majority of its membership was always out of work. In the Seventies there was a vast schism between the right wing of the union, who never attended meetings, and the left wing who were politically active. Thus, for example, a completely reasonable motion suggesting that Equity should adopt a branch and delegate structure would be carried at a General Meeting only to be overturned by an expensive referendum of the entire and largely dormant membership. Then the left would call an Extraordinary General Meeting to overturn the result of the ballot, at which someone like Harry Secombe or Tommy Steele would get up and bang on about how privileged everybody was 'to work in this great business that we call show'. Then the referendum decision would be rescinded, and the whole pointless and time-consuming cycle would be repeated.

The dispute between Equity and the fringe started in 1969 when Charles Marowitz had tried to produce a season of eight new American plays at the Open Space paying the actors on a profit-share basis. Equity threatened to suspend the actors for three months if they played for below the minimum wage, so Marowitz was forced to cancel the shows. Marowitz and Ed Berman, who ran Inter-Action and faced the same problems, drew up a letter of protest. They suggested that Equity grant the fringe special exemption and reasonably pointed out that they were providing jobs for Equity members who otherwise would be unemployed. Marowitz somewhat blew it by comparing Equity's stance to the Russian invasion of Czechoslovakia. As soon as the papers got hold of the story Equity backed off and the American season went ahead. Instead of grasping the nettle and working on a scheme to unionise the fringe, Equity kept its head down and hoped the whole thing would go away. Fringe companies played in Equity theatres, the 'Come Together' Festival at the Royal Court being a prime example, and everyone just got on with it until the banning of *The Knowledge* reopened the can of worms.

As a result Equity formed a Fringe Committee to come up with a fringe contract, and I was asked to sit on it. The committee met regularly for a couple of years and agreed on very little. There was little or no common ground between the ways that companies operated. Some were Collectives, some were Cooperatives, some were Collective Cooperatives, and I imagine that some were indeed Cooperative Collectives. Some wanted Equity membership, some didn't. Nobody wanted to become a Management. Footsbarn lived as a democratic non-materialistic community and grew their own vegetables, chickens, etc. They believed that if they got Equity wages they would become leeches on society. Live Theatre insisted that all their actors came from a Geordie working-class background. Red Ladder proposed their own collective contract as a model. This involved a clause insisting that members of Red Ladder were allowed to smoke only one cigarette an hour. Ed Berman suggested that fringe companies should only play in theatres with less than fifty seats. France Rifkin from Recreation Ground maintained that any theatre worker or community media operative that worked over forty hours a week was exploiting him or herself and therefore should pay him or herself overtime or withdraw his or her labour. North West Spanner feared that unionisation would lead to professionalisation and thus revolutionary Socialists who had started doing theatre as a political weapon to create propaganda and agitation would be replaced by left-wing actors, active in their union but with little or no other political work behind them, who basically would want to play all the big parts. Meetings most resembled those of the People's Front of Judea in *Monty Python's Life of Brian*.

Eventually the committee came up with a draft contract proposal that accommodated Cooperatives and Collectives only to have it thrown out by Chairman Kenneth McClellan, who then proposed his own version. McClellan reiterated that Equity Members would only be allowed to work on Equity contracts and these were only available to Managements who paid at least Equity minimum. Cooperative companies and Collectives would have to become Managements, and the Arts Council would be encouraged to stop funding any company that couldn't afford to pay Equity rates. We were back to square one. He then disbanded the Fringe Committee and pushed his proposals through the Equity ruling council. At an AGM McClellan described the fringe as 'a lot of hole and corner enterprises working under conditions too makeshift for their experiments to be valid' and spoke of 'the folly and conceit of amateurs'. The AGM overturned his proposals and passed a motion demanding a fringe contract. The right organised a referendum and overturned the motion. Enough was enough.

Sixty alternative companies formed an alternative trades union called the Independent Theatre Council (ITC) and another one called the Association of Community Theatres (TACT) and something else called the Informal Meeting of Fringe Theatre Administrators (IMOFTA), and I imagine they all had some more meetings.

In 1978 Equity at last came up with a fringe contract and began the block unionisation of the fringe, granting membership to everybody who had been excluded for most of the decade. In the Eighties, Thatcher did away with the closed shop rendering the whole debate irrelevant.

Hull Truck toured all three shows in the repertoire throughout the summer of 1974 playing all over the country. We also developed a line in large-scale storytelling kids' workshops where we worked for a number of days in council estates. We arrived with a truck full of jumble-sale clothing, dressed up the kids in bizarre make-up and costumes and conducted Wild Man from Borneo hunts all over the neighbourhood. The Wild Man could only be pacified by the kids telling him silly jokes. In Bishop Auckland the Wild Man failed to put in appearance altogether when Pete, changing into his leopard-skin leotard, was unavoidably detained in a prefab in the enthusiastic embrace of one of the local mothers. In Bootle a group of pissed-up Scousers wazzed on us from a road bridge. At the Great Yorkshire Show we hijacked the Pernod lorry.

The Knowledge opened at the Bush Theatre on 11 November. The show started off slowly, but this time the critics were on our side:

'Beautifully performed, very, very funny—Don't miss it!'

(*Time Out*)

'Marvellously funny and very expressive indeed, *The Knowledge* takes an utterly frank look at contemporary life and spits it into the theatre rich and raw.'

(*Guardian*)

'This is a commentary on life today, how we live it and why, which seeks to draw no conclusions, nor does it dictate where we are expected to align ourselves… it is simply a slice of life with the nerve endings left unsealed.'

(*The Stage*)

In those days the only way to get backstage at the Bush was to go through the pub downstairs, out along Goldhawk Road and up the back stairs. There was no backstage lavatory so actors frequently pissed in pint pots and emptied them out of the window. Occasionally people would wander in off the street. Pete Nicholson was late for a cue one night evicting a skinhead who was looking for the strippers who performed regularly in the back bar. By the second week the notices kicked in and the phones started to ring. By the end of the run there were long queues for returns. We had managed to generate a buzz and some punters saw the show two or three times. Our share of the box office for the last week was one hundred and ten pounds, which meant that we had broken even. The Bush run resulted in two major developments. The Arts Council increased our grant and gave us client status and Tara Prem, producer of BBC TV's 'Second City Firsts', saw the show and loved it. Hull Truck and the Bush became firm friends and from then on we regarded the theatre as our London home.

Back in Hull nobody gave a shite.

6

Hello Prestatyn

The increased Arts Council subsidy meant that at last we could pay everybody an almost living wage and stay in cheap B&Bs rather than dossing on floors. The prospect of endless nylon sheets was far less daunting than staying with people who had hated the shows and thought we were filthy junkie smut-peddlers. It also meant that we had to become an educational charity and pay National Insurance. Until now I had handled most of the administration, but it was becoming impossible as we were constantly in rehearsal or on the road. By now I had moved into a bigger flat in Coltman Street and converted half my bedroom into the company office. I decided that it was time to get a proper Administrator.

Barry Nettleton was a local music-scene wheeler-dealer. He had trained as a photographer, run various folk clubs and had been the brains behind the Brick House, Hull's Arts Lab Underground music venue. He became a rock promoter, presenting headline acts including The Who at the City Hall, and he promoted the Mott the Hoople gig that Kevin went to in *Children of the Lost Planet*. He had lost a packet when several bands failed to show up and was now running music events at Hornsea Floral Hall and The Magic Garden at the Humberside Theatre (Hull Arts Centre had changed its name to Humberside Theatre in a desperate attempt at cultural rebranding). Barry had booked us for a few music gigs and only once tried to rip us off. He was a cross between John Peel and Harvey Goldsmith, and he was exactly what we were looking for.

Dave Ambrose and Mary East left and were replaced by Cass Patton, who returned to the company, Alan Hulse, an actor from Bradford who had been in The General Will, and an actor called Simon who had been with the York Shoestring Company. I also signed up a local lad, Steve

Marshall to be musician and roadie. Steve was a musical genius and electronics wizard who built his own synthesisers from diodes and stuff he bought from a mail order catalogue. He was no use as a roadie. He couldn't drive. We started work on the new show, *Oh What!*

I had decided to explore a selection of characters from a wider range of backgrounds with wider range of conflicting philosophies. I was interested in examining the culture clash between working-class characters and middle-class liberals and the lack of any genuine attempt to bridge the divide. Pete Nicholson had met a bloke in a pub in Beverley who he remembered from school. The guy was a soldier on leave from duty in Northern Ireland. He got drunk and told exaggerated stories of gangbangs on the Bogside. Pete decided he wanted to base his character on him. Rachel Bell devised Celia, a graduate enthusiastically embracing vegetarianism, ecology and the spirit of 1967 on a private income. She was pregnant by her absent boyfriend. Cass Patton decided to investigate Mandy, based on a girl she had met who was an assistant fashion editor for *Cosmopolitan*. Alan Hulse was Joe, a trades unionist and a lathe operator in an engineering works, who sang in pubs and had a chip on his shoulder. Steve, who was to compose the music, had nothing to do until the story had emerged, so we devised a character called Tez—a local lad getting together a Space Rock band, The Chromium Plated Megaphone of Destiny, and dreaming of stardom on the dole.

After the first week of rehearsals, Simon from York quit for personal reasons, and I decided, against my better judgement, to create a character for myself. Devising a character and devising the play the character appears in is a truly schizophrenic experience, and one that I have never felt the urge to repeat. I'm sure my choices were influenced by the knowledge I had of what other people were playing. I was thus breaking all the rules, but it was the only way at such short notice that I could get the show together. I came up with Ray, a technical college lecturer and International Socialist, based on someone I had known in Doncaster. Ray was bright, but sexually inept, and concealed his inadequacies behind political posturing and jargon.

As usual we created the characters' life histories and background stories. We decided that Brian, the squaddie, and Tez the would-be rock star, had vaguely known each other from school so we gave them a collective background, working out teachers they had known and sports they had played. I orchestrated that Celia and Mandy were at university together five years before the play started and set up a series of improvisations to explore their relationship. We discovered that there wasn't one; they couldn't stand the sight of each other. There was no chance of them meeting up five years in the future except by accident, so I needed to find a way in which they were forced together in order to explore the obvious antagonism between them. I decided to make them sisters. What this meant was that we created new parents and family for them. We worked out that their father was a sociology lecturer. We decided why their paths had diverged so widely.

After several weeks of improvisations the story went like this:

BRIAN, *back from a tour of duty in Belfast, sits in the pub getting pissed. He meets* TEZ. TEZ *is forming a band.* BRIAN *wants his hole.* CELIA, *stoned and pregnant by her absent boyfriend, is visited in her country cottage by urban sophisticate sister* MANDY, *who had been sent to find out what is going on.* JOE *is* RAY's *lodger.* RAY *and* JOE *are invited to* CELIA's *cottage. They play charades and* RAY *takes the piss out of* JOE's *ignorance of French movies.* CELIA *and* JOE *go for a walk.* CELIA *thinks* RAY *should take some acid.*

JOE. Doesn't it kill your brain cells?

CELIA. Yeah, but you've got plenty left.

JOE. But isn't it just… wrong?

CELIA I don't think there's such a thing as right or wrong.
    I just think it's a matter of opinion.

RAY *snogs* MANDY. *She laughs at him.* CELIA *realises that her boyfriend isn't coming back. In the pub* BRIAN *has not had his hole.* TEZ's *band has split up.* JOE *announces he is moving out of* RAY's. RAY *goads him, throws a dart at* TEZ *and picks a fight with* BRIAN. BRIAN *is left alone.*

The End.

Each of the characters had a song that reflected their character either in style or in content. Some of them were purposely ironic. Soldier Brian got up and sang the Irish rebel anthem 'Kevin Barry' in the pub. Joe, also a pub singer, crooned a Tony Bennett-style ballad about the joys of being working class:

Working class is what I'm proud to be
In this life you don't get nowt for free
Go down to the Chinese takeaway
Get Kung Foo Flied Lice—refuse to pay
Slant-eyed bastards rob you blind
They don't mind.

Celia had a sensitive folk-rock number about the simple life:

Where the curlew soars aloft
Chervil and Eglantine
We will build a grey stone croft
Of functional design

We will be friends of the earth
Respect Ecology
We will show the worth
Of low impact technology.

Tez's band played a space-rock number:

Set your controls for the heart of the void
We're on a star truck with Hawkwind and Floyd
We've got a million heads
We've got a ton of red leb.

I wanted the show to be a combination of front-foot entertainment and close-up naturalism. The actors, with months of one-nighters and hundreds of kids' shows under their belts, now knew how to do it.

Oh What! opened at the Birmingham Arts Lab on Good Friday, 27 March 1975 in a snow storm—and it went down a storm. Anthony Everitt in the *Birmingham Post*, who by now was a big fan and who later became head of the Arts Council, offered the following:

In the best satire one recognises one's acquaintances, friends and sometimes even oneself among the characters on stage. According to this criterion Hull Truck Theatre Company's latest show *Oh What!* scores high marks. The company brilliantly parodies what used to be called the counterculture. *Oh What!* is not simply a collection of character studies. It offers, implicitly at least, a Marxist class analysis, and we are left pondering the need for radical social change.

It is quite possible that the play offered a Marxist class analysis, but it had never been my intention. The characters in my plays were not there as symbolic protagonists in the class struggle. They were not ciphers. They were three-dimensional human beings. There were no heroes and villains. All real theatre is political in as much as it illustrates the way that human beings behave towards each other. The challenge is to find a better way to go about it.

Then we devised yet another kids' show. We were getting quite good at it.

GRANNY CALLS THE TUNE

Granny and young Waldo Wheeze have gone for a day out at the Much Dumpling Village Fête to see Pop Star Malcolm Sequin.
However, their peaceful day out turns into a dangerous and exciting adventure when they cross swords with the strange and deadly Vivienne Viper and her nasty chum Sid the Spiv.

Who put the spiders in the lucky dip? Will Malcolm get out of
the sack?

(Etc., etc., etc...)

The truth of the matter was that we still needed to tour the kids' shows
as, despite the critical success of *The Knowledge*, regional bookers still
found it difficult to come to terms with the content of our main work.

We toured both shows throughout the spring. In Aldershot we were
accused of being unpatriotic and giving succour to the enemy. In a
church hall in the New Forest the venue organiser drummed up an audience by bicycling round the village with a loud hailer. In Milnthorpe the
parish council walked across the stage during Scene Two to attend a
council meeting in the dressing room. In Nottingham Ken Campbell
decided to watch the show from the wings and enjoyed it so much he
stayed for several days.

While the company were at the Bush playing *The Knowledge,* Tara Prem had
asked me to come up with a proposal for a half-hour television play. She
knew and understood the nature of the work and appreciated that whatever I came up with would at best be a possible route map. I sent her a
treatment.

'Second City Firsts' was the brainchild of David Rose, Head of
English Regions Drama and probably the most visionary and inspiring
producer that television has ever had. 'Second City Firsts' were half-
hour television plays by new writers and directors that went out on
BBC 2 at prime time on Saturday nights. It is impossible to imagine
anything like that getting past the corporate lickspittles who run
television today.

Writers and directors who lost their TV virginity on 'Second City
Firsts' include Alan Bleasdale, Willy Russell, Ron Hutchinson, Ian
McEwan, Peter Gill, Tony Bicât and Les Blair.

The idea I sent to Tara was very simple: Rosie lectures at the Polytechnic. She is involved in organising events for International Women's
Week and Gestalt therapy. She lives with John, a belligerent conceptual-
ist painter interested in linguistic philosophy and drinking. Living in
the same house is Suki, who runs a boutique and makes trousers on a
loud sewing machine. She is interested in old movies and herself. Kevin
is one of Rosie's students. He is naïve and nervous. He comes round to
Rosie's house to read her some of his poetry. The play would be called
The Writing on the Wall.

Tara liked the idea so Hull Truck became the first fringe company
commissioned to devise a piece specifically for television.

We devised the play over a three-week rehearsal period in Birmingham and recorded it on 12 June at Pebble Mill. We got one day in the studio, camera rehearsing in the morning and afternoon, and recording the show with four cameras for two hours in the evening. The play was Hull Truck lite. With only three weeks to devise the piece we explored territory that was familiar, and so the characters lacked real bite. We also had the usual horse-trading over language. I recall sitting in a panelled boardroom and agreeing to trade two buggers for one shit, two farts and a nincompoop. The studio set up meant that we could not include songs, although Steve Marshall wrote the incidental music. Despite all the obvious drawbacks *The Writing on the Wall* did, however, present an accurate picture of a bunch of characters not usually represented on television a the time. When the wardrobe department discovered that Pete Nicholson was playing a student they predictably provided him with a duffel coat and a college scarf. The television critics moaned about lack of plot and how improvisation wasn't as good as Alan Ayckbourn.

Alan Hulse decided to leave the company at the end of June. He thought we were a bunch of shit-head hippies. In Birmingham he had trashed the People Show set. He thought they were a bunch of shit-head performance artists. He wanted to work in a Socialist theatre company committed to revolutionary politics so he went off to play the elephant's arse in an exciting new production of Brecht's *Mann ist Mann* in Hampstead. Fortunately we had taken *Oh What!* off the road until the autumn so I took over as Sid the Spiv in *Granny Calls the Tune,* and we spent the summer touring adventure playgrounds and festivals with the kids' show. We became adept at fighting off stray dogs and children. At one gig on Shepherd's Bush Green, Waldo Wheeze managed to kick an Alsatian over the heads of the crowd, which takes some doing. We also worked up a new pub show/cabaret entertainment called *The Melody Bandbox Rhythm Roadshow.*

On tour I had spent days rummaging through junk shops and had built up a collection of 78rpm records of Forties and Fifties variety artistes. I also had a collection of sheet music and scripts from long forgotten radio performers and comedians. *The Bandbox* was a recreation of a long forgotten radio show in the style of *The Billy Cotton Bandshow* or *Workers' Playtime.* Everyone had characters. I was Cuddly Dudley the compere, an Archie Rice character who also sold cheap nylons to the ladies in the audience. Rachel and Cass were Maxine and Laverne, The Grace Notes—Sisters in Song, who did a posh Beverley Sisters act. Pete Nicholson maintained his old Cheeky Reg Cleethorpes—'He's Cheeky!'—character and specialised in comic songs and emotional ballads. Steve and Thurstan Binns were the Sam Masarella Trio. There were only two of them. Thurstan was a criminology lecture from the local technical college who played drums. He was part of the Hull Truck auxiliary for years.

The show featured sing-along standards, comic turns, dreadful old gags and audience participation. Wherever we played became Prestatyn and the audience were cast as a studio audience at the recording of an episode of a Forties radio show.

CUDDLY DUDLEY. HELLO PRESTATYN!!

AUDIENCE. HELLO CUDDLY DUDLEY!!

It was one of the most successful shows we ever did. Sometimes the audience dressed up too.

Alan Hulse was replaced by David Hatton, who had been a founder member of CAST—the first anarcho-syndicalist political theatre company in Britain. Their name stood for Cartoon Archetypal Slogan Theatre. Dave was a consummate actor with a wide range of experience from Jane Arden's *Vagina Rex and the Gas Oven* at the Arts Lab in Drury Lane to *Hope and Keen's Crazy Bus* and playing the dwarf who gets burnt to death in Pasolini's film of *The Canterbury Tales*. He had started out as Master Carpenter at Bristol Old Vic and he played the Jew's harp. In *The Melody Bandbox Rhythm Roadshow* he played Arnold Wedgett—a dapper BBC type in a dinner jacket who did novelty songs, his particular favourites being 'I've Never Wronged an Onion' and 'The Spaniard Who Blighted My Life'.

At the end of the summer I had to rehearse David into *Oh What!* Although I had taken over in *The Knowledge*, I had never faced the problem of working a new actor into an already existing role plus acting in the same scenes with him. What we effectively did was to work backwards. I explained to David the nature of the character and then we invented a life history, as usual roughly based on someone Dave had known in the past. We then worked on the background circumstances and the relationship between Joe and Ray and eventually set up new versions of the original improvisations. The result was astonishing in that seventy per cent of the dialogue was the same. I have to admit that I was probably subliminally influencing the direction of the scene from within, although that was never my intention. David had never seen the play and had no knowledge of the scenario, only of the character he was asked to create.

Oh What! went back on the road in the autumn of 1975, arriving at the Bush in November. This time there was almost universal approval from the critics and we became a hot ticket:

'Hull Truck is a very special company which should be seen.'

(*The Times*)

'Leaving the theatre, the customers in the Irish pub downstairs stood around the television watching the big match. They looked less real than the actors upstairs.'

(Frank Marcus, *Sunday Telegraph*)

The critics were, at last, beginning to realise that devised plays were a valid form of theatrical endeavour. Mike Leigh's *Babies Grow Old* had recently transferred from The Other Place in Stratford to the ICA Theatre with similarly ebullient notices.

In *Time Out* Dusty Hughes described me as 'a polar bear with halitosis' and we had a rave review in *Gallery*—a soft-core porn magazine that added a whole new dimension to the meaning of self-abuse.

Hull Truck were enthusiastically embraced by the metropolitan glitterati as a bit of authentic Northern rough. At dinner parties the host or hostess would thoughtfully supply us with beer, believing that we would not be used to wine. Kenneth Tynan came to the show and praised the piece, correctly singling out Rachel Bell's remarkable performance. He invited me on to an edition of *Arena*—a television programme he was hosting—to discuss the future of the fringe, and sent a crew along to the Bush to record excerpts from the play. The *Arena* panel discussion was useless. Trevor Griffiths had a lot to say between takes but completely dried up on camera. Roland Rees talked at length about his exciting new production of *Mann ist Mann* at Hampstead. I made a plea to the Government for better funding and a coherent arts policy. The event would have been enlivened by Pip Simmons, but he overslept. Tynan seemed to want the fringe to storm the winter palaces of the West End, and seemed surprised and almost hurt when we told him we weren't interested and that our audiences were elsewhere.

We also had a visit from the Workers' Revolutionary Party, who accused us of patronising the working class. We lived in one of the poorest streets in one of the poorest cities in the country. We told them to fuck off.

In the London Theatre Critics' Awards of 1975, *Oh What!* was mentioned in dispatches by Michael Billington, Michael Coveney, Robert Cushman and John Elsom, and Rachel Bell was nominated for the Most Promising Newcomer prize.

We went back to Hull to regroup and plan our next show. Everyone in the company decided to stay on, and Alan Williams came back. I decided to drop out of the shows apart from *Melody Bandbox*, to which Alan now contributed a character called Lonesome Tex Fetlock, a wistful yet strangely drunken cowboy crooner.

At the time, I described *Bridget's House* as a death-of-the-Sixties play. I think I must have realised that by 1976 the ideals of the love generation had gone up in smoke, that, despite the best efforts of the revolutionary Socialists, Capitalism was far from surrendering and that the age of Aquarius had signally failed to usher in much harmony and under-standing, never mind sympathy and trust abounding. The characters in *Bridget's House* were older, but then so were the actors, and most of them had developed an arguably healthy dose of cynicism. *Bridget's House* was a much more personal play than *Oh What!*:

> BRIDGET (Rachel Bell) *is in her late twenties and newly divorced. She makes her living as a landlady having acquired, with her ex-husband, a number of run-down houses that she rents out to students.*

> JONATHAN (Peter Nicholson) *is a hospital porter who is training to be a Christian Youth Leader and coaches the youth club football team.*

> MO (Cass Patton) *is twenty-eight and wants a good time. She signs on, smokes dope and gets laid. She looks and talks tough. She isn't.*

> ANDREW (Alan Williams) *is very bright and a talented painter. He is a nihilist and full of wild schemes and fantasies.*

> MATHEW (David Hatton) *lectures in Behavioural Psychology at Hull University. He is small and pompous and hoping to screw Bridget.*

> BENNY (Steve Marshall) *is Mo's much younger boyfriend. He is a bit of a local legend in as much as he used to be in a band and went to London to find fame and fortune.*

The play starts with Bridget out on a date with Mathew:

> MATHEW. Why do you always wear black?

> BRIDGET. I'm in mourning for my life.

> MATHEW. Mm, what?

> BRIDGET. Chekhov.

> MATHEW. Ah. I'm sorry; I missed the allusion.

> BRIDGET. I wear black 'cos I'm fat and it makes me look thinner.

The play centres on Mathew's attempts to pull Bridget and his failure to do so.

Amongst other topics, the play discusses Behavioural Psychology, Affiliative Behaviour, Marcus Garvey and the Black Star liners, the Lamed Wufniks, Slim Whitman, the Permissive Society, the Great Beast 666, Big-gles, Tammy Wynette, Nietzsche, Roxy Music and the Clitoral Orgasm.

Andrew and Bridget unite to take the piss out of the others. Their friendship is the strongest in the play but is shattered when, after an evening in the pub, Bridget seduces Mo's boyfriend Benny. Jonathan's Christianity is revealed as being little more than self-justifying priggishness. Andrew is incapable of facing up to emotion and hides behind smart-arse, fanciful rhetoric. Bridget has built up so many defensive walls that she is similarly unable to sustain a relationship and Mathew wonders, 'Why can't a woman be more like a rat?' It's a play about emotional dysfunction.

Bridget's House opened at Lanchester Polytechnic on 24 March 1976 and was on the road for a year touring with *The Melody Bandbox Rhythm Roadshow* and the last of the Hull Truck kids' shows *The Gormless Ghoul of Castle Doom. The Gormless Ghoul* was truly dreadful. We had had enough of being bitten by dogs and children so devised a show that could only be played indoors and one that made full use of Steve Marshall's Wagnerian synthesiser soundtrack and enthusiasm for special effects. Wimbo the Wonderdog reappeared as a character in a creaky tale of bats, rats, spiders, vampires, the mad scientist Dr Glockenspiel and his unspeakably unfunny assistant Brunhilde, but our hearts were not in it. The show's failure was further compounded by the fact that none of the kids knew what a ghoul was and remained unmoved throughout.

After four years on the road we had built up a loyal following, and the critical success of *Oh What!* meant that we were booked into a wider range of venues. Even so, we often faced a hostile reaction to the content of the work, and there were frequent calls for us to be banned.

In *Bridget's House* two scenes in particular caused the most fuss. One was the Gratuitous Swearing Scene:

MO *and* BENNY *are in the kitchen.*

MO. How much bread have you got?

BENNY. How much have you got?

MO. I've only got a couple of quid.

BENNY. I've only got a quid really.

MO. What are we going to do then?

BENNY. See Slim Whitman.

MO. Who?

BENNY. Slim Whitman, he's on at the ABC tonight.

MO. Who the fuck's Slim Whitman?

BENNY. You've heard of Slim Whitman.

MO. If I'd heard of fuckin' Slim Whitman I wouldn't be fuckin' asking, would I?

BENNY. Fuckin' Slim Whitman—'Rose Marie', The Yodelling
Cowboy—a legend in his own lifetime.

MO. Oh wow! What a fantastic evening listening to a fuckin'
Yodelling Cowboy!

BENNY. He's fuckin' ace.

MO. Well, how come I've never fuckin' heard of him?

BENNY. Well, you would have done if you had any fuckin' sense.

MO. We could put the bread together and get a three-quid deal.

BENNY. You can get dope anytime.
How often does Slim Whitman come to Hull?
Anyway you can't get any decent dope in Hull.

MO. Yes, you fuckin' can.

BENNY. No, you fuckin' can't.

MO. You fuckin' can.

BENNY. You'd get fuckin' ripped off.

MO. Would I fuck.

BENNY. Course you fuckin' would.
I can get Pakki Black at sixteen quid an ounce.

MO. You fuckin can't.

BENNY. I fuckin' can.

MO. Where can you get Pakki Black at sixteen quid?

BENNY. Well, I haven't got to spread it around.

MO. That's because you can't fuckin' get it.

BENNY. I fuckin' can.

MO. Where?

BENNY. Dooley.

MO. Dooley can't get Pakki Black at sixteen quid an ounce.

BENNY. Well, he can for me.

MO. Well, he can't for me.

BENNY. That's because you don't fuckin' know him.

MO. Course I fuckin' know him, man. I've known him years.
You don't fuckin' know him.

BENNY. I fuckin' do. I've known him years.

MO. Well, how come I've never seen you round his place then?

BENNY. Yeah well, you're fuckin' stupid buying *Physical Graffiti*.

MO. Fuck off. Led Zeppelin are the best band in the world.

BENNY. Fuck off. Anyway it's the producer that counts.
Look at Phil Spector.

MO. Who?

BENNY. You haven't heard of Phil Spector?

MO. Pardon me for living. NO.

BENNY. Phil Spector invented the Wall of Sound.

MO. I thought Led Zeppelin invented the Wall of Sound.

BENNY. That was the Wall of Speakers, Phil Spector was the
sound of the Sixties. Do you remember the Sixties?

MO. I fuckin' lived in them, man.

BENNY. It was Soul. Soul was the sound of the Sixties.

MO. I thought The Beatles was the sound of the Sixties.

BENNY. I mean the early Sixties—they were the fuckin' Sixties.

MO. You were fuckin' six in the early Sixties.

BENNY. I fuckin' remember them.

MO. You fuckin' don't.

BENNY. I fuckin' do.

MO. You fuckin' don't, man.

BENNY. There's no point in talking to you. You're fuckin'
dumb.

> BENNY *starts to exit.*

MO. Where the fuck are you off to?

BENNY. I'm going to get some bread off me mam and see a
living legend.

> BENNY *exits.*

MO. Well, fuck you then.

> *Blackout.*

It's a scene about status not about swearing or drugs.

The other scene that the audiences had difficulty with was the Gratuitous Sex Scene:

> *The kitchen—early evening.* BRIDGET *is fixing a plug and* MO *is fixing her
> make-up. They are discussing* BRIDGET's *ex-husband and her recent divorce.*

MO. So why did you marry him in the first place?

BRIDGET. My parents didn't like him. It was an adolescent rebellious gesture. They were quite right. However, you must bear in mind that we were married in the summer of 1967 and summer was a 'love-in there' and we young folks, we wore flowers in our hair and danced in the streets and loved one another and all that shit. It wasn't till later I discovered that he was a pig.

MO. You didn't get on?

BRIDGET. Er, no. We were totally sexually incompatible.

MO. Didn't you make it with each other before you got married?

BRIDGET. Well. Yes we did but it was all rather forbidden fruity in those days. Subsequently, I discovered he was a pneumatic driller if you know what I mean.

MO. Only too well.

BRIDGET. The longer, the harder, and the louder I screamed the better he liked it. As long as he was satisfied, bugger if I was.

MO. Yeah, well, for some guys sex might as well be wanking in a cunt.

BRIDGET. How delicately put.

MO. Well, it's true. I mean for a chick it goes a hell of a lot deeper than that, doesn't it?

BRIDGET. Yes. That is true. I mean, let's face it… most men wouldn't know what a clitoris was if it jumped up and bit them on the leg.

MO. I was with this guy once and he was banging away and I said, 'Hey, steady on. Take it easy', and he said, 'Are you trying to tell me I'm no good in bed?' So I said, 'Yeah.'

BRIDGET. Did you?

MO. Course I did. I can't be doing with that kind of shit. And he said, 'Tons of chicks have told me I'm fantastic in bed.' I mean, he just didn't realise that they'd been faking orgasms left, right and centre. I mean, it's the easiest thing in the world to pretend to come, isn't it?

BRIDGET. It's just as well really. You know, he gets what he wants and he rolls over and starts snoring and you're lying there in the wet patch. And as a bit of an afterthought he may roll over and say, 'Oh, was that all right?' And you say, 'Oh yes, terrific!' Anything to get rid of the sod.

MO. Well, I will say that for Benny...

BRIDGET. Is that the pretty young man with the nice teeth?

MO. Yeah. Credit where credit's due. He gives you a bloody good time in bed. I mean, he's a fantastic fuck.

BRIDGET. Fancy.

MO. It's just when you get out of bed that the trouble starts. I mean, I've no objection to him fucking my body. It's just that he will keep trying to fuck my brains. I mean he's a loud-mouthed little punk with fuck-all to be superior about.

BRIDGET. Ah. I was subjected to the most extraordinary dose of male superiority the other day. Basically, I was giving this guy the elbow because I found him totally physically repulsive, and he simply could not believe that I did not wish to be touched. Therefore I must be playing hard to get. He simply couldn't believe there was any kind of relationship but a sexual one.

MO. Well, they are the best kind, aren't they?

BRIDGET. Quite frankly, given the level of intelligence and sensitivity displayed by the majority of men, I think you're better off having a wank.

MO. Some guys are all right.

BRIDGET. I feel it's a matter of standards really, don't you?

MO. Anyway I'm off to the Welly Club.

BRIDGET. With the toothpaste kid, no doubt?

MO (*exiting*). No. Fuck him. What I want is a nice deaf mute with a big cock.

Blackout.

The opinions expressed by Mo and Bridget in the scene chimed with the opinions of most of the young women in the country, yet every time we played it there were noisy walkouts and murmurs of shocked disapproval. On several occasions couples split up during the course of the scene. In Gainsborough we had to give a female audience member a lift home in the van after her husband had driven off in a huff.

Despite all the gratuitous sex and swearing we were invited by the National Theatre to open the newly built Cottesloe Theatre with *Bridget's*

House—the first fringe company to play at the National. We thought they were taking the piss. I subsequently discovered that 7:84 had also been asked but had turned it down as politically unsound.

The invitation from the National was perceived to be such a big deal in Hull that it became a news item on BBC Radio Humberside. There had been a subtle shift in our reputation. Previously we had been seen as a bunch of profane hippy gypos. We were now a bunch of bigheaded, and presumably rich, Southern snobs. The local junk shops started trying to overcharge us.

In the event the opening of the new National Theatre building was way behind schedule, so instead of playing the Cottesloe they moved *Bridget's House* to the Young Vic. When we arrived a swarm of stage managers unpacked the van and dumped everything on the stage. We put up our own set as usual but there was one major problem. There was a three-foot wide strip of gold paint running through Bridget's kitchen. It was apparently an important feature in a production of *Troilus and Cressida* that was opening a week later. I asked the production manager to paint it out. He went apeshit. It wasn't gold paint; it was pure gold leaf and had cost a zillion pounds. I told him that it was even less likely that Bridget had a three-foot-wide zillion-pound strip of gold leaf running through her Coltman Street kitchen and asked him to get rid of it. He solved the problem by cutting a piece from a brand new stage cloth and breaking it down to match the Young Vic stage. This cosmetic operation cost more than our entire set.

The week at the Young Vic was spectacularly mediocre. We never conquered the space and the performances were under par. Perhaps we were intimidated by playing under the banner of the National. Harold Hobson came to review the show for the *Sunday Times*. The next night he turned up at the theatre again after the performance and sent his chauffeur to fetch Pete Nicholson. Pete, still in costume, sat in the back of the car and gave Hobson the exact chapter and verse (John 3:16) for Jonathan's Bible quotation in Scene Two. He didn't like the show very much, but he cared enough to get it right.

At the end of the run the swarms of stage management reappeared— we hadn't seen them all week—to help with the get-out. It usually took us twenty minutes to pack the van, but this time it took over an hour as the National crew randomly slung everything into the back and we had to take it all out and start again. We were happy to set off for Oxford and an easy week of *Bandbox* performances at the Festival.

On the Monday lunchtime Barry Nettleton got a phone call from the production manager at the National. The stage management wanted their gratuities. They were demanding that we tip them sixty quid a man for helping with our get-out. There were eight of them. We pointed out that we had not asked them to help, that they had only got in the way and that they had presumably been paid as usual for not turning up all week.

They were asking us to shell out nearly five hundred pounds for no reason whatsoever at a time when our company wage was thirty pounds a week. I asked the production manager what their reaction would be if we told them to shove it up their arse. He replied that we were perfectly entitled to refuse, but if we did he would make sure that no fringe company ever played the National Theatre again. I told him it was blackmail and hung up. An hour later he called back. The lads had agreed to do it for the equivalent of a bottle of whisky a man so could we send a cheque? Barry was furious and called the Arts Council. The Arts Council advised us to pay up and agreed to reimburse us. At the time they were proposing huge cuts to community and touring companies.

We spent the summer touring all three shows including a week playing in Portakabins in the as-yet-unfinished Milton Keynes. One regional Arts Association tour was so badly organised that we frequently played to single figures. In one venue we found all our publicity material, still unwrapped, under the administrator's desk. In another, the entire audience of two knocked on the dressing-room window to ask directions to the theatre. Radio Humberside gave us a regular Friday lunchtime slot to broadcast the *Melody Bandbox* live from the foyer of Humberside Theatre. There was a delicious irony in a pastiche live radio show being broadcast live on a pastiche radio station.

In November we returned to the Bush. We stayed in theatrical digs in Gunnersbury with The Flying Fontaines—a roller-skating act who had once entertained the troops in Vietnam. Despite the hiccup at the National we were still flavour of the month and sold out the entire run. The critics were pretty much all on board and again rejoiced in Rachel Bell and her performance as Bridget. They had also finally got over their phobia of improvised plays. I celebrated by going to see The Sex Pistols at the Royal College of Art.

Earlier that year Peter Wilson, Artistic Director with Howard Gibbins at the Bush, had come up with the wheeze of turning Bill Tidy's *Daily Mirror* cartoon strip *The Fosdyke Saga* into a musical entertainment. *The Fosdyke Saga* was an epic tale of a Lancashire Tripe dynasty and their endless vendetta with the evil Roger Ditchley. Bill had no idea who we were and thought the whole enterprise was doomed to failure but said yes anyway so we set off to find a writer. David Edgar was otherwise engaged on something important, so Alan Plater signed up for the job. It proved to be an inspired choice. Wilson, Plater and I went to see Bill in Southport. We had a drink in his local pub then went to his local Trattoria where we had a boozy Italian businessman's lunch then we went back to his house in Birkdale where we had a lot of wine and played snooker with his brother-in-law who was plastering the kitchen then we had some grappa and went home. Bill told Alan: 'Your job is to glue my bubbles together, so why don't I leave it to you?' And he did. I asked Bernard Wrigley—the Bolton Bullfrog—to write the music. Bernard had written songs for the original Bolton version of the Ken Campbell Roadshow. I put together a cast who I thought would be good at cartoon acting and who had a huge range of performance skills. The idea was to use everything I had learnt from years of kids' shows, cabaret and bag escaping to make the most raucous piece of rough theatre imaginable. Roger Sloman from East 15, who had done time with 7:84, Mike Leigh and Campbell, was patriarch Josiah Fosdyke. Jane Wood from the original Roadshow was Rebecca Fosdyke. Scunthorpe-born Malcolm Ranson, fight director and funny-walk expert, was Albert Fosdyke. Kevin Elyot, now an esteemed playwright, was Tom Fosdyke and played the piano. Penny Nice, a brilliant comedienne and singer, was Victoria Fosdyke. And Philip Jackson, who could play anything, proved it by playing Roger Ditchley, Ben Ditchley, a reporter, a prison warder, another reporter, King George the Fifth, a pitman, Emily O'Malley, Schmidt, Baron von Richthofen, a newsboy, the Salford Ripper and several other pivotal roles. We rehearsed on the stage of the Bush at the same time as *Bridget's House* was playing in the evenings.

Alan's script was fast and furious, and when we discovered that he was happy for us to take liberties with it we embraced the opportunity enthusiastically. Just as Bill's original cartoon strip satirised a particular genre of literature we decided with Alan that the production should satirise current styles in theatre as well. The piece started out looking like a particularly earnest agitprop Stoke documentary about the socio-econo-mobility of the indigenous working class within the class structure of post-Industrial Revolution Lancashire but quickly deteriorated into an anarchic romp, giving a good kicking to *Oh What a Lovely War*, Joint Stock, Women's Theatre, Gritty Northern Kitchen Sink Drama, *Play for Today*, Brecht, Ewan MacColl and Plater's own *Close the Coalhouse Door* on the way. Di Seymour's set was a cartoon version of a Victorian toy theatre with Tidy-inspired backdrops that the actors changed like lightning while simultaneously changing costume.

Some of the stunts we pulled in *The Fosdyke Saga* were: A Massive Pit Disaster. A Steam Train. A Women's Suffrage Movement Wrestling Match. A Zeppelin Raid on an Innocent Tripe Works. The First World War. A Mid-Air Dogfight with some Evil Fokkers. The Angel of Mons.

An Erotic Dance with a Hammer. A Tripe Fight with the Audience.

My own favourite moments were: Penny Nice pregnantly inflating herself with an ill-disguised foot pump while singing 'I'm a disenchanted maiden whom a rotter did besmirch'. Sloman crushing Phil Jackson's bollocks in a slow-motion stroboscopic Kung Foo Fight played out to Isaac Hayes singing 'Shaft'. And Jane Wood as Emmeline Pankhurst whacking theatre critic Milton Shulman over the head with a rolled-up copy of *Socialist Worker*.

The show was entirely and joyfully politically dubious. We would never get away with it now...

Enter SALFORD RIPPER. *He spies* REBECCA *and* VICTORIA.

RIPPER. Aha! Women of the Streets!

JOSIAH. Ey up, that's a bit strong, old lad...

RIPPER. I have no quarrel with men. Only avenging myself on t'opposite sex.

REBECCA. Apprehend him, Josiah. He's mad!

RIPPER. I must rid the world of interfering, cackling women.

JOSIAH. Pity he's mad. He's got some good ideas.

The Fosdyke Saga was a huge cult hit and long queues for tickets formed round Shepherd's Bush Green. Tripe Fever gripped the City. Punters returned several times and brought their own tripe to fling at the cast. We were invited on *Nationwide*—the television news programme—and triped the interviewer. Terry Jones from the Monty Python team took us all out for a pizza. There was talk of West End transfers, and Tara Prem wanted to record the show for the BBC. Professor Albert Hunt writing in *New Society* thought that we had invented an entirely new theatrical language. John Barber in the *Daily Telegraph* thought the production recalled Joan Littlewood in her heyday. Mike Hirst said that the spirit of Charivari was alive and well. David Edgar said that we had set back British political theatre by twenty years. Years later Phil Jackson described what we were doing as 'pratting about in a life-enhancing fashion'. I think he got it about right.

So let us all now join together in the uplifting Fosdyke Anthem, 'Fosdykes Arise':

Tripe, it is grand
Tripe, it is noble
In every land
Tripe, it is global
Better by far then fowl, fish or weevil

Let there be tripe, and banish all evil
Fosdkyes Arise
Fosdykes Arise
Lift up thine eyes
See the Fosdykes Arise!

Bridget's House went on tour to Holland playing the Mickery Theatre in Amsterdam. The Mickery was a legendary date for British touring groups. Artistic Director Ritsaert ten Cate founded the theatre on his farm in Loenersloot near Utrecht in the late Sixties and then moved to an old cinema on the Rozengracht in Amsterdam. In the twenty-odd years of its existence the Mickery mounted seven thousand performances of seven hundred productions and welcomed everybody from People Show to Pip Simmons and from the Wooster Group to Wim Zomers. Arguably Ritsaert did more for British alternative theatre than anybody else. He was a wonderful and generous spirit, and everyone who played there was well paid and well looked after by the theatre and its staff.

The Mickery audience did not know what to make of *Bridget's House*. Although it is true that a fair proportion of them were stoned out of their trees and were used to a more visually pyrotechnic form of experimental performance; it is equally true that the show had hit the buffers. We were all aware that since the Bush something was wrong, but we didn't know how to fix it. After the run in Amsterdam we were due to go on a tour of one-nighters, organised by the Mickery throughout Holland and Belgium, but before setting off we took a week out to work on the show. I decided to go back to basics. On the premise of making the show more accessible to audiences who didn't have English as a first language we went through the play ditching anything that wasn't absolutely necessary. We also went back to the original objectives, and I made sure that the actors knew exactly what they were up to at any given moment. We found that the show was now twelve minutes shorter. We called it the Dutch version. It worked a treat and we got standing ovations almost everywhere we went. What had happened of course was that we had got rid of all the junk—the self-indulgent embellishments that had crept in over the year. If a new line or a piece of business gets a laugh or a reaction, the temptation for the actor is to keep it in. Eventually all these additions clog up the storytelling and the play is suffocated. Similarly, lack of concentration on objectives can result in generalised emoting, and if you get a whole company doing it you are fucked. I should have known. Joan Littlewood frequently had the same problem. She once gave the following note:

> Can we stop regarding the audience as morons, cut out the rub-
> bish, get back the tension, pace and atmosphere. Can we stop
> waving our arses all over the script, overacting, BULLYING
> laughs out of the audience and playing alone for approbation.

The Dutch version became the authorised version of *Bridget's House* from
then on.

The Fosdyke Saga transferred from the Bush to, of all places, the ICA
Theatre. Penny Nice and Jane Wood had unfortunately to leave owing
to prior engagements, but were brilliantly replaced by Elaine Donnelly
and Mary Sheen, who had been in the original production of *Fings Ain't
Wot They Used T'Be*. The entire run was sold out.

For the Dutch tour of *Bridget's House* we were based in Amsterdam
and ferried around Holland and Belgium by the Mickery stage
management in an old school bus rather than using our own truck. I
think they had had problems with English companies getting lost
and/or arrested so preferred not to take the risk. Everyday we set off
early for Leiden or Winschoten on Enschede or Den Haag or
Groningen or Tournhout and every night drove back late to the
Museum Hotel. Also staying in the Museum Hotel were Ken Campbell
and the Science Fiction Theatre of Liverpool, who were performing
the eight-hour Discordian epic *Illuminatus!* in the Mickery. The two
companies seriously bonded.

Liverpool artist Pete Halligan, inspired by Jung's dream of Liverpool
being the Pool of Life, founded the Liverpool School of Music, Language, Dream and Pun in Mathew Street, a stone's throw from the
original Cavern Club. He invited Ken, who had been converted to Science Fiction by Brian Alldiss, to come up with some sort of a show. Ken
wandered into Compendium Books in Camden Town and came out
with the *Illuminatus Trilogy* by Robert Anton Wilson and Robert Shea
because there was a picture of a yellow submarine on the cover. Appropriately *Illuminatus* is the ultimate tale of synchronicity, telepathy,
conspiracy, sex and drugs and rock 'n' roll and a world controlled by a
sinister secret organisation responsible for everything from Kennedy's
assassination to the sinking of Atlantis. Ken adapted the book with
Chris Langham, and together they formed the Science Fiction Theatre
of Liverpool and produced the play. Why Science Fiction?

> Science Fiction is the discipline of thinking sideways, and thus
> jerks the mind awake with unexpected syntheses... Science Fic-
> tion takes nothing for granted and examines concepts old and
> new with the innocent quality of a child or a Martian. Science

Fiction moves with equal aplomb towards either sense or non-sense. In so doing it often makes us think which is which.

Ken was looking for something new. He thought that fringe theatre had become a business run by the prefects and that Establishment theatre had even less to offer.

> If I wanted to know some new things tonight (say I don't get totally pissed by six), I've got a whole fresh mind, I've had quite an invigorating day, it would be good to go out and be illuminated on some point, wouldn't it? What theatre would you be likely to be illuminated in?

Ken and Chris put together an amazing and eccentric cast including Jim Broadbent, Bill Nighy, Neil Cunningham, Andrew Dallmeyer, Chris Fairbank, David Rappaport ('He may not be the smallest man in the world but he's fucking close'—K. Campbell), Prunella Gee as Eris, Goddess of Discord, and George Harvey Webb, the fiddling Dramaturg from East 15 as Carl Gustav Jung and Aleister Crowley. Also in the show was the other Alan Williams. (The *other* Alan Williams was a Liverpool impresario and club owner, who had once managed the Beatles and had given them away. He had reputedly told John Lennon that he knew people in show business and that Lennon would never work again.) Bill Drummond, who later became KLF and burnt a million quid in an ornate situationist gesture, designed the sets.

The show was a theatrical miracle combining mind-bending ideas with inspired stagecraft, impossible acting, a puppet show with dolphins and a full-length rock musical. You had to be there.

Life in the Museum Hotel had its moments. Brian Rix, Hull-born farceur turned producer, arrived with an idea to produce both *The Fosdyke Saga* and *Illuminatus!* in a huge cinema in Kilburn. *Fosdyke* would play weekdays and *Illuminatus!* weekends. Rix sat through half of the *Illuminatus!*, announced that it was a bit hard on the old bottom and was never seen again. Ironically Peter Hall invited Ken to take the show to the National, where *Illuminatus!* triumphantly opened the finally completed Cottesloe.

Back in England *Bridget's House*, in the new improved Benelux version, toured until the end of March 1977, winning nominations for Most Promising Actress for Rachel Bell and a nomination for Best Musical in the London Critics' Awards.

Tara Prem was as good as her word, and we made a television version of *The Fosdyke Saga* recording several performances at the Haymarket Theatre in Leicester using the Pebble Mill *Match of the Day* outside broadcast crew. We added drummer Charlie Grima to the team. Charlie had previously worked with Roy Wood's Wizzard and can still be seen every year on Christmas Day *Top of the Pops* miming to 'I Wish It Could Be Christmas Every Day'.

At the end of the tour the *Bridget's House* company split up. Some of us had been together for two and a half years and it was time to move on. Rachel, Pete and David Hatton went off to have proper careers as proper actors, and Cass and Steve sold their souls to rock 'n' roll. The real Alan Williams stayed on. We had come a long way in five years.

7

The Ghost of Electricity

In April 1977 I held auditions for a new company. I decided to advertise in *The Stage* and *Time Out* and see who turned up. After five years I wanted to expand the range of the company and tell stories about a wider spectrum of characters. I felt that I had exhausted the potential of chronicling the death throes of the counterculture. I told Peter Ansorge in an interview in *Plays and Players* that I wanted to make plays about vicars and taxi drivers and to work with older actors, but as always the character of the work was determined by the range of the actors in the company—actors prepared to spend a year living in a van and working for what was just about a living wage.

I had five hundred applications. After interviews in London and Manchester and a series of workshops at the Oval House, which involved improvisation and songwriting, I put together a company with a bewildering collection of talents.

David Threlfall had just left Manchester Polytechnic School of Theatre. This would be his first professional stage appearance, although he had been in Mike Leigh's television film *The Kiss of Death*. Heather Tobias was a LAMDA graduate who had been in *Tommy*. Kathy Iddon had worked at the Open Space and the Roundhouse and toured Europe with rock bands. Robin Soans had trained at RADA, had a degree in Philosophy and Jurisprudence and wrote for *The Two Ronnies*. Colin Goddard came on board as musical director: he was an experienced session musician and had been in the Lennox Avenue Blues Band. Mia Soteriou had trained as a concert pianist before doing English at Oxford. And then there was the real Alan Williams.

Among those who auditioned but failed to make the company were the eminent playwright Doug Lucie, and Graham Fellows, who became both Jilted John and John Shuttleworth.

As a result of the success of *Bridget's House* and the company's never-ending touring, the Arts Council had increased our grant, and we at last moved into our own premises. We rented an old printing works in the old town by the river, next door to William Wilberforce's house and the Transport Museum. Here we had an office and two large rehearsal spaces plus storage and set-construction space. The reputation of the company was such that Barry Nettleton was able to book a six-month tour for the new show without any indication of what it might be about or indeed what it was called. The new company took up residence in Hull at the beginning of June in 1977, and the show was scheduled to open at the Traverse in the second week of the Edinburgh Festival.

All I knew was that I wanted to make a play about love and marriage, and that it was set in Hull. The casting meant that I had the potential for three couples, but I had no idea who would go with who, or indeed if anybody would go with anybody. As usual I started working with the actors in isolation on building characters. I gave Robin and David the brief of coming up with somebody who worked as a communicator in some way. Robin was interested in a visionary Socialist architect, a Vietnam War photographer, and a guy who he had known at school who always wanted to be a vicar. Perhaps my frivolous comment to Peter Ansorge was a piece of serendipitous synchronicity. We went along with the vicar. Robin then set about researching ecclesiastical training and inventing a background that sent his character on that particular journey. So now I had a play about love, marriage and religion.

David Threlfall's journey was more picturesque. We were sitting in The Abercrombie pub in Manchester one lunchtime when a bunch of young men came in for a drink They all wore suits, and David noticed that a number of them had shoes with gold chains or bars on them. It was some kind of mid-Seventies fashion statement. David decided he wanted to play someone who wore such shoes and drove a Cortina. We reasoned that he possibly worked in advertising or marketing. David thought he should be a reporter on a local newspaper and again remembered someone from school who interested him. The boy had only been there for a couple of terms. His father was in the military so the kid had to change schools frequently. To cope with this, and to instantly make friends, he had developed a talent for impersonations and jokes. He knew every *Monty Python* sketch and *Goon Show* script and communicated only in funny voices.

Alan wanted to play someone he had met at a bus stop who had just come out of prison and claimed to have a metal plate in his head. Mia wanted to base her character on someone foreign—Mia is Greek—and was interested in an Italian girl she had seen bottling for a busker in

Oxford, and an out-of-control cousin of hers who kept running away. Heather wanted to play her Protestant distant relative from Northern Ireland. Kathy wanted to be her old head girl. I decided that we would work out a character for Colin Goddard when I had more of an idea of the tale I was going to tell. Everybody went off to research and create life histories.

Every evening we met up to rehearse as a band and started working on the material that would become part of the cabaret show. All the company sang and most played several instruments and we quickly knocked up a set of Sixties material that encompassed Tamla Motown standards like 'Jimmy Mack' and 'Mickey's Monkey' to Hedgehoppers Anonymous's 'It's Good News Week', The Pink Floyd's 'See Emily Play', and 'Telstar'. We played a regular Friday-night gig in The Old Bell pub on Anlaby Road. A local promoter wanted to sign us up for a summer season at a caravan park in Mablethorpe. We were also asked by the Junior Chamber of Commerce to provide some sort of entertainment for the Queen's visit to Hull as part of the Silver Jubilee celebrations.

Robin and I wrote a pastiche fifteen-minute Shakespeare play called *As You Lump It*, which we performed from a cart in the marketplace, and we sang a few madrigals. Whether or not Her Majesty was amused is still a matter of conjecture.

Back in the rehearsal room it became obvious that Kathy's character Meg and Robin's character Alex swam in the same cultural pool and should meet. Alex decided to spend a year doing VSO in Africa, and so I sent Meg on the same journey. They got together and fell in love and from then on we plotted the twelve years of their relationship together up until the time of the play. They married. Alex was ordained and eventually came to a parish in Hull where he conducted experimentally liberal services with folk music and passages from John Robinson's *Honest to God*. Meg organised knitting circles and coffee mornings for Sri Lankan orphanages. Robin walked around Hull in character and in a dog collar. He found that passers by either smiled at him or passed by on the other side. People who had previously seen him out of character in Ladbrokes were quietly confused.

Alan's character Trevor is in Hull prison. He hears voices in his head. His metal plate has become a transmitter for messages from dead people about the Kennedy assassination. Prison visitor Meg—Kathy's character—goes to see him. Trevor becomes her project. She promises to see him after he is released. On his release he hangs around the railway station late at night. Mia's character Mel was hitchhiking round the country. We took her out in the van and dropped her off somewhere outside Selby and she hitched the fifteen miles back to Hull in character. She ends up late at night in the railway station. She meets Trevor and moves in with him. They develop a non-sexual, but strangely tender relationship based on mutual need and petty crime.

Mel indulges in a little light shoplifting so I sent Mia out in character to do some robbing, having first tipped off the shop owner that she was coming. Not only did she successfully nick stuff from the forewarned bookshop, she got away with shoplifting from several innocent stores as well.

Threlfall's character Philip works as a reporter for the *Hull Daily Mail*. He compiles the quiz and competitions page. In addition to speaking exclusively in funny voices, he has a Day-Glo Emu puppet that he entertains people with. He also suffers from asthma. Heather's character Julie works as a secretary in a bank. She meets Philip in a bar and they go on dates. She won't sleep with him until they get engaged. So they get engaged. Julie is enthusiastically planning the wedding. Philip is not prepared for marriage. He is equally unprepared for life.

The new rehearsal room meant that we could create environments for the characters so each of the couples had a room of their own to work in. Over a period of weeks I brought the couples up to the present day and then set about structuring the improvisations that would lead to the events of the play. I realised that Threlfall's character Philip needed someone other than Julie to talk to, so Colin Goddard became his mate Wayne, and they became a silly lads double act.

The play chronicled the disintegration of the three relationships. The marriage between Meg and Alex was arid. They had never had children, and Alex had become totally preoccupied with his work. He was also pompous and a bully. Meg was unfulfilled and lonely but sublimated her pain in charitable works. She goes round to see Trevor, having visited him in prison, and meets Mel. She convinces herself that Mel and Trevor are experimenting with Black Magic. Philip and Julie are getting married in Alex's church so they go round for instruction on marriage with Alex who explains the true nature of love in a scene of staggering hypocrisy. By the end of the play Philip and Julie have split up; Mel has run away, leaving Trevor alone and mad; and Alex and Meg's relationship is in tatters. And Wayne has to marry his girlfriend who he has knocked up.

Although Colin was ostensibly musical director, everybody worked on the songs, with Robin and Mia both writing tunes and everybody writing lyrics. Once again the variety of musical styles reflected the diversity of the characters in the play. Meg's song became a Kurt Weill pastiche:

I've got to concoct a riddle-me-ree for the children's page in
  the parish magazine.
I've got to go shopping and I can't have the car because Alex
  says he needs it for his meeting with the Dean.
Mrs Green's collecting for spastics and I mustn't forget to thank
  her
And remind her that she's going to be included in the knitting
  list for dishcloths for Sri Lanka.

Trevor's song was a Johnny Cash number about the Kennedy assassination. Mel had a Patti Smith-style song. There was a happy-clappy hymn
called 'Hand in Hand'. Philip had a proto-punk tune composed entirely
from the themes of TV soaps. And Philip and Julie shared a love duet
which we thought of submitting as the Irish entry for the Eurovision
Song Contest.

After constructing the basic scenario I decided that the show should
open and close with two contrasting short sermons from vicar Alex.
Robin and I wrote them together. The first was on the theme 'Who is
your house open to?' and established the ideals of selflessness that Alex
ostensibly subscribed to and which were equally neglected by all the other
characters in the play. In the last sermon Alex described the torture
undergone by a Christian missionary in Pinochet's Chile. My aim was to
contrast true tenacity of spirit with Alex's self-righteous piety. Neither
speech could have been achieved solely through improvisation although
they were to an extent written in character. It was the first time I had
used scripted material in a devised piece. They were created for a particular dramatic effect and to accentuate a particular theme in the play.

Gemma Jackson designed a pastel-coloured all-purpose set dominated by a pulsating pink Valentine-card heart.

A Bed of Roses opened at the Traverse at the Edinburgh Festival and quickly
sold out. The reviews were ecstatic, and we won a Fringe First Award.
Then we set off on the road. The Sixties cabaret show had now become
Bunny Scuffs' Teen Tempo Disc Date. Threlfall was DJ and host Bunny Scuffs—
a character yet again inspired by a pair of shoes, or in this case a pair of
fluffy kids' slippers he saw on Hull market. Bunny was a cross between
Tony Blackburn and, erm... a rabbit. His catchphrase was 'Are you a-
hoppin' and a-bobbin'? And audiences frequently were. The three girls
were The Bobtails: Ruby Beaver, Connie Ling and Stubby Dago. Robin
was Jonathan Jonnies. Alan was Del Failure. Guitar hero Colin Goddard was Eric Bendix. The show expanded to include an
audience-participation teenage-love test 'How Passionate Are You?',
culled from the pages of Boyfriend magazine. We were now sufficiently

financially secure not to have to do a kids' show, a blessing for which I was personally extremely grateful, as I had run out of crap ideas.

Both shows went down well on the road, but we still sometimes encountered resistance to the content, despite there being neither a reefer nor a fuck on display. In Chesterfield we were thrown out of a hotel for putting Mia in a wardrobe.

Arriving at the Bush in January 1978 we received an astonishing critical reception.

> 'In terms of truth and dignity, Hull Truck's A Bed of Roses makes everything in the West End of London from Shaftesbury Avenue to the Strand seem positively tawdry by comparison.'
>
> (Herbert Kretzmer, *Daily Express*)

> 'A triumph of desolation and humour... A Bed of Roses is a brilliant alliance of satire and special pleading.'
>
> (*Guardian*)

> 'It is one of the few examples of contemporary theatre which is hilariously funny, extremely moving and physically frightening almost simultaneously... a small masterpiece, particularly recommended for those readers who don't go to theatre.'
>
> (*Time Out*)

> 'The show is above all else, a total vindication of director Mike Bradwell's improvisational working methods.'
>
> (Michael Coveney, *Financial Times*)

I think it would be fair to say that we had got a result. It would equally be fair to say that *A Bed of Roses* was not entirely a bed of roses. Some of our most loyal supporters felt that we had sold out, abandoning the counter culture by introducing characters (like a vicar and his wife) who could be refugees from the plays of Terence Rattigan or John Mortimer. *Plays and Players* thought that the characters had been selected 'off the peg from any of television's light-entertainment factories'. The Workers' Revolutionary Party again castigated us for patronising the working class. The production also suffered from its own success in that we all got big-headed. The Bush was packed to capacity every night, and the great and the good fought for tickets. The actors were overpraised, and the performances became self-indulgent and melodramatic. David Threlfall's asthma attack in the second act sometimes lasted several hours. Everybody was showboating, and the audiences, who had decided that we were the dog's bollocks, encouraged such misbehaviour. There was talk of glamorous agents and film offers and lucrative television roles. Stuart Burge, who was temporarily running the Royal Court, offered to transfer the show to the main house for a short season in March, and we accepted.

Back on the road we came down to earth and gave the show an over-haul. I had learnt the lessons of *Bridget's House* in Holland, and we went back to basics, stripping away all the embellishments and simply telling the story. It worked.

The Royal Court run was a sell-out and the culmination of the tour. The show received several nominations in the London Critics' Awards, and David Threlfall won Most Promising Actor for what had been his professional stage debut. It seemed that, at last, the critics had bought into the idea of improvised plays. Mike Leigh's *Abigail's Party* at Hampstead Theatre had been a popular success, selling out twice before being adapted into a BBC TV *Play for Today*, and winning every award in sight for Mike and Alison Steadman, who played the monstrous Beverley. Leigh followed up *Abigail's Party* with the bleakly unsettling but brilliant *Ecstasy* (1979) and *Goose-Pimples*, which transferred from Hampstead to the Garrick in 1981 and which, on account of Antony Sher's portrayal of a pissed-up Arab, almost resulted in the cancellation of a state visit by King Khalid of Saudi Arabia. *A Bed of Roses* had been a huge hit and had introduced the work of the company to a much wider audience, but it also changed the company for ever.

Hull Truck had always attracted people who wanted to be in Hull Truck. They believed in the work, the working method and what we were trying to say. To an extent they also believed in working outside the Establishment and were not particularly interested in commercial the-atre per se. A majority of the members of the early companies went on to work in music, design and other fields. Some of them never worked in theatre again. The success of *A Bed of Roses* inevitably meant that the company provided performers with a platform to show off their talents and could be seen as a stepping stone to apparently more prestigious or lucrative work in better subsidised or more commercial entertainment emporia. Hull Truck had become a useful vehicle.

The *Bed of Roses* company all left at the end of the tour, and I decided to take a break from devised plays. I wanted to try something different and experiment with a variety of styles. Accordingly over the 1978—9 season I directed four wildly diverse projects.

The Great Caper by Ken Campbell was first produced at the Royal Court in 1974. I saw the show with Warren Mitchell in the cast, but thought that the production did not do the play justice. My encounter with Ken and the *Illuminatus!* in Amsterdam had whetted my appetite for anarchic frol-ics, so when John Ashford from *Time Out*, who was by now running the ICA Theatre, asked me to come up with something for his Visionary Theatre Season I decided that *The Caper* fitted the bill.

The play tells of one Eugene Grimley who, discovered by the prophet Ion Will in a state of dysfunction in a London Tube station, turns out to be harbouring a sperm of mind-boggling significance. The pair embark on a quest to find the perfect woman to share it with. The journey takes them from the crumpet strasse of Tel Aviv to the frozen tundra of Lapland and involves a Hare Krishna cake vendor, a man called Geoffrey, a distressed Lapp and a natty farter. It's an Erisian tale of sex, synchronicity and the single-mindedness of ferrets. Ken Campbell was enthusiastic but thought the play probably needed updating so we sat down to do a rewrite. After a couple of days we realised that we were writing a completely different play so abandoned it and went back to the original. I cast Jim Broadbent as Eugene Grimley and Derrick O'Connor as Ion Will. Steve Halliwell, who thus far had failed to become a rock star, rejoined the company to compose the music and to play the Krishna cake man, the Lapp and the farter. There was also rather a lot of shagging and nudity. The play opened in Newcastle where the real Ion Will, who had been at school with Ken in Ilford and a Guru in Penang, announced that he thought that the bloke playing him was rather good. Derrick O'Connor had gone beyond the call of duty. The text suggests that Will has turned his bottom mandrill-mauve by disciplined mind control and speciality yoga. At the Royal Court Warren Mitchell wore a tasteful prosthetic ring piece. Derrick had dyed his arsehole with potassium permanganate. He was asked to leave several hotels and a gay bar in Gateshead as a result. Broadbent had to perform what Ken thought should be the greatest fuck ever, so he took us off to Raymond's Revue Bar to research. Jim favoured the more modest approach with the result that Grimley carefully folded his socks and Y-fronts before embarking on the epic bout of congress.

The Great Caper was such a departure for Hull Truck that the critics were baffled. The most gratifying review came from the *Norwich Evening News* who said:

> Is not such a thing illegal? It is certainly unpleasant and is every
> bit as corrupt as the strip clubs in London.

It was the first time that I had tried using devising tactics on a scripted play. Essentially this entails taking the characters out of the play, working out their backstories and relationships in the usual fashion and in the usual detail and then returning them to the narrative. Steve Grant in *Time Out* clearly spotted this:

> Mike Bradwell's Hull Truck are a company used to dealing in the
> garbled mass of communicated thoughts known as improvisatory
> theatre and it is quite fascinating to watch their skill at clothing

any character with a recognisable history (past and future). Thus Ion Will becomes an Old Kent Road shaman, a perfectly recognisable character who would have probably been a roadie with The Pink Floyd in 1968 and ten years later wound up selling ties on Oxford Street.

He also said that seeing the play felt like being cornered for two hours in a pub by a raving but amiable drunk. Which was fair enough.

Doug Lucie had auditioned for the *Bed of Roses* company but hadn't got in. He had been at Oxford with Mia Soteriou and had written a couple of darkly funny and edgily political plays for OUDS. He fancied himself as the new David Hare, but with integrity. I asked him to write a play for Hull Truck, thinking that he would come up with an acerbic piece about punks and squats and Socialist public schoolboys sniffing glue. He came up with *The New Garbo*—a play about Hollywood actress Frances Farmer. Doug had been inspired by reading a chapter about Frances in Kenneth Anger's *Hollywood Babylon* and had set out to research her story, primarily from her ghost-written and posthumously published 'autobiography', *Will There Really Be a Morning?*

Frances Farmer was born in 1913 in Seattle. While studying drama at Washington State University she won a competition in the Socialist newspaper *The Voice of Action*. Her prize was a trip to the Soviet Union. Despite opposition from her mother, who accused her of being a Communist and an atheist, Frances made the trip on her own, visiting Stanislavsky and the Moscow Art Theatre. She was given a contract with Paramount and moved to Hollywood, where she starred in *Rhythm on the Range* with Bing Crosby, and *Come and Get It* based on the novel by Edna Ferber. She was hailed by the Paramount publicity department as 'The New Garbo'. Frustrated by the banality of the Hollywood studio system, she broke her contract and went to New York to work with the leftist Group Theatre appearing in Clifford Odets's *Golden Boy*. The production was a big hit, and Frances had an affair with Odets. In New York she became increasingly politically active but left The Group when Odets dumped her. Frances continued to work both on stage and film but got a reputation for being a drunk, trouble and possibly a nymphomaniac, and was dropped from or walked out on several projects. She was arrested in 1942 for driving with headlights in a wartime blackout zone and put in jail. At her trial she threw an inkwell at the judge and punched a nurse and a policeman. She was sent to the psychiatric ward of LA General Hospital and diagnosed with manic depressive psychosis. She briefly moved back to Seattle with her parents, but her mother had her committed to a mental institution where she was given both electro-convulsive and insulin shock therapy. In the autobiography Frances claimed that she was abused by the nurses, who forced her to eat her own shit, and was used as a sex slave by the doctors. She was released after five years and made several attempts at a comeback but was deemed to be too ill or too unreliable. She converted to Roman Catholicism and died of cancer in 1970, maintaining to the last that she had never been mentally ill.

This is pretty much the story we started with and the one that Doug dramatised in his script.

I cast Lally Percy from East 15 as Frances. She had been a member of the Glasgow Citizens' Company and had the necessary capacity for both danger and glamour. Kevin Elyot played Clifford Odets and Bing Crosby, and Bridget Ashburn and Tony Scannell played everybody else. Di Seymour was designer.

We started out researching the lives of the real characters and inventing the lives of the ones that Doug had made up. He was very keen to knock the script around, and scenes were rewritten daily, often on the back of fag packets. He came up with a glorious set piece at a Hollywood masked ball, during which Frances does a striptease while reciting Emily Dickinson's poem 'The Soul Has Bandaged Moments', and another in which, in a burst of Method enthusiasm, she successfully impersonates a hooker in an LA speakeasy. After a couple of weeks of investigating the material we felt that something was missing. The story didn't seem to add up. Frances might have been an alcoholic and a nuisance, but she was also intelligent, articulate and talented, and her descent into madness seemed to be impossibly swift. The autobiography didn't hold water and, despite the brutal descriptions of life in the institution, failed to get to the heart of the tale. The motivations were all wrong.

One morning on her way into rehearsal Di Seymour bumped into the playwright Trevor Griffiths. She asked him what he was up to. He told her that he was about to write a play about Hollywood legend Frances Farmer. When he had recovered from the shock that Doug had beaten him to the punch and that we were already in rehearsal, he told Di that he had been inspired to write the play because of a new book on Frances that had just been published in America—a book that told a different version of the story. *Shadowland* by Seattle film critic William Arnold floated the theory that Frances had been targeted by Hoover's FBI, who thought her a Communist agitator and a Red menace. They had conspired with her mother to have her sectioned and incarcerated. In Western State Hospital she had been forced into undergoing a transorbital lobotomy. Frances had been the Jane Fonda of her generation and had suffered the consequences. The bogus autobiography was part of the cover-up. We had a copy of *Shadowland* rushed over from America and rewrote the play to incorporate the new material, working on the text up to and beyond opening night.

We told the story in fourteen short sharp episodes starting off with a recreation of a song and dance number from *Rhythm on the Range* called 'The House Jack built for Jill' and including scenes in the asylum, a threesome in Clifford Odets's bed and a graphic description of the techniques used in lobotomy. Between the scenes we constructed a series of fake period radio broadcasts and commercials that juxtaposed the banality of the Hollywood machine with the complexity of Frances's predicament.

The show went on tour and in London played at the King's Head where it was much appreciated by Rod Stewart and Bianca Jagger, and received a mixed bag of reviews, including the following from the *Evening News*:

> If you don't rush to see this one you'd be a fool. But I'm preju-
> diced. To me this recreation of the life of Frances Farmer is so
> fascinating that I can't stop raving.
>
> (Caren Meyer)

The 1982 film *Frances* starring Jessica Lange was much influenced by *Shadowland* and included the lobotomy scene. Several years later William Arnold recanted and maintained that he had made the whole thing up, but I am not so sure. There is a mysterious coda to the story, as we shall shortly see.

I wanted to stage Flann O'Brien's *The Dalkey Archive* because it seemed unstageable.

The story goes like this: Two decent Catholic boys, Mick and Hackett, on a swimming trip to the gentlemen's swimming pool on the rocky beach below encounter the injured and mad scientist De Selby. De Selby entertains them with vintage whiskey made last week and claims to have mastered the secret of time and also to have met John the Baptist. He is planning to destroy the world. Assisted by De Selby, Mick and Hackett dive down below Dublin Bay where they meet Saint Augustine in a cave and discuss Pelagian philosophy. Mick sets off to save the world. On the way he discovers Police Sgt Fotterell, who believes that men can turn into bicycles and vice versa, and several priests. Eventually he finds James Joyce, who is not dead but working as a potboy in a pub in Skerries. Joyce claims no knowledge of *Ulysses* and his only writings have been pseudonymous pamphlets for the Catholic Truth Society. He plans to become a Jesuit. Mick's girlfriend Mary announces she is having a baby.

I asked Alan McClelland, an old bugger who had acted with Micheál mac Liammóir and been a founder member of Belfast's Ulster Group Theatre, to provide a rough adaptation and George Harvey Webb to explain Pelagian philosophy. Neither was entirely successful.

A half-Irish/half-English cast wrote, rewrote and improvised the piece over a four-week rehearsal period. We were flying by the seat of our pants. McClelland played De Selby. Oengus MacNamara and Arthur Kelly played Mick and Hackett. Steve Halliwell, fresh from *The Great Caper*, played the several priests, Saint Augustine and the fiddle. John Blanchard played James Joyce. Blanchard was in his late fifties. He had retired from the navy and taken up acting late in life. He stayed with the company for two years. Designer Gemma Jackson set the play in a bar in a Dublin pub, which was transformed by a series of secret panels, false walls, disappearing cabinets, smoke and mirrors into countless exteriors, interiors and the undersea world of Dalkey Bay. The whole magical edifice was topped with a holy painting of the blessed Virgin riding a bicycle.

The Dalkey Archive opened at the Bush and went on tour, including a potentially foolhardy trip to the Project in Dublin. Evelyn O'Nolan, Flann O'Brien's widow, came to the preview. She sat in the front row with the Brother and a dozen moonfaced cousins and cleared off straight after the show. We thought she had hated it. On press night I was standing outside the theatre in the rain waiting for the critics to pour themselves out of the pub next door. The pub was holding a month-long happy hour and the show should have started half an hour ago. There was a screech of brakes and a bright-green Mini did a handbrake turn into Essex Street and shuddered to a halt. Out got the widow and presented me with a crate of John Power whiskey for the cast. 'Brian would have approved,' she said.

We also took the show to the Long Wharf Theatre in New Haven, Connecticut, the first time we had toured America. We had been billed in the local newspaper, the *Trumbull Times*, as 'a wacky zany British comedy troupe with a particular brand of imaginative humor', but despite this the show went down well, particularly with the Joycean scholars from Yale just up the road.

The Long Wharf is a particularly prestigious theatre, with a rich and enthusiastic subscription audience. On the opening night they threw a party for the great and the good, and a host of important showbiz folk came up from New York for the occasion. I got chatting to an elderly and distinguished playwright who had written plays for the Group Theatre. I told him about *The New Garbo* and asked him if he had known Frances Farmer. He said that she was beautiful and witty and clever, and she had been destroyed by the FBI because of her politics. The party went on late, ending up on a beach somewhere. Early next morning I got a phone call in the Duncan Hotel. It was the distinguished playwright from the night before phoning from New York. God knows how he got my number. 'About Frances Farmer,' he said, 'just forget everything I said last night. Okay?' And he hung up.

Alan Williams had written a one-man show for himself, *The Cockroach That Ate Cincinnati*. The central character was in some ways a combination of all the characters Alan had created in the devised plays. Our hero tells us of his passionate obsession with rock 'n' roll and how he believed it would change the world. It didn't and he now feels he has been betrayed. Moreover he has discovered an obscure single recorded by an American band called Remo and the Juggernauts in the late Sixties on the Elektra label. The A-side is an unspectacular version of The Byrds' 'Eight Miles High'; the B-side accurately predicts the future of rock music for the next fifteen years, including optimistically the death of Elton John. Elektra deny any knowledge of the band or the recording. The predictions on the record and a vision in Wolverhampton confirm his destiny as an avenging angel sent to complete the unfinished business of the Sixties. He decides to shoot George Harrison.

The Cockroach was a remarkable piece of work, in which Alan managed to combine zeitgeist conspiracy theory, the unhealthy *Paul is Dead* predilection for deconstructing meaningless pop lyrics, the Manson Family, and Wayne Fontana and the Mindbenders—and this was several years before Mark Chapman shot John Lennon in front of the Dakota building. The character's observations on Bob Dylan were particularly telling:

> In Dylan we were fortunate to find a poet so obsessed with rhyme that meaning went out of the window: a poet that didn't know what he was writing about from one stanza to another—'The ghost of electricity howls in the bones of her face'—totally meaningless—We were lucky to have him!

We did a try-out performance in a lecture room at the ICA as part of the Visionary Theatre Season and a short run at the Bush, where the show became a cult hit and even got enthusiastically reviewed in *Sounds*:

> Hilariously funny and as sharp as the razor that's reduced his hair to a hatcheted uneven fuzz. *The Cockroach* is probably the nearest you'll come to meeting Syd Barrett these days.

Over the next couple of years Alan wrote and performed two sequels: *The Return of the Cockroach* and *The Cockroach has Landed*. We toured them successfully round Britain and Europe, occasionally performing the whole

Cockroach Trilogy on one day. This was a mammoth feat of endurance as each of the shows was ninety minutes long. In 1981 we were invited to the Toronto Festival, where Alan won the Best Performer Award and became so popular that he stayed in Canada for fifteen years. He wrote three more solo shows: *The King of America*, *The White Dogs of Texas* and *Dixieland's Night of Shame*, which made up the *King of America Trilogy*. He became a performing legend and sold out shows the length and breadth of North America, winning universal approbation—except in Vancouver, where he was assaulted in the street for being blasphemous about Dylan. He made two film versions of *The Cockroach* in 1995 and finally got the whole thing out of his system.

The Science Fiction Theatre of Liverpool were also working on a project for the Visionary Theatre Season. Ken Campbell called me up suggesting that I should help out because 'It's going to make everything else look like bollocks'. The event was *The Warp*—the most amazing piece of theatre I have ever been involved in. One day someone will write a book about the whole mad adventure but this is not it. However...

Whilst browsing the Esoterica shelves of Compendium Books one day, Ken heard tales of *Alternative Three*, a publication that revealed the truth behind the secret Russian/American plan to colonise outer space and to evacuate planet Earth. This book was considered to be such conspiratorial hot poop that the publishers, Sphere, had pulped the whole print run and denied any knowledge of its existence. Samizdat copies could, however, be had at a garage in Holloway. Ken discovered that the garage was entirely staffed by Forteans, the spokesman for whom was Neil Oram, a poet, traveller and mystic. *Alternative Three* unfortunately turned out to be a prank, so Ken decided to dramatise Oram's life story instead. From early days as a Fifties Beat poet improvising verse in the House of Sam Widges coffee bar in Soho to becoming a founder of the Findhorn Community in Scotland, Neil had been at the centre of all things alternative. Ken and Neil holed up in a Welsh cottage and five days later emerged with over one thousand pages of what was to become *The Warp*.

The Warp was the chronicle of Phil Masters—a thinly disguised Oram—and his quest to discover his own female consciousness and thus to tap into a higher plane of reality, becoming at one with the cosmos. The journey started in medieval Bavaria and moved swiftly via reincarnation and psychedelics to Colonial Rhodesia, Swinging London, Speakers Corner, Torquay, Revolutionary Paris, Turkey, Syria, Israel, Loch Ness, Yorkshire and the cosmic battleground between Good and Evil. On the way he meets Krishnamurti, King David, Bhagwan Rajneesh, Buckminster Fuller, Several Flying Saucer Folk, François Truffaut,

Ouspensky, The Loch Ness Monster, Heathcote Williams, the Church of Scientology, and Gurdjieff. Needless to say there were also lots of drugs, nudity and fucking.

The idea was that there would be ten plays over ten days at the ICA and on the twelfth day the company would perform all ten. Ken thought that the whole cycle would last ten hours. He was wrong.

Campbell assembled a company drawn from *Illuminatus!* veterans Jim Broadbent, Bill Nighy and John Joyce; experienced actors Helen Cooper, Joolia Cappleman, Steve Williams from the RSC and Dave Hatton from Hull Truck, plus the Campbell irregulars—performers drawn from a vast array of improbable backgrounds including sculptor Mitch Davies, clown Barbara Abrakadabra and her grasshopper circus, Claudia Egypt, the golden whore of Poona, Chris dePiss, Swami Volvo Bus Nisanga, Suzanne Crowley, the great niece of the Great Beast, and George Harvey Webb, who played Buckminster Fuller and the fiddle. Russell Denton, who had been an actor at Bolton when Ken was running the Roadshow, played Phil Masters—a part that turned out to be ten times longer than King Lear. In all fifty actors played more than two hundred parts. There was a band who played everything from South African Swing to a punk version of 'Mr Tambourine Man'.

The whole thing was rehearsed in three weeks in a Scout hut in Kentish Town. I arrived at the end of the second week. It was pretty chaotic. Ken would cast a scene, rehearse it until he was sufficiently entertained and then move on. Sometimes the scene would be rehearsed again but mostly not. Any outbreak of naturalism would be punished with the cry, 'I don't want fucking real. I can get fucking real at home. I want REMARKABLE.' By the end of Week Two nobody could remember who they had played in Week One. I set up a table outside the gents and announced that I was Dialogue Coach. This meant first sorting out actually who was in which scene, what play the scene was in, and if Ken had ruthlessly recast it with someone funnier. Then I tried to explain who the characters were, what they were doing in the play and what on earth they were talking about. It wasn't always easy. I also worked with Russell, who had decided to learn his gargantuan part as one long speech, devising a cueing system based on coughs, nervous twitches and nose-picking by which his fellow actors could tip him off when it was his turn to speak, or to shut up.

The week after Christmas we moved into the ICA. It was snowing. We worked a tag directing system. Everyday I would rehearse scenes in the café and then send them down to Ken who staged them in the theatre. When either of us got bored we would swap or go to the pub. We communicated by appointing a daily runner whose job was to pass on notes and messages and roll the joints. The design concept was that the audience stood in the middle and the action was played out on a series of stages that ran around the walls of the theatre. The sets would be changed as the action moved on. The floor of the theatre was covered with a thick layer of peat. The original plan had been to rent out shooting sticks to the punters who would stick them in the turf and watch the action like toffs at Ascot. The sticks never arrived and the peat housed swarms of vicious gnats, mosquitoes and horse flies disturbed from their hibernation by the stage lighting. They were hell in the nude scenes.

Play One opened on 2 January 1979. The company regularly performed feats of the impossible. On the second day I was rehearsing a long and complicated scene containing twenty pages of obscure Gurdjieff philosophy. The elderly Rep actor playing the part didn't know the lines and didn't have a clue. I sent a message to Ken. The reply came back: 'Sack the cunt and find someone else.' I determined that the first actor to walk through the door would get the part. In walked Bill Nighy. He straight away accepted the task, learnt it in the afternoon and, word perfect, performed the role that very evening in addition to playing the Chinese Ambassador and a comic policeman.

Next day we had a visit from the high-powered lawyers for the Church of Scientology, who had got wind that the play included an accurate dramatisation of their 'auditing' practices and highlighted their belief in aliens. They came armed with an injunction to stop the show that night. Neil, who had been through their entire psychic rigmarole and knew that the play told the truth, refused to give way, suggesting politely that they should fuck off. The whole day was spent in heated negotiations over a mung bean salad in the ICA canteen. Ken ran rings around them. Possibly they believed that he too was an alien. In the end the Scientologists gave up in exchange for a few minor script changes and a programme note stating that the play was not intended to be an accurate representation of their spiritual procedures. Which it most definitely was.

The full cycle was first performed on the weekend of 18—19 January. The show started at 10:45 on the morning of the 18th and the bemused spectators and cast staggered out into the snow at 8 in the morning of the 19th. Russell Denton had been on stage for over eighteen hours, excluding a couple of one-hour meal breaks, a half-hour beer break and a pause when he went for a shit in Play Seven, leaving the Syrian Customs Officers to fill in with an improvised ethnic dance routine. Ken supervised the entertainment from the lighting box, occasionally blacking out any scene or actor that bored him.

There had never been a performance like it, and there were many remarkable deeds performed. Here are just a few of them:

Jim Broadbent, wearing a shoulder-length wig, playing Dutch vegan hippy Bob God, whose mantra was 'If you chew well, you screw well.'

Steve Williams as Rimmie taking his first acid trip while eating a full English breakfast. Rimmie pours a bottle of ketchup in his eye, uses a fried egg as a powder puff, inhales baked beans up his nose and blows them out again and finally sticks the sausage in his pants.

Steve also played a gobby parrot.

Helen Cooper playing François Truffaut.

Neil Oram spontaneously taking over from Russell to play himself in a sequence where he makes an impossible journey smuggling dope across Paris in the middle of the 1968 riots.

Man mountain Bunny Reid as King David, the Tramp who wandered the West End believing that he kept planes in the air by mind control, eating a huge raw onion and taking a piss.

The arrival at four in the morning of a minibus carrying the entire Haverstock Hill ashram of the followers of Bhagwan Rajneesh to participate as extras in the Poona sequences.

The Grasshopper Circus.

The Warp went on to the Roundhouse, a disused cinema on the Edinburgh Fringe, Germany and the Liverpool Everyman Theatre, where Ken had taken over briefly as Artistic Director. After the final performance Russell Denton gave up acting and became a gardener. There were no mountains left to climb. Ken revived the show twenty years later with his daughter Daisy playing Phil Masters. As critic Michael Coveney famously declared:

From now on the world will be divided between those who have lived through *The Warp* and those who have not.

The show was a total celebration of life. Some of it was brilliant and some of it was truly terrible. It was sexy and chaotic, profound and profane, and confirmed Ken as a visionary magician and impresario capable of inspiring his performers to achieve the impossible. A true genius who stood head and shoulders above the overhyped theatrical pygmies of today.

In addition to all this activity Barry Nettleton and I had decided to open our own theatre in Hull. In the spirit of Stratford East we wanted a theatre that would present the best new writing while being both provocative and entertaining. We even contemplated the occasional classical revival. The company would continue to tour, but we would also produce in our home base. Through local docker/playwright Dave Marson we got an entrée with East Hull MP John Prescott. Marson and Prescott had been at Ruskin College, Oxford together. Marson's analysis of Prescott proved to be perspicacious: 'He may be a thick cunt but he might be Prime Minister one day.'

With Prescott on board we negotiated a peppercorn 99-year lease on a disused listed Georgian grain warehouse in the Old Town down by the river, almost next door to our rehearsal rooms. Hull was about to embark on its Eighties programme of gentrification. The building was much too big for us, but we got carried away with our own ambition and came up with a scheme that incorporated a 214-seat theatre, a 180-seat cinema, studio workshops for local artists and community organisations, plus a restaurant and a bar where doubtlessly we imagined performing iconoclastic late-night alterative cabaret to the appreciative folks of North Humberside. We engaged an architect, who drew up plans and made a model. We signed up Hull trouser-dropping farceur Brian Rix to head up the £750,000 Appeal Fund and we launched the whole thing at a grandiose event in the Lyttelton foyer of the National Theatre with a rousing speech from Shadow Arts Minister Andrew Faulds. For twenty-five quid you could become a Hull Truck Angel. In exchange you got a shite ceramic badge, and your name would be permanently recorded on the Roll of Honour in the foyer. We raised fuck all.

In the summer of 1979 I put together a company to work on a new devised piece. I recruited John Blanchard from *The Dalkey Archive*, and Bridget Ashburn from *The New Garbo*. Mark Brignal, Hamish Reid and Rosalind March came through an intensive workshop process. Stephen Warbeck, who was musical director as well as being an actor, I had known from his work with Bubble Theatre. Fran Brookes was a complete discovery. A year earlier I had done a post-show discussion after a performance at the Chapter Theatre in Cardiff. The whole thing was extremely tedious, although I remember a heated discussion with a couple of Nigerian postgrad students who claimed that there was no homosexuality in Africa. At the end I asked for questions and a cheeky girl put her hand up and asked how you got a job with Hull Truck. I gave her our address and told her to write in next time we advertised for actors. She did, so I auditioned her. It was obvious that she had a special talent, although she did lie about playing the violin. Nonetheless I gave her first job. When she joined Equity she changed her name to Frances Barber.

Such was the reputation of the company and the thirst from the bookers for a new devised play that we were able to book a whole seven-month tour in advance, starting at the Traverse for the Edinburgh Festival and ending up in Derby via a month at the Bush, three weeks in Hull and gigs in Birmingham, Newcastle, Lincoln, Cardiff, York, Sheffield, Belfast, Bradford, York, Loughborough, Sunderland and Milton Keynes.

For the first time I had a company with ages ranging from twenty-two to sixty, so I was able to explore the generational divide, or so I thought. My theme was Education, and my central idea was that those who teach are not necessarily any more emotionally continent than those whom they are teaching. It would also involve the fading embers of Sixties utopianism dying out in a provincial university. We started out as usual, building characters.

John Blanchard was Tony, a recently widowed academic who taught French Literature at Hull University. He has one daughter, Monica, played by Bridget Ashburn, who works in London in publishing and is married with a young family. Mark Brignal played Alan, deputy headmaster of a local comprehensive school. He is married to Sarah, played by Rosalind March. They met at teacher-training college in the mid-Sixties and have been married for twelve years. They have no children. Alan still plays at the local folk club.

Stephen Warbeck was Martin, a young political science tutor and colleague of Tony's who lectures on *les événements soixante-huit* despite having been at public school at the time. Frances Barber and Hamish Reid were his two students: Kath, a romantic Trotskyite, and Hugh who was a Scottish Nationalist.

John and Bridget had the difficult task of creating a shared backstory that included inventing the character of Tony's wife and Monica's mother, the circumstances of their lives together and the nature of her recent death. We spent some time investigating the idea that the family might be Christian Scientists but in the end could not make it stick. They invented a cottage in Brittany instead. We sequestered a room at the University, and John and Stephen researched and gave lectures in character. Stephen decided that Martin also ran the local *cercle Français*.

I set up the first meeting between characters Kath and Hugh at a Freshers' Disco constructed in the rehearsal room in High Street. It was a disaster. They obviously hated each other: the whole thing ended in a row after about two minutes. I needed to get the characters together in some way, so I set up the improvisation again. This time I turned the music up so loud that they couldn't hear each other speak. They ended up dancing and became mates. Exactly as it would have been at the real Freshers' Disco.

I decided to call the play *Ooh La La!* I liked the idea of it sounding like a risqué French farce when it was unlikely to be anything of the kind.

At the same time as we worked on creating the play we started working on music. We had had many requests to bring back the *Melody Bandbox Rhythm Roadshow*, so I decided that the new cabaret would be along the same lines but with a nautical theme. It was to be called *SHIP AHOY!*:

> You'll be swinging to starboard and grooving on the poop
> when those saucy songsters with the nautical air heave to in
> your port of call.

> All your chums from the *Melody Bandbox* have signed on for a
> cruise in the Med, so there's gonna be fun in the sun as you
> travel the globe humming your glum times away.

> (*Etc., etc., etc...*)

As usual, the idea was to rehearse *Ooh La La!* in the daytime and work on music in the evenings, gradually putting together the set that would form the basis of the cabaret. Also as usual, I wanted to do a couple of unannounced gigs in local pubs to get the company used to performing together. For the first time in the history of the company this became a problem. A couple of company members who had been working in a more conventional Rep set-up decided that they had to be paid overtime for what they considered to be extra music rehearsals.

Having just finished working on *The Warp*, where fifty actors worked twenty-four hours a day for a couple of months for little more than their bus fare, I thought this was a bit rich. Barry and I were cast in the role of exploitative management. It ran counter to all the principles that Hull Truck had been founded on. It was not a good omen. We didn't have the money to pay overtime anyway so the music was under-rehearsed. The try-out gigs were pretty much a shambles although Warbeck entirely embraced the spirit of the notion, enthusiastically sitting in on piano with the real life Humberside Stompers at the local jazz club.

Back in the rehearsal room the story of the play had evolved...

There were three groups of characters: Tony and Monica, Alan and Sarah, Hugh and Kath. They were all linked together by the interventions of Lothario, Martin, who beds both Kath and Sarah. In the end Alan and Sarah split up, Monica confronts the truth about her past, and Hugh and Kath decide they hate each other after all.

Stephen Warbeck wrote all the music except for Alan's sensitive and maudlin folk ballad about his lost love, which Mark Brignal wrote himself. Someone described the style as being a cross between Weill and Satie and I think that's pretty accurate although I would put Jacques Brel on the list.

MARTIN'S SONG

I first went to Paris in '71
Camus in my rucksack—*L'Étranger*
Thought I was committed, grew my hair at school
But Prefects don't have guns—CRS
Sitting on the Right Bank I was dreaming of the Left
Days of May in mind my feet were getting wet
Jean Claude was a Maoist and his friend was reading History at
    St-Denis
Buñuel's *Exterminating Angel* was the film that we all went to see
Paris—*L'Amour*
Paris—*Tristesse*
Paris—*Au Revoir*

Ooh La La! opened at the Traverse on 4 September. The senior reviewer from the *Scotsman*, who had never seen the company before, hated it, particularly Hugh's Scottish Nationalist rant. Hamish went down to the newspaper's office intent on beating him up, but was fortunately denied admission. Despite this the show sold out.

The play was too long and too slow and occasionally self-indulgent, and I worked at tightening it up on the road. We also sold out for three weeks at the Humberside Theatre in Hull, where we had finally become accepted. The *Hull Daily Mail* said that 'it leaves you feeling that you have seen too much of your best friend's private life'.

We opened at the Bush in January 1980. Although there were still qualms about the devising technique, the critics mostly understood what we were up too and took the play seriously:

'Quite the best play on contemporary themes in the last six months. It knocks the West End into a cocked hat.'

(James Fenton, *Sunday Times*)

'Shot through with the marvellous Hull Truck mixture of sharp observation and delicate parody.'

(*The Listener*)

'Scenes of sexual and intellectual confusion are played with an extraordinary capacity for charging social stereotypes with an intensely personal subtext.'

(Irving Wardle, *The Times*)

All the critics rightly praised Frankie Barber for her performance as Kath, and she was nominated for Best Newcomer in the London Critics' Awards.

John Barber in the *Telegraph* moaned about lack of plot and thought that the songs were a mistake. Victoria Radin in the *Observer* decided that here, if it was anywhere, was the new British musical.

Personally I thought that we were lucky to get away with *Ooh La La!*

The father-and-daughter subplot between Tony and Monica was pretty bogus. The actors had failed to engage with each other, so I had had to make most of it up, and as such it felt inorganic. John Elsom in the *Listener* thought that the episode had 'something of the subtlety of a Henry James story' so it just goes to show there's no accounting for taste. The show continued on the road until the end of March.

It had not been the happiest tour. *SHIP AHOY!* had capsized early on. Mark Brignal was playing the lubricious compere, Dennis Cream, a cross between Des O'Connor and Archie Rice. On the day of the first performance some of the company decided that Dennis's jokes were too sexist. I pointed out that this was entirely the point, but alas to no avail. God knows what they would have made of *The Macintosh Cabaret*, Reggie Cleethorpes and the Rape of the Sabine Women. Mark and I rewrote the whole routine in a motorway service station from a couple of kids' joke books we had bought in the garage. It was hardly cutting-edge. Similarly we had had to cancel our booking at Queen's University in Belfast, as it was perceived by some company members as tantamount to entertaining the troops. I went off to devise a play for BBC Pebble Mill.

Over the previous couple of years I had spent many a merry evening travelling between Harwich and the Hook of Holland on the midnight ferry. I had commuted between *Bridget's House* in Amsterdam and *The Fosdyke Saga* at the Bush, and *Fosdyke Two*—the tripe sequel—had done a Dutch tour. Every voyage was packed with surreal drunken incident, and I thought the trip would make an ideal background for an improvised television play. I persuaded BBC TV producer W. Stephen Gilbert to take the journey himself, and he had such a merry time too that he commissioned the play. I had a budget for four central characters, half a dozen subsidiary characters, five weeks' rehearsal and a cast research trip to Amsterdam, returning on the night boat.

Months earlier I had roped in Jim Broadbent and Phil Jackson, and we had created a couple of characters, Stewart and Clive, who came from Retford. They were old schoolmates who had grown up together. Clive had inherited his father's garage business that was going bust and Stewart was the youngest Co-op White Goods Department Manager in the

East Midlands. Both were now married with kids. Clive wins a trip to Amsterdam in a Rotary Club raffle. His wife doesn't want to go, so he and Stewart set off on a dirty weekend.

Helen Cooper from *The Warp* came on board as Nelleke, a nutty Dutch art student on her way to London to participate in an EST course. EST— Erhard Seminars Training—was a self-improvement psychotherapy craze prevalent at the time. It involved paying two hundred quid to spend forty-eight hours in a central London hotel hyperventilating while being denied food, water or the use of a lavatory. Chris Fairbank from *Illuminatus!* played Billy, a pissed-up squaddie from Liverpool with a broken ankle, on his way to spend his leave with his auntie in Speke.

We worked on the background of the characters for a couple of weeks in Birmingham, then we went off on the recce. The idea was that the actors spent a night and a day wandering around Amsterdam in costume and character and then came back on the boat. We would not actually improvise on the return journey, but the experience would provide material we could feed into the improvisations back at Pebble Mill. We were accompanied by an understandably nervous BBC first assistant clutching a wad of BBC guilders.

After checking into the American Hotel the cast set off on their adventures. Phil and Jim decided that Clive and Stewart would head for the Red Light district. Outside a club we saw a neon sign that read 'VERY GOOD LIVE FUCKING SHOW', so the BBC man forked out the guilders and in we went. Clive and Stewart got a seat at the front. I skulked at the back with my notebook. All went well as we sat down to enjoy a particularly gymnastic bout of coupling between a doctor and a nurse. Suddenly Jim stood up and gestured to cut the improvisation and to come out of character. I rushed over.

'I'm sorry,' said Jim, 'but I just can't carry on.' I imagined that he had been offended or traumatised in some way. 'It's not that,' said Jim, pointing at the impaled nurse. 'It's just that I was at LAMDA with her...'

Stewart and Clive continued their wanderings around the Red Light district ending up in a Country and Western Bar. Stewart went home to bed. Phil and I decided that Clive would probably have gone with a girl from a window but 'didn't do the job properly'. Fairbank as Billy spent the night drinking with a load of squaddies and ended up falling in a canal. Helen Cooper went to the art college and spoke Dutch. Next day Stewart and Clive went souvenir shopping for clogs and windmills. Billy nursed his hangover with several hairs of the dog, and Helen went to the art college and spoke some more Dutch.

Back in Birmingham I worked with the actors who would play the smaller parts. Kenneth MacDonald from *It Ain't Half Hot Mum* was the barman. Steve Williams, who ate Rimmie's psychedelic breakfast in *The Warp*, was a grumpy sanyasin. Eric Richard from *The Bill* was a builder on his way home from Düsseldorf. Pippa Sparkes was Carrie, a lonely au pair. And Eric Allan from *Bleak Moments* worked at a Yorkshire racehorse stables.

We recreated the whole bar and disco area of the boat in the top floor cafeteria at Pebble Mill. We stocked the bar with booze. The improvisation started at midnight and ran all night.

Clive and Stewart set up camp in the empty disco. They haven't booked a cabin so are planning to stretch out a bit later. Nelleke arrives, and they try to chat her up. Stewart dances with her to the Bee Gees' 'Stayin' Alive'. Drunken Billy arrives and nearly gets into a fight with Clive but apologises, and reluctantly they allow him to join their table. Billy tries to get off with Nelleke. As the long night progresses they discuss their jobs, their lives, their wives, Kandinsky, Skoda, Lawrie McMenemy and the uncomfortable silence between the cradle and the grave. Clive thinks he has caught a dose, and Stewart asks Nelleke to send him a postcard: Stewart Britton, Co-operative Department Store, Retford, Notts.

Nothing much happened except life itself.

We spent a fortnight distilling, cutting and shaping the fifty-minute play and recorded it over three days in the BBC studios. It's still one of the best things I have done. *Games Without Frontiers* was broadcast on a Saturday night at 9 pm on BBC 2 after the FA Cup Final. One would doubt the likelihood of a single drama being afforded such a prime slot today, let alone a devised one. The BBC wiped the tape. West Ham beat Arsenal one-nil.

I was shagged out after devising two projects in less than a year, so I decided to concentrate on scripted work again. The next season Hull Truck toured two new plays: *Mean Streaks* by Alan Williams and *The Day War Broke Out* by Peter Tinniswood.

Mean Streaks is set in a holiday chalet in Morecambe. Norman Usher, an unsuccessful petty criminal from Manchester takes his ex-singer girlfriend Phoebe and his retarded twenty-three-year-old brother Frank for an October holiday on the glamorous Lancashire Riviera. They take along nerdy Laurence as Frank's companion/carer. Laurence had to sleep in a sleeping bag in the kitchenette. Alan himself played Norman, Arbel Jones played Phoebe, Malcolm Sherman played Frank, and Chris Jury played Laurence. It rains the whole week and the sad quartet are stuck in the holiday chalet playing endless games of Monopoly and bickering. Hell is other people. Norman bullies Phoebe. Norman bullies Laurence. Norman fails to sell a car-bootful of bootleg David Bowie albums and dreams of holidaying in New Orleans. Laurence, a Dungeons and Dragons devotee, claims that he has friends in Nuneaton. He tells Frank of his many adventures in the Kingdom of Thwoth. His character is an elf called Braxalotl. Frank wants to be a dwarf called Elvis. Phoebe has a go at Frank. Frank has a panic attack. Laurence gets the blame and is sent packing, but not before wheedling money out of both Phoebe and Norman.

Alan and I worked with the actors on building characters in exactly the same way as we had done in the devised plays and ideas, dialogue and detail unearthed during the process were incorporated in the final draft. I thought it was a terrific play. Nobody else did though.

We opened at Edinburgh, where in our usual spirit of cavalier entrepreneurism we had decided to run our own Festival venue. In partnership with Actors Touring Company we had hired a church hall some way out of the centre of town. We had a marquee with a bar and café, organised our own box office and ran shows day and night. In many ways this was the precursor of the Pleasance, the Gilded Balloon and the Assembly Rooms. We lost a fortune.

The critics didn't like the characters or the story, and, although the play sold well on the road, the audiences that we had built up for the devised work couldn't get their head around the fact that we were trying something new. Alan had written a play about what came to be known as 'the underclass' in a way that was neither patronising nor sentimental, and as such it should have been celebrated. *Mean Streaks* was taken off after two performances at the Scunthorpe Civic Theatre. The *Evening Telegraph* proclaimed:

> Surely local man Mike Bradwell should have known that such profanity and the baiting of an unfortunate spastic was not suitable fare for the workaday folk of Scunthorpe.

It was great to be back.

I had met Peter Tinniswood a couple of years earlier when I had persuaded Jenny Topper at the Bush to commission a Christmas show from him. We were looking for a quirky and compelling seasonal entertainment that would become the successor to the enormously popular *Fosdyke Sagas*. I had been a big fan of Tinniswood's since reading *A Touch of Daniel* and the Brandon trilogy of novels that Peter then adapted into the innovatory TV sit-com *I Didn't Know You Cared*, a series that prefigured *The Royle Family* by several decades. Peter had come up with *Wilfred*, in which Philip Jackson memorably metamorphosed into a full-size French poodle. It was a big hit and I wanted to do more work with Tinniswood.

While working on *Games Without Frontiers* at Pebble Mill I had approached David Rose with the suggestion of commissioning Peter to simultaneously write a stage play for Hull Truck and a television version of the same play for the BBC. It was a bit cheeky, but everyone had had such a merry time on *Games* that he agreed. I then went to Peter James, running the Crucible Theatre in Sheffield (Tinniswood's home town), and suggested a co-production of the stage version between Hull Truck and the Crucible. This is how it worked: we would rehearse the stage version for four weeks in Sheffield before opening the show there. After the Sheffield run we would head off to Birmingham where we would rehearse and record the TV version. We would then take the show on the road for a couple of months, culminating in four weeks at the Bush. The TV version of the play would be broadcast on the evening of the last performance in London, again in the prime-time Saturday-night BBC Playhouse slot.

Peter Tinniswood and I shared a love of music hall and variety and had endless discussions about the relative merits of Bob and Alf Pearson, Elsie and Doris Waters, Nat Jackley and the like. It therefore came as no surprise that Peter decided to set his play in the backstage world of a seedy second-rate touring nostalgia show presenting tribute impressions of long-dead variety turns. A bit like the *Melody Bandbox Rhythm Roadshow*, really.

The Day War Broke Out centred on Rob Wilton impersonator Albie and his wife, fellow impressionist and stooge Carla. The other character in the piece was the show's lubricious manager and Albie's boss, Reg Atack. Kenneth MacDonald played Albie, Dee Anderson played Carla, and David Hatton—back in the Truck again—played Atack. All the action took place in the dressing room during and between shows. As in most of Tinniswood's work, the play was about fantasy and reality, and the characters swapped roles and impersonated each other, exposing the truth and lies behind their various relationships. In the end the audience is unsure about what has been real and what has been imaginary. And of course the whole thing has been imaginary. The BBC became energised about a sequence in which Albie, impersonating Carla, is sexually assaulted by Atack, who is after a bit of illicit humpo, but David Rose convinced the higher powers that it was artistically kosher, so we got away with it.

The TV version included scenes recorded in front of an audience of pensioners in the Palace Theatre, Redditch. This gave us the opportunity to immortalise Dave Hatton's spirited version of 'I've Never Wronged an Onion' and to include Rob Wilton's aside to G.H. Elliott, the Chocolate Coloured Coon: 'Hardly worth blacking up for, mate.'

One of the OAP extras had himself been a variety artiste. As Uncle Windy he had performed a speciality balloon-sculpture act and during breaks in filming entertained the crew by making pornographic balloon dolls with unfeasibly exaggerated privates.

At the end of the tour of *The Day War Broke Out* I decided that I would take a sabbatical year at the end of the next season. I had run out of steam. Our audiences and bookers, although appreciating the scripted plays, constantly demanded new devised product and I had no new ideas. In *Ooh La La!* I felt I was repeating myself. I was also fed up with being constantly on the road. My house in Hull had been burgled three times in the last year when I was away. The truth of the matter was that I was equally fed up of living in Hull. My house, which I had bought for £800 out of the TV money, was scheduled for demolition, so I had let it go to seed. The residents of the neighbourhood were all keen to be shipped out to faceless satellite ghettos with a promise of improved sanitation. There were, however, a couple of locals who wanted to stay and who wanted the Victorian terraces to be preserved. There was a meeting at the Guildhall so I went along. The local barber got up and made an impassioned speech about preserving the community. He was howled down and physically attacked by a group of women who erroneously believed that his intervention would prejudice their move to the rural bliss of Orchard Park Estate. They kicked him as he fell. He had a heart attack and died on the floor of the Guildhall. When I remonstrated with the leading harridan she spat at me shouting, 'Get your fucking priorities right; clean your fucking windows!'

The plans for our own theatre had also hit the rocks. The local council had annexed our warehouse scheme and come up with an even more grandiose plan of their own for a two-million-quid arts complex including a 600-seat theatre and a conference hall. Fuck knows what they planned to do with it, but it was no longer a scheme that had any relevance to what we had envisaged. Meanwhile, the 150-seat Humberside Theatre, which would have been an ideal venue, lurched on from financial crisis to financial crisis with no discernible artistic policy whatsoever. Reluctantly we pulled out of the project. We had spent fifteen grand of our own money on it, and the council tried to charge us a further fifty grand for what they described as necessary renovation work. Hull Truck had come a long way in ten years, but we had certainly lost most of the pioneering zeal of the early days. Despite best efforts we had become a management, with all the administrative red tape and bullshit that goes with it. We may still have been regarded as a fringe company, but we were the acceptable face of the fringe, and as such were perilously close to becoming the Establishment.

I planned the tenth birthday season and set off for Toronto with Alan Williams and the *Cockroach Trilogy*.

The Cockroach was the hit of the Toronto Festival, winning several awards. The show transferred to a bigger venue and the run was extended by three weeks and then a further three weeks. In Toronto I met up with British director Pam Brighton, who had just quit at Stratford, Ontario, and had been running the Toronto Free Theatre. I asked her if she would like to take over Hull Truck for a year, and she accepted. I left Alan in Canada and went off to California on a road trip with my girlfriend. It was there I decided that the whole sabbatical idea was a cop-out. What I really wanted to do was to leave the company altogether. I phoned Barry from a payphone in a motel outside San Diego. We decided to keep it a secret.

Back in England we began work on Alan Williams's new play *Dwygyfylchi*. For the first time we rehearsed in London where all the company were based, as indeed was I, my vandalised house in Hull now having been demolished to build a car park. There were two main problems with Alan's piece. The first was that nobody understood or could even pronounce the title, which was the name of the Welsh village in which the play was set. The second and more pressing problem was that the script was in early draft stage as Alan had been preoccupied with becoming a comedy icon in Southern Ontario. We changed the title to *In Dreams* and decided to fix the script in rehearsal.

After initial work in London we moved to Dwygyfylchi, where we took over the Glynywrog Guest House, working on character background and improvising on location while Alan wrote the script. During our Welsh retreat Prince Charles married Lady Di and there was a bonfire. Chris Jury wandered the hills drunk, and in character and frock coat, and saw a ghost.

We opened *In Dreams* at the Liverpool Everyman and then went on the road playing the Tricycle in London, a bunch of regional dates and ending up at the Battersea Arts Centre. There was some great writing and excellent acting in *In Dreams*, but the show never entirely gelled and could not be counted as a major triumph. A couple of years later Alan rewrote the play and produced it at the Prairie Theatre Exchange, where it was a popular success with the theatregoers of Winnipeg.

While *In Dreams* was on tour I started work on *Still Crazy After All These Years*, my last devised play for Hull Truck. I wanted to do a play set in London, and I wanted to do a play about the hip London media. I went to Jenny Topper and Simon Stokes at the Bush, and we decided on a co-production between the two companies. We would rehearse the play for twelve weeks in London, open at the Bush at Christmas and then tour until April. Instead of a formal rehearsal room we hired a furnished flat not far from the theatre in gentrified Hammersmith Grove, which gave us two bedrooms, a living room, a pine kitchen and a bathroom with a bidet to play about in.

I decided on a four-hander and I decided that we wouldn't use music, although in a way we did. I cast Roger Davidson, Thirzie Robinson from *Illuminatus!*, Helen Cooper from *Games Without Frontiers* and Jonathan Kydd, who had recently left Hull University Drama Department and who I had seen in an Edinburgh revue singing a pastiche music-hall song called 'The Yodelling Dog Boiler'. Designer Geoff Rose, who also designed *Ooh La La!*, was in rehearsal from day one.

I gave the actors the brief of coming up with characters who could be involved in some way with contemporary metropolitan media culture. Eventually we decided that Roger would play a rock journalist, Thirzie would be a painter, Helen would be a fashionista, and Jonathan would be a would-be rock star specialising in synthesiser pop. We set about building characters and researching the London scene. Roger became Nick, a public schoolboy from Sheffield who got sent to Stowe because his parents moved to Germany. He goes to Bristol University, where he meets Thirzie's hippy-dippy character Libby. They get married with a Hare Krishna ceremony in a field. Libby goes to Camberwell School of Art where she meets Maddie, Helen Cooper's eccentric French art student. Jonathan played Alex Tyle, a Wykehamist with a private income who sells his uncle's Picasso to finance his recording career

On 29 November, halfway through rehearsals, we held a Hull Truck tenth birthday party at the Lyric Theatre in Hammersmith. We didn't have it in Hull as by now most of the people who had worked with us had gravitated to the Metropolis. It was a raucous and fashionable evening enjoyed by the great, the good and numerous stars of showbiz. There were two bands and David Hare was cloakroom attendant. I announced my resignation and introduced Pam Brighton who in turn announced that she was going to produce *Diary of a Hunger Striker* by Peter Sheridan—a play about Bobbie Sands. Things were certainly going to be different...

Back in the rehearsal room the *Still Crazy* story evolved.

Nick has become a music producer for the BBC recruiting bands for *The Old Grey Whistle Test* and the *John Peel Sessions*. Libby has put her artistic aspirations on hold as she brings up two-year-old Barnaby with help from a Buddhist nanny. They live in stylish dope-smoking affluence on Primrose Hill in a house crammed with the detritus of contemporary design. Helen's character, Maddie, has set up her own fashion design business and is preparing to launch her collection based on roman togas. Alex Tyle (Jonathan) is preparing to release his single on his own label, Reptyle Records. He has made a promo video in which he dances like a robot in a Johnson and Johnson suit and shoots an inflatable dummy of Paul McCartney in celebration of the new music. We made the video for twelve quid with students from the Royal College of Art. We discover that Nick and Maddie have been having an affair for years and that Libby does not know. Alex comes round to Primrose Hill and shows Nick his dreadful promo in the hope of getting included in Nick's new music documentary. Nick counters by playing Dylan's 'Visions of Johanna' with the memorable 'ghost of electricity' lyric.

The entire second half of *Still Crazy After All These Years* was based on one master improvisation. It was the first time in ten weeks that Jonathan Kydd had met any of the other actors. The story of the breakdown of Nick and Libby's marriage was told mainly in subplot. The actual dénouement, when Libby learnt of Nick's affair, was wordless, conveyed entirely by an exchange of looks between the characters. In the final analysis it was a play about the loss of ideals, selling out, the creeping terror of domesticity, crap music and Thatcherism. And about leaving Hull Truck.

We opened at the Bush on 18 December 1981, exactly ten years since arriving in Coltman Street for the first time. The entire run at the Bush sold out in advance, and the London glitterati turned out in force. They all thought it was about them, and in a way they were right. Rock legend Dave Edmunds turned up wearing exactly the same pair of Robot shoes as Jonathan's character, Alex, wore in the play, and several BBC couples claimed that Geoff Rose's painfully accurate set was based on their flats.

The press sort of liked it. There was the usual 'lack of plot' guff and questions about the working method, and a general feeling that chronicling the foibles of trendy NW1 media folk was like shooting fish in a barrel. They mostly missed the bigger picture.

> '*Still Crazy* is witty, sad and affectionate about people who grew up in the Now Generation finding that it's later than they think. Not a gesture is forced; not a line of dialogue. It is a model of how a small play can be a great deal bigger than most in the West End.'
>
> (*Evening Standard*)

> 'Acted with such superlative truthfulness; four lovely performances. You won't find many better ensembles anywhere. The play is a fine testament to Bradwell's truth-digging decade with Hull Truck.'
>
> (Michael Billington, *Guardian*)

'Where Mr Bradwell goes next I don't know, and neither I believe does he; but he has behind him ten years of the richest, sharpest and funniest work in British theatre.'

(Robert Cushman, *Observer*)

The show went on the road and sold well, although we still had occasional problems with the content; I was attacked at a Q and A in Bristol about drugs and swearing. *Still Crazy* returned to the Bush for another sell-out run in April and that was that.

After the last performance everybody went to the Ajanta on Goldhawk Road for a curry. Pam Brighton, Peter Sheridan and some of *The Diary of a Hunger Striker* team came too. They had been to see our show and hated it. The evening ended in a fight when Geoff Rose told a particularly graphic joke involving an Irishman having anal sex with a gorilla. What a very long and very strange trip it had been.

In fact *Hunger Striker* became a big hit and played the Roundhouse successfully but, despite the company moving into Humberside Theatre when Lincolnshire and Humberside Arts booted out the incumbents, Pam decided that Hull Truck was not her scene and quit after a year. Barry Nettleton and I headhunted John Godber, whose work I had first seen at the National Student Drama Festival when he was at Bretton Hall College of Education.

A couple of years later when Godber's own *Up and Under* and *Bouncers* were the talk of the town, John was invited to appear on the *Terry Wogan Show*. Wogan asked him what sort of plays Hull Truck performed. 'I just want to do plays me Mam and Dad would like,' said Godber.

I never went back.

In April 2009 Hull Truck opened a brand-new £15 million glass-and-steel theatre on the site of the old Yorkshire Electricity Board building on Ferensway. The project was paid for by the Arts Council and the European Regional Development Fund. The complex boasts a 440-seat main auditorium, a 134-seat studio theatre, a rehearsal space, an education space, offices, a green room, extensive workshop space, several bars, a café/restaurant and corporate entertainment facilities, where business customers, looking for new ways to raise their profile and promote their brand, are afforded the opportunity to impress their clients in Hull's new home of theatrical discovery and innovation. There are two Artistic Directors, an Associate Director, a General Manager, an Administrator, a Touring Coordinator, a Development Coordinator, a Financial Controller, two Financial Officers, an Education Manager, an Education Assistant, an Education Intern, a Manager of Marketing and Sales, a Marketing Officer, a Marketing Officer (press/PR), a

Marketing/Press and PR Assistant, a Sales Manager, a Theatre Manager, two Duty Managers and countless others. They are currently recruiting a Chief Executive Officer at a salary of £60,000 a year. I hope that together they may long continue to provide popular and provocative entertainment to the workaday folk of North Humberside.

Fell in love with a fan heater
Fell in love today
Fell in love with a fan heater
But it blew away...

8

Moving Swiftly On

For the next twelve years I worked as a freelance director and writer in theatre, film, television and radio. These are some of the things I did.

Immediately after leaving Hull Truck I directed a touring version of *The Night They Raided Minsky's* for the New Vic Company and went to Japan as part of something called the TOYP Conference organised by the Osaka Junior Chamber of Commerce. TOYP stands for Ten Outstanding Young People. I was England. When I got to Tokyo I discovered that I had been sponsored by Margaret Thatcher. It was all a ghastly mistake. The other Outstandings were international businessmen and corporate executives, except for the editor of the *Christian Science Monitor*. I gave a lecture on skinheads, went to the Sumo fights with the Canadian Ambassador, spent a night in a Buddhist monastery run by a gay Texan, and met the Crown Prince and Princess, now the Emperor and Empress. On my return I directed Doug Lucie's *Hard Feelings*—a play about a bunch of Oxford graduates living in Brixton and managing to ignore the Brixton riots outside. *Hard Feelings* started out as a tour for Oxford Playhouse and then transferred to the Bush. We then made a television version for BBC TV's *Play for Today*. The excellent cast throughout were Frances Barber, Chris Jury, Di Katis, Jennifer Landor, Ian Reddington and Stephen Tiller.

I then directed Dusty Hughes's *Bad Language* for Hampstead Theatre— a play about sex and post-structuralism at Cambridge. Alan Rickman, Prunella Gee and Kevin Whately were in the cast as well as Robin Lermitte, who now reads the weather report on television. At the Bush I directed Terry Johnson's *Unsuitable for Adults*, set in the world of alternative cabaret with Joanne Pearce, Tim McInnerny, Felicity Montagu and

Saul Jephcott as a useless escapologist. I then became part of the Almeida Theatre Company.

The Almeida was started by Pierre Audi, who had been at Oxford with Doug Lucie and Mia Soteriou. Pierre had discovered the abandoned medical institute and carnival novelty factory in Islington a couple of years earlier, and I went with him to see it. We had to crawl in through a broken window. In 1984 the company of directors, designers, actors and writers mounted two productions. The first was a remarkably silly version of *Hedda Gabler*, in which I was grossly miscast as Eilert Lovborg. The whole experience was so dreadful that I decided never to act again. I then directed the second show, Helen Cooper's *Mrs Gauguin*, which told the story of Gauguin's wife, the indomitable and Danish Mette Gad. With designers Tom Cairns and Anthony McDonald we created a Nordic water-world of showers and rain and steam diametrically opposed to Gauguin's more sumptuous palette, and the whole production, with music by David Owen, became a remarkable piece of poetic and visual theatre. Rachel Bell from Hull Truck played Mette and Don Sumpter played Gauguin. Paul Jesson played Emile Schuffenecker.

In 1984 Max Stafford-Clark asked me to become Associate Director at the Royal Court. To this day I have no idea why, as our styles of directing are a million miles apart. Max enticed me to join with the prospect of *Tom and Viv* by Michael Hastings or *Aunt Dan and Lemon* by Wallace Shawn. Inevitably Max directed both these shows himself, and I got *An Honourable Trade* by G.F. Newman and *Susan's Breasts* by Jonathan Gems. Gordon Newman's play was an almost Jacobean political satire loosely inspired by the Cecil Parkinson affair and an unfortunate incident allegedly involving the then Home Secretary, Sir Leon Brittan. Margaret Thatcher appeared as a character, and Richard Wilson played an MP who is booted into the House of Lords after an affair with an underage schoolgirl. There was a great deal of fuss about the content of the show, Max was threatened by the Chair of the Board, and we sought legal advice from Michael Mansfield QC. Mansfield said that it was borderline, but that the Tories would look utterly foolish if they decided to take out an injunction. At the first preview the stalls were stuffed with lawyers from the DPP, but we never heard a thing. Whatever impact the show might have had was effectively annulled when, on press night, the IRA bombed the Grand Hotel in Brighton in an attempt to assassinate Thatcher and her cabinet thus rendering our puny theatrical squib irrelevant.

Jonathan Gems described *Susan's Breasts* as a pharmaceutical comedy. It revolved around a group of fashionable amoral modern Londoners being fashionably amoral in modern London. The feminists at the Court wanted to change the title to *The Phases of the Moon* but we resisted.

Max asked me if I would like to direct a classic. I suggested *Uncle Vanya*, but decided to quit the Court when the script-approval panel decided that Chekhov's masterpiece was no longer politically acceptable. They felt Sonia was portrayed as too much of a victim. I was also pissed off that they turned down my suggestion to do a panto.

Around this time I also directed a musical version of *Charlie and the Chocolate Factory* for Leeds Playhouse when the original director pulled out at a fortnight's notice. The production toured Britain for two years, went to Australia, played at Sadler's Wells and was seen briefly at the Dominion in the West End. It was a shower of shite.

I directed *Flann O'Brien's Hard Life* at the Tricycle as a suitably surreal fantasy in which Flann turns into a thirty-foot Pope. The brilliant veteran Irish actor David Blake Kelly played Mr Collopy. There's a point in the script where Flann describes seeing a touring Shakespearian production in which the aged Anew McMaster, playing Hamlet, remains rooted firmly to the spot while Laertes 'did all the lepping and the rapier work'. In rehearsal Blake Kelly revealed that as a young man he had been in McMaster's company touring Ireland and had, indeed, been that very Laertes. Kerry Crabbe's script also contained the following lyric to be sung to the tune of 'Carrickfergus':

Flann O'Brien,
Brian O' Nolan
Myles na gCopaleen
Three names, one man.
He also wrote as Brother Barnabas
But that last handle
Proved an also ran.

In 1986, back at the Bush, I directed Nick Darke's *The Oven Glove Murders*, an acerbic take on the *Chariots of Fire* British film revival. Designer Geoff Rose and I opened up the normally boarded windows overlooking Goldhawk Road and built a *trompe l'oeil* set on the roof outside so it seemed that Mark Wing-Davey, as the supremely untalented movie director Garstang Galt, was actually fondling his Oscar in an office on the other side of the road. The stunt was equally successful when Tim Roth as the thrusting young producer nightly fell out of the window and, to screams from the audience, seemingly plunged to his death in the street below.

Terry Johnson and Kate Lock adapted their award-winning television play *Tuesday's Child* for the stage. The original had been a fifty-minute duologue between a Catholic priest and a young girl, played by Kate herself, who comes to confess that she is pregnant. She is also a virgin. Terry and Kate expanded the piece for an optimistic West End producer adding several characters and a prequel in a Wexford old people's home. It didn't really work, and they should have probably left it alone. I directed it at Stratford East with Eileen Atkins, Mike Angelis, Chris Jury and a chicken. On the opening night impresario Eddie Kulukundis told Eileen that it would run in the West End for three years. It didn't.

Since leaving Hull Truck I had written a couple of screenplays that disappeared into development limbo, but as a result I was approached by actor-producer Richard Johnson to come up with an idea for his new film company, United British Artists. I started work on *Happy Feet,* a film set in Yorkshire in 1960 about a bunch of kids from a mining village who go to Scarborough to compete in the East Coast Classical Dance Festival. I didn't think there was much hope of it ever seeing the light of day.

At the Lyric Hammersmith, I directed Christopher Douglas's *Scout's Honour,* in which a leftish Community Centre is haunted by the ghost of a Fascist Scoutmaster played by John Fortune. Also in the cast were Rachel Bell, Nigel Planer, Steve O'Donnell and Dr Palfi the Laughologist, a clown who had served in Vietnam, playing Spinach, a clown who had served in Vietnam. The play was subsequently turned into the television comedy series *Tygo Road.*

Writer Helen Cooper, designer and performance artist Geraldine Pilgrim and I formed a company, Potemkin Productions, to produce Helen's play, *Mrs Vershinin,* at the Riverside Studios. The play centred on events in the Vershinin household as the story of Chekhov's *Three Sisters* unfolds in the Prozorov household down the road. Geraldine's stunning set featured a vast greenhouse/conservatory with a fallen tree smashed through the glass roof. Rick Fisher did the lighting. Stephen Warbeck did the music. The production was chosen for the Theater der Welt Festival in Hamburg.

Richard Johnson and United British Artists decided to go ahead with *Happy Feet,* and Julie Walters agreed to play the central character, Yorkshire dance teacher Dora Jackson. To my utter amazement Richard and Julie announced that the film would be their next project at a press launch on the beach at the Cannes Festival.

Peter Ansorge had recently taken over as Head of Drama at the newly formed Channel Four TV and asked me to devise a play for their new drama slot, which had the dubious generic title of 'Four Play'. Accordingly I decided to make a piece about a group of women at an Anne Summers sex toys party. Ann Scott of Greenpoint Films came on board as producer, and I spent the spring locked up in a house in Camden Town with actors Lizzie McInerney, Veronica Roberts, Julie Legrand,

Su Elliot, Julie Peasgood and Natasha Morgan as we improvised what became *Chains of Love*. Broadcast on 11 November 1989 the play achieved record audience figures and prompted a letter from Mary Whitehouse, who described it as 'a very cheap exploitation of women's sexuality—and men's for that matter'. She was also concerned about:

> ... a jelly mould shaped like an erect penis and soap moulded in
> the same way and although the vibrators were not actually shown,
> the motor noises were heard and no doubt was left in the minds
> of the viewer as to what was making the noise. The whole play
> was pathetic and sordid, bringing the more lurid aspects of sex
> shops into one's living room at a time (9 pm) when many quite
> young children would still be watching.

At the Lyric Hammersmith I directed two plays by Richard Zajdlic—*Cannibal* and *Cock and Bull*—for his company Ratskins and took them on a short tour.

By now Richard Johnson had persuaded Yorkshire Television to come on board as co-producers of *Happy Feet*. It was to be their first feature film. With the YTV team I spent weeks location-hunting around Yorkshire and started auditioning the kids at local ballet schools. I took Julie to a dance festival in Skegness to meet local teachers. Richard flew to LA to prise a deal memo out of Hemdale, producers of *The Terminator*, who were supposed to be backing the film. He moved into the Chateau Marmont on Sunset Boulevard and camped in their office. Back in Leeds, YTV were panicking. We were due to go into pre-production and they were already spending money they didn't have. Hemdale wouldn't sign the memo. Yorkshire TV pulled the project and I went off to Canada to work with Alan Williams. Alan was teaching at the University of Winnipeg and had formed a company with ex-students called the Rude Players. We did two devised pieces: *Rock is Dead*, which was about an obnoxious nerd and his obsession with the legendary missing Doors rock opera, and *Fun in Manitoba*, about a *Penthouse*-reading Zamboni driver and a woman who claims to be a witch. We took the plays to the Edmonton Fringe performing in a fake grain elevator.

Max Stafford-Clark decided to run a series of short political plays at the Royal Court written by people who didn't normally write for theatre. These included Julie Burchill and David Hart, the man who orchestrated the defeat of the miners' strike for Thatcher from a suite at Claridge's. In case the non-writers failed to come up with anything Max included a couple of proper playwrights in the mix. One of them was Doug Lucie. Doug perspicaciously wrote a play called *Doing the Business*, a showbiz satire in which a successful Oxford-educated producer agrees to finance his old OUDS director chum's political theatre season if he dumps all the cutting-edge stuff and replaces it with an anodyne production of *The Caretaker* starring Mel and Griff with Billy Connolly as the tramp. I cast Nick Dunning and Nicholas Woodeson. It was a riot.

Brendan Behan's brother Brian wrote his first play at the age of sixty-three and took it to Nick Kent at the Tricycle. The play was very roughly based on Brian's Uncle Padser and began in the Behan household in Dublin. The second half was set in London on the building site for the 1951 Festival of Britain, where Brian, himself a Communist shop steward, had led a strike for improved safety measures and better conditions. In the Behan tradition the script was practically non-existent, so Brian would come up with a basic idea, the actors would improvise the scene and then Brian would provide suitable Behan dialogue such as:

He's so mean he wouldn't give a ghost a fright.

Where there's a will there's a widow.

May you be shot with balls of your own shite.

And my particular favourite:

I wish I was back in Dublin wishing I was back in London wishing I was back in Dublin.

We then bunged in some songs, some of which were by brother Dominic but without permission as the brothers had not spoken for eighteen years after Dominic tried to charge Brian for bed and breakfast when he visited him for Christmas. Eventually we got to the point in the script where the Brendan character was threatening King George VI with a revolver shouting 'Die the death of an English dog!' When I asked Brian what happened next he escaped out of the jakes window leaving a note that said, 'I hope my good comrades will come up with a suitable ending.'

Ann Scott of Greenpoint was determined to save *Happy Feet*, so she bought it from UBA and took it to the BBC to produce as an independent. Astonishingly they agreed, so we filmed it over the summer of 1990 in Scarborough and Buxton with a cast of thirty kids from Hull, Lincoln and Doncaster dance schools. Julie Walters had to drop out as she was having a baby, but Phyllis Logan took over magnificently. Derrick O'Connor played the love interest. Chris Jury played the twat interest. Fred Pearson played the Mayor of Scarborough and Jim Broadbent selflessly provided a beautiful cameo performance as Man in Shop. John Naylor played the miner's son who wins a scholarship to the Royal Ballet School. Stephen Warbeck again did the music, and the film was selected as the BBC Christmas movie. Julie Walters later played a dance teacher in another film about dance schools in a northern mining community.

I spent the next year writing film scripts that didn't get made, including *Albion Rocks*, set in Glastonbury, based on the Ruralist Brotherhood of painters and *James and Julian*, about two sixteen-year-old public schoolboys who in 1964 try to make a remake of Truffaut's *Jules et Jim* with the housemaster's fifteen-year-old daughter in the Jeanne Moreau role. I also worked on an abandoned *Arena* documentary with Van Morrison, and gave Sting acting lessons. They didn't work.

I directed Catherine Johnson's *Dead Sheep*, again at the Bush. *Dead Sheep* told the story of three recovering female alcoholics on an Outward-Bound expedition up the Brecon Beacons with a born-again Christian midget. The cast was Katrin Cartlidge, Kate Hardy, Gary Love, Gwen Taylor and the vertically challenged John Key. Geoff Rose's set included real turf, a running stream and an hydraulic mountain that appeared in a cloud of dry ice to the dwarfs' chorus from *Das Rheingold*.

After the fall of the Berlin Wall I spent some time travelling in former East Germany. I spoke to workers and artists, writers and political agitators, and several pre-war Communist Party members who had fled Hitler and now feared they would be rounded up again. I spent some time in Eisenhuttenstadt (originally Stalinstadt) on the Polish border. I discovered secret Stasi tunnels and hundreds of abandoned obsolete Russian tanks in the woods outside Potsdam. I went to the trial in Cottbus of the Nazi skinheads accused of burning down an immigrant hostel. I eventually came up with an idea for a television series that I pitched to Peter Ansorge of Channel Four on the phone. I told him that the theme would be *The Simpsons Go to East Berlin*. In fact it was about an American steel-company executive and his family and their adventures among the Ossies after the husband is sent to oversee the privatisation and asset-stripping of the East German steel industry—a reunification comedy. Ansorge commissioned a three-part series, Ann Scott joined as producer and I went off to write it making frequent research trips back to East Germany.

At the same time I also managed to direct Doug Lucie's *Grace* at Hampstead, a play about American Cultural Imperialism, which the Royal Court had turned down. Anna Massey played the eccentric English aristocrat who is forced to sell her country house to an American evangelical church. *Grace* was an astonishingly accurate metaphor for what would become Bush's foreign policy. It was pretty much dismissed at the time as paranoid exaggeration.

Channel Four enthusiastically accepted the scripts for the East German series, which was now called *I Am A Donut* in homage to Kennedy's '*Ich bin ein Berliner*' declaration in 1963. Ann Scott and I went location-hunting. We arranged to shoot at the EKO Stahl steelworks in Eisenhuttenstadt and in the Stasi tunnels. We signed up a German co-producer and were offered a sound stage at the newly reopened Babelsberg studios where Josef von Sternberg shot *The Blue Angel*. I cast Anna Kohler from the Wooster Group as Conni, the German female protagonist. On the Friday before we were due to start pre-production Channel Four pulled the entire series. They also cancelled productions by Snoo Wilson and Tony Marchant. They had decided to sack their audience and planned to concentrate on less provocative drama that would appeal to a broader market. I suspect the advertising department had done some focus groups. I was gutted and seriously broke. I had lost a year's work overnight.

Sometime later I turned *I Am A Donut* into a radio series and it was broadcast on BBC Radio Four in 1997.

I directed Richard Zajdlic's *Rage* at the Bush with Nicky Henson and Sue Johnston in the cast and spent a year writing countless abortive treatments for film projects. This all came to a head when I was asked to write a thriller for Cinema Verity, a prominent independent production company. This was really not my scene, but I actually had what I thought was a good idea based around a eugenic conspiracy hatched up at Peterhouse College, Cambridge, by a right-wing don and an ugly bunch of Thatcherite ministers. I was disabused by the teenage script associate, who told me that university-educated characters were no longer acceptable as they didn't play well with their target social demographic. Things were no better at the BBC where creative producers were rapidly being replaced by management consultants with MBAs. As Tony Garnett pointed out in July 2009, 'The BBC hired McKinsey's and ended up as McDonalds.'

I realised that I was flogging a dead horse trying to write for film and television. I needed get back into the theatre and I needed to go to work every day.

Roger Davidson, Thirzie Robinson and Helen Cooper in *Still Crazy After All These Years*, Hull Truck, 1981

Anjela Bell and Alan Rickman rehearsing *Bad Language* by Dusty Hughes, Hampstead Theatre, 1983

Diana Katis, Ian Reddington and Frances
Barber in *Hard Feelings* by Doug Lucie,
Oxford Playhouse and the Bush, 1983

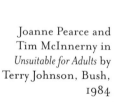

Joanne Pearce and
Tim McInnerny in
Unsuitable for Adults by
Terry Johnson, Bush,
1984

Meeting the Crown Prince and
Princess of Japan, TOYP
Conference, Tokyo, 1982

Filming *Happy Feet* in Scarborough, 1989. My daughter Flora is on the tricycle ⎯⎯⎯⎯

Left to right: Killian McKenna, Howard Lew Lewis, David Blake Kelly and Heather Tobias (corpse: Paul Boyle) in *Flann O'Brien's Hard Life* by Kerry Crabbe, Tricycle Theatre, 1985

Celia Robertson and Paul Bettany in *Love and Understanding* by Joe Penhall, Bush, 1997

Left to right: Joanne Pearce, Nicola Redman and Ona McCracken in *Shang-A-Lang* by Catherine Johnson, Bush, 1998

Howie the Rookie by Mark O'Rowe, Bush, 1999
(above: Karl Shiels; right: Aidan Kelly)

Bette Bourne as Quentin Crisp in *Resident Alien*
by Tim Fountain, Bush, 1999

Paul Sparks and Elizabeth Reaser in *Blackbird* by Adam Rapp, Bush, 2001

Left to right: David Bamber (at piano), Oliver Jackson, James Hornsby, Mark Drewry, David Schofield and Shaun Prendergast rehearsing *The Glee Club* by Richard Cameron, Bush, 2002

Julia Ford and Mark Monero in
adrenalin… heart by Georgia Fitch,
Bush, 2002

Nicholas Tennant in *A Carpet,
a Pony and a Monkey* by Mike Packer,
Bush, 2002

Suzan Sylvester,
Amanda Hale and
Debbie Chazen in
Crooked by
Catherine
Trieschmann,
Bush, 2006

Outside the Bush, 1997

9

Here Comes the New Boss

I took over the Bush Theatre in 1996 almost by mistake. I was directing Richard Cameron's *With Every Beat*, a play about a man who was
trying to beat the world long-distance drumming record, at West Yorkshire Playhouse when I heard that Dominic Dromgoole, who was
running the Bush at the time, had resigned. I called him up and as a
joke told him that I was thinking of applying for his job. 'You won't get
it in a million years,' he said. So I applied.

The Bush Theatre was founded in 1972 by Brian McDermott, who
had also founded the King's Head. Pub theatre was in the ascendant.
There was a lot of talk about demystification, breaking down the barriers of bourgeois theatre and bringing Beckett to the bar room, etc., but
the real reason was that a lot of pubs had spare upstairs rooms and land-
lords were happy to rent them out cheaply, even to fringe theatres, if it
meant bringing in more customers. The Bush had originally been
Lionel Blair's dance studio. In twenty-five years it had become one of
the most important new-writing theatres in the country, launching the
careers of Stephen Poliakoff, Robert Holman, John Byrne, Ron
Hutchinson, Terry Johnson, Doug Lucie, Billy Roche, Catherine Johnson, Richard Cameron, Jonathan Harvey, Richard Zajdlic, Naomi
Wallace, David Eldridge, Victoria Wood and many, many others. The
100-seat theatre had also been the London home of my company, Hull
Truck. I loved the intimacy, the close-up magic. It's impossible to tell
lies on the Bush stage. You will be found out. It was and remains the
only theatre I ever wanted to run.

As soon as I arrived the theatre closed down for six months. The
Bush Hotel, above which the theatre lives, had originally been a sweat
and sawdust Irish bar run by Tommy Conway and his family from Cork.
Nobody went in there much except for a few eccentric regulars and the

BBC production team from the *Terry Wogan Show*, which was recorded at the Shepherd's Bush Empire next door. There were strippers in the back bar on Sunday lunchtimes and the occasional Irish show band, and the pub and theatre rubbed along pretty well together save for the occasional fight and the odd fire. By 1996 things had changed for the worse. Tommy Conway had long gone and the Shepherd's Bush Empire had been turned into a rock venue with bands every night, so the Bush bar was crowded with Goths, Metal heads, Punks and punters determined to get arseholed before the gig. To make matters worse the pub landlord had decided to run a mod disco in the back room and refused to turn the volume down. All this made the experience of going to see a play at the Bush fairly intolerable. The critics often described the theatre as being located above the most revolting pub in London. Happily, Allied Domecq, the owners, were about to change all that. The pub was going to be totally refurbished, rebranded and reopened in January 1997 as The Fringe and Firkin.

I started out at the Bush with two guiding principles: that we were a writers' theatre, which meant that the writers and the plays must always be at the heart of the equation, and that no one was being paid enough to have a bad time.

The Bush, like most fringe theatres, had started out as a collective and I felt that it was important that the theatre should be run in as non-hierarchical a way as possible. There was a full-time staff of eight, including me, producing nine shows a year. It was not unusual for staff members to work fourteen hour days at least six days a week. I wanted everyone to own the work we put on and to be genuinely part of a collaborative process.

Everybody who takes over a theatre or indeed any organisation inevitably starts by pissing on the lamppost to announce his or her agenda. The Bush was already in a strong position artistically when I arrived: there was successful team in place headed by General Manager Deborah Aydon and Literary Manager Joanne Reardon. There were, however, a few things that I wanted to change. In my application for the job I had stressed the need to move out of the pub and find new premises. The pub was a shit-hole, and the backstage facilities were medieval. The office was in a dank damp basement without natural light, and we had no rehearsal room, workshop or wardrobe space. There was a certain amount of sentimentality and nostalgia about what is, of course, a wonderful acting space; but I felt that after twenty-five successful years the time had come for the Bush to have the facilities it deserved. I remained unconvinced that the Fringe and Firkinisation of the pub would solve any of the problems. The reasons for the move were not just cosmetic. Despite the unparalleled track record for discovering and producing the most exciting new writers around, the Bush was still considered to be a semi-professional pub/fringe theatre by the funding bodies. Our closest competitors in London were the Royal Court, Hampstead, Soho Theatre and the Almeida, all of whom had received vast Lottery grants to build new or refurbish old theatres as well as a subsequent increase in revenue funding to run them properly. The Bush was being marginalised and was seen by both the public and the theatre Establishment not as an important theatre in its own right, but as some kind of stepping stone to a glittering career in better-subsidised or more commercial emporia.

In fact there had been schemes to move out of the pub almost from the moment that the theatre opened, including moving into the cinema next door and taking over the Whitehall in the West End, but none of them had got very far. A scheme to take over an old electricity-generating station opposite the BBC in Wood Lane had seemed promising, but Dominic Dromgoole had abandoned the plan, preferring to stay put. The time had now come for the Bush to step up a gear. We were a Premiership team with a Fourth Division stadium. I decided that it was time we were promoted. My intention was to find a space in which we could recreate the intimate Bush magic but with improved facilities for both the production team and the audience.

I also decided to refurbish the Literary Department. Under the guidance of Literary Manager Joanne Reardon, the Bush had a terrific team of readers, drawn from a variety of backgrounds, all of whom had the increasingly rare ability to actually read a play and assess its potential. Every one of the thousand-plus scripts we received each year was read, and every writer received a report, hopefully with advice and encouragement. Promising scripts were given a second read and then passed on to the Literary Manager and ultimately the Artistic Director, who would meet with promising writers and offer dramaturgical suggestions. A number of successful writers had been discovered from the unsolicited script pile, most notably Jonathan Harvey, Catherine Johnson and Sharman Macdonald.

I decided to introduce a workshop, rehearsed reading, and script-development programme into the process.

There is a lot of crap talked about workshops. There is a lot of crap talked in workshops, and a lot of workshops are crap. There is a feeling among some writers and directors that any script-workshop process is a waste of time as the word of the writer should be sacrosanct. Indeed one very celebrated director/playwright goes so far as to suggest that no play in the history of world theatre has ever been improved by the intervention of either a dramaturg or a director.

Although I disagree with this view, I am no big fan of workshop culture per se. It has become the practice of theatres both here and in America to spend an inordinate amount of time and energy working on plays that they have no intention of ever producing. Theatres frequently give a play a rehearsed reading or a workshop in order to get rid of it. Producers can then convince themselves that what is in fact an exercise in box-ticking is in some way beneficial to the writer and in addition provides work for the legions of assistants and associates that most theatres seem to need these days. In America there are dozens of writers with strings of awards and glittering prizes to their name who have never actually had a play produced.

For me the purpose of a workshop is to work with a bunch of bright actors and the writer with the aim of trying to make the play better. This involves discussing character, through-line, plot, politics and the writer's intentions, to make sure the play says what the writer wants to say in the way he or she wants to say it. It's not about imposing your will on the play. It's about illuminating to the writer ways in which his or her play might work better. My idea was only to workshop plays that I felt there was a definite chance of us producing.

I decided to increase the number of plays we commissioned each year. In common with most new-writing theatres we only had sufficient funding to commission the more established writers, and I wanted to offer seed commissions to encourage a wider range of novice playwrights. I also instituted something we called pro-active commissioning. The idea came about because of Catherine Johnson.

Catherine is one of my favourite writers. She is funny and clever and fearless. I saw her first play, *Boys Mean Business*, about a bunch of ne'er-do-wells on the front at Weston-super-Mare at the Bush in 1989, and fell in love with her writing. I directed her next play, *Dead Sheep*, at the Bush in 1991. Catherine won the Thames Television Best New Play Award for the show, but spent the two hundred pounds' prize money on a taxi back home to Bristol to avoid the sexual advances of a prominent Shakespearian producer. So obviously she was the first writer I commissioned when I took over the theatre.

Catherine wanted to go to Butlins. She had heard about the Seventies-revival weekends when hundreds of Seventies music fans in authentic Seventies costumes spent the weekend getting totally pissed listening and dancing to the now middle-aged survivors of Sweet, Mud,

Black Lace and the Bay City Rollers. It was too good an opportunity to miss. We went together to Butlins Bognor Regis. As a result Catherine decided to write *Shang-A-Lang*, a play about forty-year-old rollerettes shagging a Rollers tribute band. Catherine told me that she wanted to write the play because she was 'totally fucked off with Bridget Jones and her fucking diary'.

Pro-active commissioning essentially involves matching up an idea or a location with a writer and sending the writer off on a research trip; thus Toby Farrow went to stay in a Shepherd's Bush backpackers' hostel, Tracy O'Flaherty went to the Labour Party conference in Brighton and Michael Wilcox went, reluctantly, on a Saga holiday to Torremolinos.

I needed to find extra funding to do all this. My plan was to guilt-trip all the television and film companies who had profited enormously from exploiting Bush writers over the years into coughing up for the script-development programme.

The pub was due to reopen as the Fringe and Firkin in time for Christmas. It didn't, so we had plenty of time to plan the spring season. We also produced a couple of shows elsewhere. *Kiss the Sky* was a psychedelic rock musical by Jim Cartwright. It had been produced a number of times in a number of venues and with a number of different titles. Sometimes it had been *Stoneground*. Other times it had been *Eight Miles High*. All versions were essentially a compilation of great psychedelic anthems hung round a pretty feeble plot, all of which took place at a Free Festival in a field somewhere in Lancashire sometime in the Sixties. The book was dreadful, dumb and sexist, and I was stuck with it. The show was already programmed when I arrived, and a contract had been signed to hire the Shepherd's Bush Empire next door. The script was so embarrassing that I commissioned Jim to write a new version. This was even worse and mostly consisted of a crude line-drawing of a forty-foot Buddha with slogans like 'Ladies, Burn Your Bras!' written all over it. He claimed to have been inspired by the Becks' script for *Paradise Now*, which I had foolishly shown him. Worse still, he wouldn't let us change a line. In desperation I pleaded with Alan Williams to come back from Canada to play the narrator and recruited genius musical director Neil McArthur and a team of terrific actor/musicians. The music was superb. We even pulled off a live version of Frank Zappa's 'Call Any Vegetable'. The lighting by Jenny Kagan was out of this world—the technical rehearsal took longer than the actual Woodstock Festival—but despite all our best efforts it was impossible to disguise the fact that there was no plot and no characters. The show had a small cult following, but the critics demolished it. The Bush would have gone bust had the show not been paid for with the compensation money from Allied Domecq for the six months' closure of the theatre. It was a dreadful start.

Joanne Reardon and I started to programme the new season. It seemed to me that there were several tiers of Bush writers. First there were the established playwrights who had worked there for years like Snoo Wilson, Tony Bicât and Doug Lucie. Some of them, like Stephen Poliakoff and Mike Leigh, would need to be coaxed back into the fold. Then there were the current Bush writers like Richard Cameron, Catherine Johnson and Richard Zajdlic and the up-and-coming writers like David Eldridge, Samuel Adamson and writer-in-residence Conor McPherson. Then there were beginners like Rebecca Prichard and the completely new writers yet to be discovered. Any Bush season should include new plays from all these categories of writer. In addition I thought it important to bring into the Bush the most exciting work from both the Edinburgh and Dublin Festivals, and to work with touring companies including those specialising in devised work. I also wanted to collaborate with visual theatre and performance companies. I was fortunate to find that there were already several good plays in the Literary Department cupboard. It has become common practice for incoming Artistic Directors to dump all the plays and playwrights developed or commissioned by their predecessor. Some even dismantle entire Literary Departments. I think this is more lamppost-pissing.

The show I programmed to reopen the theatre was Richard Cameron's *All of You Mine*, set, like most of Richard's work, in South Yorkshire. The play is a lament for the mining community and a family splintered by the events of the 1984 Miners' Strike. It's warm-hearted, witty, unsentimental and political in the true sense, and it had the magic ingredient that singles out a Bush play: it had Soul.

Conor McPherson had scored a big hit just before the theatre closed for refurbishment with *This Lime Tree Bower*, the first of his plays performed out of Ireland. Dominic had seen it at the Dublin Festival and brought it over. The Bush had a great track record for premiering Irish writing, having introduced London audiences to Billy Roche, Sebastian Barry and Ron Hutchinson. Dominic had also wangled a Pearson Television Writer's Residency for Conor, which bizarrely involved him having to pretend to live in Leicester. The play Conor wrote was *St Nicholas*—a monologue about a middle-aged Dublin theatre critic who falls in love with a young actress from the Abbey Theatre and ends up pimping for vampires in Covent Garden.

Conor, who was also directing the piece, wanted comedian Dave Allen to play the central role so we went off to see him. Dave loved it, but turned it down as he thought he would never be able to learn the lines. I asked Conor who he wanted to try next. He said he wanted somebody 'like Brian Cox'. I suggested Brian Cox: he was just mad enough to do it. Cox had recently moved into a house in Los Angeles to spend more time with his movie career. I sent him the script. Two days later Brian called. 'You fucker,' he said, 'now I have to come all the way back to England to do this fucking play. It's brilliant.'

When you become the Artistic Director of a theatre you get invited to all sorts of glittering functions and literary agents take you out to lunch. Literary agent Alan Radcliffe took me out to lunch and gave me a copy of *Plutonic*, a new play by Joe Penhall, which had been commissioned by the Royal Court but they had turned down. The play was about a married thirty-something couple, Neil and Rachel, who are both doctors. Their lives are totally destroyed by the arrival of Neil's old chum, mad, bad and dangerous-to-know Richie, a charming dope fiend and hedonist. Joe claimed that the Court had turned it down because it was too middle-class. He also had an improbable story along the lines that they had already designed the poster with a skinhead showing his arse and that the play didn't fit the design concept. Joe wrote a new draft and changed the title to *Love and Understanding*, and I agreed to put it on. I couldn't understand how the Royal Court missed it. Several years later the Court had a big hit with *Under a Blue Sky* by David Eldridge, which I had commissioned, but turned down. It went into the West End. The artistic policy of any theatre inevitably reflects the taste of the Artistic Director. Sometimes they get it wrong. That's the way it goes.

The Fringe and Firkin opened in January 1997. The Firkin brand had originally been associated with the brewing of real ale and indeed the pub now had its own microbrewery where the mod disco used to be. The other unique selling points of the Firkin chain were alliteration and double-entendre. The pubs were supposed to attract 'students'. Allied Domecq clearly believed that they were doing us a favour by tying the theatre into their branding so we were astonished to find that that the themed beers on tap were variously called Fringe, Thespian's Revenge, Shakes Beer and Luvvy Ale. There was also a cabinet full of Firkin memorabilia including scratch 'n' sniff Firkin jock straps and a sick bag which carried the slogan 'Afore ye gag buy the Firkin bag' and a cartoon of Hamlet throwing up. There was, however, a proper dressing room, with a proper lavatory so that the actors didn't have to piss in beer glasses backstage. Despite now being decorated with posters and photographs of past productions and tastefully themed as a pastiche Victorian brothel, the pub was still a shit-hole. Most of the clientele did not know there was a theatre upstairs and if they did they couldn't give a fuck. It is possible that this arrangement prevented us from getting carried away with our own significance but the truth of the matter was that the refurbishment had not made much of a difference. We still had to move out.

Simon Usher's production of *All of You Mine* did very well and *St Nicholas* was a smash. Conor wrote:

> We opened. Press night had about twenty-five critics. I sat waiting for the moment when Brian says, 'Mmm. I was a bollocks to all the other critics. And I'll tell you why, because it was this: They were all cunts.'

> I could remember writing that line one afternoon when I was living in Leicester. I could remember my mischievous self-satisfaction, thinking what a great fellow I was altogether. And now here it was, ringing out over a room full of critics. There was a silence like someone had pressed the detonator and nothing happened. And then bang, the place erupted. We were all playing.

I directed *Love and Understanding* myself. The cast was Nicholas Tennant, Celia Robertson and the relatively unknown Paul Bettany. Es Devlin designed the set. Joe Penhall worked very closely with the cast and with Es, and both the script and the design evolved considerably during the three-week rehearsal period. I think that it is absolutely crucial to have the writer in rehearsal when working on a new play. There are, of course, times when an inexperienced playwright can screw things up by impatiently demanding to see the finished result at the read-through, but, by becoming part of the collective process of putting the play on, the writer frequently discovers new ways to make the play work and the actors have a far greater understanding of what the writer is trying to say. Having the writer in the room also prevents directors and designers embarking on some fanciful concept to enhance their own artistic reputations, rather than concentrating on the text and the characters. This is why a number of prominent directors prefer to work with writers who are dead.

Love and Understanding opened on 2 May 1997—the day after the Labour landslide in the General Election. We had only managed one public dress rehearsal/preview owing to illness, and everyone was exhausted having stayed up all night to watch Michael Portillo being humiliated in Enfield. For one night only we changed Paul Bettany's line in the first scene from 'You'll be blaming the Government next' to 'You'll be blaming the *last* Government next.' We got a huge round. For some reason the play, despite being a dark and often bleak comedy, seemed to embody the hope that many people felt after eighteen years of the Tories.

The reviews were good, the actors and Joe were praised to the heavens, and a couple of days later we got a call from Westminster. Chris Smith, the new Labour Minister for the Arts, wanted to come and see the show. Presumably he had arrived in his new office and decided that it would probably be a good move to see some Art. An aide picked up a copy of *Time Out*, saw that *Love and Understanding* was their number one Critics' Choice and booked him in. Understandably Deborah Aydon and I thought this was an opportunity to tap him up for more funding for the Bush and for the arts in general, so we rounded up a couple of the more presentable Board members, and invited him and his partner to dinner after the show at Renezio's Pizza Parlour. To our surprise he accepted the invitation.

It was a strange evening. The Fringe and Firkin was packed both with our punters and several hundred death-metal fans on their way to a gig next door. Chris Smith's security man gave us the ministerial red box for safekeeping. We stashed it in the dressing-room lavatory. We bought Chris a pint of Luvvy Ale. He didn't seem terribly impressed. All went well until after the interval. Just as the second half was about to go up I got a desperate message from stage management. There was a madman threatening the cast with a bottle and trying to get on stage. I went round the back. A Bulgarian metaller trying to break into the gig at the Empire had climbed the wrong fire escape and ended up backstage. He was lost, confused, violent and off his tits on whizz. I grabbed him by the collar and booted him down the stairs and out of the pub. I then realised that I could have been stabbed and became a gibbering wreck for the rest of the evening. Dinner with Chris Smith was fine. He was relaxed and charming, and listened intently to our arguments for improved funding. We got the impression that he would have preferred to be Secretary of State for Health.

The Tory policy for the arts had been a disaster. Thatcher had no idea what the arts were for, and would probably have abandoned funding them all together if she could have got away with it. Under the Conservatives, theatre, and indeed all branches of the arts, had to submit to the diktats of the free market. Their mantra was that culture should serve the economy. Lefty theatre practitioners lacking in business skills clearly could not be trusted to run their own organisations efficiently so were downgraded and replaced or superseded by placemen or women from the world of commerce or usury. A typical advert in the *Guardian* at the time would read: 'Birmingham Rep seeks Chief Executive—No previous experience in theatre necessary.' The most grotesque manifestation of this practice was the appointment of the Conservative Peer Baroness Detta O'Cathain as Chief Executive of the Barbican. O'Cathain had previously run the Milk Marketing Board. Obsessed with targets and the bottom line, during her tenure she sacked over forty members of staff and alienated everyone in the building. She had no understanding of the need for an artistic organisation to work collaboratively in pursuit of the art and indeed seemed to despise the people she worked with. She even imposed a dress code and banned RSC actors from using the public bars and restaurants if 'improperly' dressed. After a vote of no confidence from the staff she was eventually removed but with an alleged golden fuck-off payment of £300,000.

The prevailing orthodoxy also dictated that theatres should strive to increase the amount of financial support they derived from corporate and individual sponsorship and donations. The governing bodies demanded public and private initiatives in which state subsidy and Lottery funding would depend on matching sums being raised from business and similar sources. In response, arts organisations created yet another tier of administration—the Development Managers and Consultants—a new breed of fundraisers who, like the new breed of Chief Executives, also prioritised financial gain over artistic integrity. At the same time Marketing Departments, with all their attendant voodoo, blossomed like flowers in the spring, and theatres that had previously been successfully run by an Artistic Director, a General Manager and a part-time Publicity Officer found themselves supporting whole departments of the new Executive Classes and their several assistants. God knows how Hull Truck had managed for all those years without them. All the above characterised themselves as 'wealth creators' as opposed to the self-indulgent writers, actors and directors, who merely created the stuff they were selling. Accordingly they voted themselves the kind of inflated salaries that they imagined they would command in the private sector. We were witnessing what playwright Doug Lucie perspicaciously described as 'the revenge of Business on Culture'. Disappointingly the Arts Council, supposedly free from political bias but now stuffed with Thatcherite apparatchiks also paying themselves fat salaries, embraced all this monetarist nonsense. Surely under New Labour things could only get better. Fortunately the Bush did not as yet suffer from most of this malarkey. We were merely undervalued and skint.

The Bush was funded by the Arts Council via the London Arts Board and by the local borough of Hammersmith and Fulham. The council funding was always in peril, as local councillors both Tory and Labour had little time for the arts, and certainly none whatsoever for a new-writing theatre. They would have preferred to spend the money on clowns in the shopping precinct, kids' face painting or the kind of activity that Deborah Aydon pithily categorised as 'cunts on stilts'. A sympathetic councillor had insisted that our funding was ring-fenced by the Mayor's office, but we were constantly told that this could not last and that we were lucky to get any funding at all. The Catch-22 was that you could only get Arts Council/LAB funding if you received subsidy from the local authority. Fortunately Sue Timothy at the London Arts Board was an old friend from Hull Truck days. She agreed that the Bush had been underfunded for years and also was entirely sympathetic to our plans to move, but warned us that it was unlikely that there would be any more Capital Lottery funding for new buildings and certainly not in London. It was beginning to dawn on the authorities that millions of pounds of Lottery funding had been squandered on white-elephant projects: the stable door was about to be shut. It seemed that the Bush had already missed out on the bonanza as far as a new building was concerned. Sue advised me instead to apply for the Lottery to fund the Writers' Development Programme under the A4E (Arts for Everyone) new-projects scheme.

She also conscripted me on to the LAB New Writing panel. This was a group of theatre professionals who met several times a year to advise on grants for writers. It seemed to me a straightforward business; we would allocate funding to interesting new writers to write plays and to theatres to put the plays on. This was not the case. At the first meeting I sat bemused as a bunch of people, who, as far as I could tell, had never written, acted in, directed or produced a play, argued for hours about initiating cross-discipline strategies to facilitate improved provision for Pan-Asian dramaturgical input in South East London. Nobody mentioned plays at all. It became clear to me that most of the participants were not in fact experts in the arts. They were experts in meetings about the arts. In the pub I confessed to Paul Sirett, the Soho Theatre Literary Manager, that I hadn't got a clue what anyone was talking about. He hadn't either. This was the first time I had come across the new language of 'Artspeak'. It would not be the last.

The situation in the pub deteriorated rapidly. After a couple of fights, a stabbing, and wholesale and conspicuous drug-dealing, the landlord posted bouncers on the doors and searched everybody coming in. Not surprisingly this was not popular with our customers. The bouncers were rude and aggressive, and, let's face it, a body search should not be part of an evening out at the theatre. We had many complaints, but the whole thing came to a head during the run of feminist Sphinx Theatre's *Goliath*, adapted by Bryony Lavery from the book by Beatrix Campbell, when a number of women refused to have themselves or their bags searched and were refused admission. This included the writer and director of the play.

I complained to the pub manager, who said that he would be happy to see the theatre closed down. If we didn't like it we could fuck off.

I complained to Allied Domecq. The strange irony was that the corporate wing of Allied Domecq thought that the Bush was a good thing, and were trying to be supportive and well intentioned when they came up with the Fringe and Firkin branding. They also owned the Gate Theatre in Notting Hill and had even sponsored a playwriting award. In addition they were major sponsors of the Royal Shakespeare Company. Ian Oag, the head of Corporate Affairs, came to see a show with his family, who cowered in a corner of the bar, but declared that there was nothing he could do: the pub was one of Allied Domecq's few money-spinners.

There were two further outstanding productions during the season. The first was the remarkable *Disco Pigs* by Enda Walsh produced by Corcadorca, which I had seen at the Dublin Festival. Actually I had not seen it at the Dublin Festival because I couldn't get in, but the buzz about the show and the company was such that I was determined to book them. Everyone at the Bush thought I was mad, even more so when they read the script which appeared to be incomprehensible. I persuaded the Traverse to take it for the Edinburgh Festival, and the show sold out both there and at the Bush, transferring to the West End and touring the world. The performers Eileen Walsh and Cillian Murphy, in his first ever role, were superb, and Enda won both the Stewart Parker and George Devine Awards.

Nicole Kidman came to see it at the Bush. She went to the Empire next door by mistake. Not surprisingly they let her in. It was only when she found herself surrounded by punks with Day-Glo Mohican haircuts watching New Model Army that she realised she was in the wrong theatre.

Playwright Terry Johnson brought me the script of *Caravan* by Helen Blakeman, a student on David Edgar's MA Playwriting course at Birmingham University. The play was a dirty sexy tale of a Liverpool family on holiday in a caravan in North Wales. Over the course of the action both of the teenage daughters of the house are impregnated by the same man, and the elder daughter steals her mother's boyfriend. It was a remarkable first play, and I programmed it straight away. Gemma Bodinetz directed and designer Bruce Macadie built a completely see-through yet functional caravan on the Bush stage. Helen Blakeman won both the George Devine Award and the Pearson TV Award the next year, two in a row for Bush writers.

The Roundabout Theatre in New York had got to hear about *St Nicholas* and Brian Cox's performance in it. They asked if they could put on a benefit performance for one night only as part of a series of special events for their rich supporters and subscribers. There was no fee but they would pay Brian's and Conor's expenses and put them up at a posh hotel. Brian was keen, so Deborah and I agreed, in exchange for maximum publicity for the Bush in all their marketing material. We saw it as an opportunity to take our work to a wider audience. When I worked at the Royal Court in the early Eighties the theatre had a symbiotic relationship with Joseph Papp's Public Theater and productions regularly travelled both ways. I was looking for a similar arrangement between the Bush and an American theatre. *St Nicholas* went down a storm and we got to meet the great and the good and the theatrical aristocracy of New York in one long weekend. Doug Hughes, who had just taken over the Long Wharf Theatre, invited us over to New Haven for lunch. He wanted our production of *Love and Understanding*, and he wanted to swap it for his production of *A Question of Mercy*, an AIDS euthanasia drama by David Rabe. Over lunch he told us how the last English theatre company to play the Long Wharf had abandoned their set in a container in the parking lot, where it had slowly rotted for several years until the theatre had to pay the Department of Sanitation to take it away. I hadn't the bottle to tell him that it was the Hull Truck set for *The Dalkey Archive*.

Deborah and I naïvely thought the exchange would be straightforward. We were not prepared for the bureaucratic nightmare that is American Equity. We were similarly unprepared for the shark pool that is New York theatre. Primary Stages signed up Brian to perform *St Nicholas* Off-Broadway. It was essentially the Bush production. Same actor, same director, different chair. Brian even wore the suit we had bought him. The Bush never saw a nickel or received a credit. I even had to pay for my own ticket on press night.

Joanne Reardon went off on maternity leave and was replaced as Literary Manager by playwright Tim Fountain. Tim was supposed to be Joanne's maternity cover, but she decided not to come back so he got the gig. Tim's ebullient personality and impeccable bad taste played a significant part in the success of the Bush for the next three years.

I launched the New Writers' Development Programme with a huge twenty-fifth-birthday gala bash at the Duke of York's, where the Royal Court were living in splendid exile while their Sloane Square base was being rebuilt. We presented extracts from memorable Bush productions over the past twenty-five years, involving where possible the original casts. Alan Rickman flew in from LA to appear in Dusty Hughes's

Commitments and the original *Fosdyke Saga* cast threw tripe at the well-heeled audience but the highlight of the evening was top TV writer Lynda La Plante, reincarnated as actress Lynda Marchal, performing a scene with Simon Callow from Snoo Wilson's *Soul of the White Ant* in a thick South African accent while lying horizontally behind a makeshift bar. During the curtain call Lionel Blair tap danced on stage to the overture for *Mack and Mabel* with a birthday cake. He had never heard of the theatre but enjoyed the party. The show raised over £10,000, although the Royal Court did try to sue us for ruining their new carpet.

Anyone contemplating organising a fundraising gala should always avoid involving events coordinators, party organisers, function consultants and similar members of the vampire class. Many a theatre has found itself expending vast amounts of time and energy coordinating such an event, only to find that all the money raised has gone to pay the inflated fees of the professional consultants hired to help them organise it in the first place.

My efforts to guilt-trip film and TV companies into funding the writers' project met with a mixed response. Miramax wanted a 'first-look' deal, but didn't want to pay for it. Humphrey Barclay at London Weekend Television, however, was happy to contribute in return for suggestions for new comedy writers. Vanguard, an American development company run by kitchen-surface magnate and writer Wes Moore, paid us a retainer to find them potential film projects. I had several meetings with Peter Ansorge, who by now was Head of Drama at Channel Four, and we began to plan a scheme for Channel Four to support and possibly transmit Bush plays.

At the same time I invited Peter Stevens to join the theatre's Board. The Board at the time was chaired by Tracey Scoffield from the BBC. Three of its members were ex-Artistic Directors of the theatre. Among the rest were the legendary TV producer Kenith Trodd and playwright Christopher Hampton. They were loyal and supportive and completely hands-off when it came to artistic decision-making. I thought, however, that if we were going to find or build a new theatre we needed a hard hitter on the team. Peter Stevens had been General Manager at the National Theatre with Peter Hall, and had overseen the building programme there. He had been in at the beginning of Nottingham Playhouse with John Neville and had run the Shakespeare Festival in Stratford, Ontario. He had also been an assessor for the Arts Council advising on Capital Lottery funding for several of the new building projects. He was tough and outspoken, and as a fan of the Bush and our work, he readily agreed to come on board.

I opened the 1998 season with *Martin and John*, an adaptation of Dale Peck's novel *Fucking Martin*. The show had been a big Edinburgh hit and won a Fringe First Award a couple of years previously. It sold out to an almost entirely male gay audience some of whom complained that we had female box-office staff. The play was truly dreadful.

We followed this with Snoo Wilson's *Sabina*—a play about Carl Gustav Jung and his patient and lover Sabina Spielrein. I had originally commissioned Snoo to write a panto, but he came up with this instead. The show was directed with surreal glee by film director Andy Wilson and featured Paul McGann and Susan Vidler, with Mark Long and Jeff Nutall from the People Show. *Sabina* was also a sell-out; every night the Jungians and the Freudians battled it out over pints of foaming Luvvy in the pub downstairs. As far as I know, no theatre has ever lost money producing plays about gays or psychotherapy.

The original cast reunited to rehearse *Love and Understanding* for the Long Wharf. In the intervening nine months Paul Bettany was already on his way to becoming a star. We cut the play slightly, tightened it and, I think, improved it. My friend the actor Nicky Henson had given me some advice about playing American audiences. 'Don't pause,' he said. 'If you pause they think it's the intermission.'

There had been the usual problems with work permits, visas and American Equity, but we thought that we had found a way round them. The deal was that Long Wharf would essentially mount a new production of *Love and Understanding* with the British actors, director, designer and lighting designer, and we would mount a new production of *A Question of Mercy* with their American cast and crew. There were three actors in our company and four in theirs, so no Americans were knowingly deprived of work. In addition the Long Wharf paid Equity a sizeable bond and guaranteed that the American actors would be paid LORT-scale wages and expenses at the Bush, which were at least twice as much as we could afford to pay our own actors. We cleared all this with British Equity, who said that all this was fine and fulfilled the terms of the reciprocal agreement between the two unions. What could go wrong?

The reception we received in New Haven was overwhelming. The theatre staff were friendly and supportive beyond the call of duty. Celia Robertson later said that it was like being licked to death by kittens. We arrived to find that the show had already sold out, so we agreed to extend the run. There was a meet-and-greet where we were bombarded with love and muffins for several hours, and then we settled down to the business of rehearsing. At this point a man who announced himself to be the local Equity convenor turned up and insisted on holding a private meeting with the actors. He told them that under American Equity rules each foreign actor must pay the equivalent of a month's salary to become a temporary member and furthermore each actor had also to pay $800 medical-insurance cover before they were allowed to perform. He wanted $2,000 from each of them. The actors told him that they had been advised by their own union, British Equity, that under the reciprocal agreement this was not in fact the case and politely suggested that he shove it.

He said that if the fees were not paid Equity would not allow the show to open. I had a meeting with Long Wharf Artistic Director, Doug Hughes. It was clearly sharp practice and probably blackmail. He agreed with me but paid the subs anyway and bought more doughnuts. I think he should have called their bluff. When the American actors arrived at the Bush, no one from Equity turned up, and there was no mention whatsoever of fees or insurance. The problem still exists today, but strangely not in the case of the National Theatre or the Royal Shakespeare Company.

The Long Wharf is a subscription theatre with a subscription audience, most of whom are over sixty-five years of age, so it was with some trepidation that we approached the first preview. After a couple of minutes Paul said 'Fuck'—no reaction. A few minutes later Paul said 'Cunt'—no reaction. Celia took off all her clothes—no reaction. Then Paul lit up a cigarette and thirty-five people stormed out complaining of being exposed to passive smoking in infringement of their civil rights. In fairness the subscription audience respected and admired the show. They praised the acting and the writing, but didn't really understand it. They failed to empathise with the predicaments of the characters in the play. It was only during the extension period that the show found a younger audience. Yale University is only a mile or so down the road, but the students rarely make it to the theatre. Press night was packed and glamorous. The *New York Times* turned out, and all the local critics praised the show. Veteran producer Arthur Cohen planned to move it Off-Broadway and invited me to lunch and to look at possible theatres.

Arthur lived in the Dakota building, and his Broadway office was crammed with photos of the stars he had worked with, including Zero Mostel, Ingrid Bergman and Rex Harrison, and fading posters of over a hundred of his hit shows including *On Golden Pond* and *The Music Man*. He was famously careful with money, so we took lunch in an 8th Avenue self-service Chinese cafeteria with a dollar-ninety noodle special and toured the theatres by bus—Arthur had a senior citizens' bus pass.

The *Times* review was never published so the transfer never happened. Even Arthur would not risk moving the show without the blessing of the all-powerful *Times*. He did, however, manage to wangle a substantial donation to the Bush Writers' Development Programme from the Billy Rose Foundation. He was a true man of the theatre.

A Question of Mercy was a disaster in London. The actors hated each other and the critics hated the show. They thought it was worthy, preachy, self-indulgent, sentimental and a string of American pseudo-psychobabble. I thought that they were xenophobic and had entirely misread the play, but the damage was done, and the Long Wharf never sought to repeat the exchange.

Peter Ansorge suddenly left Channel Four, scuppering all our plans. I arranged a meeting with the new Head of Drama, Gub Neal. The meeting took place the morning after a particularly emotional press night, and Deborah and I had raging hangovers. Gub was prepared to support the Bush and our writers but in return wanted tangible results—plays that could in some way be turned into television drama, and preferably plays that could become pilots for series or serials. This was a bit of a tall order as stage and television plays often have a different agenda and are not necessarily mutually compatible. I came up with a scheme on the hoof. We would commission twelve new writers to write twelve new one-act plays. The Bush would develop and workshop them all. Channel Four and the Bush would decide on the best two and the Bush would produce them as a double bill. Channel Four would have first dibs on all the material produced. Channel Four would pay for the lot. To our immense surprise Gub agreed. It would cost them a hundred and forty grand. The whole thing was to prove an administrative and artistic nightmare.

Deborah was also battling with the current nightmare, the application for Arts for Everyone Lottery funding. We had decided to apply for the full whack of £500,000 to set up and run a three-year programme. We hoped to fund a new office and a bigger marketing budget out of the scheme, as well as the workshops, rehearsed readings and extra commissions. Lottery applications were notoriously complicated, so much so that consultancy firms had sprung up charging ridiculous sums for advice. In some cases their fees were larger than the grants being applied for. Deborah did ours on her own, staying up night after night trying to devise new ways to use the word 'Access'.

I had always been a big fan of the National Theatre of Brent and its founder, writer, director and chief executive Desmond Olivier Dingle (alias Patrick Barlow), so I was happy to play a small part in enabling Desmond to finally mount his major, but sadly unproduced, work, *Love Upon the Throne*. The play about the Charles and Diana love story had been commissioned by Nottingham Playhouse, but abandoned when the

Princess was killed in the car crash. I decided that sufficient grieving time had passed, so we co-produced it with Assembly at the Edinburgh Festival where it was a popular success, probably not least because the *Daily Record* described it as 'sick filth'. After the Festival the show came down to the Bush and on to the Comedy Theatre in the West End.

As usual Tim and I went to Edinburgh in search of new talent. There is always a certain amount of hysteria at the Festival as punters, critics and producers alike charge about like Gadarene swine looking for this year's big hit. It's like a bad student party where a bunch of gatecrashers run around trying to find where they have hidden the booze and then steal it all. Eventually a handful of shows will emerge that win Scotsman Fringe Firsts, Herald Angels, Vimto Awards, etc., etc., and are garlanded with hype and praise. Three months later they turn up in London and everyone wonders what all the fuss was about. 'Were we drunk?' they ask. Undoubtedly we were. I usually make a point of going to see the show with the most stupid title. Obviously there is no guarantee that this will work, although one year I did see Manchester students Rik Mayall and Ade Edmondson in a play called *Death on the Toilet* written by a teenage Ben Elton.

One of the much hyped shows that year was *Moscow-Moscow*. The publicity strap line promised: 'Three gay Americans trapped in a Jean-Paul Sartre-like existentialist hell improvise a musical version of Chekhov's *The Three Sisters*.' I went with Tim, Sarah Kane, Vicky Featherstone and Traverse Artistic Director Philip Howard. It was so bad that we all decided to give up theatre.

As a result of our earlier research trip to Butlins, Catherine Johnson had been working away on *Shang-A-Lang*. The plot was deceptively simple. Pauline, Jackie and Lauren, three lifelong friends from Bristol, go on a Seventies-revival weekend at Butlins Minehead to celebrate Pauline's fortieth birthday. As teenagers they have been Bay City Rollers fans, and it is still Pauline's dream to meet Woody. What happens is that they get pissed, Lauren and Jackie shag two members of the Rollers' tribute band and Pauline outgrows her teenage fantasy. In Catherine's first draft most of the action took place in two adjacent chalets, one for the girls and one for the boys. During the workshop we came up with the idea of using one room to represent both chalets, as all Butlins chalets look the same. Consecutive scenes therefore took place in the same set, culminating in a scene in which both sets of characters, the girls and the boys oblivious to each other, played simultaneous scenes in the same location. During the scene the actors swapped costumes as the boys changed out of their Roller gear and the girls changed into theirs. It was a good stunt. I cast Nicola Redmond, Joanne Pearce and Ona McCracken as the girls, and Stevie Graham and Peter Jonfield as the boys. Geoff Rose did the design. The show opened with the girls performing a karaoke version of Sweet's blockbuster 'Blockbuster', and was an evening of loud, vulgar, politically incorrect full-frontal joy. In addition to impersonating the Rollers, Stevie Graham and Jonfield were also the Sensational Soul Brothers, blacking up to perform James Brown's 'Sex Machine'. The play also had real depth and insight and was a great piece of genuine popular theatre. After selling out the Christmas run at the Bush we took *Shang-A-Lang* on a number-one tour, playing, in some cases, theatres with over a thousand seats. This helped to demolish the myth that Bush shows only worked in our intimate space. The secret is always to tell the truth. On a bigger stage you just have to tell it bigger.

In Northampton, the local paper reviewing *Shang-A-Lang* said, 'This is the kind of thing that prevents Northampton from becoming a city.'

At the beginning of 1999 we were told that we had been successful in our Arts for Everyone Lottery application. We did not get the full five hundred thousand, but enough to put most of our plans in motion. It meant that we could mount one extra in-house production a year, that we could increase the number of commissions we issued, concentrating on providing support to relatively unknown writers. We could pay the writers and readers more and increase the number of workshops and rehearsed readings we provided to serve the development of the new commissions. We would pay the actors, designers and directors involved proper fees. We also decided to extend the work we did with the National Student Drama Festival. We actually bought a working computer, and we made plans to move the office out of our foetid basement into somewhere suitable for human habitation. The Lottery grant would last for three years.

At about the same time the Arts Council commissioned consultant Peter Boyden to prepare a report on the current state of theatre in the country, decimated by the disastrous Conservative arts policies. In the eighteen years of Tory enterprise culture, over a quarter of the regional producing theatres had been forced to close. Those that were left were running a collective deficit of £6 million, which was more than their total annual subsidy. As well as a financial deficit, most theatres had an artistic deficit as well. New writing was almost invisible as theatres favoured safe programming that would not offend the bodies both public and private, local and national, that held the purse strings. Even the major subsidised venues became a risk-free zone, churning out interminable productions of deservedly neglected European classics played out on Expressionist sets filched from Ruth Berghaus's recently published book of theatre design. Things indeed could only get better.

Although this was obviously good news it become increasingly clear to us that the neither the Arts Council nor the National Lottery had any intention of financing or even helping the Bush to find a new space. I had to come up with a new plan. Around the corner from the Fringe and Firkin was another Allied Domecq pub, The Richmond. It was also a Victorian pile with many unused rooms and sufficient space to build an extension. It was also virtually empty with a diminishing band of local regulars just like the Bush had been before the Empire became a rock venue. It certainly wasn't making money, and I reasoned that there were many more pubs in the same situation throughout London. Up to now the model for pub theatre had been to run a pub with a theatre in it. My idea was to run a theatre with a pub in it. In the spirit of the times I wrote a report with the hugely portentous title of *Reinventing Pub Theatre for the New Millennium*. The wheeze was simple. Allied Domecq or some other brewery chain would give us a rundown West London pub with good transport connections. We would gut it and build a hundred-seat theatre with proper backstage facilities, office and rehearsal space and a small workshop. A bar and bistro area run by the brewery would be part of the scheme. The bar would be open during pub hours but would be orientated to the needs of the theatre and its audience. It would not have a jukebox, but there could be after-show cabaret in the bar. It was not a million miles from the original idea for the Hull Truck Theatre in the old grain warehouse.

I presented the report to the Board and sent a copy to Ian Oag at Allied Domecq. I pointed out the scheme would look good in terms of Corporate Responsibility, and it might even make them a few quid.

The 1999 season opened with *In Flame* by Charlotte Jones. The play was brought to my attention and produced in conjunction with thrusting young producer Matthew Byam Shaw. Many years ago I had directed Matthew in a devised show at Bristol University. The show ended with Matthew standing on the roof of the theatre with a traffic cone on his head shouting, 'I am Superjew.' He had helped me run the gala, and I had found him a place on the Board because I thought he had good taste.

In Flame was an odd tale set in both Victorian England and the present day, and was stylishly directed by Anna Mackmin with a couple of entertaining if superfluous dance routines, one involving a wheelchair. The show attracted a cult following and transferred briefly to the West End. Charlotte Jones moved on to write for more glamorous playhouses.

The season continued with three consecutive in-house productions: *Howie the Rookie* by Mark O'Rowe, *Card Boys* by Mike Packer and *Dogs Barking* by Richard Zajdlic.

Howie the Rookie came through the post. Tim gave it a second read and quickly passed it on to me. I had read a previous play that Mark had written for a Dublin youth theatre, which showed promise, but this was something else. Written in Dublin street slang, the play flew off the page like Joyce on crystal meth. There are two unrelated characters, the Howie Lee and the Rookie Lee. In interconnecting monologues the Howie tells the first half of the story, which involves a chase through night-time Dublin to beat up the Rookie, who has infected a mattress with scabies, and culminates in the violent death of his five-year-old brother, the Mouse. In the second half the Rookie faces a punishment beating for accidentally killing a gangster's Siamese fighting fish until he is saved by the Howie, avenging the death of his brother. It's visceral, it's violent, it's sexy, it's gloriously funny, it's about redemption and it has the power of Greek tragedy. I went to Dublin and recruited Aidan Kelly and Karl Shiels, two brilliant young actors. Es Devlin did the set—a savage strip of tarmac and barbed wire lit with fluorescent tubing.

The monologues in *Howie the Rookie* have to be played on the front foot. They are told in the present tense—unlike, say, *St Nicholas*, which is told in the past tense. This requires a different energy, the energy of stand-up comedy. We started off by watching tapes of Bill Hicks. In rehearsals we decided that what we were going for was stand-up *drama*. I was adamant that the actors talked to the audience rather than at them. They had to believe that the actors were telling the tale to each of them personally, and telling it for the first time. I rehearsed Karl and Aidan separately and secretly. I wanted each of them to find their own rhythm and style of storytelling and not to be influenced by one another. We also hit on the idea of storyboarding: imagine that you go and see a movie and then go to the pub and tell your mates about it. You are describing what you have just seen, shot by shot. For the major descriptive passages Karl, Aidan and I sat down and worked out what the movie version of the scene was like, or the strip-cartoon version. Where were the close-ups? Was this a tracking shot? It must have worked because almost every night as the Rookie described the final carnage as the Howie is impaled on a set of railings before being ploughed into by a Hiace van, audience members turned away and hid their eyes. They couldn't bear to watch… what? A bloke standing on stage telling them a story.

Howie was a bit of a sleeper. The reviews at the Bush were fine and the audiences were OK, but we clearly suffered from the peculiarly English prejudice about monologues. It's as though the audience feel in some way short-changed if they know no one else is going to come on. Straight after the London run we were invited to open the brand-new Civic Theatre in Tallaght, where Mark O'Rowe comes from and where the play is set. The show was a sensation in Dublin, quickly transferring to the Andrews Lane Theatre in the city centre. The real fuss, however, started later in the year when we took *Howie* to Edinburgh.

Mike Packer's *Card Boys* was an everyday story of lowlife folk. Card boys are the guys that stick up the cards in phones boxes advertising hookers, and the play is set in the street-savvy world of pimps, prostitutes, part-time villains and dope dealers. Simon Usher's production was graced by a brilliant performance by Willie Ross as the Geordie wino, Teddy. Willie, who starred in Alan Clarke's film *Rita, Sue and Bob Too*, started out as a comic on the northern club circuit. In *Card Boys* he said 'cunt' one hundred and forty-seven times, which I think may be some kind of record. One night he set his pants on fire.

I also directed Richard Zajdlic's *Dogs Barking*. I had directed a couple of shows for Richard's company, Ratskins, several years earlier and also *Rage*, his previous play at the Bush in 1994. *Dogs Barking* is a deeply unsettling play about love gone wrong. After the break-up of their relationship Alex, played by Raquel Cassidy, tries to evict her borderline psychotic ex-partner Neil (Tony Curran) from their shared flat. The play warns that material success will not shield you from hurt and violence. Since our Bush production in 1999 *Dogs Barking* has been performed all over the world. On the strength of the play Zajdlic disappeared into the world of television, whence he has never emerged.

According to critic Aleks Sierz the three plays in the spring season were classic examples of 'In Yer Face' Theatre, whatever that might be.

We launched the Channel Four scheme, now called 'Breaking In', with a posh party at Teatro. Our slogan was 'No Cops, No Docs, No Vets.' According to *The Stage*, I said that:

> We want writers to bring their imagination to TV drama. We want this to encourage writers with vision and imagination back into television. Too many dramas are based on conventional genres, and there is a bogus premise that the single play is dead.

Gub Neal said that the collaboration gave Channel Four 'the opportunity to do for television drama what *Trainspotting* did for Film Four'. We vowed to continue the scheme until we got sacked.

Ian Oag from Allied Domeq got back to me. He was incredibly impressed with the *Reinventing Pub Theatre for the New Millennium* document, and he was going to present the scheme to his Board of Directors. He was convinced that they would go for it, and indeed suggested that we should open a chain of Bush Theatre Pubs throughout the country. I told him that I thought that this was a bit over-the-top and that we should probably concentrate on one at a time. Nonetheless it looked like we had got a result.

My excitement was tempered by Deborah Aydon's decision to leave the Bush after six years. She had been headhunted for the job of Executive Producer with the Rough Magic Theatre Company in Dublin. They had ambitious plans to open the first new-writing theatre in Ireland in a dilapidated Viking Wax Museum, and Deborah would spearhead the scheme. I was sad to see her go. The Board of the Bush decided that rather than advertise for a new General Manager they would advertise instead for an Executive Producer. I think that they had been impressed by Deborah's new job title. The argument was that 'Executive Producer' would attract a better class of applicant than 'General Manager'—Peter Stevens thought that it was a piece of needless window-dressing. He believed that the running of the theatre should be in the hands of the Artistic Director and was suspicious of extra executives with important titles. I said that they could call the job whatever they liked as long as the actual job description stayed the same. There were four candidates on the short list for the Executive Producer post. Two of them were surprised to learn that they would not be in charge of artistic programming. The best candidate by far was Fiona Clark. Fiona had been working in commercial theatre with producer Danny Moar at Bath Theatre Royal, where she had run the Ustinov Studio. She was ruthlessly ambitious. She got the job.

The season continued at the Bush with two touring productions, *High Life* by Lee MacDougall and *Mainstream* by David Greig, a performance piece that we had commissioned and co-produced with Scottish company Suspect Culture. *High Life* was a Canadian comedy about a bunch of incompetent morphine addicts trying to rob a bank. With Nigel Planer, David Schofield and Paul Barber from *The Full Monty* in the cast, producer David Johnson hoped it would go into the West End. It didn't.

In addition we produced a new version of Adrian Pagan's play *The Backroom*. Adrian had been a stage manager at the Bush, and this, his first play, had won the Soho Theatre's Verity Bargate Award the year before. Soho had produced it for a handful of workshop performances at the Pleasance. I thought it was terrific but needed more work. I asked Abigail Morris at Soho to consider a co-production but she wasn't interested, so I commissioned Adrian to write a new draft. *The Backroom* was a Feydeau-style farce set in a gay brothel in Earls Court. It packed out the theatre throughout the long hot summer of 1999, when the lack of air conditioning made theatregoing particularly uncomfortable, especially for those members of the audience who turned up in leather trousers.

Tim Fountain and I used some of the A4E money to commission new plays from Richard Cameron, Catherine Johnson, Lin Coghlan and Helen Blakeman, plus new writers Georgia Fitch, Tracy O'Flaherty and Kofi Agyemang. We sent Jonathan Hall off to stay at a gay B&B in Blackpool and Mike Packer infiltrated a group of ticket touts ending up in Belgium for Euro 2000. David Eldridge went to Dover where the National Front had organised violent demonstrations against asylum seekers and the local paper had referred to immigrants as 'human sewage'. Tim and I also tried to find a project for Bette Bourne.

Bette, originally called Peter Bourne, had been a rising young star in the Sixties, touring in Shakespeare with his contemporary Ian McKellen and appearing in the West End. In the Seventies he came out, became a founder member of the Gay Liberation Front and started a radical drag-queen commune in Notting Hill Gate. Inspired by the American Queer company Hot Peaches, Bette formed the drag cabaret outfit Bloolips and toured Europe with shows like *Slung Back and Strapless* and the Roman epic *Get Hur*, eventually conquering New York where Bette became a legend in his own lipstick. I had seen several Bloolips shows at the Drill Hall, but was completely blown away by Bette's performance as the castrato singer La Zambinella in Neil Bartlett's chamber opera *Sarrasine*. Tim and I met Bette on several occasions to talk about ideas and scripts. None of them was much good. One day Bette started to tell anecdotes about his friend of twenty years, Quentin Crisp. They were much more exciting than the yet another turgid pastiche of *Zoo Story* we had been discussing. On the way back to the office Tim had an epiphany on Shepherd's Bush Green. Why don't we get Bette to play Quentin?

Bette was unconvinced but brightened up when I told him that if we got it right the show could be his pension scheme. He agreed to write to Quentin for permission. Mr Crisp wrote back:

> I give my permission for Mr Bourne to impersonate me as fully and for as long as he likes.

In a burst of nepotism I commissioned Tim to write the script.

Howie the Rookie opened at the Assembly Rooms in Edinburgh and, with five-star reviews across the board and the Herald Angel Award for Best Production, became the must-see sell-out hit of the Festival. Karl and Aidan were treated like superstars. Mark Russell invited us to tour the show to Performance Space 122 in New York, and Wes Moore from Vanguard booked us into the Magic in San Francisco.

The Channel Four plays turned out to be a nightmare. Deborah Aydon had spent months negotiating with the twelve writers and their twelve agents to commission twelve treatments, twelve one-act stage plays which were also twelve television plays which were twelve pilots for twelve potential television series or serials. Both the Bush and Channel Four insisted that everybody got the same deal, but the agents didn't.

Several writers found it difficult to reconcile the conflicting demands of a one-act stage play and a TV series, and a couple of them never got past the treatment stage. The final choice of the two plays we were going to produce became a tug of love between the producing entities, and the resulting compromise ended up serving neither. The winners were Sam Adamson with *Drink, Dance, Laugh and Lie*, about a children's television presenter blackmailed into appearing in a gay porn film; and Mette Bolstad's *One Life and Counting*, about a family of Norwegian Elvis impersonators who win a girl in a raffle.

I thought it would be in the spirit of the enterprise to give two bright young directors, Angus Jackson and Sacha Wares, the opportunity of directing the plays. This also proved to be a mistake, but it wasn't their fault. We had managed to choose the two most technically difficult plays in the bunch. One was set in a trailer and one was multi-locational, involving a bed-sit, a bus stop and a blowjob. Both featured multiple TV screens, video technology and complicated soundtracks, and we were presenting them as a double bill on one evening. I engaged the brilliant Es Devlin as designer but even her talents were stretched. The writers and directors clearly saw the whole event as a golden opportunity to break into television, and so were unwilling to compromise their exciting visual concepts for the greater good. The scripts, though fun, were not exactly the greatest either.

The read-through went very well. Both casts were excellent, and Gub Neal from Channel Four announced that he thought both plays were superb and would make terrific single dramas, possibly on film, etc., etc. We never saw him again. The technical rehearsal took days, and the crew didn't sleep for a week, but the previews went well. The press night was a fiasco. It was normal practice at the Bush to limit the press-night audience to eighty. This is because the seats are uncomfortable at the best of times, but when the audience are packed in like pilchards it can get claustrophobic as well. As part of the deal Channel Four had demanded a VIP allocation of forty tickets. Not a single one of them turned up. The audience therefore comprised thirty critics plus the Bush staff and anybody we could round up from the pub at the last moment. The atmosphere was dreadful. There were no laughs and the plays died on their feet. At the post-show party the writers, directors and actors stood sullenly in corners, silently accusing us of letting them and their plays down. They were probably right.

I had been so keen to prise money out of Channel Four that I had initiated a project that failed to satisfy either party. The upside was that twelve writers got a commission and an introduction to Channel Four. The Bush got a free production and a heap of heartache. I think that Channel Four should have had the confidence just to give us the money to do what we do, putting on plays and developing new writers, rather than tying it in to an unsatisfactory hybrid end-product. Channel Four probably felt they shouldn't have got involved in the first place. They certainly never repeated the experiment. Some days you eat the bear; some days the bear eats you.

A meeting with Ian Oag to discuss the next stage in *Reinventing Pub Theatre for the New Millennium* was suddenly cancelled. Allied Domecq had sold all their pubs. The Fringe and Firkin had been sold on to an outfit called Punch Taverns. The whole scheme was off. Fiona and I desperately searched *Who's Who* to find out if anyone on the Punch Board or Corporate Executive had the slightest interest in the arts and could be persuaded to take up the project but, by the time we had found out that there wasn't anybody, Punch Taverns had sold the pub on to Bass. Bass had no knowledge of our existence whatsoever. They told us that they once again planned to refurbish and rebrand the pub. This would be twice in less than four years. In terms of finding a new space we were back to where we had started.

Tim's technique in writing *Resident Alien* was to read everything that Quentin Crisp had written and steal the good bits. The next stage was to interview him in New York. Quentin, as always, gave a performance. This gave Tim the idea for the structure of the play. He then stole the plot from *Waiting for Godot*. This is the plot:

It is winter. Quentin Crisp is in bed in his New York apartment watching Oprah Winfrey under the blankets. The apartment has not been cleaned for many years. Quentin slowly gets dressed, puts on his make-up and explains to us that he has an appointment with a Mr Brown and a Mr Black who want to take him to lunch and talk to him about style. They are late; so to pass the time he tells us his life story and how he comes to be living in the last rooming house in New York. It snows. The doorbell rings and Mr Crisp goes out to lunch. Interval. Mr Crisp returns. It wasn't them. Quentin tells us more about style instead. He cooks an egg. Mr Brown and Mr Black telephone and rearrange the lunch meeting for the next day.

Bette had known Quentin for years, and his characterisation transcended impersonation, turning what could have easily become a cabaret act, albeit an hilarious one, into a profound and moving testimony to Quentin's inspiration and courage. He had been *out* in the Twenties, the Thirties, the Forties, the Fifties, the Sixties, the Seventies, the Eighties, the Nineties, and here he was, still tinting. Bette's wig, however, was terrible. It looked like he had stuck his head up a dead badger.

The play opened at the Bush on 10 November and was greeted enthusiastically by the critics. The *Financial Times* critic said that Bette was 'one of the most compelling performers that he had ever seen on a stage', and that Bette 'as much as Crisp was one of the stately homos of England'.

I went on holiday to Cuba. On 23 November in a guest house in the middle of a rain forest I got a telegram from Fiona in the office: 'By now you will have heard that Quentin is dead...' I had heard nothing.

While Tim, Bette and I were rehearsing, Quentin had given an interview to the *Daily Telegraph* in which he said that he was dreading the show and thought that we were going to send him up. Despite being ill he then announced that he would return to England, something he had long vowed he would never do, to tour his own one-man show. Perhaps he wanted English audiences to have one last opportunity to see the real thing. He spoke to Tim on the phone and, ever contradictory, wished us luck and suggested that we should join forces to publicise both shows. He even arranged to take tea with Bette on Geoff Rose's brilliant set, which forensically recreated his famous East 3rd Street room on the stage of the Bush.

On Sunday 18 November with 'a hernia as big as an orange', Quentin flew into Manchester for the first leg of his tour. He was driven to his digs in a boarding house in Chorlton-cum-Hardy. After a cup of tea and several glasses of brandy he retired to his bed. Next morning he was dead. The policeman who attended the scene was called PC Sissey. Our show, which started out as a celebration, had become a requiem. At the end of the play Quentin pours himself a generous glass of whiskey and raises his glass—'To life, a funny thing that happens to you on the way to the grave.'

In December we moved into the new office. It was a vast improvement. It had windows. For the first time we had luxuries like enough computers, printers, a photocopying machine and a working phone system. Fiona installed a computerised box-office system, which was also a vast improvement. Previously whoever answered the phone took bookings, writing them down in a ledger and issuing cloakroom tickets. The move also marked the beginning of a subtle change in the culture. Deborah and I had run the office by simply talking to people and having conversations in the pub. Now there were schedules and memos and agendas and meetings and minutes and reports. The Administrator had mysteriously become the General Manager, and there were plans to recruit an Assistant General Manager. Suddenly there were Heads of Department and Line Managers and Targets and Staff Appraisals and Disciplinary Procedures, all of which seemed more appropriate for a multinational conglomerate or a branch of the Civil Service rather than for a radical theatre company with a full-time staff of eight. It seemed that in exchange for increased efficiency we had to accept a load of spurious and anally retentive business practice. It suddenly dawned on me that I was twenty years older than everybody else at the Bush. They were all Thatcher's children.

The New Millennium season kicked of with *The Maiden's Prayer* by American writer Nicky Silver, directed by Sarah Esdaile and containing a terrific performance from Eric Loren as several American homosexuals. Simon Block's *A Place at the Table* was a brilliant satire on the dumbing down of the television industry and the predominance of focus-group culture. Script Associate Sarah (Joanne Pearce) meets disabled playwright Adam (Eddie Marsan) with a view to producing his fringe hit play for television. Sacrificing all her principles for career advancement she first persuades him to turn it into a sit-com and then dumps it altogether. It was a great antidote to the Channel Four debacle.

The Glasgow Citizens' Theatre toured in with Harry Gibson's adaptation of Irvine Welsh's *Filth*. Tam Dean Burn violently played a violent bent copper with a missing wife, a drug habit and a talkative tapeworm. During the run of the play Tam had an altercation with a barman in the pub downstairs, who took his revenge by taking a dump on the set.

Fiona and I began negotiations with the new owners Bass about the future of the Fringe and Firkin. Bass ran three different pub chains, each with its own special identity and target demographic. We hoped that they would choose the brand that chimed most sympathetically with the needs of the theatre. Some hopes. The three possibilities were: All Bar One, described as stylish, cosmopolitan and female-friendly with a mature guest basis; O'Neill's, a pastiche traditional Irish pub with a warm welcome, live music and great craic; and Scream, aimed at 'students and like-minded individuals' with a quirky attitude to life and style and with a logo adapted from the Munch painting. Scream pubs were similar vomitaria to the Firkins, but without the urban sophistication. Bass chose O'Neill's.

The pub and the theatre would have to close over the summer for rebuilding and rebranding. The Bush had evolved from being a genuine Irish pub into a bogus Irish pub in less than thirty years.

The Boyden Report, commissioned by the Arts Council, was finally published. It concluded that theatres had been inadequately funded since the beginning of the Eighties and that many companies were operating on a deficit and close to bankruptcy. The report recommended that funding mechanisms and organisations should be overhauled and that £25 million would have to be found just to stop the rot. In response the Government pledged to increase Arts Council funding from £252 million to £337 million over the next three years. This was great news, but the increase in funding came at a price. New Labour had their own agenda.

The Government thought that the arts were elitist, but they also believed that they could be transformed into a catalyst for social change. The Arts Council, although theoretically politically impartial, once again became an agent for Government policy. Theatres would now have to prioritise social and sexual inclusion, cultural diversity, education, education, education, disability, outreach and access. They were charged with developing new audiences and embracing multiculturalism. They had to overhaul their artistic programmes to appeal to audiences from a wider spectrum of society and with a wider ethnic balance, while simultaneously offering innovation and excellence. They had to outreach into their local communities and schools, and provide value for money for the stakeholders. God knows when there would be any time to put on plays. Their funding levels would now be assessed on their achievement of 'measurable success factors', although nobody seemed to know what these were. There was also an implicit suggestion that organisations failing to meet these targets were institutionally racist, sexist, ageist, homophobic and disabilist.

The ideals behind all these initiatives were exemplary, and you would have been hard pushed to find anyone in theatre who disagreed with them. The problem was that most of the directives were ill-conceived, spurious, and often contradictory exercises in box-ticking. The transformative power of theatre and of art lies in the work itself. Sometimes that work is difficult. Sometimes it's offensive. It is imperative that access to theatre is available and affordable to all, especially people who claim that it's only for snobs or toffs or white people, but you do not achieve this by making the work less challenging or less offensive to satisfy notions of inclusivity. It would be possible to make a public swimming pool more attractive to non-swimming tax-paying stakeholders by draining all the water. But it would no longer be a swimming pool.

Whilst initiating all this utopian social engineering, New Labour, ever relaxed about the filthy rich, managed simultaneously to embrace Tory market-driven enterprise culture and the cult of the managerial classes. Arts practitioners found themselves becoming increasingly schizophrenic as they tried to serve both monetarist and socially inclusive agendas.

The Arts Council issued a list of eight priorities that they expected theatres to address in order to qualify for increased funding:

A better range of high-quality work.

Attract more people.

Develop new ways of working.

Education—we expect funded theatres to place education at the heart of their work.

Address diversity and inclusion—we expect the theatre community to develop work that speaks to diverse audiences. We want to see an increase in the workforce from the non-white population.

Develop the artists and creative managers of the future.

An international reputation.

Regional distinctiveness.

It seemed to me that the Bush fulfilled most of these conditions. I was unsure as to exactly what the regional distinctiveness of Shepherd's Bush was, but I was certainly prepared to find out. Sue Timothy, still hanging on at the London Arts Board, thought that we were definite candidates for a funding uplift. She did, however, warn me that we might have a problem in terms of our education work. Although we provided free dramaturgical support and encouragement to over a thousand new writers every year, and now had in place a comprehensive Writers' Development Programme, this apparently did not count. It was the wrong sort of education.

I believe that theatre is educational per se. I think an involvement with theatre and drama from as early an age as possible is as important to the future of our children and to the health of our society as maths and spelling. Nevertheless I pointed out that as we only had a full-time staff of eight and as they were fully engaged in producing eight shows a year, commissioning writers, building audiences, developing new ways of working, running workshops, organising both national and international touring, dealing with the refurbishment, and going about the actual business of running a theatre, there was no time available for us to offer workshops on Brecht to bored teenagers. Another problem was that the content of most of our work was apparently not considered suitable for anyone under sixteen. I couldn't see what more we could do without diverting funds away from our core purpose of discovering, nurturing and producing new writing to create a whole new department and in doing so possibly compromising the nature of the work. Sue saw my point.

Meanwhile, we carried on with the season. I directed Helen Blakeman's new play, *Normal*. Helen had become our writer-in-residence as a result of the success of *Caravan*, but *Normal* was a very different kind of play altogether. Strange and dark, the piece took as its theme Münchausen syndrome by proxy, a psychological condition by which a parent or carer harms or injures a child in order to win praise for their subsequent devoted care of, and attention to, the child. The play centres on the relationship between Merseyside mother Joan and her daughter Kate and the secrets they share. It's also about self-harm, plastic surgery and phone sex, and it ends in violence and death. *Normal* is difficult and uncompromising and was a huge step in Helen's writing. I cast Marion Bailey, Lisa Ellis, Ben Crompton, Sam Graham, Chris Barnes and Emma Pike, and I think we made a really good job of it.

Producer Adam Kenwright came to the first preview. He said that he wanted to take it into the West End. Adam brought producer Sonia Friedman to the second preview. She wanted to transfer it too. They were convinced that the critics would love it. I was not so sure. The critics didn't like it very much; in fact most of them didn't get it. We heard no more from Adam and Sonia.

We followed *Normal* with *Mrs Steinberg and the Byker Boy* by Michael Wilcox, in which a Newcastle Socialist charity shop is transformed into a thrusting market-driven business by a gay work-experience student. The play, a not particularly subtle allegory for the rise of New Labour, also contained some steamy gay sex and a magnificent central performance by Theatre Workshop's Miriam Karlin as Mrs Steinberg, whose seventieth birthday we celebrated on stage.

It was becoming increasingly obvious that in the long run we still had to move ahead in finding a new space. Fiona believed that we needed to change the nature and complexion of the Board to achieve this. She decided to organise a Board of Directors' Development Day. She was also encouraged by the Arts Council to conduct a 'Skills Audit' in order to determine if the Board members had the right skills and talents needed to take the theatre forward. They even recommended an arts professional consultant who would act as facilitator for the exercise. Barbara Matthews had been General Manager of Cheek by Jowl but was now carving herself out a consultancy career. I was not convinced that she knew any more about theatre than I did and thought that we could save ourselves the fee but, in the spirit of harmony and with a degree of curiosity, agreed to go along with the exercise.

The day did not start well. Chair Tracey Scoffield read out a letter of resignation from Peter Stevens. Peter thought that the whole Development Day caper was a nonsense. He didn't want be associated with a theatre that indulged in what he called 'babbletosh'; he thought that the Skills Audit was insulting and as a result was not prepared to sit on the Board any longer. In retrospect I know that he was right and that he could see the trouble ahead, but at the time I thought it was over-the-top and an unhelpful gesture. If he thought it was a bunch of bollocks, why didn't he just turn up and say so?

There then followed a lot of talk about Corporate Governance, and Barbara Matthews drew some diagrams on a whiteboard. The Skills Audit apparently revealed that we needed to appoint new Board members with expertise in Development and Fundraising, Accountancy, Marketing, Press and Public Relations, Capital Lottery Projects and Information Technology. Unfortunately the only Board member who possessed any of these skills had just resigned because of the Skills Audit. Barbara suggested that the Bush recruit sympathetic executives from the City or the world of Corporate Finance. Also in the future we would need to commission consultants to prepare a Business Plan, an Options Analysis and a Feasibility Study, and we would have to appoint a full-time Development Officer and no doubt desks full of wealth creators. I said that the greatest, and indeed only, asset that the Bush had got was the work, and the success of the work was a result of the collective involvement of everybody in the theatre. I was not prepared to pay self-important consultants vastly inflated fees when we were still paying a pittance to the writers, actors, directors and designers—the real stakeholders who genuinely subsidised the theatre with their time, their talent and their labour. I thought that it would be a betrayal of everything the Bush stood for.

The secret was to find a way to build a new theatre without compromising either the work or our ideals. I didn't want us to become a boutique theatre like the Donmar or the Almeida. I just wanted to be better at being the Bush. I don't think Barbara Matthews was particularly impressed with my speech, and I soon realised that I was possibly fighting a losing battle. The line had been drawn and the curse had been cast. Around this time Fiona told me that she wanted to be Joint Chief Executive Officer. She felt her lack of significant status meant that she could not hold her head up in elevated Executive company.

Jim Nicola from the New York Theatre Workshop wanted to take *Resident Alien* to New York. The Workshop was on the up having successfully transferred *Rent* to Broadway. Jim had known Bette from Bloolips days, and Quentin had lived two minutes away from the theatre, so it seemed the perfect gig. I went over to view the space, and Fiona went over to do the deal. Everything seemed to be in place. Then Nicola changed his mind. He wanted to mount his own production with Bette playing Quentin. His rationale was that the Bush was not sufficiently experienced a theatre to organise the transfer to New York, that the fee was too expensive and that New York Theatre Workshop were producers not presenters. This was a complete *volte-face*, and we were furious. We did, however, hold the rights to the play so there wasn't much he could do without them. We soon discovered that Jim's manoeuvre was standard New York Theatre Workshop practice. They wanted to give the impression that they had discovered the show in order to big up their reputation with their subscribers and to secure the lion's share of any Broadway transfer. After weeks of negotiation we hammered out a deal. They would produce it in association with the Bush. It would essentially be our production, but they would pay for the new set and the rehearsal costs. We would split the profits. It cost them far more than if they had just toured in our production as originally agreed. The Bush would open both *Resident Alien* and *Howie the Rookie* in the same week in two Off-Broadway theatres two blocks apart. I told the very expensive publicist that the Workshop had hired that I thought this might be a good selling point. 'Nah,' he said, 'who gives a fuck about Howard the Duck?'

As part of the increased theatre subsidy generated by the Boyden Report, the Bush received a modest uplift in revenue funding from the Arts Council. Ironically it was just about enough to cover the cost of the enforced closure and pay for the refurb. Financially we were effectively at a standstill. Our direct new-writing competitors, the Royal Court, Soho and Hampstead, received proportionately far more spectacular increases, but this went mostly to offset unseen increased running costs incurred as a result of building new theatres. Hampstead, for instance, apparently now had an astronomical window-cleaning bill.

The pub was refurbished over the summer, and so was the theatre, Fiona supervising the transformation. The box office and foyer had always looked like a Pollock's Victorian Toy Theatre long abandoned by a disinterested child, but now was sexy and modern, and for the first time the theatre had real seats. The pub was now O'Neill's, and the walls were hung with harps, shillelaghs, artistically foxed sepia photographs of James Joyce, Brendan Behan and Flann O'Brien, and framed copies of the sheet music for 'How Are Things in Glocca Morra?' and 'The Rose of Tralee'. To celebrate all this paddy-whackery, we opened the new season with *Hijra* by Indian playwright Ash Kotak.

Hijra was a big sprawling mess of a play. Tim and I had worked on it for months. We were in danger of dramaturging it to death, so in the end we decided that the only thing left to do was to put it on and see what happened. What happened was the play caused quite a fuss. *Hijra* is as far as I know the only Gujarati gay coming-out transvestite magical-realism eunuch sex farce ever performed in Britain. The plot is really quite simple.

In-the-closet Indian gay Nils from Wembley is taken by his mother to find a bride in the Bombay wedding season. She fixes him up with Sheila, but Nils fixes himself up with Raj, a trainee cross-dressing hijra he meets on the gay-cruising beach. Smitten with love, Nils smuggles Raj back to England where he poses as Nils's new wife Rani. Then Mum and Sheila turn up and there's a lot of jumping in and out of saris until the mystical guru Hijra weaves a magic spell and everyone ends up happy and homo in Harlesden. Director Ian Brown imported a Bollywood cast from Mumbai and, except for the occasional death threat, a jolly multicultural time was had by all.

Tim, Bette and I arrived in New York to remount *Resident Alien* the week before Christmas. It was freezing, and New York Theatre Workshop still hadn't signed the contract. There were forty-three people at the read-through, mostly called Larry, and we had doughnuts, muffins, bagels, Honey Nut Loops, muesli, crunchy granola and a double-cinnamon hazelnut chocolate-chip wheat-germ skinny lo-cal decaff. Bette smoked a cigarette. The Larrys nervously eyed the sprinkler system. Rehearsals began. Bette is an Alternative Diva in the East Village and behaved like one. At the costume fitting there were rows of new coats and hats and shirts and jackets, and Bette rejected them all. The wigmeister from the Met was called away from dealing with Pavarotti to sort out the syrup. Christmas came and went, and we moved into the theatre to rehearse on the set. The snow machine blew up three times. They should just have cut a hole in the roof. Outside the worst blizzard for fifteen years was raging. I got a call from PS 122. The set for *Howie the Rookie* and Fiona were stuck in Washington, and the visas for the actors had gone missing. We started the tech for *Resident Alien*. Bette didn't like his spotlight but now loved his wig. Scott on the box office was crocheting him a new shawl. Fiona and the *Howie* boys arrived, and we went straight into the tech at PS 122 then back to the tech at the Workshop, trudging through the snow. Jim Nicola still hadn't signed the contract. *Howie* opened at PS

122 after only one preview. I missed the opening because of the dress rehearsal for *Resident Alien*, but when I got back to the theatre everyone was ecstatic. Ben Brantley from the *New York Times* had been in. This was clearly a big deal. New York theatre folk are Pavlovian about the *Times*. The British Council, who had initially refused to back the show, now threw a party for us in a bar decorated with British red telephone boxes. We were their new best friend. Next day was the first preview of *Resident Alien*. Big Warhol posters of Bette went up in the foyer. The Bush's credit was nowhere to be seen. As the audience arrived Fiona and I were in the middle of a stand-up row with the Workshop Administrator. We told him Bette would not go on unless he signed the contract and changed the poster. We were not bluffing. He signed the contract. Bette was magnificent. Everyone talked Broadway, and Tim went to Joe Allen's.

Early next morning Fiona called me from the airport. She was on her way to Chicago to negotiate a gig for *Howie*. The *Times* review had come out and it was a rave. I went down to the news-stand to buy a copy; when I came back there were eleven messages on my machine. The *really* big deal *Times* review is when you get a colour photo and the review is printed above the fold. We had one of those. It's the theatrical equivalent of winning the Lottery.

The message from Wes Moore from San Francisco said:

Hey man, are you riding around in a Chevy with roses in your buttonhole?

The message from Lighting Designer Brian McDevitt said:

Hey man, you're fucked. From now on it will be nothing but uptown Jews.

Ben Brantley in the *New York Times* said:

Both actors are excellent. What these young men have in common is the ability to make language a living, growing organism. They make us hear the world with new ears in a way that only fine theatre can. *Howie the Rookie*, at Performance Space 122 through Jan 27, gives you that priceless, delirious high that comes from hearing words made flesh.

Later that morning I bumped into the Theatre Workshop's very expensive publicist putting up the corrected *Resident Alien* posters outside the theatre. He looked sick. Howard the fucking Duck indeed.

Howie was the talk of the town, and Wes Moore was determined to set up a lucrative Off-Broadway transfer with a major producer. He took Fiona and I off to see Fred Zollo. Zollo was brash, rude and self-important. We thought he was an arsehole, but Wes said he was the real thing.

We went to look at the Jane Street Theatre in the seedy ballroom of a flophouse hotel down by the river in the West Village. The theatre previously housed *Debbie Does Dallas*. The hotel previously housed the survivors from the *Titanic*. It was the perfect venue for *Howie the Rookie*.

Ben Brantley came to see *Resident Alien*. Everyone treated him like royalty. As the curtain went up a very large and very noisy woman pushed him out of his seat. She was a major donor to the theatre. Jim Nicola went white as a furious Brantley had to clamber ungainly over two rows to find a new place to sit. We all went to the pub next door.

The opening-night party was at the Cooper Diner, Quentin's favourite restaurant. They used to give him free whiskey if he sat in the window to attract custom. In traditional style the *Times* review arrived just after midnight. In any other circumstances it would have been a terrific notice but it was never going to match up to *Howie*. Brantley loved Bette though, and we partied long and hard. Next morning I had breakfast with playwright Michael Weller. 'You have been twice blessed, my son,' he said. 'Twice blessed.'

With both shows selling out and queues around the block I flew back home. Wes and Zollo were going to transfer *Howie* in the spring, and Bette was the Queen of East 3rd Street. If you can make it there you can make it anywhere. In London the theatre had flooded: one of the bar staff had blocked the drainpipe with his underpants.

10

Same as the Old Boss

In fact there were queues round the block in Shepherd's Bush as well. I had booked in the National Theatre of Brent for the Christmas season.

Patrick Barlow and John Ramm as Desmond Dingle and his assistant, Raymond Box, had elected to revive *The Messiah*, almost certainly the most profound yet at the same time highly popular oeuvres ever known in the entire British theatre. First performed to massive universal acclaim in 1983, *The Messiah 2000* proved to be a radical yet moving update of the original award-winning text, including many specially researched brand new sequences culled from the very latest biblical findings. Initially Desmond had demanded a live donkey and a children's choir, but eventually settled for an opera singer to assist the ensemble company of two re-enact the birth of Jesus, including all of the best loved characters, Jesus, Joseph, the Virgin Mary, the Archangel Gabriel, Herod, God and many more. A particularly profound exchange went as follows:

MARY. I'm having a baby.

JOSEPH. When's it due?

MARY. Christmas.

The 2001 season opened with Kay Adshead's *The Bogus Woman*, a co-production with the Red Room, which we brought in from Edinburgh. Kay researched her play with help from the Medical Foundation for the Care of Victims of Torture, the Refugee Council and detainees from the Campsfield Detention Centre:

> I simply couldn't believe what I was hearing. I could not believe that the violation of human rights of vulnerable people was happening in England in 1997 and, more shocking still, in the first year under a Labour Government for which I had waited for

eighteen years. I have written my play because I hope it will give people an insight into what it can really be like to seek asylum in this country. I also hope it may change minds.

The Bogus Woman tells the story of a young African poet and journalist, superbly played by Noma Dumezweni, who, after witnessing the killing of her family and baby, and after her subsequent rape, seeks asylum in Britain and is treated with appalling cruelty. It was a fine piece of agit-prop theatre. Michael Billington in the *Guardian* suggested:

> A powerful, passionate piece of theatre that if seen widely enough might change hearts and minds. If I were Greg Dyke, I would put it straight on to BBC TV and invite Home Secretary Jack Straw to respond in the course of a properly focused rational debate.

The *Independent* further advised:

> Words in Adshead's hands are bullets. Brace yourself and see this play—preferably with Jack Straw strapped in beside you.

We invited Jack Straw but he was otherwise engaged. The *Daily Telegraph* thought that the play presented only a one-sided view. Too fucking right.

Howie the Rookie opened at the Magic Theatre in San Francisco with Tom Waits in the first-night audience. He told Aidan Kelly that he really dug the words. The boys flew to LA to audition for a Jerry Bruckheimer war picture and Wes Moore continued to work on raising money for the transfer. The show broke box-office records at the Magic. *Resident Alien* closed in New York having failed to move to Broadway but winning two Obie Awards.

In March the Chair of the Arts Council, the Blairite management guru Gerry Robinson, announced that he was abolishing all ten of the Regional Arts Boards. They would be replaced by local branches of the Arts Council, no longer independent, but centrally controlled from London. This expensive manoeuvre was spun as an exercise in cost-cutting, streamlining and integration, but was in fact a hostile takeover. The new organisations were stuffed with New Labour fundamentalists eager to implement the doctrines of social inclusion and targetology. Thus the London Arts Board became Arts Council, London, with a fine and expensive new logo and rebrand. Sue Timothy had had enough and went off to organise the Touring Department.

Tim Fountain resigned as Literary Manager. He wanted to spend more time with his penis. In addition to the success of *Resident Alien*, Tim had also branched out into the field of directing. He had convincingly mounted *Puppetry of the Penis*, an overextended rugby-club stunt in which a couple of Australian comedians torture their cocks into unlikely and painful positions in order to represent a Big Mac, the Eiffel Tower or the fall of the Communism. The dick-trick show had proved to be popular with the ladies and was about to embark on a national tour. He was also writing a play about Julie Burchill for hasbian comedienne and chanteuse Jackie Clune. He felt that he could no longer give the post of Literary Manager the attention it deserved, and he was fed up with reading crap plays. I was sad to see him go.

Before he left we again took a Bush team to the National Student Drama Festival in Scarborough, where we had become theatre company-in-residence. Every year we provided a selection of practitioners who supplemented the vast cornucopia of educational events already available by offering masterclasses, workshops and mentoring in acting, directing, writing and design. This time we took Bette along to run a workshop on how to play Lady Bracknell. The student productions on show are usually a lively mix of new plays, classics and devised work. There's also always new dance, some visual theatre and a smattering of performance art. Every year someone announces that they are reinventing the language of theatre. This inevitably seems to involve the use of polythene sheeting. It's an inspiring and wonderful event. After each performance there's a public discussion and criticism session that frequently ends in tears and violence. In 2001 the heated debate involved a particularly vociferous mob of post-structuralist fans of Derrida and Roland Barthes railing against conventional playwrights and declaring entertainment to be bourgeois and all notions of plot or character inherently fascist. During a break in hostilities I went out onto the promenade for a breath of fresh air only to be joined by the *enragés* desperately tapping numbers into their mobile phones. I asked a passing student what was going on. 'They're all calling their mums,' she said. 'They want to know who shot Phil Mitchell in *EastEnders*.'

In New York Fred Zollo and Wes Moore postponed the Off-Broadway transfer of *Howie the Rookie*. They were having trouble with American Equity organiser Flora Stamatiades, who had decided that we had conned them when we took the show to PS 122 and the Magic. In New York we had tenuously claimed to be part of an international performance festival and San Francisco had ignored Equity entirely. Equity now demanded that Zollo had to guarantee that two American actors would appear in the London West End in exchange for the *Howie* actors appearing Off-Broadway in New York. It would take time to arrange. Karl and Aidan were pissed off as they had turned down work, but there was little anybody could do, and so the show was rescheduled for Jane Street in early September.

In May we brought in *Among Unbroken Hearts* by Henry Adams from the Traverse, a bleak and poetic piece in which a pair of Glaswegian smack addicts get back to their roots in a highland farmhouse. Continuing the junkie theme I followed this up by directing Adam Rapp's remarkable *Blackbird*. The play had arrived in the post the previous year, and I was immediately impressed by its beauty and brutality. I met Adam in New York and within ten minutes had agreed to produce the play and bring over an American cast. Adam was the hot new writer on the block. He had started out hating theatre. His brother Anthony was a child star, and Adam had spent his youth being dragged along on regional tours of *Oliver!* by his mother, who was a nurse in Joliet Prison (c.f. *The Blues Brothers*). He became a juvenile delinquent gangbanger and so was sent off to reform school, military college and then a Catholic university, where he became a basketball star. He won a playwriting fellowship to Julliard and had published a couple of novels. His play *Nocturne* had just been accepted by the American Repertory Theater. *Blackbird* was workshopped by Lee Breuer of Mabou Mines at PS 122 and turned down by every theatre in America. Subscription audiences would not approve of the plot or the characters.

Operation Desert Storm veteran Baylis lives in a squalid apartment in a Canal Street industrial building. He is crippled with a herniated disc and is incontinent. He blames 'sand nigger' nerve gas. He lives with his junkie trick-turning girlfriend, Froggy, who he has met in a strip club. She has hepatitis. It is Christmas Eve. In the course of the evening we discover that Froggy is pregnant with her own father's child. *Blackbird* is a love story.

We cast Elizabeth Reaser as Froggy, and Paul Sparks as Baylis. American Equity tried to insist that we had to pay West End rates but we told them that it was none of their business and secured the work permits anyway. We rehearsed in the cellar of a Baptist church in Shepherd's Bush. The church also ran a vagrants' drop-in centre so rehearsals were frequently interrupted by winos and the terminally confused. It all seemed to fit in with the play. The actors were superb. The rehearsals were intense and dangerous; we decided that we would take no prisoners. The show split the audience and critics alike. Some people walked out. Some people fainted. It remains one of the best productions I have ever done, and I think is one of the most important plays the Bush has ever produced. *Blackbird* has subsequently been performed throughout America and Adam directed a film version in 2006. He was also nominated for a Pulitzer Prize.

Nicola Wilson took over as Literary Manager. She had been senior reader at the National Theatre and had seen every new play in London in the past five years. She had an encyclopedic knowledge of new writing and the rare gift of being able to read a script. She was fun and witty and loyal to the writers, fighting hard for increased commission fees and demanding respect for their talents. The role of Literary Manager is central to the success of any theatre and is at least as important as that of Executive Producer or General Manager. It is their job to help to find the plays, organise the readers and the script-development programme, handle the unsolicited script pile, widen the horizons of the theatre by discovering new playwrights and encourage the Artistic Director to take risks. The relationship between the two is paramount. It has recently become a trend for theatre managements to downgrade the Literary Manager role, according it similar significance to that of Corporate Hospitality Coordinator or Diversity Compliance Officer. This is a mistake. There are many things a theatre can do without. Plays are not one of them. Nicola had a complete sense of what the Bush was about and an especially highly evolved bullshit detector. She played a major part in the success of the theatre for the next three years.

Tim Fountain had initiated a scheme with the Japan Foundation as part of the Japan 2001 Cultural Exchange, in which we undertook to organise a series of rehearsed readings of plays by contemporary Japanese writers. The first two plays in the series were *Fireflies* by Toshiro Suzue and *Time's Storeroom* by Ai Nagai. *Fireflies*, which apparently examined 'loss of subjectivity among contemporary urbanites', was a sad little play about love and loneliness. A couple on a date sit in a bus-station café drinking rancid milkshakes. A man pretends to be a horse. In Japan, 'fireflies' is also the expression used to describe the people who stand outside bars, cafés, shops and offices smoking on their own in the dark.

Ai Nagai is Japan's leading female playwright. She is at the same time popular and politically radical—a sort of feminist Alan Ayckbourn—and runs her own company Nitosha, which means 'Two rabbits'. *Time's Storeroom* is the first part of her *Post War Life History Play Trilogy*. In the play the poor but proud Shinjo family are forced to face up to the impact of Sixties consumerism when a geisha with a television moves into their spare room. There's also a satirical look at revolutionary student politics and a subplot about a rather peculiar but highly sexually charged amateur writers' circle. There's a cast of sixteen so in the spirit of the exercise I decided to direct the reading with a cast of sixteen. The literal translation we were sent from Japan was academic, impenetrable and unsayable, so Nicola and I cut forty pages and rewrote it in two days. We substituted 'The Esso sign means happy motoring' and 'We are the Oval-teenies, little girls and boys' for a couple of incomprehensible Japanese 1960s TV adverts. We took fifty minutes off the running time, but it was still three hours long. We assembled an all-star cast including Gerard Murphy, Sheila Reid, Celia Robertson, Susanna Bishop, our writers-in-residence Georgia Fitch and Tracy O'Flaherty and a bunch of students from LAMDA. The Japan Foundation flew Ai and Toshiro over for the gig. They asked to sit in on rehearsals. When we arrived at the theatre we discovered they had brought with them a party of twenty including translators, producers, directors, dramaturgs, the Head of the Tokyo International Arts Festival and Akihiko Senda—chief drama critic for the *Asahi Shimbun*. They all had cameras. After hours of muffins and bowing, we started to rehearse, the Japanese contingent trying resolutely to follow the proceedings in their Japanese scripts. After lunch they gave up and went shopping.

Amazingly the reading the next night was a triumph. The theatre was packed with both English and Japanese punters, and everyone got high on the total anarchy of the occasion. After the show the Japan Foundation invited me to be a guest at the Tokyo International Arts Festival later in the year. Nobody ever mentioned the missing forty pages.

As a follow-up to the Board Development Day, Fiona dragged me off to an Arts Council-sponsored seminar on 'How to Cull Your Board of Directors'. I imagine it wasn't actually called that, but that was certainly the business in hand. The burden of the argument was that boards of arts organisations were generally speaking clogged up with old-fashioned practitioners and well-meaning lefties who were either unable to cope with the dog-eat-dog realities of development and fundraising or who were insufficiently multiculturally diverse and therefore should be replaced. The seminar would instruct us how best to go about it. The day involved a lot of role-playing games that hovered emotionally somewhere between Gestalt therapy and Harvard Business School. There was a selection of techniques one could use in order to manipulate board members, one of which was that you could always use your sexuality. There was also a suggestion that organisations make a rule restricting board membership to between three and five years. Most of the Bush Board had been there for decades. Help was, however, at hand. Somewhat conveniently, a networking consultancy called Arts and Business had set up a Board Bank to provide arts organisations with new improved board members from the business community, who had the necessary financial, legal and commercial expertise required.

I realise that I am probably making a grotesque generalisation here, but I think it's a safe bet that nobody on the Board Bank's list of potential candidates had ever been to a show at the Bush and had probably never heard of the place. I also think it likely that they held opinions that would be philosophically, politically and morally at odds with those of the majority of writers, directors and actors that had made the theatre such a success. I firmly believe that anyone who works in any profession predicated on self-interest, greed, and that exists predominantly for financial gain without social purpose, has no place in any arts organisation in any capacity whatsoever. Theatre in particular is in the business of challenging and offending the Establishment and should not associate itself with anyone in whose best interest it is to preserve it. The day did not go well.

The sad truth of the matter was that the Arts Council/Government fixation on increased private funding meant that even an organisation as unsuited to entrepreneurism as the Bush had to find more money from private sources. Despite selling out virtually every performance in the season we were still financially screwed and the three-year A4E funding for the Writers' Development Programme was about to come to an end. We had moved into the new office, and we now had paid front-of-house and box-office staff. We also appeared to have doubled the number of people engaged in administration. We had to raise an extra forty thousand a year just to stand still and part of the responsibility for this fell on the shoulders of the Board. In Britain we were increasingly moving towards the American model where, for example, members of the Board of the Magic Theatre, San Francisco, were individually expected to raise $50,000 as a condition of their continued membership. Most of our Board members came from publishing, television, theatre and the arts. Three of them were ex-Artistic Directors of the theatre and none of them had either that kind of money or the time or the inclination to raise it. They were all, however, completely dedicated to the Bush and understood its history, purpose and ethos. They were the keepers of the holy flame; it would be disastrous if they were replaced by a bunch of suits who worked in the City and occasionally went to the Donmar.

At the beginning of August Fred Zollo pulled out of the Off-Broadway transfer of *Howie the Rookie*. He had to put down a deposit of sixty grand to secure the theatre and just as he was about to sign the cheque, American Equity moved the goalposts yet again. They now demanded a bond of $50,000 in addition to two American actors appearing in the West End at the same time as *Howie* played in New York. Fred was so frustrated that he just gave up on the whole thing, and although Wes Moore fought to raise the money the gig was called off.

Mark, Karl and Aidan were sad and angry. They blamed the Bush and who could blame them? It would have been easy to say that if you can't take a joke you shouldn't have joined, but once again American Equity had conspired to deny American audiences the opportunity to see an important piece of contemporary theatre. *Howie* was produced a couple of years later at the Irish Arts Centre in New York with an American cast, smoke, strobes and a soundtrack. Adam Rapp said it was shite.

Tim and Bette remounted *Resident Alien* at the Assembly Rooms in Edinburgh for the Festival, where it was once again a sell-out and won the Herald Angel Award. They then set off on a world tour playing Australia, Europe and America twice before another London run. They remounted the show yet again in 2009 selling out twelve weeks at the New End. Bette's pension scheme seems still to be secure. At the Festival Nicola and I saw *The Age of Consent* by Peter Morris at the Pleasance and decided to bring it to the Bush in the New Year. At every Edinburgh Festival there's a 'shock, horror, ban this perverted load of filth' show and this year *The Age of Consent* was it. The play is a pair of intercut monologues. In the first Stephanie, a young single mum tries to push her six-year-old daughter into a showbiz career encouraging her to flaunt her tits and teeth while ignoring possible abuse from a shady producer. In the second Timmy, who has murdered a child in a manner not dissimilar to the killers of Jamie Bulger, awaits release from a secure youth institution. It caused a huge fuss but was in fact a complex and morally challenging examination of childhood and the loss of innocence. The show contained two brilliant performances from Katherine Parkinson and Ben Silverstone. We booked it in for January.

On September 11th two planes flew into the World Trade Center in New York. September 11th had been the planned opening night for *Howie the Rookie* in Jane Street.

Fiona and I flew to Japan for the Tokyo International Festival. Fiona had successfully wangled a place on the trip in exchange for a lecture on 'How to be an Executive Producer'. After a thirteen-hour flight we were whisked straight from the airport into a Festival International Visitors Programme reception, a tea ceremony and a British Council reception, followed by an hour-long subway and train journey in the rush hour and the rain to the Setagaya Theatre, where we saw a four-hour version of *Uncle Vanya* in Japanese followed by another reception and a meet and greet with the director and the actors. 'I hope your body conditions will be a good one,' said Itchimura San, the Festival Director, optimistically. This pretty much set the agenda for the next few days. We had hours of lectures on post-war Japan and the role and history of contemporary Japanese theatre. Half a dozen contemporary writers showed us films of their work and explained how they were more significant than the other contemporary writers, and there were countless receptions, banquets, discussion forums, Q and As, theatre visits and a dinner with the Minister for Culture in a restaurant on top of a skyscraper. We spent hours on the subway every day. In the middle we were flown to Shikoku Island to see a new play by Ai Nagai's company Nitosha in the local theatre in Kochi. It was Sunday afternoon but the place was packed. The play, which seemed to be about the preservation of a local traditional inn, was impenetrable, but the punters loved it. Next morning early we flew back to Tokyo for a conducted tour of the new National Theatre, a couple more discussions on adaptation, and a Chinese banquet. At the end of the trip Itchimura San invited us to take bring a show to the next Festival two years hence. He said he wanted something that was representative of contemporary British theatre. He wanted it 'In Yer Face'.

Back in Shepherd's Bush we presented two more Japanese plays in the rehearsed reading series: *The Happy Lads* by Hideo Tsuchida and *Far From the River* by Koji Hasegawa. *The Happy Lads* was an anti-war play—a sort of Japanese *The Long and the Short and the Tall*. *Far From the River* was a two-hander about a schoolteacher who goes to visit a Yakuza (Mafia) boss to find out why his son no longer attends school. As usual there were dozens of directors, dramaturgs and dignitaries watching the rehearsal. At one point David Westhead who was playing the Mafia boss asked what a particular line meant. There was consternation in the Japanese ranks. It was rather like one of those Bateman cartoons: 'The Actor who dared to ask a question'. After several minutes of discussion the answer came back: 'Westhead San, it mean he has killed his wife.' After the reading Shuko, who had been our translator in Tokyo and was now a friend came up to me in the pub. 'Bradwell San,' she said, 'I have seen this famous play many many times in Tokyo in Japanese and I never knew killed fucking wife.'

The Bush Theatre's Thirtieth Anniversary season in 2002 kicked off with *The Age of Consent*, which successfully opened after Christmas and managed to transcend all the prurient comment about content it had engendered in Edinburgh.

Next up was my production of *The Glee Club* by Richard Cameron—a play set in 1962 about a group of Yorkshire coalminers who form a close-harmony vocal group to raise money for charity. The journey we took with *The Glee Club* is a good example of how the dramaturgical development process works. Richard's first draft had the six characters and their essential stories, but the order of the telling seemed arbitrary and confusing. The narrative dashed about between a number of locations and time zones, the style was inconsistent and so the motor of the play was dissipated. Richard and I, in conjunction with Literary Assistant Jenny Worton, gathered together a team of experienced actors including Paul Copley, Alan Williams and Phil Jackson, and we spent a couple of days reading the play and unravelling the tale. The actors found ways to make the structure work and, together with Richard, thrashed out the style of the piece. An idea emerged that the characters all did impersonations, especially of their own and each other's wives. Richard wrote a second draft which, as an exercise, set the entire play in one room to see if it was possible. We organised a rehearsed reading to see how this would play with an audience. The reading went well. The story now worked, but the play had become claustrophobic, and we realised that we had to open it out again. We also needed to concentrate on the nature of the music and the comic songs. All we knew at this point was that we wanted to include 'Funiculi Funicula' and 'You Always Hurt the One You Love'. We worked out where the musical numbers should come and how they should comment on either what had just happened or prepare us for what would happen next. I brought designer Bruce Macadie and lighting designer Rick Fisher on board. We decided that it was crucial to include scenes in the pithead baths and worked out a way to build fully practical showers on the Bush stage. We liked the idea of the characters singing filthy songs while showering naked. Richard decided on a new ending, wrote the third draft and, though it still needed fine-tuning, we set a date for rehearsals. I brought in Mia Soteriou, who I had first worked with on *A Bed of Roses* in 1977, as musical director. Mia and I chose the songs. We decided to open the show with it a rousing number called 'A Gay Ranchero', because it had a Mexican theme entirely inappropriate for South Yorkshire and was an innocent comment on the underlying homophobia of some of the characters. We also recycled a couple of songs from *The Melody Bandbox Rhythm Roadshow* including a spirited version of 'Istanbul' with a sand dance routine in the style of Wilson, Keppel and Betty.

In the cast were David Bamber, Mark Drewry, James Hornsby, Oliver Jackson, Shaun Prendergast and David Schofield. Mark was the last person we cast. He was born in Doncaster and was born to play Walt. We couldn't have done better. Also he needed the gig. The previous month he had been busking on the Tube.

Each of the six characters in the Glee Club has a problem. Nineteen-year-old Colin wants to be a Billy Fury. Happily married Jack is having an imaginary affair with a posh childhood sweetheart. Scobie's wife is having their fourth child. Bant has lost his wife to the ballroom dancing Ringtons tea man. Widower Walt has abandoned his son to a grim children's home. And organist Phil is accused of touching up choirboys. We rehearsed over January in the gloomy Baptist Church cellar. Richard rewrote as we went. We all realised that we were on to something, and rehearsals were euphoric. After three weeks we planned the first run-through for the Friday. On the Thursday evening on his way home from rehearsals Mark Drewry was knocked off his bike by a taxi. He had extensive injuries and fell into a coma. Fiona Clark went to the hospital and stayed all night. I broke the news to the rest of the cast next morning; everyone was shattered and in shock. Although none of us wanted to admit it, it was obvious that Mark was seriously ill and there was no way that he would be able to continue with the show. I decided that the only thing we could do was to get on with it, and get on with it straight away. I called Rod Smith who had worked on the play in the early stages. I told him the dreadful tale. 'I'll be there in an hour,' he said, and he was.

That afternoon I made the cast go ahead with the first run-through as planned, with assistant director Jamie Reid playing Walt and Rod watching. It was heart-breaking. Over the weekend Mia taught Rod all the songs, and we started back at the beginning again on the Monday. We had a week to go. I have never seen a team of actors work so hard and so unselfishly. Whatever egos had been flying around instantly disappeared as we pulled the show together. At the end of the week we recorded a tape of the songs and sent messages to Mark, who was still unconscious. Sadly he didn't respond.

The Glee Club opened on 22 February 2002. The response from the audience was amazing, and response from the critics was over the top. Michael Billington wrote a rare overnighter in the *Guardian* awarding us an equally rare five stars. The other critics were similarly excited:

'Richard Cameron's drama—splendidly warm, sad and funny— has all the hallmarks of a hugely appealing popular hit.'

(*Daily Telegraph*)

'*The Glee Club* has some unforgettable musical numbers and laughs by the shovel-load. It never patronises its characters and offers its ideas and insights with humour and a respect for emotional truth. A night to remember.'

(*The Stage*)

The phones started ringing and never stopped. We could have sold out the entire run several times over. We extended the show by a week and added extra matinees. West End producers circled round like vultures. Bill Kenwright called to ask if the show had legs. Michael Codron came to see it and called me next morning. 'Good God, Michael,' he said. 'David Bamber is hung like a fucking stag!' Despite all this enthusiasm no one seemed prepared to put their money where their mouth was. It was a great show with a great script and great acting, but it had no stars so...

Nicola Wilson and I set off for the National Student Drama Festival in Scarborough taking with us Mark Ravenhill and Catherine Johnson, who gave a talk on the writing of *Mamma Mia!*. We were in the middle of the usual NSDF round of argument, plays, all-night drinking, poker, performance art and inappropriate sexual behaviour when Fiona called to say that an offer to transfer the show had come in from maverick producers Julius Green and Ian Lenagan. Their previous projects had included *Saucy Jack and the Space Vixens* and the Russian anarchist performance troupe Derevo. The deal was that they would produce in partnership with Bush Productions Ltd—our commercial wing of which Fiona was now apparently Managing Director. All we had to do was to come up with investors. Fiona spent the rest of the week trying to raise the money. By Friday we were on, and the show was scheduled to open in three weeks' time at the Duchess Theatre. In keeping with Bush Theatre principles all the actors were paid the same and billing was alphabetical. I suspect Catherine Johnson put up a large part of the investment, but characteristically she kept quiet about it.

Bruce Macadie redesigned *The Glee Club* for the proscenium at the Duchess. Surprisingly the stage there is a couple of feet narrower than the one at the Bush. I had a week's rehearsal in which we gave the show a service, tightening it up and removing some of the less convincing embellishments it had picked up during the run. We had a couple of previews and opened in the West End. Again the critics got behind the show. 'It deserves to run and run,' said the *Guardian*, and there were rave reviews from the red tops who never came to the Bush. The next day I went into rehearsals for *A Carpet, a Pony and a Monkey* by Mike Packer. As part of the proactive commissioning stunt we had sent Packer off to Belgium with the ticket touts following England in Euro 2000—the European Football Championship. *Carpet etc.*, the play inspired by his trip, is a farce about football, racism, fame, money, deceit, lies and gambling. The biggest gamble was to open it during the World Cup.

On 28 April we mounted a huge Thirtieth Anniversary Gala at the Royal College of Music. Rather than a celebration of the theatre, this whole event was conceived as a high profile fundraiser ostensibly to pay for the continued Writers' Development Programme and also to launch a new and improved Patron Scheme, which was supposed to provide new and improved opportunities for Individual and Corporate giving. We clearly had to raise money if we were even going to think of finding a new space.

Despite having a much larger administration staff than ever before, it was felt necessary to hire a specialist fundraising development consultant to help arrange the event. Against my better judgement I went along with the scheme, believing that it was for the greater good and an exercise in the redistribution of wealth.

The idea was to have a champagne reception, a star cabaret, a posh dinner and a celebrity auction. Punters would buy a table with an attendant celebrity and during the course of the evening they would be systematically fleeced for the good of the cause. The female staff members were instructed to wear Wonderbras. I had imagined that it was the expert fundraiser's task to drum up both celebrities and marks, but this was not the case so I was forced to call in favours and raid my address book. In the end Victoria Wood did the cabaret, *The Glee Club* boys sang a couple of songs, Jim Broadbent introduced the evening and Richard Wilson did the auction/raffle. Rich people bought celebrity-laden tables and enthusiastically donated, waving around wads of fifty-pound notes in an attempt to buy Amanda Burton's marigolds from *Silent Witness* and other exciting showbiz prizes. The entire Bush staff worked beyond the call of duty to make the evening work at the same time as mounting three in-house productions, and the event was in its own terms a huge success. Personally I felt uneasy about the whole thing. I felt somehow that the integrity of the Bush had been compromised and cheapened and that we should have celebrated thirty years of achievement with a huge party for the writers, actors and theatre staff that had made it possible, not by sucking up to hedge-fund managers. If they believed in the work of the Bush they should not need a *vol au vent* with Felicity Kendal to make them open their wallets.

The highlight of the whole event for me was when I went out for a fag and bumped into Ken Campbell who had gatecrashed the do.

CAMPBELL. I've discovered this amazing performer called
    Mouse who is capable of immeasurably improving any play
    in the entire canon of world theatre as we know it.

ME. What does Mouse do, Ken?

CAMPBELL. She takes off her knickers and blows multi-
    coloured liquid out of her arsehole. Just imagine that in *The*
    Wild Duck.

A Carpet, a Pony and a Monkey opened to good reviews but indeed suffered from the World Cup in terms of audience numbers. It was very much a play for people who don't go to theatre, and they are a difficult crowd to attract. *The Glee Club* lasted a mere six weeks in the West End, closing on 1 June. There were no stars in it and it wasn't *The Full Monty*. During the run at the Duchess we did a midnight matinee to raise money for Mark Drewry's family and parents, who had to travel from Doncaster to visit him in hospital. Mark never regained consciousness and died eighteen months later. I heard the sad news while rehearsing Richard Cameron's next play, *Gong Donkeys*.

Fiona organised annual appraisals. As executives we were appraised by the Board and in turn we appraised the line managers and the line managers appraised the staff. The whole thing was a ridiculous piece of American-Corporate-status-fixated toss and completely inappropriate for an organisation like the Bush. Appraisals involved a SWOT analysis, which was supposed to quantify Strengths, Weaknesses, Opportunities and Threats. There was also a handy chart which illuminated this in some form or other. I had to appraise Nicola. It felt like a prefects' meeting at a minor public school. I didn't do it again. As part of her appraisal Fiona asked the Board to make her Joint Chief Executive. They turned down her request.

Over the summer we rehearsed *Stitching* in the theatre. *Stitching* was a new play by Anthony Neilson which we co-produced with the Red Room and which was destined for the Traverse at Edinburgh. Neilson decided to write the play during the rehearsal period based on discussions and improvisation with the actors Selina Boyack and Phil McKee. He wanted it to be what he called 'transgressive theatre'. Having no idea what the play was going to be about we billed it as his 'most intimate and explicit work to date', which seemed to cover all the bases. Anthony started to write after the second week of rehearsal and then did a major rewrite after the sneak dress-tech-preview at the Bush and another one after the tech in Edinburgh. The play is about a young couple, Stuart and Abby. Abby falls pregnant, and the couple test their relationship by exploring sexual fantasy, sadomasochism, masturbation, internet porn and genital mutilation. It goes to some very dark places indeed. Stuart describes how he used to wank off over photographs of naked Jewish women waiting to be gassed in Auschwitz, and there is mention of the Moors Murderers.

The opening at the Traverse caused yet another Edinburgh shock-horror torrent of filth outrage and multiple walkouts. Strangely enough this time the flames of controversy were fanned by some prurient stringer on the *Guardian* phoning up the mother of one of Brady and Hindley's victims for an understandably incensed quote. The show sold out, of course, as a result. Once the fuss had died down the play got the response it deserved with a clutch of five-star reviews, a Fringe First and a Herald Angel Award. Once again we had worked the Edinburgh magic. Back at the Bush the critics were equally enthusiastic about this shocking odyssey to the darkest depths of sexuality.

'*Stitching* is one of the most exciting plays of the year... I left the theatre with my pulse and my mind racing.'

(*Time Out*)

'*Stitching* explodes with power, discipline, integrity and sheer psychological accuracy... Neilson's writing has a terrible beauty.'

(*Sunday Times*)

'It's not my job to tell the audience a rose is beautiful. Everybody knows that. My job in to see if there is a way to make turd beautiful.'

(Anthony Neilson)

Our production toured throughout Europe during 2003, ending up at the National Theatre of Slovenia in Ljubljana. The play has subsequently been produced throughout the world and was banned in 2008 in Malta.

It may just be possible that there are as many clichés in 'In Yer Face' Theatre as there are in Boulevard Comedy.

Playwright Dusty Hughes and visionary television producer Kenith Trodd both left the Board to be replaced by people with experience in fundraising and the City. One of them suggested at a Board meeting that as the majority of our audience was aged between twenty and thirty we should consider ways to a change our demographic by programming shows that might appeal to an older and financially more secure clientele. Our core audience were paying off student loans and were consequently not wealthy enough to join the exciting new Patrons' scheme. I ignored the suggestion.

Despite making thirty grand on the gala we were still short of money. Nicola and I worked out a plan to do three shows for the price of one and a half. As part of the A4E scheme we had developed three exciting plays by first time writers and decided to produce all three in a short festival under the banner 'Naked Talent'. The plays were *adrenalin... heart* by Georgia Fitch, *Falling* by Shelley Silas and *Untouchable* by Simon Burt.

Each play had the usual rehearsal period and ran for three weeks, but they all shared a common set and lighting rig. In fact we would have found it difficult to attract audiences for three totally new first plays by unknown writers on the trot, so the idea of the season was to build up momentum and sell it as a voyage of discovery. It more or less worked.

I directed *adrenalin... heart*, which was an exceptional piece of writing about addiction that pushed the boundaries of form between direct address, flashback, naturalism and rap poetry. With two stunning performances from Julia Ford and Mark Monero, the play changed rhythm and tempo to reflect the drugs the characters were taking and the mood they were in. It was totally original. I decided that this was the show we would take to Tokyo.

The New Year kicked off with *The Drowned World* by Gary Owen, a Paines Plough show that we had seen in Edinburgh, set in a futuristic dystopia where the ugly rule and the beautiful are hunted down and killed. On 15 February 2003, the day of the last performance, everyone from the theatre went on a demonstration against the forthcoming war with Iraq. A million protesters marched through London to a rally in Hyde Park. Blair took no notice.

Our next show was former Bush Artistic Director Simon Stokes's production of Doug Lucie's *The Green Man*, which we brought in from Plymouth Theatre Royal. Doug Lucie is one of my favourite writers. I first met him when he auditioned as an actor for Hull Truck and I had commissioned and directed his play *The New Garbo* about the tragic life of Frances Farmer. I had directed *Hard Feelings*, both at the Bush and on television, *Doing the Business* at the Royal Court and *Grace* at Hampstead. I had also directed *Love You Too* at the Bush in 1997 with Susannah Doyle, Miranda Foster, Sam Graham and Rhys Dinsdale in the cast. It was a wonderful, dark, witty and perspicacious play about love and politics. The critics had for the most part dumped on it, perplexingly comparing it unfavourably with Patrick Marber's *Closer*, a play it comprehensively outshone in both soul and substance.

The Green Man is set in the early hours of the morning in an unfashionable London pub, where a bunch of whisky-soaked anglers prepare to go on a carp-fishing trip. It's a play about greed and lies, and is a trenchant analysis of the New Labour project. The dramatic events on the set of the fake pub upstairs were no match, however, for the dramatic events in O'Neill's—the real fake pub downstairs.

The pub manager had initially agreed to rope off a space for theatre customers before the show and in the interval, but this was swiftly abandoned and audience members were often unable to get served at all. The bar staff and bouncers were rude and abusive, and we had many complaints from our public, all of which were ignored by the landlord and the regional manager. On Saturdays when Queens Park Rangers played at home the pub was frequently colonised and trashed by visiting supporters. Millwall thugs graffitied the theatre foyer with BNP slogans. On a couple of occasions the police on horseback threw a protective cordon around the building, and the matinee had to be cancelled without warning. Noise levels were intolerable and requests to turn the volume down were met with hostility and aggression. We just had to get out. The situation was further complicated by the Hammersmith and Fulham

Council, who decided to revoke our club status and forced us to apply for a Public Entertainment Licence.

The Bush had still been operating as a theatre club. Most of the other small-scale theatres founded in the late Sixties and early Seventies, such as the King's Head, the Orange Tree, Soho Theatre, The Open Space and the Theatre Upstairs at the Royal Court, had started out this way. The original purpose of club status was that performances were for members only and were therefore beyond the jurisdiction of the Lord Chamberlain and his smut hounds. Indeed several theatres became clubs in order to mount particularly controversial productions. The other bonus was that theatre clubs could operate under a less strict set of regulations than theatres that had to comply with the conditions of a Public Entertainment Licence. In real terms it meant that our idiosyncratic seating, aisle space and fire exits were officially legal, which was just as well as it would have cost us a fortune to reconfigure them. Several local authorities had plugged the loophole years ago, but Hammersmith and Fulham had failed to notice and we were certainly not going to tell them. Unfortunately Fiona, while researching the implications of new Health and Safety regulations, inadvertently managed to tip off the Borough Surveyor, and we had a visit from the local council. They told us that we were no longer allowed to function as a private members' club. We had to apply for a Public Entertainment Licence; this would only be granted if the theatre complied with technical standards for places of Public Entertainment. The theatre would be inspected by the London Fire Brigade and the council's Licensing, Environment and Safety team. If we failed the inspection, we would be closed down.

I tried to plead that the Bush had functioned safely and legally for thirty years but to no avail. All we could do was carry on as normal until the inspection.

We opened Simon Burt's *Got to Be Happy*, and Nicola and I set off for the National Student Drama Festival. On arrival in Scarborough I turned on the television in my hotel room to see live pictures of the American Army pulling down the statue of Saddam Hussein in Baghdad and Bush announcing the triumph of Freedom and Democracy. Nicola and I ran workshops on character, plot and story structure and wrote a play about a goat with fifteen fifth-formers from a school on Guernsey. I also did a Q and A with Mike Leigh, who was funny and inspirational. After the talk we saw a performance piece apparently about Sylvia Plath by the Paper Birds—a group of young women from Bretton Hall College of Further Education. The show involved petticoats, fish tanks and talcum powder and some of it was in French.

Rather late on in the proceedings one of the Sylvias cheerfully announced 'I'm a dirty girl, I am' in English to which Leigh equally cheerfully replied, 'Well, that's a fucking bonus.'

Back in London I began rehearsals for a new play by Catherine Johnson, *Little Baby Nothing*, which we had been working on for a while. The play takes place one summer on the roof terrace of a flat in Bristol, where widowed mum Anna lives with her fourteen-year-old daughter El. El and her best friends Erin and Joby are would-be Goths, who try to raise the devil and the dead, and who perform homemade rituals with sheets and candles and vodka and Marilyn Manson. Despite all this, it's a warm-hearted and sensitive play about mothers and daughters and loss and love. The terrific cast were Suzan Sylvester, Jem Wall and newcomers Alice O'Connell and Jenny Platt from East 15. Tom Daplyn, who played Joby, deserved a special award for sticking a lighted candle up his arse while wearing a Cradle of Filth *Jesus is a Cunt* T-shirt with a picture of a wanking nun on it. It was long way from *Mamma Mia!*, but deserved to do just as well.

After the first preview of *Little Baby Nothing*, a member of the theatre staff had her drink spiked by someone in the pub who then tried to bundle her into a car. We were pretty sure that the man who did it had earlier been drinking with the bar staff but couldn't prove it, so decided not to call the police. Our complaint to the pub management went ignored.

During the third week of the run we got the results of the Environment and Safety inspection. To qualify for a Public Entertainment Licence we had to reduce the number of seats in the theatre from one hundred-plus to eighty. We had to move all the fire exits, install new emergency lighting and totally reconfigure the aisles and backstage area. The theatre had to close immediately and could only reopen when we had complied with the findings of the inspection and been granted the Licence. *Little Baby Nothing* still had a week to go so we applied for a stay of execution, but the council remained unmoved. I decided to ignore them; I told Fiona that I would do the time.

It was fortunate that the whole licensing business had just about coincided with the closure of the theatre over the summer, but it was still a huge blow. We would have to completely redesign the auditorium and find an extra £20,000 to pay for it all. The disappearance of twenty seats also meant a potential twenty per cent loss in box-office income. The Arts Council response was less than sympathetic. They effectively told us that, as the Bush now only had eighty seats, they would have to reconsider our future level of funding based on our decreased value for money owing to our decreased capacity. We were getting screwed from all directions. The Arts Council had just spent £70,000 changing its name from Arts Council *of* England to Arts Council, England—an investment that obviously represented immeasurable value for money to its many stakeholders. Since the departure of Sue Timothy, I felt that there was no longer anyone at the Arts Council who understood what the Bush was for, or valued our contribution to the theatrical wealth of the nation. What they did want from us, however, was a Cultural Diversity Action Plan.

This was yet another spurious initiative by which theatres had to devote time and energy to preparing a document which set out the means by which the theatre intended to achieve a wider and more inclusive ethnic balance of writers, actors, directors, designers, executives, administrative staff and audience. My policy statement could not have been clearer:

> It is the policy of the Bush Theatre to discover and nurture the best new theatre writers from the widest possible range of backgrounds and produce their work to the highest possible standards for the widest possible audience.

This would apparently not do, in as much as it did not detail how we were going to recruit more black playwrights or Chinese box-office staff or attract more Asian punters.

It seemed to me that the Government policy, rather than increasing the number of people who enjoy and benefit from the arts, was likely to have the opposite effect. Pigeon-holing everybody into particular kinds of ethnicity or orientation was divisive rather than inclusive. There was a danger of ghettoising the experience. There's no such thing as Black Theatre or White Theatre or Women's Theatre or Gay Theatre or Disabled Theatre or Fringe Theatre or Alternative Theatre. There's only Good Theatre and Bad Theatre. The scramble for socially inclusive box-ticking meant that directors and administrators were tempted not to programme work based on the quality of the Art or of the Artistic experience, but rather on the ethnic or cultural identity of those making it. There also seemed to be a diversity league table based on degrees of Colonial Oppression or Imperialist Guilt.

In the spirit of genuine enquiry I asked the Arts Council for clarification, citing two Bush plays I was hoping to produce. One was written by an Indian Jewish lesbian about two white middle-class heterosexual couples living in Surrey. The other was by a middle-aged middle-class white male writer about black and Asian gay teenagers on a housing estate in Bradford. Which play was more appropriately diverse? I think they thought I was taking the piss.

All this was even more confusing as, while the theatre was forcibly closed for the summer to reconfigure and reduce the seating, I was working with the Iraqi/American writer performer Heather Raffo on *Nine Parts of Desire*. Heather's father is Iraqi and her mother is American. Heather is Roman Catholic. After the first Gulf War she travelled to visit her family in Iraq, and the play was based on a series of interviews she conducted with a wide range of Iraqi women about their experience of living under Saddam Hussein and in a war zone. Heather played all the characters. Her purpose was to bring home to Western audiences the common humanity we share with imagined enemies and the obscene consequences of violence, shock and awe. The recent Allied invasion made the piece even more powerful and poignant, as Heather, in common with thousand of Iraqi exiles, had no idea if her family in Baghdad had survived the American bombing.

Producer Richard Jordan had seen a workshop version in New York and brought it over to Edinburgh. He showed me the script and I immediately agreed to co-produce the play at the Bush, although we had absolutely no budget. The show in Edinburgh was a bit of a mess. The production was overcomplicated with performance-art cliché and inappropriate mime, and the structure was all over the place. Back in London, Heather and I cut and reshaped the piece to give it a stronger dramatic drive. The theatre had been completely stripped back as part of the reconstruction to reveal bare walls and layers of crumbling paint and plaster, some still blackened from the fire fifteen years previously. Heather thought it symbolised the al-Amiriya bomb shelter where in the first Gulf War four hundred and eight civilians were massacred by American smart bombs. We decided to leave it as it was but called in a couple of Iraqi artists living in London who graffitied the walls with bright chalk murals.

The performances at the Bush were charged and emotional. After the show, Iraqi exiles and American visitors frequently talked in the bar for hours. It seemed to me to be the ultimate example of Cultural Diversity in action. No one from the Arts Council bothered to turn up.

Nine Parts of Desire was further developed by The Public Theater in New York and then opened at the Manhattan Ensemble Theatre, where it sold out for nine months, and Heather won the Lucille Lortel Award for Best Solo Show.

Nine Parts of Desire is an example of how Art can remake the world.

(John Lahr, *New Yorker*)

With our Public Entertainment Licence and reduced capacity seating firmly in place we continued with the autumn season. As part of the refurbishment, the front-of-house office and lighting store had been converted into the Corporate Hospitality Suite. The idea was that the Board would host regular Patrons' Cultivation Events where they would invite hedge-fund managers and the like to see the show, give them a glass of Cloudy Bay and some *amuse-bouches* in the interval and let them mingle with the actors afterwards. We would also have the odd celebrity on hand for them to hobnob with. They would be so overwhelmed by the art and the cultural bonhomie that they would fork out to join the Patrons' scheme immediately. The Corporate Hospitality suite was so they didn't have to brave the potential dangers of the pub downstairs like our regular but impoverished punters. I really tried to go along with these Brown-Nose evenings, but found it enormously difficult to sell the Bush to people who had no real interest in the nature and purpose of the work. I also thought it significant that Cultivation events only happened during the run of shows deemed suitable for prospective donors. Plays featuring politicians, lawyers and media folk were OK. Plays with glue sniffers in Peckham were not. *Airsick* by Emma Frost did not qualify as a Cultivation event.

Airsick, following on from Georgia Fitch's *adrenalin... heart*, was yet another astonishing first play from a woman writer, and also one that successfully experimented in form without compromising the impact of the content. The play, which I directed, was about black holes, sex, self-worth and hepatitis, with fine performances from Celia Robertson as the central character, sculptor Lucy, and from Peter Jonfield as her miserable old cockney fucker dad. Susannah Doyle as the much abused Scarlet teased, rejoiced and horrified in a series of utterly filthy monologues. Es Devlin build a jet-black hydraulic set that transformed from a hospital to a dinner party to a jumbo jet and back again almost at the flick of a switch.

> This is an evening that's as near to perfect bliss as you can get
> without dropping an E.
>
> (Aleks Sierz, *What's On*)

The show was a co-production with Simon Stokes at Plymouth Theatre Royal. While setting up the production, Fiona met architect Ian Ritchie, who had designed the award-winning TR2 production centre at the Plymouth Theatre. Ritchie lived in West London and was a big fan of the Bush. He had also been hired by Chelsfield to design the new White City Centre, a one-million-square-foot, £1.5 billion leisure and retail complex and the largest building project in Europe. Ritchie was a radical architect: his plans included a Roman forum with columns and natural ventilation and a thousand sheep grazing on Shepherd's Bush Green. He also had plans for the Bush.

To gain planning permission for such a huge development from the local authorities it is not unusual for the rapacious speculator to have to offer to build something beneficial to the community as a quid pro quo. This can either be social housing or some kind of local amenity. The scheme is called Planning Gain and involves Section 106 of the Town and Country Planning Act. Ian Ritchie proposed that the planning gain for the White City site would involve building an arts complex with new library, a cinema and a new theatre for the Bush. He would design it to our specifications and the developers would build and pay for the shell. We would have to find the money to fit it out.

It seemed like great news, although Ian warned that he had to get Chelsfield to agree to the deal. Even so it finally looked like we were getting somewhere. Personally I would have preferred to convert a found old building, but Ian's plans were exciting and visionary, and we would hopefully be part of a community rather than marooned in some ugly glass box in a deserted shopping mall—a fate which had sadly overtaken so many new British theatres built in the past thirty years. Ian set out to negotiate on our behalf.

Earlier in the year I had commissioned Richard Bean to write a Christmas show. He vaguely thought he might write about religion. Nicola and I christened the project *Mr Bean's Christmas Turkey*.

In the end Richard wrote *The God Botherers*—a viciously funny play about the impossible task faced by Western aid workers in the fictitious African state of Tambia. The play is simultaneously cynical and humanitarian, which is a difficult trick to pull off. It's even-handedly offensive to everybody, and as such provided a splendid seasonal entertainment and one of which I was suitably proud.

The autumn season had been a complete sell-out, but the reduction in capacity had meant a significant fall in box-office revenue. It was impossible to meet the earned income/subsidy ratio demanded by the Arts Council with only eighty seats. We also had to face up to the fact that, for financial reasons, the touring companies now preferred to play theatres with a greater capacity than ours. The relationship with the pub had failed to improve, and there was an increased amount of theft as security was extremely lax despite the Neanderthal bouncers. A survey showed that the pub was a major deterrent to our audience. There was another problem on the horizon.

Although we were now legal in terms of the Public Entertainment Licence we were about to become illegal under the Disability Discrimination Act. It's true that the Bush had, and still has, major access problems for the disabled. In the past we had always carried wheelchairs, sometimes with their occupants aboard, up the staircase to the theatre, but this practice was now banned because of Health and Safety regulations. To provide a wheelchair lift and other necessary disabled facilities would involve major structural modifications to the building and a vast amount of money. We had until October 2004 to make the changes. The brewery had no interest whatsoever in undertaking the project and, as the Bush is a Grade II-listed building, may not have been allowed to make the necessary alterations even if they had wanted to.

Fiona and I came up with a plan. There was no time to wait for Ian Ritchie's Chelsfield scheme to bear fruit and no guarantee that it would happen anyway. We decided that we would look for accommodation elsewhere while working on a long-term new venue. The new space would have 120—150 seats and would preserve the Bush's intimate atmosphere. It would provide us with rehearsal and workshop space and have proper facilities for our audience. In the meantime we would scout every theatre space or potential found space in London for a temporary home. To address the problem of value for money and box-office receipts, we would set up major national and international tours of our work and possibly curate seasons of Bush plays in other theatres. We would move out of the pub by the end of the next year.

We opened 2004 with *A Feast of Stephens*—a mini-season of two plays by Simon Stephens—and I re-rehearsed *adrenalin... heart* for Tokyo, Fiona Bell taking over from Julia Ford, who was having a baby. In the space of a week we flew to Japan, set up and teched the show on a completely new set, gave five performances plus a series of workshops and Q and As, did some serious clubbing, flew back to London and set up, previewed and opened *adrenalin... heart* back at the Bush again. In Tokyo we performed at the Setagaya Theatre Tram playing to packed and enthusiastic houses. Simultaneous translation surtitles were projected onto tall screens on either side of the stage. The translator, who claimed to have read the play over a hundred times, had clearly done a good job and the audiences seemed to follow every word. They even laughed at a couple of obscure jokes about the Arsenal team that nobody got in England. What on earth is the Japanese equivalent for 'If Sol Campbell was a lager, what sort of lager would he be?'

The discussions were challenging. Audiences appreciated the play and the acting, and obviously related to the characters' predicament as they were clearly moved and often distressed at the end. We were, however, constantly told that there was no drug addiction in Japan, which I knew to be untrue. To admit to the problem would apparently have meant loss of face.

Back in London *adrenalin... heart* took on a new lease of life and found favour with the critics.

'Fitch's writing had me hanging on every heartbeat.'
(Alistair Macauley, *Financial Times*)

'One of the best plays I have ever seen on addiction. The flawless production with performances of rare, raw emotional power from Fiona Bell and Mark Monero left me emotionally trembling.'
(John Peter, *Daily Telegraph*)

The Arts Council's reaction to our plan to move and seek temporary accommodation while working towards finding a new space was puzzling to say the least. On one hand they intimated that they would not continue to fund us if we stayed in the pub, while on the other hand they were certainly not going to help with capital funding for a new building and would not commit to continued revenue funding if we were to move out. On top of all that they now demanded that we commission an overpaid consultant to conduct a Feasibility Study and an Options Analysis to determine how feasible our scheme was. We would have to pay for this ourselves. I thought the whole thing was pointless. I saw no reason why the Arts Council should dictate to us, as they had no intention of supporting the scheme anyway. I didn't care if the scheme was *feasible* or not. What mattered was that the move was *necessary*, and therefore ways had to be found to make it happen. I have no interest in feasible theatre. I am only interested in the impossible. I also wanted to know why Hampstead, Soho, the Almeida and the Royal Court were all deemed worthy of new buildings and the Bush was not. Was the Arts Council prepared to see the Bush go to the wall? There were several theatres in London that were clearly failing both financially and artistically. Would it not be possible for the Arts Council to arrange for the Bush to take one of them over, just as Hull Truck had taken over the failing Humberside Theatre? Instead of a reply we were advised that we had to pay greater attention to monitoring our Cultural Diversity Action plan.

We were told that we had to find out what proportion of the 1,500 unsolicited scripts we received through the post every year came from ethnic minority writers. I asked how they proposed we should do this. The first suggestion was that we should check to see if the writers had ethnic-sounding names. I pointed out that Britain's most successful black playwright is called Roy Williams. The next suggestion was that we sent each writer a form on receipt of their script asking them to state their gender, ethnicity, sexual orientation and whether they were disabled. I said that I couldn't see what possible relevance the information had in judging the worth of the play and refused to do it. Their next piece of nonsense was supposed to provide an audience-ethnicity profile. Box-office staff were to be instructed to ask punters what their ethnic origins were when they phoned up to buy a ticket. Fiona said that if anyone asked her for details of her ethnicity she would tell them to fuck off and mind their own business. We also drew the line at front-of-house staff counting black faces at the door.

All this data would no doubt be used to check if we were complying with diversity targets or quotas, but no one ever told us what those targets were. Oddly enough, at the same time as all this was going on, the Arts Council Touring Department was backing a high profile tour of *The Glee Club*.

We had planned to take *The Glee Club* on the road after the West End run had finished but couldn't raise the money, so when Bolton Octagon Theatre asked Richard if they could do the play it seemed like a good opportunity to remount it and take it on tour. I redirected the play with Jim Hornsby and Ollie Jackson from the original cast augmented by Stefan Bednarczyk, Steve Garti, Colin Tarrant and Michael Burns. We trimmed it slightly and changed a couple of the musical numbers and once again it went down a storm. After a month in Bolton we went on to the Galway Festival where, along with Steppenwolf from Chicago, the Bush was billed as one of the world's leading theatres. Later in the year the show, which was a Bush/Bolton co-production supported by the Arts Council and a pilot scheme for their new touring initiative, went to Leeds, Exeter, Oxford, Ipswich, Warwick, Sevenoaks, Sheffield and Southport. The play was enthusiastically received everywhere except for Leeds and Sheffield, where they thought we were a bunch of Southern poofs. A merry time was had by all with the added bonus that the Arts Council could no longer bang on about us not providing value for money, as they had been our partners in providing it.

Steve Thompson was a maths teacher. He wrote a first play called *Absolute Privilege* loosely based on the experiences his wife had working as a night lawyer at *The Times*. A friend of his borrowed it and sent it to Terry Johnson. Terry phoned Steve up and said, 'I have read your script and think you should do this for a living.' Terry sent it to the Bush. Reader Adrian Pagan said that he thought that Steve was the most exciting new writer since Doug Lucie. I read it. Nicola worked with Steve on a new draft. We changed the title to *Damages*, and we put it on. That's how things worked at the Bush.

Damages is set late at night in the offices of a red-top newspaper. The play takes place in real time. The editor has gone to see *The Lion King* and is therefore uncontactable, so the assistant editor Phil, the night editor

Baz, the duty libel lawyer Abigail and the veteran revise sub-editor Howard are left to negotiate the legal and moral minefield of whether to splash with *Topless Blue Peter Presenter in Love Triangle* or go with *Teenage Rapists Horror*. Will the ink hit the paper before the shit hits the fan? Roxana Silbert expertly directed Amanda Drew, Paul Albertson and Phil McKee from *Stitching* with John Bett from 7:84 as the estimable Howard.

The play was a popular success especially with journalists and media types and extended for several weeks over the summer. There was a lot of West End talk and Steve won the Meyer-Whitworth Award. We made him writer-in-residence.

> Sharp, slick and howlingly funny, Steve Thompson's first play is a modern *The Front Page* with balls. I haven't laughed so much or so loudly in a theatre for a long time.
>
> (Lyn Gardner, *Guardian*)

One would not have readily imagined that Poland joining the EU would have much impact on the Bush, but strangely it did. West London has always had a substantial Polish community, but the scrapping of immigration controls meant that hundreds of thousands of additional Polish workers descended on London and most of them ended up in Shepherd's Bush. The bar staff in O'Neill's were usually Aussie, Kiwi or South African backpackers, but overnight they were replaced by cohorts of strapping blonde lads and lasses from Krakow and Wrocław. We had been annexed by Poland. This new population was desperate for entertainment and the pub manager, spotting a gap in the market, determined to plug it by running a Polish disco in the pub every Thursday night. As a result every Thursday night the pub was besieged by literally hundreds of Polish builders, plumbers and plasterers trying to get in. The crowd far outnumbered the maximum capacity of the bar and so the doors were often locked early in the evening. This meant that Bush audiences couldn't get in and sometimes couldn't get out. The noise levels were unbelievable, and most performances upstairs were punctuated by ear-splitting bursts of 'The Final Countdown' or the drunken and sentimental communal singing of 'Lady in Red'. In addition the Polish DJs often spiced up their set with strobe lighting and smoke bombs. The smoke set off the fire alarm, and we frequently had to stop the show until the fire brigade arrived and showed the bar staff how to turn off the alarm system.

Fiona and I continued our search for a temporary home. We considered Riverside Studios, but this would have meant merging our organisation with theirs, and we would have lost both our identity and autonomy. I set up a meeting with Nick Hytner and asked him if we could borrow the Cottesloe for six months. He gave me a talk on *Henry V* and looked at his shoes. Ian Ritchie continued his negotiations with Chelsfield, and the Board appointed a new Chair.

Tracey Scoffield had given up the post the previous year as her workload running BBC Films meant she couldn't devote enough time to the job. Long-time Board member Richard Phillips, a showbiz lawyer and Bush devotee, temporarily took over as the Board sought to recruit the right kind of financial big-hitter. They recruited John Shakeshaft. John was a corporate finance and investment manager and at the time was also a Managing Director of ABN AMRO bank. Before that he had been a Managing Director of Barings, an Executive Director at Morgan Stanley and worked at the Foreign Office, where he learnt to speak twelve languages before quitting to make serious money. He took me out to lunch at a Turkish restaurant. He ordered in Turkish. He told me how he had grown up in Liverpool and as a schoolboy been a regular at the Everyman. He remembered seeing *John, Paul, George, Ringo... and Bert*. I liked John and I thought he sincerely wanted to help the Bush, but I felt that theatre was not for him a matter of life and death and that as a banker and businessman he would never be able to embrace the necessary irreverent and subversive attitude you need to understand how the Bush works and to appreciate the work that it does. It may be fair to suggest that I am exhibiting prejudice here, but I would be more prepared to accept the appointment of a banker to the board of a theatre if it coincided with the happy but unlikely event of a playwright being appointed to the board of a bank.

Fiona and I introduced John to our Arts Council officer. She said that we should roll out some toolkits and set up some milestones. No, I don't know what she meant either.

In October we produced the first full-length play by Chloë Moss—*How Love is Spelt*—which was, according to Alex Sierz in *The Stage*, 'a Bush classic, an evening of quiet but emotionally true revelation'. Also in October we learnt that Chelsfield, who were developing the White City complex had been taken over by Multiplex, the firm that was also building Wembley Stadium. Ian Ritchie thought that this was bad news. He described them as 'a bunch of hairy-arsed Aussies'. Consequently he didn't hold out much hope for the inclusion of a new theatre for the Bush in the revised plans, although he would continue to lobby on our behalf. There was also the remote possibility of the theatre being included in another property-development scheme in Paddington Basin.

At Christmas I directed Richard Cameron's new play *Gong Donkeys*. Richard had discovered that in the late 1850s Charles Dickens and

Wilkie Collins visited Doncaster ostensibly to write about the St Leger, but more likely as a front for an assignation between Dickens and Ellen Tiernan, a young actress who was appearing in town. 'Gong Donkeys' was the expression Dickens invented to describe the drunken and lunatic folk of Donny, who make a noise somewhere 'between a gong and the braying of an ass'. In Richard's play, the tale of Dickens's clandestine romance is re-enacted by two daft lads, a fat lass and a fourteen-year-old schoolboy, as part of a fantasy game on a Yorkshire allotment. *Gong Donkeys* is a play about the need we all have for stories and storytelling. Richard and I dedicated the production to Mark Drewry.

Nicola Wilson resigned as Literary Manager to travel and become full-time proper writer—goals that she has subsequently achieved. I was sad to lose her. We had a great partnership and she had made an enormous contribution to the Bush. Nicola was replaced by Abigail Gonda, who had previously run the script department at Theatre503. By the end of 2004 we still had no concrete plans for a new building and we had failed to find a temporary home. So we stayed where we were.

The 2005 season opened with *Bites* by Kay Adshead in a co-production with The Red Room and Kay's company, Mama Quillo. It didn't really work. Kay's enigmatic play took the form of a banquet at the end of the world and the seven scenes were supposed to symbolise the seven courses from soup to nuts. The stories see-sawed between George Bush's Texas and Afghanistan and were a series of thematically linked surreal parables about War, Greed, Famine, God, Death and Global Inequality. Some of it was in verse. With *Bites* up and running I went up to Edinburgh to direct Sharman Macdonald's *The Girl With Red Hair*.

The Bush had discovered Sharman in 1984 when Alan Rickman, then reading scripts to supplement his meagre income as an actor, picked her play *When I Was a Girl I Used to Scream and Shout* out of the script pile. Simon Stokes's production eventually transferred to the West End and won loads of awards. *The Girl With Red Hair*, which I commissioned, had taken two years to make it to the stage. The play was set in a small Fife seaside town. Simultaneous scenes were played in a café, on the seashore, in a graveyard and on a rooftop. Even the genius and ingenious designer Robin Don pronounced it impossible to stage at the Bush. He thought we should turn it into a film. There was also a cast of eight, which, ridiculously, the Bush couldn't afford unless we spent the rest of the year doing monologues. I tried everywhere to rope in a co-producer including the National, the Traverse and Sheffield Crucible, but had no takers. Nicola and I had despaired of ever getting it on until she persuaded a friend of hers to organise a rehearsed reading with a student cast at the Royal Scottish Academy. Mark Thompson, who had recently been appointed Artistic Director of the Royal Lyceum in Edinburgh, turned up, fell in love with the play and asked if he could come in on the show. We then needed a London venue large enough to take Robin's seaside set so I persuaded Hampstead to join us, and we split the costs.

The Girl With Red Hair is a play that works almost entirely on atmosphere. It's a poetic meditation on loss and loneliness. There is precious little in the way of a plot, no dramatic action to speak of, and the tale unfolds languorously over one hot day in summer.

The play divided audiences and critics alike. Some thought it was slow, whimsical and insubstantial. Others thought it lyrical, mesmerising and cathartic. Michael Portillo, writing in the *New Statesman*, described it as 'an upmarket soap opera'. The Scottish local press were particularly consumed by the arrival of Sharman's daughter, Keira Knightley, on press night:

> Who does so-called Hollywood film star Keira Knightley think she is turning up at the opening of her mother's play last night in a chauffeur-driven limousine? Why can't she get the bus like everybody else?

In London *The Girl With Red Hair* played to about fifty per cent capacity at Hampstead over three weeks, which in terms of audience numbers is roughly the equivalent of selling out for three months at the Bush. I imagine that the Arts Council thought this was value for money.

Building work had started on the Multiplex White City development, but without any sign of the proposed new home for the Bush. Ian Ritchie found that his original plans were being diluted and compromised. In March the *Standard* reported that Multiplex were being blackmailed by the Russian Mafia, who threatened to use snipers to shoot the crane drivers if they didn't stump up £27 million. There was no word from the Paddington Basin scheme.

Fiona and I continued the search for temporary premises. We had meetings and discussions with the Players' Theatre and Trafalgar Studios but neither of them were really suitable. I felt in both cases that the commercial organisations that ran the theatres were merely looking for someone to programme their spaces cheaply. At one point we even thought of buying the abandoned synagogue on Brook Green but failed to persuade Cameron Mackintosh to lend us a million quid.

The previous autumn director Anna Mackmin and writer Amelia Bullmore had come in to talk about Amelia's play *Mammals*. Amelia had written stuff for television and also worked as an actor with Steve

Coogan and Chris Morris. *Mammals* was her first stage play. It's a comedy about love, marriage, kids and adultery among the breeding generation, but with a sting in the tale. Set in a middle-class London suburb, *Mammals* actually seemed to me to be the perfect play for Hampstead Theatre and their audience, in as much as it represented the acceptable face of new writing—more 'On Yer Patio' than 'In Yer Face'. Inexplicably Hampstead had turned it down. The risky stunt in the play was that the children, two little girls aged four and six, were to be played by adults—a trick used to great effect in Dennis Potter's *Blue Remembered Hills*. The danger was in allowing it to become whimsical, cute and sentimental. I decided that we should go for it anyway.

The critics and audiences were all pretty ecstatic about the show and it sold out in hours generating a fair amount of West End interest:

'I cannot remember when I last saw a first play so vital, so engrossing, so fully achieved, so mature.'

(*Sunday Times*)

'If you are prepared to battle the almost-daily gun battles on Shepherd's Bush Green, it's definitely worth a visit.'

(Toby Young, *Spectator*)

As part of our mission to take the work to a wider audience and provide value for money we decided to tour the show the following spring.

There was further West End activity. Fiona Clark, in her capacity as Managing Director of Bush Productions Ltd, our commercial wing, was in negotiation about a possible transfer of Steve Thompson's *Damages* to the Haymarket. Consequently there was all the usual nonsense about star casting and approaching Richard Wilson, Michael Gambon, Sting, Jade Goody, etc., etc. In addition the Haymarket, even though they had much admired Roxana Silbert's production, felt that she should be replaced by a name director with a proven West End track record. To my eternal shame I pragmatically went along with the notion. I told Roxana truthfully that the show would not transfer with her as director. I was a spineless shit. It was a betrayal, and I knew it. I should have told them to fuck off. I think that was the moment when I realised that I couldn't do the job for much longer.

In 1996 I had commissioned Lin Coghlan to write a play. Nine years later we produced *Kingfisher Blue*—probably the greatest possible testament to the persistence and longevity of our Writers' Development Programme. Lin had written, workshopped and abandoned several plays over the years. Her original starting point had been a story about a paedophile at Butlins. Since then the play had gone through several incarnations.

Kingfisher Blue is set on a Peckham housing estate. It concerns two lost boys: Elvis, an apprentice plumber who lives in a hostel, and his four-teen-year-old mate Ali, who lives with his abusive dad. Ali needs to raise cash to visit his mother in Majorca so he wants Elvis to photograph him naked so he can sell the photos to perverts in the pub. He also tries to sell a collection of stuffed animals he found in a dead man's house. It all goes horribly wrong. Charles Spencer, writing in the *Daily Telegraph*, was sufficiently moved by the production to suggest:

> A hundred years from now, when historians are researching what life was like at the turn of the previous century, they could do a lot worse than arm themselves with a bunch of Bush Theatre playscripts.
>
> They won't find much specifically political theatre, but when it comes to small-scale plays that capture the details of ordinary lives and the still, sad and often wonderful music of humanity, the Bush is in a class of its own. Again and again, the Bush has caught the confusion and pain of a society that has lost the com-fort of religious faith and a reassuring sense of social order, but where people are still battling on, searching for something that will make sense of their fragmented lives.

I should have quit while I was winning.

Despite the enthusiastic notices, *Kingfisher Blue* played to half-empty houses. I began to get the feeling that some of the Board and indeed sev-eral members of staff were more in sympathy with the conspicuously successful and commercially viable work like *Mammals* and *Damages* than the difficult and challenging work that Lin's play represented.

Architect Ian Ritchie finally pulled out of the White City project after Multiplex was taken over by Westfield and his visionary designs were largely abandoned in favour of an ugly glass temple to consumerism. As that particular door closed another one opened in the shape of Ken Shuttleworth. Shuttleworth had worked for Norman Foster before start-ing his own company, Make. They were architects for yet another development, Riverside Embankment in Hammersmith, a scheme to build three new open-plan office blocks and some apartment buildings on a site off the Fulham Palace Road. The development would eventu-ally become a 'riverside destination, boasting extensive restaurant, café and exhibition spaces, a state-of-the-art watersports facility [sic] and a wealth of landscaped open spaces'. It was also miles from anywhere and had no proper parking. As part of the sweetener, the developers were to build a certain amount of affordable housing for key workers. One would not unnaturally assume that key workers would be nurses, teachers and the like, but more often than not they turned out to be marketing consultants or BBC middle management. Again the deal Shuttleworth had in mind was to use Section 106 Planning Gain to convince the developers to provide a new home for the theatre and thus make the project a more socially responsible proposal.

Despite the whole thing being several years in the future the Arts Council again demanded that we commission a Feasibility Study and make a Business Plan. Fiona announced that she would again seek to become Joint Chief Executive. She felt that she needed the status to front up the building scheme.

The autumn season, on the theme of 'Tainted Love', kicked off with *After the End* by Dennis Kelly, a twisted thriller that we produced with Paines Plough and had premiered at the Traverse during the Edinburgh Festival. The play is a claustrophobic two-hander. After an apparent nuclear terrorist attack Louise wakes up to find herself quarantined in an underground fallout shelter with wimpy work colleague Mark, who has apparently saved her. They eat tinned chilli and play Dungeons and Dragons until Mark declares his love and things turn nasty. After playing at the Bush the play toured nationally and internationally with gigs in New York and Leningrad.

We followed *After the End* with *Bottle Universe*, Simon Burt's third play, which I commissioned on the strength of *Untouchable* and *Got to Be Happy*. *Bottle Universe* was a special play that tackled real issues of bullying, self-harm and happy slapping and should have been seen by every fourteen-year-old in West London at least.

At our annual Arts Council appraisal we were told that we had only just managed to achieve the required proportion of Cultural Diversity. We would have failed miserably had it not been for Lin Coghlan being Irish. I asked our Arts Officer if Kay Adshead scored points on account of being Jewish. Apparently she didn't. Enough Jews went to the theatre already. We were also told that the Arts Council, England had been tasked by the Government to deliver improved provision for circus skills.

I wrote to the chairman, Sir Christopher Frayling:

Dear Mr Frayling,

I am pleased to note that the Arts Council England has chosen to prioritise the acquisition of circus skills in the latest annual review. As an ex-circus performer myself I am now keen to get back to the 'Big Top' and the 'Sawdust Ring'. Alas having reached a ripe old middle age I am no longer sufficiently agile for the more gymnastic disciplines, so consequently I have decided to retrain as a Lion Tamer.

I hope you will be so kind as to furnish me details as to where I might seek the appropriate instruction and where I might purchase a suitable lion.

Yours, etc.,

We were warned that Hammersmith and Fulham Council were contemplating cutting our grant unless we provided more in the way of education. They did not consider that putting on plays like *Kingfisher Blue* and *Bottle Universe*, or working with talented young writers with something to say, satisfied the educational conditions of our subsidy. We had to do more to benefit the local community and our stakeholders. They were particularly keen that we involve ourselves in organising an event to celebrate Black History Month. I had no idea what to do. It was impossible to rustle up a new play on a black historical theme at a moment's notice. I arranged a meeting with all the black writers, readers and members of staff who had worked at the Bush. The writers in particular thought that the whole notion was a cynical exercise in box-ticking. Fiona was adamant that we produce some kind of caper, so Literary Manager Abigail Gonda and I went to Felix Cross for advice. Felix runs Nitro, the black music/theatre company that grew out of the Black Theatre Collective. He thought that we shouldn't do it. Felix told us that he had previously worked as a musician and a stand-up comic. It was only when he began to work in theatre that his job was described as being black anything. He didn't believe that black theatre existed. In the end, to appease the local council, we ran a couple of unsatisfactory workshops. I felt that I had been coerced into organising something that was both pointless and tokenistic.

Out of the blue I got a call from John Levitt, the Chairman of the Save London's Theatres Campaign. He suggested that the Bush should relocate to the New Westminster Theatre that was under construction in Victoria. It sounded like a possible solution to our problems even though the project had a somewhat chequered history. The old art deco Westminster Theatre—home of Moral Re-Armament Theatre—closed in 2002. While its preservation and future were under discussion, the building was mysteriously destroyed by fire, clearing the way for a development company, who wanted to build a seven-storey block of luxury flats. Planning permission was granted on the condition that the developers built a new smaller theatre on part of the site. The new theatre was earmarked as a home for Talawa Theatre Company, so the

Westminster would become Britain's first purpose-built black theatre venue. The Arts Council pitched in with £4 million Capital Funding. The Millennium Commission added £1.8 million from the Lottery and the London Development Commission came up with the rest. The total cost was estimated at £9.3 million. Plans were drawn up and all was going well until in July 2005, as construction work was about to start, the Arts Council suddenly withdrew their share of the money. This was apparently because of 'ongoing issues around organisational weakness, financial viability of the building project and its artistic and business plans'. They also threatened to withdraw Talawa's revenue funding. The other backers then pulled out of the project, leaving the developers with a hole in the ground that they could only develop if the scheme included a new theatre.

Fiona and I looked at the plans. There was to be an adaptable 270-seat flexible auditorium, a rehearsal room, office space, a cafeteria—and the building was almost in the West End. With a little tweaking we could make it work. We decide to talk to the developers. The Arts Council called up in a panic and warned us off. We were to deny that we had any ambitions whatsoever to take over the Westminster on pain of death. Talawa, spurred on by leading Government race relations adviser Peter Herbert, had threatened to take the Arts Council to the High Court. They were seeking a legal review claiming that the Arts Council had failed to follow its own equal opportunity procedures. The Black Theatre Act Now lobby group even accused them of institutional racism. If a non-black Arts Council-funded company like the Bush was seen to be taking over the Westminster their suspicions might seem to be have been confirmed. In the end Talawa got their revenue funding back and the £4 million was redirected towards cross-country infrastructural support for regional ethnic centres of excellence, whatever they might be. The Westminster Theatre is still a hole in the ground.

Bush reader Tessa Topolski had discovered the young and extremely talented writer Jack Thorne a couple of years earlier. Nicola and I had encouraged and worked with him through several preliminary drafts of what was to become *When You Cure Me*, an outstanding and complex debut play.

Rachel and Peter are seventeen and have been going out for three months. They are both virgins. Rachel is attacked and raped at knifepoint. She is scarred and immobilised from the waist down, suffering from psychosomatic paralysis. She has no memory of the assault and is damaged and angry. The play chronicles the attempts of her mother, Peter and her friends to help her through a crisis none of them understands, and Rachel's journey towards overcoming her personal trauma. It's a difficult play and requires actors of great skill and bravery, willing to investigate the confusion of adolescent sexuality in a truly painful situation. The dialogue is teenage monosyllabic, and most of the action is in the subtext. The fearless actors were Samuel Barnett, Daniel Bayle, Morven Christie, Lisa McDonald and Gwyneth Strong.

> In one of the year's finest pieces of new writing, Jack Thorne paints a compassionate, gripping portrait of a fledgling relationship that is asked to bear more than many well-established marriages. A superlative evening.
>
> *(Evening Standard)*

The Board decided to go ahead and commission a Feasibility Study from a firm of theatre consultants. It would cost us about thirty grand. The Arts Council would not pay for it, so we had to find the money ourselves. John Shakeshaft proposed to get the cash from the Sainsbury Foundation. I found the whole idea hugely depressing. Why on earth were we giving in to the Arts Council's demand to pay a consultant an extortionate amount of money we hadn't got in order to discover how feasible it was for us to raise the unknown sum of money required to move into and run a building that did not as yet exist and towards the cost of which they had no intention of contributing?

The Board appointed a consultant.

It was by now obvious to me that, for the Bush to move forward, they clearly needed an Artistic Director who readily embraced the proposed strategies for fundraising and development, not someone who morally and philosophically opposed them. I should have resigned there and then, but stubbornly I decided that I had to see it through. I was determined to stay until the future of the theatre was secure.

The situation in the pub had meanwhile deteriorated even further. There were now two Polish discos a week, and they were getting out of control. It was most definitely the final countdown. In response to all this Slavic turmoil the bouncers came up with a novel plan. They banned hats. One night I was barred from entering the bar because I was wearing a trilby. I asked what the problem was and why the ban. 'If you wear a hat we don't know who you are,' said the head doorkeeper. 'Yes, you do,' I said. 'I'm the one wearing the fucking hat.'

At the beginning of January 2006 John Fox, Artistic Director of Welfare State International, one of the most exciting, influential and original theatre troupes anywhere ever wrote an article in the *Guardian* announcing that he was winding up the company.

Welfare State was started in 1968 by a tribe of artists, poets, musicians and pyrotechnicians—wayward dreamers in search of 'entertainment, an alternative and a way of life'. We would be Guardians of the Unpredictable, travelling the world, creating site-specific celebratory theatre. Eyes on stalks. Not bums on seats. Our track record demonstrates that an applied vernacular art is possible. Yet on April Fool's Day 2006 we are stopping. The arts tightrope between celebrity and surrogate social work has become untenable. All our intentions of 1968—access, disability awareness, multigenerational and multicultural participation—are established; now, though, they come before the art.

We joined to make playful art outside the ghetto. Not to work three years ahead in a goal-orientated corporate institution where matched funding and value-added output destroy imaginative excess. The art business puts jobs before vocations. Overintensive risk management, child protection, licensing, family-friendly badges and employment laws invade with a suffocating culture of smug inertia. The final straw? The day we were told that we needed a hot-work permit for a bonfire in a field. Had we swept the floor and were the overhead sprinklers working? In Cumbria we call that rain.

It was one of the saddest things I had ever read.

The 2007 season opened with two back-to-back touring productions: *Monsieur Ibrahim and the Flowers of the Qur'an* by Eric-Emmanuel Schmitt, and *Trad* by Mark Doherty, which came in from the Galway Festival. *Mammals* went on a three-month national tour with a view to coming into the West End in the spring.

When the show played Cambridge, Fiona and John Shakeshaft organised a corporate event for executives from the accountancy firm KPMG. This involved a champagne supper, a reception mingling with the stars and new frocks all round. KPMG specialise in advising the mega-rich on tax avoidance. In the past they have admitted to criminal wrongdoing in the creation of fraudulent tax shelters. I emphatically believe that this is the kind of liaison that the Bush and every other theatre should avoid like the plague, but I had no say in the matter as the whole thing was organised behind my back. No one at the Bush had a clue what I was moaning about. As long as it made money it was OK.

In an effort to appease Hammersmith and Fulham Council on the Education and Stakeholder Access front I had agreed to run a new-writing scheme in conjunction with their 'West Words Live' Festival—a month-long celebration of poetry and performance involving the literature development programmes of the eight West London boroughs. Scheduled events included an Asian lyrics competition, an Iranian documentary film festival, an evening of Arabic Poetry at the Irish Centre, an exhibition about John Betjeman and a talk from Hanif Kureishi. Our scheme was called 'Getting It On'. We were going to present rehearsed readings of twenty-four short new plays by local writers. It was a huge undertaking, and the logistics were crazy. The writers came from supportive and non-judgemental writers' groups run by the local councils in local libraries. The wheeze was that we would select the plays, and each one would be developed and workshopped by a professional director taking them to a second draft. Each writer would also have a Bush playwright as mentor, and all twenty-four plays would be given rehearsed readings using student actors from LAMDA, East 15 and the disabled-led company Graeae over four evenings at the Bush. I press-ganged Lucy Foster, Vicky Jones and Meriel Baistow-Clare into joining me as directors; we took six plays each. The mentors were Jack Thorne, Georgia Fitch, Steve Thompson and Jenny Farmer.

I had assumed that the writers would harbour ambitions of becoming playwrights. In fact only one of the writers had attempted a play before and that was for radio. Most of them had never read a play. None of them had been to the Bush. Most of them had never been to a theatre. A majority had only written a play at all because it had been set as project by the writers' group tutor especially for the festival. Most of the tutors didn't go to the theatre either. (It was elitist.) Some of the writers only went to the groups because they were lonely. The standard was not good. We decided that the best we could do was to give everybody a fun time and hopefully make a few suggestions about how their work might improve. Even this proved to be controversial. A couple of writers quit believing that we were dissing them—failing to show them suitable respect—by giving them notes at all. The Christian Fundamentalist left because the workshops were on Sundays.

The final readings played to packed houses. The Mayor of Hammersmith came to the opening night, and there was a buffet with samosas. The audiences were made up almost exclusively of the families and friends of the writers. Some of them walked out noisily as soon as their chum's play had been performed, disturbing the rest of the audience. As far as I know, not a single writer wrote another play, and neither they nor their families or friends, ever came to the Bush again. In terms of writers' development, access and social inclusion I would like to claim that we made a difference, but I seriously doubt it. The professional directors, writers and actors had invested an enormous amount of dedication, time, talent and energy into ticking another box.

Why is it that the arts seem exclusively to be the target of Government attempts at Egalitarianism? I can't see the Ministry of Defence threatening to withhold taxpayers' money from the Army if they fail to provide better provision for weapon-training workshops to Islamic stakeholders.

At the same time I asked director Paul Miller, who had often worked at the Bush and also on the Connections Scheme at the National, to come up with a list of possible education initiatives. He wrote a comprehensive document called *Bush Futures—Building a Theatre for Tomorrow*, which proposed a formidable collection of schemes. These included Bush Future Playwrights, Bush Youth Theatre, Bush Young Activists, Bush Young Ambassadors, Bush Connections, Bush Futures Mentoring, Bush Creative Apprenticeships, Bush New Directors' Group and a Bush Futures programme of new-writing workshops specially tailored for GCSE and A-level students. The problem was that we had no one to run or organise them, nowhere to do them and no money to pay for them, unless we cut back seriously on the number of productions we put on. The other consideration was that, just half a mile down the road, the Lyric Theatre, Hammersmith ran a fully functioning, well-financed and exemplary education department that already offered most of the attractions on Paul's list.

The tour ended and *Mammals* failed to transfer to the West End. The stars and presumably the director were just not big enough. The consultants began work on their Feasibility Study, and Fiona had numerous meetings with the Riverside Embankment developers, without any decision being reached.

The previous July I had been to the Summer Play Festival in New York run by the thrusting young producer Arielle Tepper. There I saw a dozen new plays and sat in on countless platforms and discussion groups. I met some fascinating writers, actors, directors and producers, and I also found a stunning new play that I was determined to produce: *Crooked* by Catherine Trieschmann from Athens, Georgia.

Fourteen-year-old Lanie and her academic mom Elise move from Wisconsin to Oxford, Mississippi. Lanie is precocious and pretentious and fancies herself as the next great American female novelist. She also has a spinal deformity and is ostracised by the kids at her new school. Lanie is befriended by Maribel, the simple and enormous daughter of the local used-car dealer and evangelical preacher, who suffers from invisible stigmata. Maribel converts Lanie to Jesus, and Lanie declares herself a Holiness Lesbian who believes in the power of the Holy Ghost and kissing girls. *Crooked* is a comedy and coming-of-age drama that also had a lot to say subliminally about the religious right in George Bush's America. The *Evening Standard* described the play as 'a small-scale crock of dramatic gold'. During the run the theatre flooded again. The bar staff who lived upstairs had blocked the drains with discarded beer cans.

John Shakeshaft asked me for my opinion as to whether Fiona should become Joint Chief Executive. I firmly believe that the buck should stop at the Artistic Director and that all decisions about the running of the theatre should ultimately serve the art and not necessarily the commerce. As I was, however, forever banging on about collectivism and non-hierarchical power structures, it would have been churlish of me to stand in her way. I told John that it was up to the Board to make the decision and that she could be the Akond of Swat if it helped to secure the future of the theatre.

Fiona and I met with the architects and Theatre Projects to work on plans for the new theatre on the Hammersmith Embankment site. The building would be over four floors. There would be a 200-seat adaptable auditorium, rehearsal rooms, offices and a workshop. There would be a purpose-built education space. There was probably a revolving restaurant on the roof. It would be a destination building, if anyone could find it. The other problem was that no one could decide who was going to pay for what, and we could not begin fundraising until we knew what we were raising funds for and how much we needed to raise.

At our annual appraisal the Arts Council grudgingly identified the high standard of plays we produced but told us that we had to find more cost-effective office and rehearsal space, that we had to complete the Feasibility Study, that we had to prepare a new three-to-five-year Business Plan, that we had to find new premises in order to achieve compliance with the Disability Discrimination Act, and provide public benefit in line with the level of Arts Council investment. And if we hadn't addressed these issues by February 2007, they would have to consider if they were able to continue funding the company in future years. In other words, if we stayed where we were they would cut our grant, and if we didn't find a new space and come up with a three-to-five-year Business Plan in the next six months, they would cut our funding entirely.

They told us that we had to do even more to satisfy Hammersmith and Fulham Council's stated funding criteria. All the time and energy we had put into the 'Getting It On' project had been deemed insufficient. Hammersmith and Fulham Council did not regard all the work we did putting on the plays as representing value for money for their stakeholders. They didn't know what we were for and couldn't care less.

Finally we were told that new playwriting was no longer a priority. The Arts Council, England had been tasked by the Government to deliver improved provision for experimental practice and street arts. It was an impossible situation.

At the same time, Chloë Moss's new play, *Christmas is Miles Away*, came in from the Royal Exchange in Manchester. Two teenage schoolfriends love the same girl. One goes to art college; the other joins the Army and gets involved in Abu Ghraib-style torture. Chloë's tale of three teenagers learning about love, sex and growing up had more to offer young audiences than a thousand education workshops.

At a Board meeting John Shakeshaft ratified Fiona's new position as Joint Chief Executive. The deal was not as I had imagined. Fiona and I would be Joint CEO until the company went into a new building, at which point the Alternative Theatre Company (the company name that the Bush had traded under since 1974) would be wound up, and Fiona would then become sole Chief Executive of the new outfit. Shakeshaft later said that he was only floating the idea as a suggestion, but you don't need a weatherman to know which way the wind blows.

I spent the hot summer directing Abbie Spallen's play *Pumpgirl* in the airless and windowless theatre. The reason we were rehearsing in the theatre was that we hadn't enough money for a rehearsal room. *Pumpgirl* was an unscheduled production. The play arrived through the post earlier in the year. I thought that it was the most exciting piece of Irish writing since *Howie the Rookie*, but this time from the North rather than the South. I quickly organised a rehearsed reading. Abbie wrote a new ending, and I persuaded the Traverse to take the show for the Edinburgh Festival. *Pumpgirl* is set in the badlands of South Armagh. The play takes the form of three interlocking monologues. The characters are the Pumpgirl herself who works in a failing filling station, walks like John Wayne and looks like his horse; Hammy, her sometime lover, who works in the chicken factory and drives stockcars; and his wife, Sinead, who has an affair with an ex-IRA market trader. It's a small-town council estate play about love, adultery and Glen Campbell that ends in a gangbang and a death.

> Abbie Spallen comes out all guns blazing with writing so sparky and intricately observed, it seems as if it might spontaneously combust.
>
> (*Guardian*)

After taking on journalists and lawyers in *Damages*, Steve Thompson decided to turn his attention to politicians and the Whips' Office in particular. We arranged for him to meet one of Blair's ex-chief whips, and he also talked to Michael Portillo, who was charming but unforthcoming, and Gyles Brandreth, who was charming and indiscreet. Steve came up with a plot involving the newly elected Tory whips defending a majority of three by lying, cheating, bullying and blackmailing their way to secure a victory on the seemingly innocuous Tents, Gazebos and Flagpoles Bill. With Boy Scouts rioting in Whitehall and the Chief Whip dressed up as Santa, the play was clearly a farce so we gave it the Ray Cooneyesque title *Whipping It Up*. Terry Johnson came on board to direct and, believing that the play had West End legs, assembled a top-notch cast with Robert Bathurst, Fiona Glascott, Lee Ross, Nicholas Rowe, Helen Schlesinger and Richard Wilson. *Whipping It Up* went into rehearsal as *Pumpgirl* opened at the Bush.

At a specially convened meeting the Board and the theatre staff gathered to hear the preliminary results of the Feasibility Study. The consultants told us that the Bush would have to go through radical changes to survive in the future. The move into a bigger space would mean that we would have to become more commercially minded. This would mean star casting and selecting shows with commercial potential. We would have to organise fundraising properly, employing full-time development consultants. We would have to change the way we operated and develop better business skills and acumen. The Bush had been successful for thirty-five years and had an enviable track record in discovering new writers. It was now, however, time for the theatre to Grow Up.

I realised that I couldn't carry on any longer. If this was the way forward I was completely the wrong person for the job. I thought that the Feasibility Study was an utter waste of time and money, and I despised the culture that it embraced. I could not, however, come up with an alternative plan. The Bush clearly needed a grown-up as Artistic Director or Chief Executive and at my age that was too dangerous a step to take.

I don't believe that theatre is safe in the hands of grown-ups.

A couple of nights later I went for a drink with Fiona and told her that I was thinking of going. She thought that I should. I went back to O'Neill's to say goodbye to the *Pumpgirl* cast, who were leaving the next day. The bouncer barred me for wearing a hat. I told him to fuck off and got banned from the pub. I resigned the next day.

I worked out six months' notice. The last show I directed was *I Like Mine With a Kiss* by Georgia Fitch, the follow-up to *adrenalin... heart*. It was a great show to go out on—a moving, relevant, witty, contemporary play by a writer that the Bush had discovered and nurtured.

> Georgia Fitch's new play is an instant Bush classic—the writing is brilliantly observed, sensual, dirty and imaginative, the acting bristles with emotional truth and the staging boasts a wonderful theatricality. A triumph of good writing and true feeling.
>
> (Aleks Sierz, *The Stage*)

After I left, *Whipping It Up* went into the Ambassadors in the West End. Literary Manager Abigail Gonda asked one of the Bush Board of Directors why the actors were no longer billed alphabetically. 'We've stopped all that Sixties hippy shit,' he said.

Postscript

Nine months later, in December 2007, and without warning or consultation, the Arts Council announced that they were going to cut the Bush Theatre's annual grant by forty per cent. They also planned major cuts to 194 arts organisations and withdrew funding entirely from the National Student Drama Festival. The threatened companies were given five weeks to appeal, but as the Christmas holidays were coming up it meant that they had only eighteen working days to prepare and submit their case. The timing was clearly *not* a mistake. Furthermore, the Arts Council refused to give reasons for their decisions. The Bush's new Artistic Director, Josie Rourke, had to invoke the Freedom of Information Act to obtain the relevant information. The Arts Council then came up with a series of different and contradictory justifications for the reduction in subsidy. The first was that the Bush had been overfunded for the past ten years, presumably since the Boyden uplift. The cut would bring the company in line with 'what is appropriate for an eighty-seat theatre and is comparable with its peers the Gate, the Arcola and the Orange Tree Theatres'. The Royal Court Theatre Upstairs is also an eighty-seat theatre but received no similar threat. The second reason was that the Bush had 'not taken sufficient steps' to find new premises and that the Arts Council had concerns about the theatre's capacity, access and locality. This was despite the fact that we had spent the last ten years trying to find a new building, that the Arts Council had consistently refused the Bush capital funding to relocate, and that they would not commit to providing revenue support for a new venue—a stance that could hardly be seen as supportive by prospective development partners. The third reason was that Bush productions did not play to sufficient numbers and therefore did not represent value for money for the stakeholders. Josie's research uncovered the fact that the Arts Council had underestimated the audience figures by two-thirds. They had failed to record attendance numbers for the West End transfer and national tour of *Whipping It Up*. In fact over 100,000 stakeholders had seen Bush productions in 2007.

I believe that the Arts Council purposely miscalculated the figures to justify cutting the Bush. Millions had been spent on rebuilding and refurbishing the Royal Court, Hampstead and Soho Theatres and providing the increased revenue to run them. Something had to go to pay for it all, and some prick at the Arts Council had deemed that the Bush was surplus to requirements.

They had not reckoned with the reaction of the public and of the theatre community.

Josie Rourke orchestrated a 'Save the Bush' campaign that resulted in national media coverage and support from the great and the good. Letters of complaint appeared in the press signed by two hundred leading practitioners, and questions were asked in the House of Commons. For the Arts Council, who had just announced that we were living in a new golden age of artistic endeavour and excellence, the whole affair was a massive own goal. The campaign culminated in an open meeting organised by Equity at the Young Vic during which Arts Council Chief Executive Peter Hewitt was accused of arrogance, incompetence, high-handed behaviour and Stalinism. Nick Hytner said that Hewitt was talking bollocks, and Miriam Karlin called for a vote of no confidence that was carried *nem con*. In its annual report Equity declared the Arts Council 'unfit to judge what is excellent in theatre'. Sir Christopher Frayling snottily dismissed the protest and later claimed that Mike Leigh had called him 'a shit' in a lift at the Algonquin Hotel in New York.

Eventually twenty-five of the companies facing cuts had their funding restored, including both the Bush and the National Student Drama Festival.

The Bush Theatre is still above the O'Neill's pub on Shepherd's Bush Green. In 2009 they had to close down for several months, as the building was declared unsafe after yet another flood. They are actively seeking new premises, but the Arts Council has again refused Capital Lottery support without offering any explanation.

They have, however, tasked the Bush to engage consultants and to commission a new Feasibility Study.

In the mid-Eighties the Society of West End Theatres gave Joan Littlewood a Lifetime Achievement Award. In her acceptance speech she told
the assembled theatrical Establishment, 'I know why you've given me this
award—it's because I've stayed away.' After the ceremony there was a do
at the Waldorf Hotel. The flunky on the door refused to let her in. Joan
had to haul her trophy out of her shopping bag to prove she was invited.
He thought that she was the cleaning lady.

Index